# THOMAS MIDDLETON

The redefinition of the Thomas Middleton canon has led to an explosion of interest in this quintessential Jacobean. Middleton's best-known plays, such as *Women Beware Women* and *The Changeling*, are now staged, filmed, and rewritten for modern audiences. But Middleton also wrote religious poetry, satires, historical allegory, prose, and less familiar plays; he collaborated frequently, even with Shakespeare. His works are rooted in his historical and cultural environment, from the growth of religious Arminianism and the Overbury scandal to the fall of the boys' companies. Here, experts in literature, theatre, history, law, and religion analyze the complex contexts of Middleton's works, clarifying debates over his religious and political affiliations. Divided into sections presenting new interpretations of the world in which Middleton wrote – as Londoner, citizen, dramatist, and early modern man – and concluding with a section on performance history, the essays cover the full range of his works, from the frequently performed to the newest attributions.

SUZANNE GOSSETT is Professor of English at Loyola University Chicago. She has edited Middleton's *A Fair Quarrel* for the Oxford Middleton, Shakespeare and Wilkins's *Pericles* for the Arden Shakespeare, and Beaumont and Fletcher's *Philaster* for Arden Early Modern Drama. She is a general editor of Arden Early Modern Drama and, with Gordon McMullan, General Textual Editor for the Norton Shakespeare 3.

# THOMAS MIDDLETON IN CONTEXT

EDITED BY

SUZANNE GOSSETT

CAMBRIDGE
UNIVERSITY PRESS

## CAMBRIDGE
### UNIVERSITY PRESS

University Printing House, Cambridge CB2 8BS, United Kingdom

Cambridge University Press is part of the University of Cambridge.

It furthers the University's mission by disseminating knowledge in the pursuit of
education, learning and research at the highest international levels of excellence.

www.cambridge.org
Information on this title: www.cambridge.org/9781107685642

© Cambridge University Press 2011

This publication is in copyright. Subject to statutory exception
and to the provisions of relevant collective licensing agreements,
no reproduction of any part may take place without the written
permission of Cambridge University Press.

First published 2011
First paperback edition 2015

A catalogue record for this publication is available from the British Library

Library of Congress Cataloguing in Publication data
Thomas Middleton in context / edited by Suzanne Gossett.
p.   cm.
ISBN 978-0-521-19054-1 (hardback)
1. Middleton, Thomas, d. 1627 – Criticism and interpretation.   I. Gossett, Suzanne.
II. Title.
PR2717.T48   2011
822'.3–dc22
2010040406

ISBN 978-0-521-19054-1 Hardback
ISBN 978-1-107-68564-2 Paperback

# Contents

# Illustrations

# Contributors

SYLVIA ADAMSON is Professor of Renaissance Literature and Early Modern English Language at the University of Sheffield and President of the Philological Society of London. Her recent publications include *Renaissance Figures of Speech* (Cambridge), which was one of *Choice*'s "outstanding title" selections for 2008, and "Questions of Identity in Renaissance Drama" (*Shakespeare Quarterly*, 2010). She was assisted in writing this essay by Hannah Kirby (M.A. University of Sheffield), a doctoral student at the University of Oxford; Laurence Peacock (M.A. University of Sheffield), currently teaching English as a foreign language; and Elizabeth Pearl (M.A. University of Sheffield), currently teaching English as a foreign language.

PASCALE AEBISCHER is Senior Lecturer in Renaissance Studies at the University of Exeter. She is the author of *Shakespeare's Violated Bodies* (Cambridge, 2004) and *Jacobean Drama* (2010). She is coediting *Performing Early Modern Drama Today* with Kathryn Prince (Cambridge, forthcoming) and researching the film adaptations of the plays of Shakespeare's contemporaries. Work on this subject has been published in *Shakespeare Quarterly* (2009) and *The Cambridge Companion to English Renaissance Tragedy* (2010).

IAN W. ARCHER has been Fellow, Tutor, and University Lecturer in History at Keble College, Oxford since 1991. He is the author of *The Pursuit of Stability: Social Relations in Elizabethan London* (Cambridge, 1991), editor of the forthcoming *English Historical Documents 1558–1603*, Academic Editor of the Bibliography of British and Irish History, and Literary Director of the Royal Historical Society.

LINDA PHYLLIS AUSTERN is Associate Professor of Musicology at Northwestern University, Illinois. She is the author of *Music in English Children's Drama of the Later Renaissance* (1992), editor of *Music, Sensation, and Sensuality* (2002), and has published articles in such journals as *Early Modern Women, Journal of the American Musicological Society, Music and Letters,* and *Renaissance Quarterly.*

JAMES P. BEDNARZ is Professor of English on the C. W. Post Campus of Long Island University, where he has received the Trustees' Award for Excellence in Scholarship and the Newton Award for Excellence in Teaching. His book *Shakespeare and the Poets' War* (2001) was selected as an "International Book of the Year" by *The Times Literary Supplement.* He is currently completing *Shakespeare and the Truth of Love,* a study of *Love's Martyr.*

ALASTAIR BELLANY is Associate Professor of History at Rutgers University and Director of the Rutgers British Studies Center. He is the author of *The Politics of Court Scandal in Early Modern England: News Culture and the Overbury Affair, 1603–1660* (2002), and coeditor (with Andrew McRae) of "Early Stuart Libels: An Edition of Poetry from Manuscript Sources" (2005; www.earlystuartlibels.net). He is currently working on several studies exploring the reputation and representation of George Villiers, Duke of Buckingham.

ANKE BERNAU is Lecturer in Medieval Literature and Culture at the University of Manchester. Her work covers particularly female virginity, medieval origin myths, and early modern and cinematic medievalisms. Among her publications is *Virgins: A Cultural History* (2007). She is currently writing on literary representations of memory and forgetting in the fifteenth and sixteenth centuries.

CAROLINE BICKS is Associate Professor of English at Boston College. She is the author of *Midwiving Subjects in Shakespeare's England* (2003), and has published most recently on female sexuality and the early modern stage in *Modern Philology* and *Studies in English Literature, 1500–1900.* She is coeditor with Jennifer Summit of *The History of British Women's Writing, 1500–1610* (2010).

ALISON A. CHAPMAN is Associate Professor of English at the University of Alabama at Birmingham. Her research concerns the aftereffects of the Protestant Reformation, with a particular focus on patron saints. Recent publications include "Marking Time: Astrology, Almanacs, and English Protestantism" (*Renaissance Quarterly,* 2008) and "Ophelia's 'Old Lauds': Madness and Hagiography in *Hamlet*" (*Medieval and Renaissance Drama in England,* 2007).

JANET CLARE is Professor of Renaissance Literature at the University of Hull. Among her publications are *Drama of the English Republic, 1649–1660* (2005), *Revenge Tragedies of the Renaissance* (2006), and *Art Made Tongue-Tied by Authority: Elizabethan and Jacobean Dramatic Censorship* (second edition, 1999). She has coedited (with Stephen O'Neill) *Shakespeare and the Irish Writer* (2010).

THOMAS COGSWELL is Professor of History at the University of California at Riverside. Having recently published (with Peter Lake) "Buckingham Does the Globe: *Henry VIII* and the Politics of Popularity in the 1620s" (*Shakespeare Quarterly*, 2009), he is hard at work (with Alastair Bellany) on two crime thrillers, one on the "murder" of James I and the other on the assassination of the Duke of Buckingham.

TRUDI L. DARBY is Honorary Senior Research Fellow in Humanities and Deputy Head of Administration at King's College London. She currently works on the influence of Cervantes on the plays of Shakespeare's contemporaries. Recent publications include "William Rowley: A Case Study in Influence" in J. A. G. Ardila (ed.), *The Cervantean Heritage* (2008) and "The Black Knight's Festival Book? Thomas Middleton's *A Game at Chess*" in Alexander Samson (ed.), *The Spanish Match* (2006).

ELIZABETH LANE FURDELL is Professor of History and Distinguished Professor at the University of North Florida. Her books on early modern English medicine and medical publishing include *Publishing and Medicine in Early Modern England* (2002) and *Fatal Thirst: Diabetes in Britain until Insulin* (2009). She edited and contributed to *Textual Healing: Essays on Medieval and Early Modern Medicine* (2005).

ANDREW GORDON lectures in sixteenth- and seventeenth-century literature at the University of Aberdeen and is Co-Director of the Centre for Early Modern Studies there. He has published widely on many aspects of the culture of early modern London, from city maps to inn signs and urban libels, and also works on early modern correspondence. A monograph, *Writing the City: Memory, Text and Community in Early Modern London*, is forthcoming.

SUZANNE GOSSETT is Professor of English at Loyola University Chicago. She has edited Middleton's *A Fair Quarrel* for the Oxford Middleton, Shakespeare and Wilkins's *Pericles* for the Arden Shakespeare and Beaumont and Fletcher's *Philaster* for Arden Early Modern Drama. She is a General Editor of Arden Early Modern Drama and, with Gordon McMullan, General Textual Editor for the Norton Shakespeare 3.

DARRYLL GRANTLEY teaches in the School of Arts at the University of Kent, Canterbury. His publications include *Wit's Pilgrimage: Drama and the Social Impact of Education in Early Modern England* (2000), *English Dramatic Interludes 1300–1580: A Reference Guide* (2004), and *London in Early Modern English Drama: Representing the Built Environment* (2008).

ANDREW GURR is Professor Emeritus at the University of Reading and former Director of Research at Shakespeare's Globe, London. His academic books include *The Shakespearean Stage 1574–1642*, now in its fourth edition; *Playgoing in Shakespeare's London*, now in its third; *The Shakespearian Playing Companies*; *The Shakespeare Company 1594–1642*; and, most recently, *Shakespeare's Opposites: The Admiral's Men 1594–1625*. He has edited *Richard II*, *Henry V*, and the Quarto *Henry V* for the Cambridge Shakespeare editions, and is currently editing *The Tempest* for the New Variorum. He is a trustee of the Rose Theatre Trust.

DIANA E. HENDERSON is Professor of Literature and Dean for Curriculum and Faculty Support at MIT. Her works include *Collaborations with the Past: Reshaping Shakespeare Across Time and Media* (2006) and *Passion Made Public: Elizabethan Lyric, Gender, Performance* (1995). She has edited and contributed to *Alternative Shakespeares 3* (2008) and *A Concise Companion to Shakespeare on Screen* (2006). Henderson has worked as a dramaturg for college and professional productions, and has collaborated with the Royal Shakespeare Company and the Actors' Shakespeare Project.

HEATHER HIRSCHFELD is Associate Professor of English at the University of Tennessee, Knoxville. She is the author of *Joint Enterprises: Collaborative Drama and the Institutionalization of the English Renaissance Theater* (2004), as well as articles in *ELH*, *Shakespeare Quarterly*, *Renaissance Drama*, *Journal of Medieval and Early Modern Studies*, and *Publications of the Modern Language Association*.

MARK HUTCHINGS is Lecturer in English at the University of Reading. He is coauthor (with A. A. Bromham) of *Middleton and his Collaborators* (2008) and editor of *Three Jacobean "Turkish" Plays* (forthcoming). His principal research interest is drama in performance, and his current project is an exploration of Anglo-Spanish relations and their intersection with English theatre.

FARAH KARIM-COOPER is Head of Courses and Research at Shakespeare's Globe and Visiting Research Fellow of King's College London. She is Chair of the Globe Architecture Research Group and is leading the research for a reconstruction of an indoor Jacobean playhouse. She is Co-Director of the Shakespeare's Globe/King's College London MA in Shakespeare Studies. Her publications include *Cosmetics in Shakespearean and Renaissance Drama* (2006). With Christie Carson she coedited *Shakespeare's Globe: A Theatrical Experiment* (Cambridge, 2008). She is currently researching a book called *Shakespeare and the Hand*.

DAVID KATHMAN is an independent scholar in Chicago, Illinois. He has published articles in *Shakespeare Quarterly, Shakespeare Survey, Early Theatre*, and *Medieval and Renaissance Drama in England*, and was a contributor to the *Oxford Dictionary of National Biography*. His current research focuses on boy actors and on inns, taverns, and places other than playhouses where professional plays were performed in sixteenth-century London.

AARON KITCH is Associate Professor of English at Bowdoin College, Maine. He has published *Political Economy and the States of Literature in Early Modern England* (2009), as well as essays on Renaissance drama in *Shakespeare Quarterly, Studies in English Literature*, and *Renaissance Drama*. His new project explores the epistemology of pleasure in the European Renaissance.

ROSLYN L. KNUTSON, Emerita Professor of English at the University of Arkansas at Little Rock, is the author of *Playing Companies and Commerce in Shakespeare's Time* (2001) and *The Repertory of Shakespeare's Company, 1594–1613* (1991). She has published widely on theatre history. Her current projects include a repertorial analysis of the commercial theatrical marketplace in 1587–93, and the wiki-style *Lost Plays Database* (www.lostplays.org), which she coedits with David McInnis (University of Melbourne).

NATASHA KORDA is Professor of English at Wesleyan University, Connecticut. She is author of *Shakespeare's Domestic Economies: Gender and Property in Early Modern England* (2002), and coeditor of *Staged Properties in Early Modern English Drama* (Cambridge, 2002) and *Working Subjects in Early Modern English Drama* (forthcoming). She has recently completed a book entitled *Labors Lost: Women's Work and the Early Modern English Stage*.

JENNIFER LOW has published articles in *Comparative Drama* and *Philological Quarterly*. She is the author of *Manhood and the Duel: Masculinity in Early Modern Drama and Culture* (2003) and is currently coediting (with Nova Myhill) a collection of essays entitled *Imagining the Audience in Early Modern Drama, 1558–1642*. She is Associate Professor of English at Florida Atlantic University.

SONIA MASSAI is Reader in Shakespeare Studies at King's College London. She is the author of *Shakespeare and the Rise of the Editor* (Cambridge, 2007) and editor of *World-Wide Shakespeares* (2005). She is editing John Ford's *'Tis Pity She's a Whore* for Arden Early Modern Drama and coediting (with T. L. Berger) *The Paratext in English Printed Drama to the Restoration* (Cambridge, forthcoming).

SUBHA MUKHERJI is Lecturer in English at the University of Cambridge. She is the author of *Law and Representation in Early Modern Drama* (Cambridge, 2006); coeditor of *Early Modern Tragicomedy* (2007) and *Fictions of Knowledge: Fact, Evidence, Doubt* (forthcoming); and editor of *Thinking on Thresholds* (forthcoming). Her current book project focuses on doubt and epistemology in early modern literature.

IAN MUNRO is Associate Professor of Drama at the University of California, Irvine. He is the author of *The Figure of the Crowd in Early Modern London: The City and Its Double* (2005) and editor of *A Woman's Answer is Never to Seek: Early Modern Jestbooks, 1526–1625* (2007). Recent publications include "Knightly Complements: *The Malcontent* and the Matter of Wit" (*English Literary Renaissance*, 2010).

CAROL THOMAS NEELY is Professor Emeritus of English at the University of Illinois, Urbana-Champaign. She is coeditor of *The Woman's Part: Feminist Criticism of Shakespeare* (1980), and author of *Broken Nuptials in Shakespeare's Plays* (repr., 1993) and *Distracted Subjects: Madness and Gender in Shakespeare and Early Modern Culture* (2004.) She has been President of the Shakespeare Association and on the editorial boards of *Publications of the Modern Language Association* and *Shakespeare Quarterly*.

MICHAEL NEILL is Emeritus Professor of English at the University of Auckland. His publications on early modern drama include *Issues of Death* (1997) and *Putting History to the Question* (2000), as well as editions of *The Changeling* (2006) for New Mermaids, Massinger's *The Renegado* (2010) for Arden Early Modern Drama, and *Anthony and Cleopatra* (1994) and *Othello* (2006) for the Oxford Shakespeare.

KAREN NEWMAN is Owen Walker Professor of Humanities and Professor of Comparative Literature at Brown University. She has written widely on early modern letters and culture and on Shakespeare and Renaissance drama. Recent books include *Cultural Capitals: Early Modern London and Paris* (2007; paperback, 2009) and *Essaying Shakespeare* (2009). Her current research on Shakespeare and cultural translation aims to historicize contemporary claims about the globalization of culture.

SIMON PALFREY is Fellow of Brasenose College, Oxford. His books include *Shakespeare in Parts* (2007, with Tiffany Stern), winner of the MRDS David Bevington Prize, and *Doing Shakespeare* (revised edition, 2010). He is founding editor (with Ewan Fernie) of the *Shakespeare Now!* series of original "minigraphs."

JENNIFER PANEK is Associate Professor of English at the University of Ottawa, and author of *Widows and Suitors in Early Modern English Comedy* (Cambridge, 2004). Her most recent work includes a Norton Critical Edition of Middleton and Dekker's *The Roaring Girl* (2011), and an essay in *English Literary Renaissance* on stage representations of male prostitutes for women.

TRIPTHI PILLAI is Assistant Professor of English Renaissance literature at Coastal Carolina University. Her recent work includes "Constructing Experiences and Charting Narratives: The Future In/Of *A Midsummer Night's Dream*" in *A Midsummer Night's Dream: A Critical Guide* (2010).

TANYA POLLARD is Associate Professor of English at the Graduate Center and Brooklyn College, City University of New York. Her publications include *Drugs and Theater in Early Modern England* (2005), *Shakespeare's Theater: A Sourcebook* (2003), and essays on early modern theatre and medicine. She is currently writing a book on the development of popular stage genres in early modern England, and their debts to the ancient Greek dramatic tradition.

ERIC RASMUSSEN is Professor and Chair of the Department of English at the University of Nevada. He coedited, with Jonathan Bate, the *Complete Works* of Shakespeare for the Royal Shakespeare Company (2007). His recent publications include *Cynthia's Revels* for the *Cambridge Edition of the Works of Ben Jonson* (coedited with Matthew Steggle, forthcoming), and an edition of *Everyman and Mankind*, coedited with Douglas Bruster, for Arden Early Modern Drama (2009).

CATHERINE RICHARDSON is Director of the Canterbury Centre for Medieval and Early Modern Studies and Senior Lecturer in Renaissance Literature at the University of Kent, Canterbury. Her research focuses on material experience: houses, furniture, and the social and personal significance of clothing. She is author of *Domestic Life and Domestic Tragedy* (2006), and editor of *Clothing Culture 1350–1650* (2004) and (with Tara Hamling) *Everyday Objects: Medieval and Early Modern Material Culture and its Meanings* (2010).

CERI SULLIVAN, Professor of English Literature, Bangor University, works on rhetorical structures in mercantile and bureaucratic literature. Recent books are *The Rhetoric of the Conscience: Donne, Herbert, and Vaughan* (2008) and *Authors at Work: The Creative Environment* (2009, coedited with Graeme Harper).

# *Acknowledgments*

I would like to thank, first, all of the contributors to this volume, who not only wrote wonderful essays but replied rapidly and cheerfully to queries despite personal difficulties of many kinds. Particular thanks go to Pascale Aebischer and Diana Henderson for struggling with the technology of modern illustration; to Darryll Grantley for arranging to have new maps drawn; to James Bednarz, Heather Hirschfeld, and Eric Rasmussen for collaborating on collaboration; to Sylvia Adamson for supervising a team of linguists; and to Pascale Aebischer, Trudi Darby, and Diana Henderson for descriptions of the National Theatre's 2010 *Women Beware Women*. Like so much of Middleton's work, this has been a happy collaboration.

I am grateful to Gary Taylor for proposing that I undertake this volume; to Sarah Stanton for helpful suggestions and support all along the way; to Rebecca Taylor for assistance with the illustrations and the editing; to Alison Thomas for sharp-eyed and careful copy-editing; and to Lacey Conley for work on the bibliography and index. As a team we are deeply thankful for assistance from librarians too many to name, on both sides of the Atlantic and at the many institutions where our contributors teach and research. We greatly appreciate the cooperation we have had from the photographic staff at the Folger Shakespeare Library, the Huntington and Newberry Libraries, the Victoria and Albert Museum, the Shakespeare Centre Library, Shakespeare's Globe, and the London Clothmakers' Hall. Finally, I would like to thank my family, as well as Gordon McMullan, for assistance and encouragement; they all yielded time that might have been spent in other ways to allow me to complete this project.

# Chronology

Dates of texts are from *Middleton* and refer to date of composition.

| Middleton/Middleton texts | Literary contexts | Cultural and political contexts |
|---|---|---|
| 1580 Middleton is born to William and Anne Middleton | | 1580 Jesuit mission established in England |
| | | 1580 Return of Francis Drake |
| | | 1580 Marlowe begins residence at Corpus Christi College, Cambridge |
| 1586 Death of William Middleton | 1586 Death of Sidney | 1586–7 Mary, Queen of Scots, implicated in the |
| 1586 Anne Middleton remarries | 1587 Kyd, *The Spanish Tragedy* | Babington Plot and executed |
| | 1588–92 Marlowe, *Doctor Faustus, The Jew of Malta, The Massacre at Paris, Edward II* | 1587 Drake defeats Spanish fleet at Cadiz |
| | 1588 Lyly, *Endymion* | 1590 Death of Francis Walsingham |
| | 1592 Death of Robert Greene | 1592–3 Plague: London theatres close |
| | 1592–3 Shakespeare, *Richard III* | |
| | 1592–3 Shakespeare, *Venus and Adonis* | |
| | 1593 Death of Marlowe | |
| | 1593–4 Shakespeare, *The Rape of Lucrece* | |
| 1597 *The Wisdom of Solomon Paraphrased* | 1596–7 Shakespeare, *The Merchant of Venice* | 1596 James Burbage builds the second Blackfriars Theatre |
| | 1596–7 Shakespeare, *1 Henry IV* | |
| | 1597–8 Shakespeare, *The Merry Wives of Windsor* | |
| | 1597–8 Shakespeare, *2 Henry IV* | |

| Middleton/Middleton texts | Literary contexts | Cultural and political contexts |
|---|---|---|
| 1598 Middleton matriculates at The Queen's College, Oxford | 1598 Shakespeare, *Much Ado About Nothing* | |
| 1599 *Microcynicon* | 1598–9 Shakespeare, *Henry V* | 1599 "Bishops Ban" on satire Middleton's *Microcynicon* burned |
| | 1599 Death of Spenser | |
| | 1599 Marlowe's *Hero and Leander* published | |
| | 1599 Shakespeare, *Julius Caesar* | 1599 Henry Airay elected Provost of The Queen's College, Oxford |
| | 1599–1600 Shakespeare, *As You Like It* | |
| 1600 *The Ghost of Lucrece* | 1600–1 Shakespeare, *Hamlet* | |
| 1601 *The Penniless Parliament of Threadbare Poets* | 1601 Shakespeare, *Twelfth Night* | |
| 1601 Middleton receives the £25 set aside for him at the time of his father's death From January he is noted "in London daylie accompaninge the players" | | |
| 1602 "Caesar's Fall" (lost) | 1602 Shakespeare, *Troilus and Cressida* | |
| 1602 Prologue and Epilogue for revival of *Friar Bacon and Friar Bungay* | | |
| 1603 *News from Gravesend* | 1603 Jonson, *Sejanus* | 1603 Death of Elizabeth I |
| 1603 Middleton marries Magdalen (Mary) Marbecke | 1603 Heywood, *A Woman Killed with Kindness* | 1603 Accession of James I |
| | 1602–5 Shakespeare, *A Lover's Complaint* | 1603 The Chamberlain's Men become the King's Men |
| 1603–4 *The Phoenix* | 1603 Shakespeare, *Measure for Measure* | 1603 Orlando Gibbons becomes a musician of the Royal Chapel |
| 1603–4 The Middletons' son Edward born | 1603–4 Shakespeare, *Othello* | 1603–4 Plague: London theatres close |
| 1604 *The Whole Royal and Magnificent Entertainment* | 1604 'A' text of Marlowe's *Doctor Faustus* published | 1604 Tobacco Tax introduced |
| 1604 *Father Hubburd's Tales* | 1604 Daniel, *Philotas* | 1604 Peace concluded with Spain |
| 1604 *The Meeting of Gallants at an Ordinary* | 1604 Marston, *The Fawn* | 1604 Convening of the Hampton Court Conference |
| 1604 *Plato's Cap* | | |
| 1604 *The Black Book* | | |
| 1604 *The Patient Man and the Honest Whore* | | 1604 Dowland, *Lachrimae* |
| 1604–6 *Michaelmas Term* | | |
| 1605 *A Trick to Catch the Old One* | 1605 Shakespeare, *The History of King Lear* | 1605 The Gunpowder Plot |
| 1605 *A Mad World, My Masters* | 1605 Munday, *The Triumphs of Reunited Britannia* | 1605 Jonson and Chapman arrested for *Eastward Ho!* |
| | | 1605 The Red Bull opens |

| Middleton/Middleton texts | Literary contexts | Cultural and political contexts |
|---|---|---|
| 1605 *A Yorkshire Tragedy* | 1605 Jonson and Jones, | 1605 The Rose closes |
| 1605–6 *Timon of Athens* | *Masque of Blackness* | 1605 Caravaggio, *Ecce Homo* |
| | 1605 Bacon, *The* | |
| | *Advancement of Learning* | |
| | 1605 Cervantes, *Don Quixote* | |
| 1606 "The Viper and Her | 1606 Fletcher, *The Noble* | 1606 Charters issued to |
| Brood" (lost) | *Gentleman* | colonize Virginia |
| 1606 *The Puritan Widow* | 1606 Jonson, *Volpone* | 1606 Union Flag |
| 1606 *The Revenger's Tragedy* | 1606 Shakespeare, *Macbeth* | 1606 Plague: London theatres |
| | 1606 Shakespeare, *Antony* | close |
| | *and Cleopatra* | 1606 *Act to Restrain Abuses of* |
| | 1606 Wilkins, *The Miseries of* | *Players* |
| | *Enforced Marriage* | 1606 Actors of the Children |
| | 1606 Death of John Lyly | of the Queen's Revels |
| | | arrested for *The Isle of Gulls* |
| | | 1606 Birth of Rembrandt |
| 1607 *Your Five Gallants* | 1607 Beaumont, *The Knight* | 1607 "Midlands Rising" |
| | *of the Burning Pestle* | 1607 Jamestown founded in |
| | 1607–8 Shakespeare and | North America |
| | Wilkins, *Pericles* | 1607 Halley's Comet |
| | | 1607 Plague: London theatres |
| | | close for most of the year |
| | | 1607 Robert Jones, *First Set of* |
| | | *Madrigals* |
| | | 1607 Monteverdi, *L'Orfeo* |
| 1608–9 *The Bloody Banquet* | 1608 Birth of John Milton | 1608 Theatres reopen and |
| | 1608 Shakespeare, *Coriolanus* | then close due to plague |
| | 1608 Fletcher, *The Faithful* | 1608 Whitefriars theatre |
| | *Shepherdess* | opens |
| | | 1609 The King's Men begin |
| | | to perform at the |
| | | Blackfriars |
| 1609 *Sir Robert Sherley* | 1609 Shakespeare, *Sonnets* | 1609 Shipwreck of *The Sea* |
| 1609 *The Two Gates of* | 1609–10 Shakespeare, *The* | *Venture* in the Bermudas |
| *Salvation* | *Winter's Tale* | 1609 Galileo's telescope |
| | 1609 Beaumont and | 1609 Moors expelled from |
| | Fletcher, *Philaster* | Spain |
| | 1609 Jonson, *Epicene* | 1609 Theatres reopen |
| | 1609 Jonson, *The Masque of* | 1609 Death of Dr. Dee |
| | *Queens* | |
| 1611 *The Roaring Girl* | 1610 Shakespeare, *The* | 1610 Prince Henry made |
| 1611 *No Wit/Help Like a* | *Tragedy of King Lear* | Prince of Wales |
| *Woman's* | 1610 Shakespeare, *Cymbeline* | 1610 Assassination of Henri |
| 1611 *The Lady's Tragedy* | 1611 Shakespeare, *The* | IV of France |
| | *Tempest* | 1610 Louis XIII becomes |
| | | King of France |

| Middleton/Middleton texts | Literary contexts | Cultural and political contexts |
|---|---|---|
| | 1611 Lanyer, *Salve Deus Rex Judaeorum* | 1610 John Guy leads expedition to colonize Newfoundland |
| | 1611 Fletcher, *The Tamer Tamed* | |
| | 1611 Jonson, *The Alchemist* | 1610 George Buc replaces Edmund Tilney as Master of the Revels |
| | 1611 Tourneur, *The Atheist's Tragedy* | |
| | 1611 Heywood, *The Brazen Age* | 1610 Death of Caravaggio |
| | | 1611 King James Bible published |
| | 1611 Heywood, *The Silver Age* | |
| | 1612 Webster, *The White Devil* | 1612 Death of Prince Henry |
| | 1612 Heywood, *An Apology for Actors* | 1612 Execution of the Lancashire witches |
| | 1612 *Don Quixote* published in English | 1612 John Dowland becomes lutenist to James I |
| | 1612–13 Shakespeare and Fletcher, *Cardenio* | 1612 Gibbons, *The First Set of Madrigals and Mottets* |
| 1613 *A Chaste Maid in Cheapside* | 1613 Elizabeth Cary, *Tragedy of Mariam* | 1613 Princess Elizabeth marries the Elector Palatine |
| 1613 *The Manner of His Lordship's Entertainment* | 1613 Shakespeare and Fletcher, *Henry VIII* | 1613 First Globe burns down |
| 1613 *The Triumphs of Truth* | 1613 Beaumont, *Masque of the Inner Temple and Gray's Inn* | 1613 Opening of the New River in London |
| 1613 *Wit at Several Weapons* | | |
| | 1613–14 Shakespeare and Fletcher, *The Two Noble Kinsmen* | |
| 1614 *Masque of Cupids* | 1614 Webster, *The Duchess of Malfi* | 1614 "Addled Parliament" dissolved |
| 1614 *More Dissemblers Besides Women* | 1614 Jonson, *Bartholomew Fair* | 1614 Pocahontas marries John Rolfe |
| | | 1614 Hope Theatre opens |
| | | 1614 Second Globe opens |
| | | 1614 Death of El Greco |
| 1615–16 *The Widow* | 1615 Donne ordained | 1615 The King's Men and other theatre companies summoned by the Privy Council for performing during Lent |
| | | 1615 Rubens, *The Death of Seneca* |
| | | 1615 Inigo Jones becomes Surveyor of the King's Works |

| Middleton/Middleton texts | Literary contexts | Cultural and political contexts |
|---|---|---|
| 1616 *The Witch* | 1616 Death of Shakespeare | 1616 Catholic Church bans |
| 1616 *Macbeth* (adaptation) | 1616 Death of Henslowe | Copernicus's *De* |
| 1616 *Civitatis Amor* | 1616 Death of Beaumont | *Revolutionibus* |
| 1616 *A Fair Quarrel* | 1616 Death of Cervantes | 1616 Rubens, *Hippopotamus* |
| | 1616 Jonson, *The Devil is* | *and Crocodile Hunt* |
| | *an Ass* | |
| | 1616 Chapman, *Whole Works* | |
| | *of Homer* | |
| | 1616 'B' text of Marlowe's | |
| | *Doctor Faustus* published | |
| | 1616 *The Works of Ben Jonson* | |
| | published | |
| 1617 *The Triumphs of Honour* | 1617 Jonson becomes Poet | 1617 Cockpit Theatre |
| *and Industry* | Laureate | destroyed in apprentice |
| | | riots and rebuilt as the |
| | | Phoenix |
| 1618 *The Owl's Almanac* | | 1618 Beginning of the Thirty |
| 1618 *The Peacemaker* | | Years War |
| 1618–19 *An/The Old Law* | | 1618 Walter Ralegh executed |
| | | 1618 Francis Bacon appointed |
| | | Lord Chancellor |
| | | 1618 William Harvey lectures |
| | | on the circulation of blood |
| 1619 *Masque of Heroes* | 1619 Death of Richard | 1619 Death of Queen Anne |
| 1619 "Burbage" | Burbage | 1619 Inigo Jones designs the |
| 1619 *The Triumphs of Love* | | Whitehall Banqueting |
| *and Antiquity* | | House |
| | | 1619 Edward Alleyn founds |
| | | Dulwich College |
| 1620 *The World Tossed at* | 1620 Bacon, *Novum* | 1620 The *Mayflower* embarks |
| *Tennis* | *Organum* | from Plymouth to Cape |
| 1620 *Hengist, King of Kent* | | Cod |
| 1620 Middleton appointed | | 1620 Gentileschi, *Judith* |
| City Chronologer of | | *Decapitating Holofernes* |
| London | | |
| 1620–1 *Honourable* | | |
| *Entertainments* | | |
| 1620–3(?) *Annales* | | |
| 1621 *Women Beware Women* | 1621 Jonson, *The Gypsies* | 1621 The Fortune burns |
| 1621 "Bolles" | *Metamorphosed* | down |
| 1621 *Measure for Measure* | 1621 Dekker, Ford, Rowley, | 1621 Donne becomes Dean of |
| (adaptation) | *The Witch of Edmonton* | St. Paul's Cathedral |
| 1621 *The Sun in Aries* | 1621 Fletcher, *The Island* | |
| 1621 *Anything for a Quiet Life* | *Princess* | |
| | 1621 Burton, *Anatomy of* | |
| | *Melancholy* | |

| Middleton/Middleton texts | Literary contexts | Cultural and political contexts |
|---|---|---|
| | 1621 Wroth, *The Countess of Montgomery's Urania* | |
| 1622 *An Invention* | | 1622 Birth of Molière |
| 1622 *The Changeling* | | |
| 1622 *The Nice Valour* | | |
| 1622 *The Triumphs of Honour and Virtue* | | |
| 1623 "St James" | 1623 Shakespeare's First Folio published | 1623 Prince Charles and Buckingham visit Spain |
| 1623 *The Spanish Gypsy* | | |
| 1623 *The Triumphs of Integrity* | 1623 Fletcher, *The Sea Voyage* | 1623 Henry Herbert appointed Master of the Revels |
| 1623 "Malfi" | | |
| | | 1623–4 Velázquez, *The Investiture of St. Ildefonso with the Chasuble* |
| 1624 *A Game at Chess*, banned after a nine-day run | 1624 Massinger, *The Parliament of Love* | 1624 Pope Urban VIII orders burning of Luther's German translation of the Bible |
| 1624 "To the King" | | |
| 1624 "Hammond" | | 1624 Cardinal Richelieu appointed adviser to Louis XIII of France |
| 1625 "Picture" | 1625 Death of Fletcher | 1625 Death of James I |
| 1625–6 "Pageant for Charles I" (Lost) | 1625 Massinger becomes principal playwright for the King's Men | 1625 Accession of Charles I |
| | | 1625 Dutch settlement in Manhattan |
| | | 1625 Death of Gibbons |
| 1626 *The Triumphs of Health and Prosperity* | | |
| 1626–7 *Farrago* | | |
| 1627 Middleton dies and is buried in St. Mary's churchyard in Newington | | |

# *Abbreviations*

Note: The abbreviations of Middleton titles (listed below) in almost all cases are taken from the Oxford *Thomas Middleton: The Collected Works*. All Middleton quotations are from this edition. Lost plays are indicated by quotation marks, extant plays by italics. Middleton plays are cited by act, scene, and line number; other works are cited by line or page number as appropriate. Introductions and other essays are cited by page and the author is credited. All quotations from Shakespeare are taken from the relevant volume of the New Cambridge Shakespeare.

| | |
|---|---|
| *Companion* | *Thomas Middleton and Early Modern Textual Culture: A Companion to the Collected Works*, Gary Taylor and John Lavagnino (gen. eds.) (Oxford: Clarendon Press, 2007). |
| *Middleton* | *Thomas Middleton: The Collected Works*, Gary Taylor and John Lavagnino (gen. eds.) (Oxford: Clarendon Press, 2007). |
| *ODNB* | *Oxford Dictionary of National Biography*, H. C. G. Matthew and B. Harrison (eds.) (Oxford, 2004–10); online edn., L. Goldman (ed.) (www.oxforddnb.com, 2007). |
| *OED* | *The Oxford English Dictionary*, 2nd edn., 1989; online edn. (http://dictionary.oed.com). |

### WORKS OF MIDDLETON

| | |
|---|---|
| *Antiquity* | *The Triumphs of Love and Antiquity* |
| *Aries* | *The Sun in Aries* |
| *Banquet* | *The Bloody Banquet* |
| *Black Book* | *The Black Book* |
| "Bolles" | "On Sir George Bolles" |
| "Burbage" | "Richard Burbage" |
| *Changeling* | *The Changeling* |
| *Chaste Maid* | *A Chaste Maid in Cheapside* |

| | |
|---|---|
| *Civitatis* | *Civitatis Amor* |
| *Cupids* | *Masque of Cupids* |
| *Dissemblers* | *More Dissemblers Besides Women* |
| *Entertainments* | *Honourable Entertainments* |
| *Five Gallants* | *Your Five Gallants* |
| *Game* | *A Game at Chess* |
| *Ghost* | *The Ghost of Lucrece* |
| *Gravesend* | *News from Gravesend: Sent to Nobody* |
| *Gypsy* | *The Spanish Gypsy* |
| "*Hammond*" | "To the worthily accomplished Master William Hammond" |
| *Hengist* | *Hengist, King of Kent; or, The Mayor of Queenborough* |
| *Heroes* | *Masque of Heroes* |
| *His Lordship's Entertainment* | *The Manner of his Lordship's Entertainment* |
| *Hubburd* | *Father Hubburd's Tales* |
| *Industry* | *The Triumphs of Honour and Industry* |
| *Integrity* | *The Triumphs of Integrity* |
| *Invention* | *An Invention* |
| *Lady* | *The Lady's Tragedy* |
| *Mad World* | *A Mad World, My Masters* |
| *Magnificent* | *The Whole Royal and Magnificent Entertainment, with the Arches of Triumph* |
| "*Malfi*" | "Upon this Masterpiece of Tragedy" |
| *Meeting* | *The Meeting of Gallants at an Ordinary* |
| *Michaelmas* | *Michaelmas Term* |
| *Microcynicon* | *Microcynicon: Six Snarling Satires* |
| *No Wit* | *No Wit/Help Like a Woman's* |
| *Old Law* | *An/The Old Law* |
| *Owl* | *The Owl's Almanac* |
| *Patient Man* | *The Patient Man and the Honest Whore* |
| *Peacemaker* | *The Peacemaker* |
| *Penniless Parliament* | *The Penniless Parliament of Threadbare Poets* |
| *Phoenix* | *The Phoenix* |
| "*Picture*" | "The Picture" |
| *Plato* | *Plato's Cap* |
| *Prosperity* | *The Triumphs of Health and Prosperity* |

| | |
|---|---|
| *Puritan* | *The Puritan* or *The Puritan Widow* or *The Widow of Watling Street* |
| *Quarrel* | *A Fair Quarrel* |
| *Quiet Life* | *Anything for a Quiet Life* |
| *Revenger* | *The Revenger's Tragedy* |
| *Roaring Girl* | *The Roaring Girl* |
| "St James" | "The Temple of St James" |
| *Sherley* | *Sir Robert Sherley his Entertainment in Cracovia* |
| *Solomon* | *The Wisdom of Solomon Paraphrased* |
| *Tennis* | *The World Tossed at Tennis* |
| *Timon* | *Timon of Athens* |
| *Trick* | *A Trick to Catch the Old One* |
| *Truth* | *The Triumphs of Truth* |
| *Two Gates* | *The Two Gates of Salvation* |
| *Valour* | *The Nice Valour; or, The Passionate Madman* |
| *Virtue* | *The Triumphs of Honour and Virtue* |
| *Weapons* | *Wit at Several Weapons* |
| *Widow* | *The Widow* |
| *Witch* | *The Witch* |
| *Women Beware* | *Women Beware Women* |
| *Yorkshire* | *A Yorkshire Tragedy* |

# Introduction

## Suzanne Gossett

> Against the model of Shakespeare as universal genius may be set the model of Middleton as a dramatist of unremitting focus on his own times
>
> (John Jowett, "Thomas Middleton")

Thomas Middleton – playwright, poet, religious and political polemicist, City Chronologer of London, and celebrator of royal entries – is a man best understood as product and producer of his own environment, and yet, as demonstrated by the success of his works on the contemporary stage and screen, is one who speaks directly to the modern world. The essays in this volume are intended to assist readers, whether students coming to Middleton for the first time or experienced scholars more familiar with Shakespeare, in placing Middleton's writings in and against the world with which they are so deeply intertwined. Here Middleton is examined in his multiple contexts – that is, in his private life; in the city of early modern London in which he was born, lived, and died; in the world of national and international events that resonated in that city; in the environment of the Jacobean theatres; in the conditions of authorship that led, for example, to frequent collaboration of various kinds; and finally in the context of current intellectual, psychological, and social frameworks.

For the reader and the scholar today the most immediately important context for reading Middleton was the appearance, in 2007, of Gary Taylor and John Lavagnino (gen. eds.), *Thomas Middleton: The Collected Works*. This was the first attempt at a complete edition since A. H. Bullen's in 1885, which was itself a reprint of Alexander Dyce's 1840 edition (see Sonia Massai's essay in this volume, p. 317). I own a copy of Bullen; I bought it many years ago in the basement of a bookstore in Cambridge, Massachusetts, and only when I took the volumes home and found a signature in one did I realize that they had belonged to the great Harvard scholar George Lyman Kittredge (1860–1941). Kittredge, one can tell from his carefully penciled notes, was well aware of the defects of the Bullen edition and was contemplating his own. But although he edited a *Complete Works of Shakespeare* (Grolier Club, 1936) and published extensively on Chaucer as well as on Jonson and the "poetasters," he never produced a Middleton. One might well ask why: was it that Middleton – sexy, violent, religious – did not speak to Kittredge's world, as he does to ours; or was it just that Kittredge, although he published extensively on philology, was defeated by the need to determine the outlines of Middleton's career before he could discuss his beliefs, his style, and his development? In Kittredge's day, for instance, it was believed that Middleton was born in 1570 instead of 1580; that *The Revenger's Tragedy* was by Tourneur; and that *The Family of Love* was by Middleton.

The situation of the current reader is different. During the nearly two-decade gestation of the Oxford *Middleton*, many scholars of the early modern period – over and above the more than sixty who actually participated as editors – became intrigued by Middleton and began new research on and interpretation of his works. In addition, Taylor and his collaborators, especially the attribution scholar MacDonald P. Jackson, worked diligently to clarify the outlines of the Middleton canon. With the now largely uncontested addition to the canon of major tragedies such as *Revenger* and *The Lady's Tragedy* (formerly known as *The Second Maiden's Tragedy*), the shape of Middleton's career appears more clearly that of a significant, multi-talented dramatist: it looks less heavily weighted towards the comedies written early for the boys, less like the limited course of a "city dramatist." The composition of tragedies stretches from *A Yorkshire Tragedy* (1605) to *The Changeling* (1622), and these are interspersed with tragicomedies, pamphlets, entertainments, and comedies for the adult players. Middleton's role as a collaborator has also become clearer with the addition of *Wit at Several Weapons* (like *The Nice Valour*, first published in the Beaumont and Fletcher folio) to his other work with William Rowley, and with *Timon of Athens*, *Macbeth*, and *Measure for Measure* recognized as different forms of co-writing with the chief dramatist of the King's Men.

The Oxford *Middleton*, by its very girth, makes clear the multiplicity of the man and his work; we need to read Middleton in context because his own contexts are multiple. Unlike Shakespeare, who did not write religious poetry, satires, Lord Mayor's shows, historical allegory, or non-dramatic prose, and whose surviving works come almost exclusively from one theatrical company of adult players, rather than from many companies of boys and men, Middleton's varied works need to be understood as responding to a series of specific situations, from the gradual growth of religious Arminianism to the rise and fall of the second group of boys' companies.

One result of looking at the range of his contexts, as the essays in this volume do, is an increase in both breadth and depth of understanding. Certain recognized masterpieces – *Changeling, Women Beware Women, A Chaste Maid in Cheapside* – gain complexity as their varied local connections are unraveled. For example, in the essays below *Chaste Maid* is analyzed in the context of London trades, of a powerful Welsh family, of Middleton's use of the supernatural, of his views on women, and of his language varieties and puns. On the other hand, because the essays explicate different parts of Middleton's world, a wide range of his works, some quite unfamiliar, figure. In the early twenty-first-century context there are works that gain a prominence they probably would not have had for Kittredge: *Revenger*, of course, which he presumably knew as by Tourneur, but also *The Roaring Girl*, with the appeal of its fighting heroine in drag; *The Witch*, for its historical immediacy and its connection to *Macbeth*; the *Triumphs* (*of Truth, of Honour and Industry, of Love and Antiquity, of Integrity, of Health and Prosperity*), which so clearly distinguish the eventual City Chronologer Middleton from Ben Jonson, the writer of court masques.

As the essays by Diana Henderson and Pascale Aebischer in this volume describe, after a long though not absolute silence, in the twentieth and twenty-first centuries Middleton has also had an active performance context. These essays demonstrate the ways in which Middleton has been newly reappreciated, rewritten, or distorted to suit us today. For example, on May 11, 2010 BBC Radio 4 ran a program on Middleton called "The Tudor Tarantino," advertised as about the "rise and fall of Thomas Middleton, the bad boy of Renaissance drama." This amusing oversimplification of the seriously Calvinist Middleton – who, when still a "boy" of 17, published *The Wisdom of Solomon Paraphrased* in seventeen chapters of rhyming sestets – demonstrates the necessity to understand Middleton in context. In the course of the program Gary Taylor called *Revenger* "an angry young man's play," which is reasonable enough considering that Middleton wrote it when he was 25 or 26 and had been forced down from Oxford by the financial malfeasance of his new stepfather. But certainly later on it was not a "bad boy" who wrote Lord Mayor's shows or who, probably with powerful political support, made satirical allusions to the notorious Howard/Somerset marriage or to the contrivances of the Spanish that frightened the English population while Prince Charles was in Madrid.

It is, apparently, both the "badness" and the familiarity of Middleton that appeals now. The BBC program featured Harriet Walter, playing Livia in *Women Beware* at the National Theatre in spring 2010, and the production's director Marianne Elliott. They noted that Middleton's language is colloquial, dark, and full of "street talk," the characters motivated by greed, sex, and criminal impulse. Elliott's production seemed designed to suggest parallels with the 2009–10 banking crisis: the crumbling portal of the Mother's house resembled a decrepit bank, and Leontio was a bank clerk rather than a factor. The Ward was a "teddy boy," and clever use of the Olivier stage revolve allowed the audience to see Bianca's rape at the same time as the two older women sat comfortably chatting in Livia's salon. On the BBC Elliott summarized Middleton's plays as about "ordinary people living ordinary lives under ordinary pressures that they find extraordinary."

The essays in this volume explicate both the ordinary and the extraordinary contexts in which Middleton, and other English men and women, lived ordinary and, in Middleton's case, extraordinarily talented lives in the late Elizabethan and Jacobean periods. These essays provide general as well as specific contexts in which to read Middleton; that is, they focus broadly on such matters as political developments in Europe and more narrowly on his personal interests and environment – for example, the food, textiles, furnishings, and tricksters that surrounded the middling sort of Londoner. They reveal the pressures on a freelance craftsman of the theatre and the complications of finding a religious position in the shifting sands of Jacobean Protestantism.

The volume begins with an essay on Middleton's own life as a "quintessential Jacobean." Mark Hutchings points out that Middleton came of age during the period of the Armada and died as the Thirty Years War was under way, and argues that "in his engagement with both foreign crises and domestic controversy," Middleton is the "principal chronicler" of the turbulent years of James's English rule. Hutchings pays particular attention to Middleton's early poems and satires: with *Microcynicon: Six Snarling Satires*, he notes, Middleton entered simultaneously "the literary community" and political controversy. It is the many communities in which Middleton lived – poetic, theatrical, legal, religious, civic, commercial, English and European – that the subsequent essays explicate.

Everything that Middleton achieved was tied to the extraordinary growth and complexity of London, so the first group of essays examines the civic context. Looking at both comedies and non-theatrical writings, Darryll Grantley shows how Middleton's London was "on the one hand a place of wit and sophistication, and on the other one that endemically permitted deception, criminality, and corruption." Catering for a London audience, Middleton exploited their familiarity with the city to create "a cultural and moral frame of reference." Andrew Gordon, using the little studied play *The Puritan Widow* as his focus, then exemplifies how Middleton drew upon "the knowledge, shared with his London audiences, of the modes of living with which specific spaces of the city were inscribed." Thus the satirical force of naming two servants "Simon St Mary Overies" and "Nicholas St Antlings" and the expression of status through architectural detail. Gordon concludes that Middleton "consistently represents the space of the city as porous," showing privacy disrupted by "the persistent affirmation of spatialized neighborhood relations."

Ian Munro delves further into Middleton's view of the crowded city with its rapidly growing population. The playwright's Lord Mayor's shows consistently present London with a "bifurcated understanding": alternatively as an idealized bounteous mother and as Error's "disorderly, shapeless and secret city," full of vice and crime. Middleton's complaints about London's vice were not merely generic; rather, "specificity of location combines with thematic preoccupations" to articulate his particular anxieties about "what London was becoming." Munro concludes by noting the "dangerous fluidity of the metonymic connections between stage and city": in *Your Five Gallants*, as a pawnbroker reads out an actual plague bill, "Middleton's theatre is not merely a representation of Error's thronged city, but one of its principal intersections."

The next group of essays provides more detailed description of the day-to-day life that lies behind Middleton's representations. Starting from a 1622 inventory of a citizen's goods, Catherine Richardson enters the household, the city's principal social and political unit. Through Middleton's representations in *Chaste Maid* and *Women Beware*, Richardson illuminates the material variety of London life, demonstrating how small objects could "signal social position" and serve as assets in time of need. But more than merely painting a naturalistic picture of material objects, she argues, Middleton "uses the household ... to explore the gendered nature of notions of private property within the acquisitive city."

As Elizabeth Lane Furdell writes, "Enjoying a long and vigorous life in Middleton's London required both a robust constitution and good luck." Recurrent plague, "new" diseases, "seasonal fevers" all threatened, killing even the heir apparent. Furdell traces the disputes over theories of healing between religion and medicine, between followers of Galen and of Paracelsus, and between the College of Physicians and the unlicensed healers who challenged it. Middleton, she shows, had opinions about all of these conflicts, as is visible for instance in the satire on the surgeon in *A Fair Quarrel*. It is no surprise that his final surviving work, the Lord Mayor's Show for 1626 (which followed one cancelled because of the plague), is entitled optimistically *The Triumphs of Health and Prosperity*.

Several of the next essays sharpen the outlines of Middleton's own positions. Noting that the circulation of money drives plot, character, and setting in Middleton's works "to an extraordinary degree," Aaron W. Kitch nevertheless differentiates this dramatist's "consuming interest in wealth and its distribution" from the attitudes of others such as Dekker and Jonson. In an equally pertinent distinction, Kitch argues that in Middleton, as in our own society, "quotidian life becomes subject to impersonal market forces," but in a play like *Roaring Girl*, although relations between people can be read through the lens of Marx's logic of commodity, the setting nevertheless remains precapitalist. "Invested in the economic realities of early modern London," the plays demonstrate the financial models jostling each other at the time. For example, in *A Trick to Catch the Old One*, Lucre's "fetishism of landed property" is outmoded, while his nephew operates successfully within the new "economy of credit." Similarly, where wealth in the comedies tends to "dissolve communal bonds," in the civic pageants that Middleton wrote for London's powerful merchants commerce "figures as a necessary catalyst for community and nation."

The world of tradesmen and guildsmen was "rapidly changing and riven with tensions" during Middleton's lifetime. Natasha Korda shows Middleton registering these tensions in plays like *The Patient Man and the Honest Whore* that juxtapose "the formal and informal economies of the city," satirizing them in pamphlets like *The Owl's Almanac*, and obfuscating them in depictions of economic transformation in his Lord Mayor's pageants. Korda points out that the playing companies adopted some of the structures of the "innovative capital ventures" of the guilds, and suggests that Middleton "modeled his professional life on the newly flexible forms of trade that surrounded him."

Ceri Sullivan offers a radical rereading of *Chaste Maid* (1613) by connecting it to Middleton's two entertainments of the same year for the Myddleton brothers – Hugh, who brought a new water supply to London, and Thomas, who became Lord Mayor. Their clan of North Welshmen had something of a stranglehold on the capital's markets, water supply, and civic affairs. If the play is read with the entertainments in mind, rather than revealing a negative view of sexual and economic incontinence, "its interests in money, sex, and water have a more local, literal, and positive value," implicitly arguing that "abundance comes from harnessing immigrant talents and natural resources on a communal basis."

The development of Middleton's civic entertainments is traced more broadly by Karen Newman, who shows how these entertainments could be "an assertion of civic power and competition with monarchical authority and its attendant ceremonies." Her analysis of the Venetian ambassador's reaction to *Industry* (1617) clarifies how specifically English these events, which produced "a distinctive urban and discursive space in which persons of different status and degree mixed," seemed to foreign visitors.

The London world could be violent and dangerous, but, as Jennifer Low demonstrates, it is a mistake to accept only the cony-catching pamphlets' description of its criminal underworld. Low, instead, points out that a frequent source of violence was the aristocracy, with their duels enabled by technical developments in steel forging. Middleton nevertheless links aristocratic violence to the confidence tricksters by repeatedly satirizing their parallel use of formulaic language. Thus, for instance, *Quarrel* connects "ritualized verbal challenges and nonsense-words." Still, Low describes how, despite James's objections and the pamphlet he commissioned Middleton to write against dueling, the custom of the duel actually reduced bloodshed and brawling in Jacobean London.

One response to civic violence was law, which Subha Mukherji identifies as "one of the most visible faces of the viciously predatory city." In the context of a "robustly litigious London," law is ubiquitous in Middleton's works, satire of law appearing in the early prose narratives as well as throughout the plays. Mukherji connects Middleton's special concern with the absurdity of legal language – in *The Phoenix* Tangle's madness is cured by a bloodletting of legal jargon – to the sixteenth-century shift from manuscript and oral assimilation to print, with the consequent proliferation of law commentaries and handbooks. Ultimately, though, for Middleton legal maneuvers were connected with "deeper concerns of ethics, usury, and justice."

The essays in the second part place Middleton's life and works in a national and international context, starting from the royal court, "the spectacular center of much of the kingdom's political life," in Alastair Bellany's words. In theory the court was an exemplar of virtue, but in Middleton's lifetime it became "indelibly associated" with immorality. Bellany shows how scandalous images of the Stuart court circulated especially through the little discussed but ubiquitous verse libel. He recounts the Overbury scandal, the greatest of the period, against the broader context of the contested power and authority of favorites. Bellany acknowledges that plays need not mimic events precisely – although some of *Witch* does – but he argues that court scandal is the context in which to read the great tragedies, including *Changeling* and *Women Beware*. Even the transformation of Buckingham "from popish Ganymede to patriot hero" in *A Game at Chess* can be best understood in the context of the revised verse libels of 1624.

The essays of Thomas Cogswell and Ian W. Archer together explain political and religious developments during Middleton's working life. The sequence of these developments clarifies the changing contexts in which, for example, Middleton first attacks and then defends Buckingham, or satirizes Puritans while remaining a Calvinist. Cogswell, stressing the voracious fiscal demands of the long Anglo-Spanish conflict and its impact on traditional modes of taxation, not only describes the political situation against which *Game* – Middleton's most daringly overt satire – must be read, but shows how the combined forces of nationalism, religion, and fiscal exigency led to conflict in a way deeply familiar today.

Archer's essay illuminates the long-raging debate over Middleton's religious position, between those who see the playwright as Puritan and those who don't. The problem arises from "the real fluidity of religious positions in Jacobean London." Archer argues that Puritanism was as much a system of practices as of belief: this helps clarify how Middleton could be a left-wing Calvinist and, notoriously, satirize Puritans. Archer draws further distinctions between religious life in London and in rural England, and between attitudes towards religious imagery in 1622, when Middleton wrote verses celebrating the consecration of St. James, and iconoclasm earlier and later. Similarly, he demonstrates how the meaning of Middleton's "Calvinist religious tract," *The Two Gates of Salvation*, altered between its first publication in 1609 and its republication in 1620 and 1627.

Trudy L. Darby's final essay in this part serves as a transition between Middleton's political and cultural worlds. For example, it places *Game* in the context of his other plays with Spanish themes as well as within the political debate over the Spanish match. Darby's broad overview describes the obsession with all things Spanish, whether cultural, literary, or linguistic. Although Spain was "the enemy," in London there was a "fruitful" business teaching Spanish; Spanish–English dictionaries multiplied; and Middleton was only one of several dramatists who could read Spanish and went directly to Spanish originals for plots.

Essays in the third part of the volume turn to the theatre. Andrew Gurr begins by establishing the "social cartography" of Middleton's theatrical life, particularly important because Middleton wrote for a "uniquely wide range of amphitheatres and indoor theatres" and for a "hugely varied" audience with an "extreme" social range. David Kathman continues by focusing more closely on the history of the boys' companies, for which Middleton wrote an entire series of early comedies. Kathman throws a new light on *Chaste Maid* by proposing that it, too, could be considered a boys' company play, one of the last of the genre. Finally he connects shifts in comic style in the Jacobean period to the disappearance of the boys' companies.

Roslyn L. Knutson, too, considers the relationship between company and style. Examining the "commercial dynamic" of the adult companies, she challenges the traditional view of a binary division in the social and economic relationship between "citizen" and "elite" audiences. Instead, she argues, by mixing "retro" features with his "sassy boy-company style of city comedy," Middleton's plays challenge "arbitrary distinctions in audience taste." In their blend of the old-fashioned and the trendy, Middleton's plays were suited to the multiple venues of adult companies like the King's Men and designed to appeal across class lines.

Middleton's writings began to be censored – his early satires were burned – before any of his plays reached the stage. Janet Clare traces different patterns in the operation of censorship by examining the three Middleton plays that attracted the censor's attention. Clare argues that the different outcomes were tied to the immediate political contexts – for example, the issue of regicide in *Lady* was "politically provocative" just after the assassination of the French King Henry IV. Occasionally Middleton himself may not have known just how far he could safely critique the court. But for his greatest success, *Game*, Clare contends, in an argument that helps explain the play's apparently inexplicable licensing, the "satirical thrust" was "consistently coded" on the page and only "activated in performance." Nevertheless, Clare shows from subsequent events that when it suited the authorities, censorship could be merely "token recrimination" to "mollify" objections.

In the final essay in this section Linda Phyllis Austern alerts readers to the "acoustic context" of Middleton's plays. Invisible and often forgotten in reading, sound was "integral to the flow of the action and its meaning." Austern looks carefully at dramatic music in context: its varying significance was "based on cultural practice, intellectual beliefs about the art, and theatrical tradition." Music featured at traditionally determined moments – for instance, the passage between life and death – and those participating in performing it also performed gender, profession, social status, and sometimes nationality.

Essays in the fourth part examine aspects of authorship less tightly tied to performance. Sylvia Adamson begins by identifying Middleton's language as the "harbinger of the naturalistic plain style that was to become dominant in the later seventeenth century." As this is especially true of the comedies, she and three of her students take examples from *Chaste Maid* to exemplify three aspects of Middleton's language: its use of sociolinguistic varieties – that is, divisions of language by class, location, and religion – to distinguish characters; puns, especially those that emphasize contradictory meanings; and variations in pronoun forms of address expressing status and power relations. Adamson concludes that even while Middleton's language pushes towards social realism, it remains limited by stereotyping and satire.

The next three essays explore a particularly important element of Middleton's authorial life, collaboration. As James P. Bednarz writes, a "limitless number of influences can be factored into the process of theatrical production" – and hence anything from the participation of the original actors to the mental activity of the modern reader can be considered, broadly, a form of collaboration – yet "one of its most revealing forms remains the most literal, the writing of a play by a pair or group of authors." Bednarz concentrates on two exceptional cases of Middleton and another author writing "a single text at the same time": his work with Webster on *Anything for a Quiet Life* and with Shakespeare on *Timon*. Heather Hirschfeld then discusses Middleton's two sustained collaborations, those with Thomas Dekker and William Rowley. For Hirschfeld there is a direct relationship between Middleton's willingness to collaborate and the variety of companies for which he wrote. She concludes that the collaborative ideal can be seen in its "allegorized perversion" in Middleton and Rowley's most famous play, *Changeling*, while the ideal itself informs even *Game*, a play Middleton wrote alone but in which he "carved out" a part for Rowley, an actor as well as Middleton's most consistent collaborator.

Eric Rasmussen completes the discussion of collaboration by raising the methodological difficulty presented once we accept a norm of collaboration: how does one determine authorship? Putting pressure on the standard view of the early seventeenth-century literary and theatrical context, which takes for granted Shakespeare's dominance even after Middleton had begun to write consistently, Rasmussen points out the "shuffling" of attributions on a variety of printed plays, from ones (mis)attributed to Shakespeare, like *Yorkshire*, to ones in which Middleton's name never appears, like *Timon* and *Macbeth*, and notes that at certain moments Middleton had more plays printed than Shakespeare. Rasmussen's essay takes us into the current scholarly context, in which arguments about attribution – and methods of attribution – still rage, and in which scholars sometimes contest their own opinions as well as those of others.

Subsequent essays in this part look at particular aspects of Middleton's choices as an author: his resistance to established genre, his non-theatrical writings, and his continuing ties to medieval forms and attitudes. Using current generic theory, Suzanne Gossett shows how from his earliest writings Middleton pushes against traditional formal limits, and argues that both a desire for topicality and consistent religious, satiric, and social attitudes led him to weaken or override traditional divisions between the comic and tragic, even when not technically writing tragicomedy. Alison A. Chapman analyzes Middleton's "adaptive impulse," his persistent engagement with prior texts, including works by Nashe and Greene, mock almanacs and testaments, plague literature and Bibles. She argues that this characteristic intertextuality "reveals not only Middleton's flair for intellectual one-upsmanship, but also his sense that literature has an overriding ethical imperative." For Chapman, Middleton's "habit of entering into conversation with other texts" is an aspect of his "fundamentally collaborative habit of mind."

Anke Bernau finds a "medievalizing tendency" even in this "most modern" of Jacobean playwrights. Middleton draws on tropes associated with the Middle Ages (allegory, magic, the chess game) and frequently gives characters the names of personified virtues and vices, as in the morality tradition. While of the plays only *Hengist, King of Kent*; or, *The Mayor of Queenborough* is set in the medieval past, the claim by its presenter, Raynulph the monk, that "Ancient stories have been best," establishes the exemplary value of that past for "patterns, mirrors, examples." Middleton's civic pageants, both the royal entries and the Lord Mayor's shows, do make reference to medieval historical precedent, paying particular attention to the contested medieval version of national origins.

The fifth part of the volume focuses on the psychological and social frameworks that provided a personal context for Middleton's oeuvre. The first two essays, by Caroline Bicks and Jennifer Panek, are broadly concerned with issues of gender. Bicks focuses on female sexuality and male views of its "secrets." Middleton devotes particular attention to the "plight of the undomesticated female body" and, most unusually, to the bastard children resulting from sex outside of marriage, an event which occurs even in such unlikely plays as *Game*. In contrast to most of his contemporaries, Middleton makes many of the advanced pregnancies in his plays undetectable, further complicating the difficulties of knowledgeable parenthood in a "pre-DNA era." Jennifer Panek uses the title of a lost Middleton play, "The Puritan Maid, the Modest Wife, and the Wanton Widow," as a template for his treatment of the life stages and prescribed behaviors of women. Middleton, she shows, was unusually "even-handed" in depicting men and women or such topics as wives and money – for example, in his plots about widows he is "more likely to satirize the mercenary suitor than the desirous widow." His views on women emerge as quite different from those of Shakespeare; rather than depicting irrationally jealous husbands and innocent wives, "on the contrary, jealous Middletonian husbands are usually punished with the cuckolding they deserve."

Farah Karim-Cooper explores "the tantalizing elusiveness of identity" for Middleton by examining his use of theatrical and prosthetic disguise. Invoking recent theoretical work on selfhood by Nancy Selleck, along with familiar analyses such as Stephen Greenblatt's *Renaissance Self-Fashioning*, she finds that for Middleton disguise simultaneously reveals and blurs essential qualities, "gesturing towards the beguilement of acting" and dependent upon "memories of identity." Most importantly, for Middleton "identity is dialogic," relying upon interpersonal exchange.

Middleton's awareness of contemporary trends emerges in Tanya Pollard's essay on his distinctive treatment of drugs and poisons. Tobacco – about which Middleton wrote several times – is the drug of choice of the idle city gallant in comedy; poison, the drug of tragedy, is often treated with sardonic wit, as in *Revenger* and *Lady*. More complexly, Middleton uses ambiguous drugs – placebos, fake poisons, virginity testers – for the plot twists of tragicomedy, including, Pollard notes, the only anti-aphrodisiac in the period's drama. She concludes that the use of these substances marks the playwright's "witty self-consciousness towards dramatic genres and their conventions."

But Middleton was not only, or always, witty. While supernatural phenomena belonged "to the sensational stock-in-trade" of the early modern drama, and Middleton repeatedly played with mock funerals and resurrections and made his witch "confessedly mortal," Michael Neill argues that it would be a mistake to assume that "thoroughgoing skepticism" was Middleton's consistent philosophical position. In *Revenger*, "a ghost play without a ghost," Vindice's condition exemplifies Freud's definition of the uncanny. In *Changeling* the sense of the uncanny is even stronger, as the "constant recurrence of the same thing" that Freud noted takes "the visible form of the phallic token" De Flores brings to Beatrice-Joanna. The ghost of Alonzo, showing his damaged hand, is, Neill says, perhaps the only one of Middleton's supernatural creations who "makes the functioning presence of the supernatural appear fully convincing," yet Neill concludes that for Middleton the context of human guile "holds the audience's gaze while the supernatural . . . keeps sliding unnervingly out of sight."

While models of tragic and comic madness were well established on the early modern stage, Carol Thomas Neely shows that Middleton pioneered his own, "the play-within-play performance by Bedlamites for the sane," and otherwise represented madness "through performative excess," blazoning his "exuberantly self-conscious art." Neely's analysis depends in part on the new scholarly attribution of *The Nice Valour* to Middleton alone. Like Middleton's other plays that include madness and "over-acting passions," *Valour* shows how "theatrical performance, like distraction, violently 'breaks' the passage of everyday time and space." Neely sees Middleton using madness "to foreground theatre's core elements: bodies and illusion, costumes and props, disguise and role-shifting." Oddly, his success in creating a theatrical Bedlam has been read backward into history and used to (mis)understand the reality of Bethlehem hospital and its practices.

The final part of the collection, "Afterlives," considers Middleton in the context of later print and performance. After recapitulating the inadequacy of the nineteenth-century editions, Sonia Massai considers why there was no collected volume of Middleton's works either during or shortly after his lifetime. While Middleton dedicated pageants and masques, he never seems to have sought patronage for any of his greatest works: "what is remarkable is the absence of dedications [or signed paratext] in any of the single-authored commercial plays published during his lifetime." Many of his best plays – for example, *Changeling* – were published anonymously; none had addresses to the reader. Yet there are dedications in the manuscript copies of *Witch* and *Game.* Hence, Massai concludes, "the visibility granted to Middleton as a major writer and playwright may therefore be a product of our desire to re-member and monumentalize him rather than his wish to build his literary reputation as a successful playwright through the medium of print."

Thus Middleton seems to have believed that his plays would live most importantly in performance, and such a hypothesis is borne out by the recent history of Middleton on stage and screen. Although Diana E. Henderson shows that, especially in adaptations, Middleton did not entirely disappear from the stage after the 1660s, she confirms that only in the second half of the twentieth century did Middleton's plays, seen as violent and overtly sexual, full of "explosive speech," come into their own again. "The theories of Antonin Artaud, Brecht's Marxist adaptations of early modern plays, the re-making of Shakespeare as 'our contemporary,' the 1960s 'sexual revolution,' and the politics of anticensorship British theatre" all contributed to making Middleton playtexts, with their representation of "privileged corruption, social deviance, and sexual power," resonate with audiences. Such resonance has continued into the period of third-wave feminism, and has permitted topical reinterpretations (e.g. Beatrice-Joanna as Princess Diana) of the kind previously familiar only in the case of Shakespeare.

Pascale Aebischer, too, analyzing twentieth-century filmings of Middleton tragedies directed by Jacques Rivette, Marcus Thompson, and Alex Cox, finds them in the tradition by which "non-Shakespearean Jacobean drama is associated with Artaudian Theatre of Cruelty and the opportunity for an alternative exploration of [modern] culture." These films vary in the extent to which they maintain either text or plot of the original: for Rivette, theatre "is the archaic medium" against which his *Noiroît* "defines itself as cinema," and "situations, characters and actions of *Revenger* take precedence over text and meaning." The films of Thompson and Cox include more Middleton but emphasize it as part of an alternative tradition, an extreme of excess and deviance. In a cinematic version of the familiar opposition, Cox's *Revengers Tragedy* [*sic*] is used to attack the "Shakespeare establishment" and his, and its, presumed political inertia and reactionary politics. Now it is Middleton who is our contemporary.

In conclusion, Simon Palfrey stands back from Middleton, entering into his present and presence, arguing that for him plot and presence were "foundational" both as technique and as "presumed theology," a sequence of relations in which "events cannot outrun their source." Like so many of the writers in this collection, Palfrey could only be writing in the current context. Only now could he find Middleton's iconic moments of "saturated phenomena" both in the familiar *Changeling* and in a play only recently attributed to him, *Yorkshire*. Yet as Palfrey says, a play is written for "future presents," the contexts in which Middleton will be read in the future.

Today Middleton seems not just acceptable but recognizable. Attacks on the obfuscatory language of lawyers, the pursuit of wealth, and the ponzi schemes of the likes of Quomodo can all be found in our morning newspapers. In a world full of avatars, a play peopled by chess pieces looks less unfamiliar. In a world where terrorists justify their actions by theology, a play where black and white are divided by religion as much as nation is less alien. In a world of assisted fertilization, the actions of Lady Kix do not seem strange. In a world of bestsellers about vampires, even making love to a skull seems possible. The context for reading Middleton, however, was best established long ago by Heminges and Condell's address in the folio of another early modern playwright: "Read him, therefore, and again, and again. And if then you do not like him, surely you are in some manifest danger, not to understand him." This volume is dedicated to assisting the current reader in understanding the works of Thomas Middleton.

# PART I

# *Middleton and the London context*

## CHAPTER 1

# Thomas Middleton, chronologer of his time

## Mark Hutchings

Of all the public events in the life of any English man or woman born in the second half of Elizabeth I's reign who lived to see the end of her successor's, arguably none were more significant than the "triumphs" over Spain in 1588, 1605, and 1623. A young Thomas Middleton at the tender age of 8 no doubt shared the joy and relief of his fellows when news of the defeat of the Armada reached London. Less speculatively, the unmasking of the gunpowder plotters and the return of Prince Charles from Madrid – both similarly marked by widespread public rejoicing for England's deliverance – each left their mark.[1] These three occasions neatly straddle the poet's formative years, the early playwriting, and the remarkable *A Game at Chess* (1624); Middleton's career coincided almost exactly with the years of James's English rule. Peace with Spain in 1604 would not only overshadow the Stuart monarch's kingship, but also to a considerable extent frame the nature and trajectory of Middleton's writing. In his engagement with both foreign crises and domestic controversy Thomas Middleton is the principal chronicler of those turbulent years. (See Figure 1.1.)

There are a number of ways of narrating the career of a writer whose standing is arguably higher now than at any time since the giddy days of summer 1624.[2] There is the writer of the city, in satirical comedies for children's companies and, less visible today, in the pamphlet form to which he turned occasionally, especially when plague closed the theatres. There is, too, of course, the writer of great tragedies later, though the firm ascription of *A Yorkshire Tragedy* (1605) and *The Revenger's Tragedy* (1606) complicates such a neat division, and indeed in the case of the latter exemplifies Middleton's experiments with genre and convention. Detectable throughout is the satirist of the court, of lawyers, and of the Church of Rome; and while his identification with a Protestant sensibility (not to say anxiety) is apparent, so too is the condemnation of hypocrisy and corruption, charges levelled close to home as well as abroad. If this illustrates both versatility and continuity, his ability to turn his hand to a diverse range of literary forms

Figure 1.1 Thomas Middleton. Frontispiece to *Two New Playes
Written by Tho. Middleton, Gent.*

and modes is testament to both the kind of career a successful writer for the
London stage might – if he was lucky – enjoy, and the mark of a remarkable
imagination. The contrast with his sometime collaborator, Thomas
Dekker, is salutary: although he had a hand in numerous plays, Dekker
was to spend seven years in debtors' prison.

Despite the Privy Council's issuing of a warrant for his arrest over the
furore caused by *Game*, it appears that Middleton may have escaped a

similar fate, and the surviving evidence, scant though it is, indicates that his
pen was sufficient to maintain him and his family; only at the very end of his
career does this situation alter.[3] Yet monetary concerns dogged his extended
family for years, and perhaps not surprisingly a critical fascination with how
social relations were determined by economic forces and circumstances
pervades the plays. As scholars are fond of pointing out, the lampooning
of the legal profession, particularly in the early plays, surely had a biographical origin, since his widowed mother, Anne, within months of William
Middleton's death in early 1586, contracted a marriage which had catastrophic consequences for the family, embroiling it in legal wrangles for
years. Thomas Harvey's actions would eventually relieve Thomas
Middleton of his inheritance, a situation of familial double-dealing replayed
(albeit with a happier ending for the heir) in one of his earliest comedies, *A
Trick to Catch the Old One* (1605). As befitting the son of a reasonably
prosperous bricklayer with his own coat of arms, the young Middleton had
entered The Queen's College, Oxford in 1598, shortly after first being
named in the lawsuit that would drag on for almost a decade. It seems,
however, that he left without taking a degree: whether this was linked to the
family's financial plight is unclear. When he came of age in April 1601 he
was given £25 by the City of London, perhaps the only legacy from his
father he would receive, since the rest was tied up in the lawsuit. But in one
of the few documented references to his activities at this time (again from
law court records) we know that from January 1601, and perhaps before, he
was "in London daylie accompaninge the players" (Eccles, "Thomas
Middleton," p. 525). So began, inauspiciously, a twenty-five-year career in
the theatre; yet even for a successful playwright it was a precarious business.
In the wake of *Game* it seems that he steadily lost favor, despite having being
appointed City Chronologer in 1620. Mary Marbeck, whom he had married
in *c.* 1603, died a year after her husband, her need to petition the city for
money an indication of her financial plight. Thus ended a career in financial
uncertainty, which for both his profession and the times was entirely
unremarkable.

   For a university-educated dramatist his literary beginnings were similarly
unexceptional. We have no direct evidence for any connection with the
London stage prior to his going to Oxford, but it may well be that he
attended plays in the 1590s. What is clear is that he had already begun
writing several years earlier and, conventionally enough, it was to poetry
that he had turned.

   At the end of the sixteenth century it was as natural for an aspiring writer
to compose poetry as it was for an impecunious poet from London to turn

to the stage, which in little more than a decade had created a new and vibrant market for literary production. In accounts of Middleton's career the earliest, non-dramatic writings tend to be dismissed or dealt with rather cursorily; even the Oxford *Middleton* relegates this material to an appendix (*Middleton*, pp. 1913–2011). While this is justifiable on grounds of quality it engenders a slightly misleading assumption that the poetry ought to be marked off as distinct from the subsequent writing. This might be questioned on several grounds. While this poetry, like all juvenilia, does not always encourage the modern critic to make the case for rereading, it is precisely as an apprenticeship that it deserves attention. Moreover, for a writer who frequently returned to and reworked material, the earliest writings can serve as more than appetizers for the main course that followed. While we may discern both a conventional, and unarguably uneven, grasp of poetic form at this time, there are also indications of the qualities that were to bring to life his words on the stage.

The early work may be divided in two. The difference in quality between the first extant work and what followed is as great as that between the greatest and least successful of the plays. Although it is possible to glimpse signs of promise, the long poem *The Wisdom of Solomon Paraphrased* demands of even its most sympathetic reader much more than it can deliver. Published in 1597, when Middleton was just 17, it was composed before he went to university, and it shows. The poem's most recent commentator, Debora Shuger, pulls no punches: "it is a very bad poem, committing some of the most execrable lines extant in the corpus of English verse." Shuger draws attention to its many deficiencies and numerous misreadings of its source, the translation of the *Sapientia Solomonis* in the Geneva Bible (*Middleton*, p. 1915). But its interest for Middleton scholars lies in its articulation of a Protestant sensibility coupled with an at times rather shrill Old Testament morality that would receive a much more nuanced and qualified treatment over the course of his career. While the religiosity of the text is somewhat conventional (though not without error), the condemnation of vice in a fallen world is a signature motif of Middleton's early drama. In lines such as

> The greedy lucre of a witless brain,
> This feeding avarice on senseless mind,
> Is rather hurt than good, a loss than gain,
> Which covets for to lose, and not to find.
> (Chapter 15, 49–52)

we may see past the awkwardness of the syntax and look forward to the later deployment of such key terms for Middleton as "lucre," "wit," and "avarice." Perhaps what the poem most effectively expresses is the speaker's frustration at the state of things: strip away the sententiousness and the seeds of an acute critique of London and the court are being sown.

Nonetheless, this first literary effort has the air of a text written in an intellectual vacuum. With *Microcynicon: Six Snarling Satires* Middleton at once enters the literary community, engaging with a public discourse – and, indeed, political controversy, for in June 1599 this was one of ten satirical books publicly burned on the orders of the Archbishop of Canterbury. The shift from the labored verse and crudely reductive moralizing of *Solomon* to the questioning of such convenient moral positioning in *Microcynicon* marks the end of Middleton's "juvenilia" and the beginning of his career proper. In this text a distinctively Middletonian voice begins to emerge – through, significantly, the introduction of dramatized characters.

*Microcynicon* consists of six poems, each of which takes a different figure for its satire. The initial impression, formed by "The Author's Prologue" and the first two poems, is that the moral sermonizing of *Solomon*, if not its literary shortcomings, is being replayed. In the opening satire, "Insatiate Cron," and the second, "Prodigal Zodon," we encounter successively the figure of the usurer and his dissolute heir. Here are archetypes of the city drama Middleton would soon embark on for the children's companies. Thus Cron is allied with the devil, his Faustian pact with gold countered by the narrator's reminder of his mortality, while in Zodon we recognize the reckless gallant who spends with abandon, spiritually and materially, his bequest:

> Well, Zodon hath his pleasure: he hath gold,
> Young in his golden age, in sin too old. –
> Now he wants gold; all his treasure's done.
> He's banished [from] the stews; pity finds none.
> Rich yesterday in wealth, this day as poor,
> Tomorrow like to beg from door to door.
>
> (Satire 2, 71–6)

So far then, so conventional; but as Wendy Wall points out, *Microcynicon* explores the ideological complexities of the genre, as in Satires 3–6 we witness the progressive deconstruction of the satirist's moral universe. Middleton alludes to Joseph Hall's *Vergidemiarum* (1597–8) and several John Marston satires, among others, as well as to Robert Greene's cony-catching pamphlets in Satire 4 (*Middleton*, pp. 1971–2). After the insularity of *Solomon*, *Microcynicon* not only establishes a dialogue with other texts – which their collective, ritual burning ironically underscored – but enables

Middleton to play with the conventions and possibilities of the genre. Crucially, this literary exploration fractures the moral framework itself. In effect, then, these six satires map out the transition from the writer's moral certainty of two years previously to a new, contingent, and altogether uncertain perspective – yet one full of imaginative possibility.

Where Zodon is mocked for his ostentatious dress, the signature of the gallant lampooned later in plays such as the collaboration with Dekker, *The Roaring Girl* – "Suit upon suit, satin too too base, – / Velvet, laid on with silver and lace" (Satire 2, 17–18) – the third poem acknowledges that the treacherousness of the aesthetic works both ways. Confected appearance may betray the wearer's vanity, but it also ensnares the viewer:

> And sin, though it be foul, yet fair in this,
> In being painted with a show of bliss.
> For what more happy creature to the eye
> Than is Superbia in her bravery?
>
> (Satire 3, 21–4)

The next line offers the familiar moral: "Yet who more foul disrobèd of attire?" But the poem has already rehearsed the inside/outside conundrum that compromises the satirist's position. No more can the narrator maintain a perspective of moral authority *outside* the world he has entered than can the reader escape the pleasure of the text. "Insolent Superbia" ends with the conventional reminder that pride will be punished: "Repent, proud princocks. Cease for to aspire, / Or die to live with pride in burning fire" (Satire 3, 131–2); but perhaps this simply serves to remind the reader that irony cuts both ways.

If the satirist is implicated in the world he portrays, so too is the reader. Like Greene's cony-catching tales, "Cheating Drone" purports to invite the reader into a world in which he is implicitly superior to, and yet analogous to, the dupe cozened by the "cheater by profession / That takes more shapes than the chameleon" (Satire 4, 1–2). Here, the moral is that of the marketplace rather than the pulpit, a shift which locates the satire in a recognizably contemporary London. In the chameleon's changeable shapes the player of roles emerges, destabilizing notions of essence and inner truth requisite for the moral paradigm. Similarly, "Ingling Pyander" challenges orthodoxies of gender and representation through a figure who anticipates Moll Cutpurse:

> Sometimes he jets it like a gentleman,
> Otherwhiles much like a wanton courtesan.
> But truth to tell a man or woman whether,
> I cannot say, she's excellent in either.

But if report may certify a truth,
She's neither of either, but a cheating youth.

(Satire 5, 25–30)

Once again, the moral judgment is more convention than conviction; crucially, however, here the speaker soon confesses that "time was I loved Pyander well" (42). The remainder of the poem is a cautionary tale, relating how the speaker was himself taken in – "Trust not a painted puppet as I have done, / Who far more doted than Pygmalion" (94–5). Not only are appearances misleading, then – as they are shown to be with Cron, Zodon, and Superbia – but just as the reader/viewer risks being seduced by the allure of the text, the satirist too is always already compromised. There is no authority position for him, who in an inversion of the Heisenberg uncertainty principle cannot but be corrupted by what he observes.

The logical conclusion is that the satirist is no better equipped than anyone else in the modern world: "Thus may we see by folly oft the wise / Stumble and fall into fool's paradise" (Epilogue, 1–2). In the oxymoronic "Wise Innocent," the final poem of the sequence, the tables are turned as the satirist himself becomes the object of the satire. Wendy Wall argues that the reader's difficulty in discerning which of the two characters is speaking at various points is deliberate, and certainly the effect is to carry through the deconstruction of the genre (*Middleton*, p. 1972). Though *Microcynicon* is putatively the first of several books, no others do or can appear, since the satirist's moral ground has been progressively chipped away. For Middleton the satirical impulse was to continue by other means, chiefly in the playhouse, for which these dialogues may well have served as a recommendation to Henslowe and the playwrights whom Middleton joined the following year. (Indeed, the Archbishop of Canterbury's actions must have dramatically raised his profile.) But *Microcynicon* may have served another purpose too. A recurring critical debate has revolved around the question of whether Middleton texts adopt "moral," "immoral," or "amoral" perspectives, an issue with implications for the representation of gender relations, for example. What this text suggests is that Middleton himself was working through this very problem, one which he recognized could not be resolved, at least not within the confines of the genre. In the plays for the boys' companies, too, it is notable that the satire – who is being attacked, who is laughing at whom – is rarely as clear-cut as it seems. The origins of such complexity arguably lie in this early trying out of different voices.

If *Microcynicon* looks forward to Middleton's writing of the city, a poem published in 1600 offers further evidence of his engagement with contemporary literary modes, and also of concerns to which Middleton would return, principally in the tragedies for which he is most lauded. *The Ghost of Lucrece* echoes in title and subject Shakespeare's *The Rape of Lucrece* (1594) and may be regarded as the first of Middleton's responses to the work of his older contemporary; later, in addition to a number of reworkings, the evidence suggests that he revised both *Macbeth* and *Measure for Measure*. Shakespeare's and Middleton's poems participate in a popular literary theme of the 1590s, the "female complaint" narrative, of which Samuel Daniel's *The Complaint of Rosamond* (1592) is most directly relevant, for it was to influence Middleton considerably (Hutchings and Bromham, *Middleton*, pp. 92–6). Perhaps the most striking feature of the poem is its dramatic qualities – striking, but not surprising, for although we cannot be certain of the date of composition, clearly he already had an eye on the stage at this time; as *Microcynicon* demonstrated, the potential of dramatized situations and plural voices increasingly appealed to the poet.

In *Ghost*, wittingly or not, Middleton first grapples with the ideological problematic of male writers ventriloquizing female characters. This he tackles head on (or seems to), a male speaker occasionally interjecting at points in Lucrece's account of "her" story – itself not only written by Middleton, of course, but arguably trapped thereby in the paradigm governing male perceptions of gender, at this (or perhaps any other) time. Arguments for textual complicity or resistance complicate the issue, but the question arises subsequently in the modern critic's sometimes uneasy appreciation of Middleton's oft-praised understanding of female psychology in characters such as Bianca and Beatrice-Joanna. What *Women Beware Women* (1621) and *The Changeling* (1622) share with *Ghost* is the subject of rape, which for Middleton is always about power rather than sexual desire alone – a strikingly modern perspective. Thus rape is configured in *Game* as the figurative threat posed to the Church of England by Rome; and for Bianca and Beatrice-Joanna, as for Castiza in *Revenger*, sexual violence is very real, bodily, and inseparable from power – as well as gender – relations. *Ghost* may be regarded then as the first of Middleton's explorations of the politics of rape, which in the plays arguably receive in their dramatization a treatment that is appropriately troubling, since it stages sexual desire and the abuse of power simultaneously. That the theme recurs in plays such as *Hengist, King of Kent; or, The Mayor of Queenborough* (1619[?]) suggests that in both its early modern resonances and Middleton's own anxieties about the precarious situation of the "pure" religion this poem prefigures concerns about the abuses that frequently coalesce around the court.

Of course, at the turn of the century all this lay ahead. The phrase on which we base our knowledge of how he made the transition from student to playwright is tantalizingly vague: "daylie accompaninge the players" suggests rather more than play*going*, rather less than play*writing*. But at some point between February 1601, when Middleton's first association with the stage is on record, and May 1602, when his name appears in Henslowe's account book, Middleton became one of the jobbing playwrights contributing to the Admiral's Men's repertory. On May 22 that year he was paid for work on a collaborative, lost play, "Caesar's Fall, or, Two Shapes"; in November he received £7 for what appears to be his first sole-authored work, also unfortunately lost, "The Chester Tragedy" (Henslowe, *Diary*, pp. 201, 206). We know nothing about how these plays fared on stage, but evidently Middleton was held in some regard, for at the end of the year he wrote a new prologue and epilogue for a court performance of the now-dead Greene's *Friar Bacon and Friar Bungay*. So began what in retrospect was a crucial period for the fledgling writer.

James's reign would provide much for Middleton to rail against, but his accession offered opportunity. He contributed to *The Whole Royal and Magnificent Entertainment*, London's welcome for the new monarch, so beginning a career-long association with the city's sponsorship of civic pageantry; but with a symbolism early moderns would have "appreciated," plague descended on the capital, closing the theatres for almost a year. However, what was catastrophic for some playwrights was perhaps fortuitous for Middleton. With Dekker he wrote two pamphlets published in 1604, *News from Gravesend* and *The Meeting of Gallants at an Ordinary* – both of which exploited the effects of plague on London – and, independently, *Father Hubburd's Tales* and *The Black Book*.

For all Londoners the plague of 1603–4 must have been a harrowing experience; for Middleton himself it carried off his sister's husband and two of their children. When the theatres reopened it was perhaps not surprising that an ironical tone suited the times. Middleton was fortunate in that his early career coincided with the rise of the children's companies, whose speciality during their brief heyday was chiefly satire. The years 1604–6 were highly significant, for he wrote no fewer than five plays for the Children of Paul's, but they were also unusual, for never again would he be identified so closely with a single company. Even in this productive period he also wrote *The Patient Man and the Honest Whore* (1604) with Dekker for Prince Henry's Men, and for the King's Men *Yorkshire* in 1605 and the following year *Revenger*. In such patterns we may read independence, talent, insecurity, exigency – a combination which underlines once again the playwright's vulnerability to forces beyond his control.

Middleton "collaborated shamelessly," but not in the sense T. S. Eliot meant: "successfully" would have been nearer the mark, judging from the apparent envy of contemporaries such as Ben Jonson (Eliot, *Elizabethan*, p. 83). All theatre is collaborative, so the distinction between sole and joint authorship is misleading: what Eliot did not appreciate, as recent scholarship has urged, is that in most cases the dramatist was in a weak position, compared to the legally protected and culturally esteemed modern "author." Shakespeare, exceptionally, became a sharer in a company; no other writer for the stage enjoyed similar security, or indeed the wealth it brought. In writing for several different companies, in different genres, with and without other writers, Middleton is nicely representative of the range of theatrical practices that characterize playmaking at this time. (See essays by James P. Bednarz, Heather Hirschfeld, and Eric Rasmussen in this volume, pp. 211, 219, 229.)

Nonetheless, as Margot Heinemann and others have found, it is tempting to trace certain patterns – *authorial*, as it were – throughout his diverse career. He would not have seen it this way, but Middleton was lucky in the reign through which he lived: domestic scandals such as the Essex divorce case and Overbury murder nicely complemented the betrayal, as many regarded it, of first the peace and then the marriage negotiations with Spain. It made for great theatre. With the benefit of hindsight the gentle satire of the city for the Children of Paul's is small beer compared to the attacks on court corruption in *Revenger*, *The Witch* (1616), *Women Beware*, and *Changeling*, to take the most notable examples. While *Game* was a spectacular conclusion to his career it is now considered to be less an *intervention* in a crisis than a brilliantly witty satire – controversial but not, despite the Spanish ambassador's complaint, politically incendiary. The great collaboration with William Rowley is subtly different. In *Changeling* the playwrights return to the cover-up over Frances Carr's macabre virginity test – a "fix" orchestrated by James himself – which had featured in *Witch*, and to her involvement in the murder of Sir Thomas Overbury, for which she and Somerset were spared death but committed to the Tower. They were released in early 1622, when *Changeling* was licensed and most likely first staged.

Along with *Game*, it was Middleton's most sustained anti-Spain play. In 1622 it offered an implied commentary on both the double-dealing at the heart of James's court and the king's all-too-cozy relationship with Spain, the principal figure of which, the ambassador Count Gondomar, would be at the heart of the 1624 cause célèbre. As such, *Changeling* was a topical and, it seems, successful play. But this topicality was to touch much nearer home when it was staged at court before Prince Charles in January 1624. There is, unsurprisingly, no surviving account of its reception, but the prince had only returned from Madrid a matter of weeks before, his father's foreign policy in ruins, and he himself an unlikely hero in English Protestant eyes, so we can but speculate about how these circumstances may have inscribed new meaning for its elite audience (Bromham and Bruzzi, *Changeling*, p. 5).

Middleton could hardly have hoped, as he watched (or imagined) *Microcynicon* going up in flames in 1599, that he would go on to write a play that would directly address the royal court with Protestant concerns about James's Spanish policy. Scholars and theorists continue to debate what we might mean by "political" when we describe Middleton, the dramatist of the city, court, law, and religion. But in his engagement with some of the key controversies of the age he was indeed the quintessential chronologer of those times.

NOTES

1. On the significance of such moments, see Cressy, *Bonfires and Bells*.
2. Evidence for the contemporary and posthumous reputation of Thomas Middleton may be found in Steen, *Ambrosia*.
3. Much of this paragraph, and biographical information elsewhere in this essay, draws on two essays by Eccles, "Middleton's Birth and Education" (1931) and "Thomas Middleton a Poett" (1957), and on Taylor, "Middleton, Thomas (*bap.* 1580, *d.* 1627)."

CHAPTER 2

# Middleton's comedy and the geography of London

## Darryll Grantley

London by Middleton's day was a tadpole-shaped conurbation, with the walled city linked to the court and City of Westminster in the west by Thames-side ribbon development, and to the suburbs in the south by London Bridge. In terms of human scale this conurbation was walkable, being approximately three miles wide east to west, and less than one and a half miles at its widest from north to south (see Figure 2.1).

Despite these spatial limitations, the city was complex and often dangerous because of its teeming population and tight juxtapositions. The texture of the rapidly growing metropolitan environment varied greatly, encompassing the more expansive elite residential areas to the west, a denser social mixture within the city involving habitation of greater and lesser prosperity, some areas like Blackfriars emerging as more fashionable, and the crowded warrens of the transpontine suburbs providing a reference point for notions of squalor and criminality. Added to this were grand commercial thoroughfares like Cheapside, open spaces such as Moorfields and Lincoln's Inn fields, and outlying leisure resorts like Islington. Middleton was born and raised in this city, but was also in other ways a son of the metropolis. From 1613 onwards he started writing for mayoral pageants and other civic celebrations, but was working for the city authorities from as early as 1604 when he contributed to their official welcome celebrations for the new monarch. In 1620–1 he wrote ten "Honourable Entertainments" for the Lord Mayor, and was appointed City Chronologer in 1620.

Middleton's commercial theatre plays also reveal a strong interest in both the society and topography of his native city, though their representation of London is less affected by his official work than by other factors. As the commercial theatre became established in London from the 1570s onwards, playwrights increasingly recognized that they were writing for a geographically localized audience, as opposed to that of the touring theatre of the earlier itinerant playing companies. The allegorically oriented drama

28

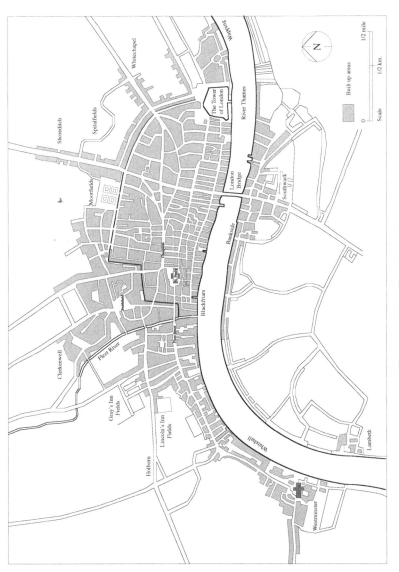

Figure 2.1 Map of London *c.* 1600.

of these troupes tended to represent the capital in terms of moral degeneracy and danger, while the 1590s commercial theatre was more inclined to
celebrate it, often with a broader nationalist agenda. By the time Middleton
was writing the situation had shifted again, with a more complex view of
London emerging in the drama, particularly as playwrights were increasingly conscious of the growing sophistication of their London audience.
Exotic foreign settings were becoming commonplace in drama, especially in
respect of their titillating dangers and threats. London, though familiar to
audiences, was often also cast in these terms, usually in the process of
constructing a picture of an urban environment requiring sharp intelligence
as a prerequisite for successful life within it. Middleton's drama participates
in this too, his London being on the one hand a place of wit and sophistication, and on the other one that endemically permitted deception,
criminality, and corruption. This latter view can be found in some of his
non-theatrical writing as well, pamphlets such as *Father Hubburd's Tales*
(1604), which often depict a tough and sometimes predatory city. But in
common with several other playwrights, Middleton was also conscious that,
catering as he was for a specifically London audience, the material city that
they inhabited could be exploited to add recognitive interest to theatrical
narratives, and even provide a cultural and moral frame of reference. Thus
his plays manifest an interest in the geography of London in a variety of
ways. In some instances he seeks to evoke its physical terrain in order to give
immediacy and impact to the dramatic action presented, in some he exploits
contemporary associations of specific localities in the metropolis, and he
also uses the familiarity with the material environment on the part of
characters to contribute to their moral and social profiles. However, in
common with most contemporary dramatists who set plays in London,
Middleton has relatively few scenes placed in named or identifiable urban
locations, most being in private interior spaces or unnamed public or
exterior ones. Where places are identified it tends to be by means of reported
rather than staged action. (See Figure 2.2.)

Despite the extremely limited scenic facilities in the early modern
commercial theatre, some locations could occasionally be suggested by
movable stage properties. The third scene of *The Roaring Girl* (1611) has
three shops "in a rank," and here the commodities on sale help to realize
the setting visually, while another recurrent location – the tavern – is
routinely evoked by means of appropriate stage properties. However,
where named urban locations are involved, they are introduced by verbal
reference, as in the following piece of dialogue from *Anything for a Quiet
Life* (1621):

Figure 2.2 Localities featured in Middleton's plays.

RACHEL CAMLET: I care not who I hurt. O, my heart, how it beats o' both
sides! Will you run with me for a wager into Lombard Street now?
KNAVESBE: I'll walk with you, cousin, a sufficient pace. Sib shall come softly
after. I'll bring you through Bearbinder Lane.
RACHEL CAMLET: Bearbinder Lane cannot hold me. I'll the nearest way over
St Mildred's Church.

(4.1.352–9)

The geographical insertion here is an economical device. By positioning
these characters in streets readily identifiable to the audience, Middleton is
able to endow both their reported action with immediacy and concreteness,
and the characters themselves with a veneer of realism.

Apart from enhancing the theatrical dynamic and interest in the dramatic
action, the evocation on stage of known public places can also contribute to
the moral and social implications of the scenes set there. The fifth scene
of *Roaring Girl* is set in Gray's Inn Fields and is a complex instance of the
signifying role of named urban space. The episode involves an assignation
between the heroine, Moll, and her ineffectual would-be seducer Laxton.
Her ascendancy over him is subtly communicated by her greater geographical mastery, and this works by drawing on the audience's awareness of
the implications of localities in their city. Laxton had suggested Holborn,
known for illicit sexual activity, as a meeting place, whereas Moll, who has a
duel in mind, has opted for Gray's Inn Fields, another dubious place but
one more readily associated with duels. Laxton arrives with a coachman,
whom he immediately sends to fetch Moll from Marylebone Park, and his
remark that it is "a fit place for Moll to get in" (4–5) indicates his assessment
of her, since this was a resort of whores. However, she arrives independently
soon after dressed as a man, her arrival and appearance immediately indicating her evasion of any form of control by him. When he finally recognizes
who she is, he suggests they go to the Three Pigeons in Brentford, a tavern
famously used for sexual liaisons, but when she wounds him in the duel, he
cries, "Pox o' the Three Pigeons! I would the coach were here now to carry me
to the surgeon's" (129–31). Moll then meets Trapdoor, whom she intends to
hire. Trapdoor is secretly trying to entrap her on behalf of others, but she gets
the better of him, this outcome again being suggested by her command of the
urban world and her own self-constructed identity within it. At one point she
tells him she is a lawyer from the Temple and that she haunts Chick Lane, an
area notorious for criminality, which has the effect of intimidating him. His
coming and going in the scene is also governed by her, as she takes him off at
the end to St. Thomas the Apostle's nearby clothing shops, in order to get
him livery. The geographical setting is quite strongly insisted upon in the

scene through the inclusion of topographically accurate detail; at one point Laxton hears the Savoy hospital clock strike, and he also sees two Innsmen and a woman walking towards Islington. The clear placing of the action in a locality that would have been a familiar part of the audience's metropolitan environment, at least by reputation, adduces a layer of experiential knowledge to their judgment of what transpires within the scene.

Localities like Gray's Inn Fields may have specific implications attached to them, but as publicly accessible spaces they also have a more neutral identity and thus offer the potential for ambiguity and ambivalence that can be exploited theatrically. This is a geographical corollary to the unstable identity of individuals that London permits and enables. Incomers to London are able to shift their identities, being freed from the constraints that would exist in smaller communities. In *Michaelmas Term* (1604–6), for instance, Andrew Lethe is able, as his name suggests, to "forget" his former identity as a poor tooth-puller's son and become an urban gallant when he arrives in London. He extends this identity shift into a geographical dimension when he lodges his whore in a constable's house, rendering its apparent respectability ironical. But this ambiguity of place characterizes many localities in London, particularly public ones. Shops are a good case in point. In Middleton's plays the legitimate trading in their ostensible commodities invariably serves as a cover for sexual transactions. This occurs in *Michaelmas*, *Roaring Girl*, *Wit at Several Weapons* (1613), *Quiet Life*, and *No Wit/Help Like a Woman's* (1611).

Taverns, like shops, are public places of association and transaction, and their theatrical utility ensures that they make frequent appearances in early modern plays. Taverns have the advantage to dramatists of allowing either arranged or random social encounters and affording access to a wide social range of people. Their ambiguity reposes in their being places of festivity and legitimate social interaction, while they also possess a potentially transgressive edge that can add a certain frisson to theatrical narratives. Especially where gaming rooms are involved, there are opportunities for their more perilous dimensions to be exploited. Middleton has two scenes set in gaming rooms in the Horn (*Michaelmas*, 2.1) and Mitre (*Your Five Gallants*, 2.4), taverns in Fleet Street. In both a countryman is inducted into supposedly "gentlemanly" comportment and attitudes. Easy in *Michaelmas* is told that he should adopt an attitude of carelessness about gaming losses if he wishes to appear a true London gallant, while Bungler in the *Five Gallants* (1606/7) is encouraged to forswear former friendships on coming to London, and indeed any notion of loyalty to friends. The air of friendly bonhomie in both instances masks not only the dangers present in these lessons, but also the process of deception that is covertly occurring in both scenes, especially in the latter play in which another apparently benign social and business space, the middle aisle of St. Paul's in 4.4, harbors similar threats, and an apparently respectable music school for ladies in 2.1 turns out to be a brothel. The theatrical satisfactions that the plays offer their London audiences often involve both a dramatic reconstitution of well-known resorts into places of hidden dangers, while allowing the urban spectators a self-congratulatory sense of metropolitan knowingness by contrast with the countryman. The ability of members of the audience to recognize the complexities and threats in these environments feeds into the way the plays invite them to see themselves.

Such scenes draw the audience in by recreating as contexts for the theatrical action localities known to the audience through experience or reputation. However, the urban geography may be used to enhance the theatrical action on a more purely imaginative level as well. In several instances of narrated action, a sense of the materiality and immediacy of that action is created by grounding it minutely in the identifiable streets and spaces of the metropolis. In act 4 of *A Chaste Maid in Cheapside* (1613), the geography of the dramatic narrative involves a combination of narration and stage action to evoke the material space. The attempted flight of the lovers Moll and Touchwood Junior at the heart of the story and some material details of it are provided in scene 2 by her brother's reaction:

> My sister's gone. Let's look at Trig Stairs for her.
> My mother's gone to lay the common stairs
> At Puddle Wharf; and at the dock below
> Stands my poor silly father.
>
> (5–8)

The scene following opens with Touchwood Junior's brother adding to the drama by describing his own earlier escape by river from sergeants pursuing him for debt. Touchwood Junior then rushes in to engage the watermen to take Moll to Barn Elms after him, and brings her in with the instruction, "Away, quick! There's a boat waits for you; / And I'll take the water at Paul's-wharf and overtake you" (26–7). This short scene is followed by one in which her family appears and her mother drags her in by the hair, Moll having been apprehended in her flight. The writing here skilfully blends urgently related narrative with economically compressed dramatic action, but the sense of realism and theatrical intensity is created by anchoring the action in known points on the Thames, London's geography being enlisted to enhance the excitement and dramatic impact.

The ways in which characters inhabit their city constitutes a not unimportant dimension of the moral construction of some figures in Middleton's comedies. In some cases this relates to the opportunities the city's topography offers for evasion, as in the case above or in *Quiet Life*, when the villainous Knavesbe, on being foiled and exposed, resolves to "sink at Queenhithe . . . [and] rise again at Charing Cross" (5.2.33–4). In *Roaring Girl*, Trapdoor expresses some suspicion of Moll (dressed as a man) when he becomes aware that she ducks and dives about the city: "I like you the worse because you shift your lodging so often; I'll not meddle with you for that trick, sir" (5.164–6). Her lack of geographical stability seems a corollary to her lack of gender fixity. Movement becomes a form of power, and it usually relates to the opportunities for shady activity offered by London's complexity and relative lack of the natural social policing inherent in smaller communities. The villainous central figures in *Five Gallants* move across the urban landscape constantly, each being associated with or practicing their corrupt or criminal activity in a particular type of locality. One example is Frip the pawnbroker gallant, who opens the play choosing from which parishes he will accept goods for pawn, rejecting those infected by plague. St. Clement's, St. Bride's, St. Dunstan's, St. Mary Maudlin's, and St. Martin's are mentioned, and the impression is created of a man decidedly in control of the material environment in which he operates. Frip later describes his rise, which involved working the city, starting with the fishwives at Blackwall, taking pickings where he could. Another character who has made good by inserting himself into the complex geography of London and negotiating it successfully is the usurer Dampit in *A Trick to Catch the Old One* (1605), who arrived in London with 10 shillings but has amassed a fortune of £10,000. He reports that he worked moving around Westminster Hall – "I would trample up and down like a mule" (1.4.50–1) – and he also describes himself as one of the "tramplers of time" working in Fleet Street and Holborn: "Here I have fees of one, there I have fees of another. My clients come about me, the fooliaminy and coxcombry of the country. I still trashed and trotted for other men's causes" (1.4.59–64).

It is not only movement in, but being knowledgeable about and known in the urban environment that confers a dubious form of power. Being able to negotiate the urban terrain is almost in itself a signifier of venality. The rogue Shortyard in *Michaelmas* is a successful negotiator of the urban landscape. Accompanied by the countryman, Easy, whom he is trying to gull, he shows himself being able to send to various tradesmen for money, and when Easy remarks on how well known he is in the city, he suggests that one should carry oneself in a bold, confident manner and take care to display oneself strategically, even to the point of choosing where one urinates: "I tell you what I ha' done: sometimes I carry my water all London over, only to deliver it proudly at the Standard; and I do not pass altogether unnoted, think you? No, a man can no sooner peep out his head, but there's a bow bent at him out of some watchtower or other" (2.1.108–13). In the case of Moll Cutpurse, her successful occupation of urban space has been demonstrated above, but her transgressiveness, for the purposes of her role in the plot and managing audience response to her, needs to be suggested but cannot be allowed to spill over into full-blown criminality. It is thus principally signalled by associating her closely with the urban fabric of London. Like Shortyard, she is well known in the city, described as "So strange in quality, a whole city takes / Note of her name" (1.103–4). When Trapdoor is hired to entrap her, he asserts, "I will sift the taverns i'th' city, and drink half-pots with all the watermen o' th' Bankside, but if you will, sir, I'll find her out' (2.210–12). Her trajectory through the play is embedded in the city's streets, and her mastery of her environment is indicated by Laxton's comment that "Sh'as the spirit of four great parishes, and a voice that will drown the city" (3.194–6). This association between transgressiveness and a familiarity with geography is something that, in theatrical terms, stretches back to the streetwise vice figures of the sixteenth-century allegorical drama.

Middleton's use of and reference to London's physical landscape in his drama thus has several purposes. Most basically it confers a form of materiality on his characters and immediacy on the narratives of the plays set in London by embedding them in public spaces recognizable to the audiences. But these are rarely neutral or innocent of implications, and their evocation on stage, through setting or verbal reference, contributes to the metaphorical framework of the plays and to the meanings they create, especially in respect of characterization. Albeit in rather different ways, the interplay between urban geography and theatre is as surely a feature of his London-set plays as it is of his mayoral pageants and other civic entertainments.

## CHAPTER 3

# The Puritan Widow *and the spatial arts of Middleton's urban drama*

### Andrew Gordon

The urban focus of Middleton's casts and locations has long been recognized in the many treatments of city comedy that mine his comic output for material, but the particular nature of Middleton's engagement with the urban environment has remained relatively unexplored. In this essay I examine Middleton's interest in what I call the "arts of living" in early modern London, concentrating on the strategies for negotiating and manipulating urban spaces explored in his plays. In doing so I take as my subject a lesser-known work, *The Puritan Widow*, one of the last of the run of plays Middleton wrote for the boys' companies in the first decade of the seventeenth century, and a play which brings the representation of urban spaces to the fore.

The play is perhaps best known for the controversy that surrounded its publication in 1608, when it was denounced at Paul's Cross in a sermon by William Crashaw. Crashaw's attack on the Children of Paul's has been examined elsewhere (Gair, *Children of Paul's*, pp. 163–6), but his particular objection to *Puritan* centered on the satirical presentation of two puritan servants under the names of Simon St Mary Overies and Nicholas St Antlings. As Crashaw recognized, Middleton was doing more than evoking well-known sites in the city; he was satirizing the cultural practices and lifestyle invested in these spaces: "Thus hypocrisie a child of hell must beare the names of two Churches of God, and two wherein Gods name is called on publikely euery day in the yeere, and in one of them his blessed word preached euerie day" (*The Sermon Preached at the Crosse*, p. 171). The infamous detail is a kind of representational shorthand in which the "predominantly social satire of Puritans" (Yachnin, "Reversal of Fortune," p. 772) constructed by Middleton draws upon the knowledge, shared with his London audiences, of the modes of living with which specific spaces of the city were inscribed.

Middleton's overt interest in the representation of urban space is more
fully developed in a curious scene in the play in which three law officers
waiting in the gallery of a grand city house find themselves confronted by a
display of "maps and pictures, and devices" (3.4.33–4). The scene draws on
the contemporary vogue for cartographic prints as prestigious consumer
ornaments, whose technological sophistication forms part of their exclusive appeal. The response of the baffled officers, however, points to the
distinction between the pleasures of viewing and contemplating these
printed images in the gallery of a wealthy gentleman on the one hand,
and the business of negotiating the spaces of the city itself on the other. As
Sergeant Puttock comments, "They say all the world's in one of them, but
I could ne'er find the Counter in the Poultry" (3.4.104–6). The three
discuss the failure of a map view of London to yield a view of this famous
prison – and since on the ground it is screened from the street by a build-
up of houses, they turn to the reverse of the map in expectation of finding
it there. The inability to comprehend the conceptual apparatus of these
two-dimensional representations, "full of circles and conjurations"
(3.4.104) is more than the conventional mockery of constabulary dullness
(Evans, "Comic Constables"). Middleton here illustrates the law officers'
concern with managing the spaces of the city that prompts Puttock to
imagine an alternative form of mapping better suited to their needs:

>                             I should
> love these maps out 'o cry now if we could see men
> peep out of door in 'em. O we might have 'em in a
> morning to our breakfast so finely, and ne'er knock our
> heels to the ground a whole day for 'em.
>
>                                  (3.4.114–18)

Puttock's fantasy substitutes the law officers able to breakfast at their leisure
while they consult their map of the city for the familiar image of a lord in his
manor consulting the map of his lands.[1] But the fantasy map, able to defy
temporal constraints and monitor the motion of individuals, is clearly
intended to point to what a map *cannot* do, and is the culmination of the
scene's three-pronged critique of urban mapping. As Puttock and his
colleagues find, the map can represent streets, but though all pre-Fire
maps of London combined elements of a prospective view with a ground
plan (Gordon, "Performing London," pp. 72–4), they could not present to
view all of a city's buildings at once. Equally, as the search of the map's
reverse reveals, there is no depth to cartographic representation of the city's
streets: interiors and internal spaces are hidden from view. Finally, and most

importantly for the officers' needs, the city map orders the space of the city, but it does not record, and cannot keep pace with, its inhabitants.

Scrutinizing the visual representation of the city thus draws attention to the multiple aspects of inhabiting urban space that a two-dimensional image cannot express. Puttock's rejection of these new-fangled artifacts implies a defense of the particular local knowledge and skills possessed by the constables – a knowledge comprising not just the layout of streets, but the recognition of places, familiarity with the ins and outs of buildings, as well as the ability to track individuals through the labyrinthine urban fabric. This is precisely the form of local knowledge, of streets, of buildings, and of the modes of inhabiting urban space, upon which the action of *Puritan* turns. But in a period when drama drew upon expanded understanding of techniques for detection and investigation deriving from increased popular participation in judicial proceedings (Hutson, *Invention of Suspicion*), the constables' claim to wield this knowledge effectively is itself brought under scrutiny.

Middleton's urban comedies frequently challenge claims to the control of urban space. The constables of *Puritan* track down their quarry to an apothecary's shop and boastfully speak of playing him like a fish when he emerges to be caught. The stakeout of locations in this manner is common practice for the officers in Middleton's comedies, from the Holborn ambush by Curtilax and Hanger in *The Roaring Girl*, to Fleshhook and Counterbluff taking up position outside the Man-in-the-Moon tavern in *Anything for a Quiet Life* – and to these we might add the checkpoint of the corrupt Promoters in *A Chaste Maid in Cheapside*, or the creditors who lie in wait with their bills in *A Trick to Catch the Old One* and other plays. In these scenarios the officers lay claim to the city's external spaces but their ability to enforce authority over the urban terrain is found wanting. The parish officers work on intelligence to locate their targets and attempt to lock down specific sites, but they are hampered by a superficiality of understanding that is analogous to the limited perspective afforded by the map image. The constables have a tendency to oversight epitomized in *Michaelmas Term* where the Courtesan escapes detection by being lodged "in a constable's house," so that "the watch that should fetch her out are her chiefest guard to keep her in" (3.5.18–22). Where the constable was often subject to caricature on the early modern stage, Middleton specifically highlights lack of spatial penetration as the characteristic flaw in his understanding.

With the spatial authority of constables confined to lying in wait outside premises, or pursuing their quarry through the streets, the evasion of their

reach depends upon applying a more acute understanding of how space in
the city is inhabited. As Puttock's fellow officer Ravenshaw concedes, "They
[scholars] will search more with their wits than a constable with all his
officers" (3.3.17–18). Middleton's urban drama thus places value upon exploiting a knowledge of the city's spatial terrain that extends beyond the open
street to embrace the various defined spaces of contemporary urban life,
including the attempts to accommodate the demands of fashionably luxuriant
lifestyles within the conditions of proximate living. In *Michaelmas* Easy
receives an introduction to the complexities of lived space in the city when
he browses the bills advertising chambers in Paul's Walk and reads of a "house
not only endued with a new fashion forepart, but, which is more convenient
for a gentleman, with a very provident back door" (1.2.139–42). In the
homoerotic terms that run throughout the play, a sexualized topography of
access combines the value of architectural display with the facility to permit
hidden movement. As Middleton makes clear, contemporary urban houses
had no greater claim to continence than the human body. In *A Mad World,
My Masters*, Citizen Harebrain's jealous supervision of his wife is given
expression in the play's succession of interior scenes that are the only urban
locations of the play, but the husband cannot exclude the opportunity for
adultery and it is his wife's virtue and not his efforts at spatial control that
keeps her chaste. In Middleton's drama authoritarian attempts at the control
of urban space are overturned by a more nuanced ability to exploit the fluidity
of the city's interconnecting spaces and their points of issue. This is nowhere
more aptly demonstrated than the realization of the constables in *Puritan* that
while they have been contemplating and imagining fantastical maps of the
city, the debtor they had arrested, George Pieboard, has made his escape via
the wealthy citizen's back door.

Derived from a contemporary jest book reinvention of the city dramatist
George Peele, the figure of Pieboard epitomizes the dramatic exploitation of
the spatial conditions that structure urban living. A refugee scholar, he
comes to London intent upon making a place for himself by the practice of
deceit in a city which "affords creatures enough for cunning to work upon"
(1.3.95–6). It is Pieboard who drives the action of the play with his scheme to
present himself as a fortune-teller and his accomplice as a conjuring man in
order to prey on the Widow. Pieboard's success is based on applying his wit
in acts of opportunistic invention that revolve around two key urban sites:
the twin houses of the Widow and the wealthy Gentleman. Pieboard's
escape from the clutches of the constables is a clear manifestation of his
ability to improvise on his urban surroundings. He correctly reads the
exterior of the house as identifying the owner among the city's most

substantial inhabitants, "for so much the posts at his door should signify" (3.4.12–13), obtaining access by interpolating the servant into his confident assertion of fore-acquaintance. Once within, he confides to the Gentleman his ruse of gaining entrance to present a commissioned masque for remuneration, with the result that the Gentleman not only agrees to sanction Pieboard's rear exit, but rewards the invention with the sum promised in his tale. In this escapade Pieboard's manipulation of the possibilities presented by the display frontage and inconspicuous back exit are as much a part of his wit as is his persuasive speech with his newfound patron.

In addition to this play on points of entry and exit, Middleton examines the nuanced expression of status through architectural detail in his representation of the two urban houses. *Puritan* explores both the social meanings and the pragmatic uses of two prestigious designed spaces in particular: the gallery and the garden. The long gallery was an architectural innovation widely imitated in grand houses from the mid Elizabethan period. Pieboard describes the example in the Gentleman's house as "a fine gallery . . . for me to walk and study and make verses" (3.4.30–1), emphasizing both the scale of the space and its associations with cultured leisure, which are reinforced by the display of maps, "very popular for hanging in long galleries" in the period (Coope, "The 'Long Gallery'," p. 65). In addition to its value as a presentational space, by virtue of its scale, lack of adjoining walls, and common incorporation of bay windows, the long gallery was also one of the few spaces in a contemporary house "hospitable to private conversation" (Orlin, *Locating Privacy*, p. 236), even while that privacy was liable to be witnessed by others. Middleton plays upon the possibilities of the gallery's spatial conditions with the interview between Pieboard and the Gentleman that takes place within sight of the constables. Pieboard is able to publicly perform the handing over of the masque and its good reception, while in demonstrating the favor of intimate speech with the Gentleman he discreetly plans his escape. His observation that the house is "most wholesomely plotted" (3.4.18) neatly encapsulates the cunning scholar's ability to harness the architectural grandeur of the building to his witty invention.

The play's other urban house belongs to the Widow Plus and is the focal point for much of the action. While it is implicitly a substantial residence, Middleton subtly undermines the claims of the household to decorous and refined living. Their eagerness to impress is satirized in the choice of what Edmond calls "the fairest room in my mother's house" (4.2.67) to play host to the conjuring of a devil, while the family are displaced offstage. This perversion of hospitality is coupled with anxiety lest "the devil should prove a knave and tear the hangings" (4.2.79–80), caricaturing the mundanity of citizen concerns. Soft furnishings aside, the threat of a devil-sparked fire reveals the superficiality of the building's finery, deconstructing architectural display in the detail of a ceiling that is "but thin plastered and [fire] 'twill quickly take hold o' the laths" (4.2.83–4). Where a long gallery features prominently in the Gentleman's house, in marked contrast the Widow's gallery is not represented onstage and is referred to only as a space of concealment rather than of elegant display, suggesting more limited proportions: "we'll steal into the gallery" (2.1.41–2), Moll tells her furtive suitor, seeking to escape notice at the sudden approach of her mother. In place of the gallery, Middleton concentrates attention on the gardens of the property. In contemporary understanding the two were closely aligned and "shared ... material and conceptual space" (Orlin, *Locating Privacy*, p. 234) as sites of decorous display and ambulatory leisure, as well as conversational intimacy away from prying ears. The Widow directs her gentleman suitors "to walk a while i'th'garden" (4.2.56–7) to divert them, indicating her pride in a space that in an urban context was indeed a luxury "found only in some of the larger houses and in the peripheral or suburban areas" (Schofield (ed. and intro.), *London Surveys*, p. 27). However, Ralph Treswell's contemporary surveys of London property reveal the compressed situation of gardens such as that of Jacques de Bees, which was accessed from the open street and overlooked by at least three different occupants (see Figure 3.1). For the Widow of Watling Street, in the very heart of the city, her urban garden is found to be not a place of seclusion but the very seedbed of her troubles. As Pieboard reveals to the audience

by good happiness, being in my hostess's garden, which neighbours the orchard of the widow, I laid the hole of mine ear to a hole in the wall, and heard 'em make these vows and speak those words upon which I wrought these advantages. (2.1.288–92)

Pieboard's opportunism exploits the close conjunction of urban spaces that not only permits him to witness the expressions of mourning and the oaths taken among the family, but having "overheard 'em severally" (1.2.110) even makes him privy to the asides that expose the private thoughts of the family members. In penetrating the privacy of the Widow's family, Middleton mocks the pretensions of the Widow's household to refined detachment from the urban environment. Pieboard's use of the information he gleans has the effect of reorienting the Widow's household towards the immediate locale, refocusing attention upon the threshold of the Widow's property and the intersection of the family home with the urban community. Predicting to the Widow the portent of a prearranged fight between his

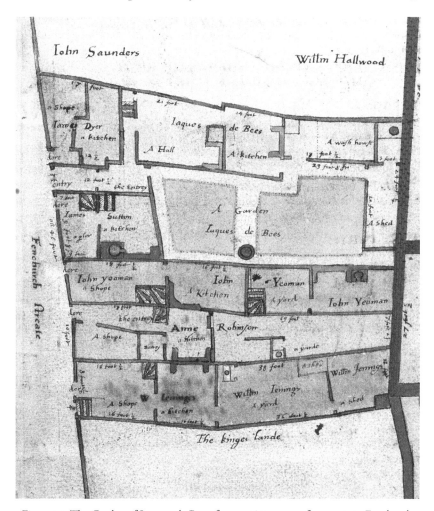

Figure 3.1 The Garden of Jacques de Bees, from a 1612 survey of property in Fenchurch
Street by Ralph Treswell, *Clothworkers' Company Planbook*, plan 3.

two accomplices, he pointedly locates it "before your door" (2.1.233–4). At
the same spot, he later stages his dramatic public intervention in the dual
processions to execution and burial, restoring Corporal Oath to life in front
of the Sheriff and assembled officers. Pieboard even enforces the participation of the Widow in the local event by directing that the restored Corporal
be carried into her house to receive sustenance. In opening her door to the
Corporal, the Widow confronts and overrules the scruples of her dogmatic

servant Nicolas – the same pedant who had earlier denied his kinsman's assertion that "thou shalt love thy neighbour and help him in extremities" (1.4.128–9) could be found in the Bible. The Widow's actions thus mark a symbolic reaffirmation of neighborliness that is a kind of spatial analogue to the reacceptance of the sex drive central to the comic plot, as she welcomes the prospect of marriage and revokes her earlier vow never to "entertain the carnal suit of man" (1.1.101).

My reading of *Puritan*, sensitive to the spatial arts of urban living, illustrates Middleton's nuanced understanding of the city's spaces and the resonant social meanings he applies to their negotiation and management. Middleton consistently represents the space of the city as porous, highlighting the interconnectedness of interior and exterior terrain. In the figure of Pieboard, an improviser responsive to the city's fluid spatial potentialities, he dramatizes the local knowledges of lived space in the city that remain unintelligible to the officers of the law. In his exploration of the cultural politics of architectural space Middleton tracks the translation of design fashions and the modes of living they imply into the urban context. In doing so he disrupts the pursuit of a decorous privacy with the persistent affirmation of spatialized neighborhood relations.

NOTE

1. The image is a common one in the surveying manuals of the period, connoting the possibility of managing the estate from afar. See McRae, *God Speed*, pp. 189–97.

## CHAPTER 4

# The populations of London

## Ian Munro

Thomas Middleton's 1613 Lord Mayor's show, *The Triumphs of Truth*, sets the scene of London in complex fashion. The Lord Mayor is first greeted by the figure of London itself, "attired like a reverend mother, a long white hair naturally flowing on either side of her; on her head a model of steeples and turrets; her habit crimson silk, near to the honourable garment of the city; her left hand holding a key of gold" (119–23). London welcomes the Lord Mayor and instructs him in how he must tend to her: "Spots in deformèd cheeks are scarce noted, / Fair cheeks are stained if ne'er so little blotted. / . . . This place is the king's chamber; all pollution, / Sin, and uncleanness must be locked out here, / And be kept sweet with sanctity, faith, and fear" (185–90). To assist the Lord Mayor in these tasks, the angel of Truth appears on a chariot (attended by Zeal) to guide him through the city, warning him that "the victory is not half won" and that on his journey through the city (both literal and meta-phorical) he will be led towards "ways more pleasant to a worldling's eyes" than the narrow path of Truth (233, 236). Soon after, the figure of Error appears, and indeed offers to lead the Mayor into the "Back-ways and by-ways" of the city, showing him "all my corners yet untold, / The very nooks where beldams hide their gold, / In hollow walls and chimneys, where the sun / Never yet shone, nor Truth came near" (310, 313–16). With Error following close behind, the procession soon comes to the "Mount Triumphant of London," an allegorical representation of the city that has been "overspread with a thick, sulphrous darkness" and occupied by Error's disciples (495). Truth exclaims, "What's here? the mist of Error? dare his spite / Stain this Triumphant Mount, where our delight / Hath been divinely fixed so many ages? / . . . We did expect to receive welcome here / From no deformed shapes, but divine and clear" (506–8, 514–15). Truth waves away the mists with her fan, revealing the ideal city beneath, but Error repeatedly covers over the Mount with mists until, at the close of the pageant, the fire of Zeal destroys Error's chariot.

In what amounts to a radical reimagining of the form and content of civic pageantry, Middleton thus presents two versions of the city. On the one hand is the traditional personification of the city as a bounteous mother, coupled with the ideal space of the "Mount Triumphant," offering a moral geometry of civic life: London sits at the center of the Mount, with Religion above her and Liberality and Perfect Love on either side; Knowledge and Modesty sit further down, with Chastity, Fame, Simplicity, and Meekness filling out the display. Such representations are the stock-in-trade of the Lord Mayor's show, which typically featured monumental visions of the city in order to present a perfect, and perfectly legible, London. On the other hand, we have Error's London, represented by mobile mists and fogs, a disorderly, shapeless, and secret city that explicitly threatens the beauty and coherence of the ideal city, staining its fair cheeks, obscuring its lines. And while the personification of London stresses that the city is "the king's chamber" (*camera regis*, an ancient title for London), Error's city has a very different spatial makeup: hidden corners and close rooms, where witches hide valuables, an urban labyrinth impenetrable by civic authority.[1]

Error's secret city is also explicitly connected to the watching London crowd. Error declares, "I can bring / A thousand of our Parish, besides queans, / That ne'er knew what Truth meant, nor ever means. / Some could I cull out here, e'en in this throng, / If I would show my children, and how strong / I were in faction" (299–304). And it is indeed this milling crowd that the procession must force its way through. The Russian ambassador's account of this show describes how the procession was surrounded by "people in masks with palms, and they carried palms with fireworks, and they threw from them sparkling fire on both sides because of the great press of people, that they might give way. And before them and behind them went soldiers, and on both sides, turning quickly and waving swords and sabres so that people would get out of the way" (*Middleton*, p. 978). In turning the procession itself into a literalized allegory, Middleton borrows a trick from Thomas Dekker's show from the previous year, which had Virtue helping the mayoral party make its way past the riotous forces of Envy. But Middleton pushes the point further, drawing the watching crowd into the space of the pageant, allegorizing the assembled populace as the symbolic impediment to the restored city. As London explains, Truth's path is that "to which place throngs / All world's afflictions, calumnies, and wrongs" (603–4).

Error's description of a secret and close city speaks strongly to the realities of early modern London, where properties were continually being extended and subdivided into smaller and smaller tenements to house the growing population.[2] At the same time, the suburban areas adjacent to the city were also growing at a ferocious rate. London's population exploded in the sixteenth century, growing from perhaps 70,000 in 1550 to perhaps 400,000 in 1650, a rate of increase made even more remarkable by the devastating mortality of the plague.[3] London grew not of its own accord, moreover, but because of massive immigration from the rest of the country; demographic estimates suggest that one in eight English lived in London for some part of their lives (Finlay, *Population and Metropolis*, p. 9). As the populations of London grew, they also became more diverse, autonomous, and fluid. The year of Middleton's birth, 1580, was also the year of the first royal proclamation against new buildings in London, a futile attempt to restrict population growth that recurred throughout the Elizabethan and Jacobean periods. Like *Truth*, the proclamation begins with an invocation of London as the monarch's chamber before moving to a more disturbing set of spaces: "great multitudes of people brought to inhabit in small rooms … heaped up together, and in a sort smothered with many families of children and servants in one house or small tenement" (Hughes and Larkin (eds.), *Proclamations*, vol. 11, pp. 466–7). Although the London that had existed was still physically visible, the crowding of London's spaces effected profound changes in how the city was understood: like the mists that stain the Mount Triumphant, or the spots in fair cheeks, crowdedness supplements the space of the city, obscuring its legibility and undermining its coherence.

Middleton's urban plays show a similarly bifurcated understanding of London, one that remained remarkably stable across twenty years of playwriting. Middleton's London (meaning the city he created) certainly contains notable civic ornaments, locations that through their age or prominence had acquired significant symbolic meaning, monumental edifices that help to anchor one's mental map of the city. Nevertheless, a much more constant presence is a city of vice, crime, and illicit sanctuary. In *Your Five Gallants*, the bawd Primero describes how some of his whores are "stol'n away at once / And married at the Savoy" (2.1.44), a district west of the city whose ancient privilege of sanctuary meant it was often employed for illicit marriages; the similar Cole Harbor, a sanctuary for vagrants and debtors in Upper Thames Street, shows up in three plays (*A Trick to Catch the Old One*, *The Roaring Girl*, and *Anything for a Quiet Life*). Indeed, a reader of the editorial glosses to Chick Lane (*Roaring Girl*), Clerkenwell (*A Mad World, My Masters*, *No Wit / Help like a Woman's*), Garden Alleys (*A Fair Quarrel*), Gray's Inn Fields (*Roaring Girl*), Limehouse (*Quiet Life*), Marybone Park (*Roaring Girl*, *Quarrel*), Rosemary Lane (*Quarrel*), Saint Giles (*Wit at Several Weapons*), Saint Pancras (*Quarrel*, *Weapons*), Shire Lane (*Quarrel*), Shoreditch (*No Wit*), Smithfield (*Roaring Girl*, *Weapons*) the Strand (*A Chaste Maid in Cheapside*), Thieving Lane (*Weapons*), and

Turnbull Street (*Mad World*, *No Wit*) might well conclude that there were few precincts of London *not* associated with thieves and prostitutes.

This portrayal of a city teeming with corruption and vice is not surprising, given the pretexts and protocols of city comedy and urban writing in general. Middleton, like Thomas Dekker, John Marston, and others, was an accomplished composer of urban satire on the model of Horace and Juvenal, a genre that seeks above all to anatomize the city, to reveal its illness in order to purge it and make it newly legible – to "discover vices and unmask the world's shadowed villainies," as Middleton puts it in the Epistle to *The Black Book* (10–11). In similar fashion, city comedy typically trades in urban knowledge and competence, offering the promise of secret knowledge, a vicarious journey into uncharted territories of the city. Even more than prose satire, Roman comedy provided the early modern dramatist with both a mechanism for urban representation and a host of appropriate character types with which to populate the city: the overbearing shopkeeper, the naive country gentleman, the jealous husband, the unfaithful wife, the conniving servant, the wealthy heiress, the braggart captain, the coxcomb, the con man, the usurer, the whore, the pimp, the thief. None of this should suggest, however, that Middleton's London is merely generic, a timeless exemplum of urban vice. Rather, specificity of location combines with thematic preoccupations in complex fashion, articulating anxieties about what London was becoming and the challenges its engrossment and fluidity presented to comprehension. In this regard, it is appropriate that Middleton's London is predominantly a place of movement, replete with points of embarkation, gathering, and transit – though scattered through with places of immobility, the prisons which threaten to capture those who move too freely through London's social and economic spaces. The populations of Middleton's London are always on the move, as demonstrated by the usurer Dampit's self-description in *Trick*:

Up in a morning and be here with his serge gown, dashed up to the hams in a cause, have his feet stink about Westminster Hall and come home again, see the galleons, the galleasses, the great armadas of the law. Then there be hoys and petty vessels, oars and scullers of the time. There be picklocks of the time, too. Then would I be here. I would trample up and down like a mule: now to the judges, 'May it please your reverend honourable fatherhoods'; then to my counselor . . . then to one of the clerks . . . then to the examiner's office . . . Then to the hall again, then to the chamber again . . . Tramplers of time, motions of Fleet Street, and visions of Holborn! (1.4.42–60)

In this vision of London's legal environs, urban crowding is figured as a congested port, with galleons and petty vessels fighting for space. Restless activity also subtends the theatricality of London's streets: the "motions of Fleet Street" connotes both movement and puppet shows, the city made into a stage by the trampling of bodies across its boards.

A key difference between *The Triumphs of Truth* and Middleton's commercial plays is that the latter rarely avail themselves of the figure of the assembled crowd as part of their representational strategies. In general, the early modern plays that show the greatest concern with urban crowding (or the greatest license in portraying it) typically stand at a remove from contemporary London: the crowds that swarm the stage in Shakespeare's Roman tragedies, for example, are difficult to find in the city comedies. Middleton also generally avoids direct use of his most immediate crowd, the theatre audience. The only play which features an explicit dramaturgical use of the audience is *Roaring Girl*, when Sir Alexander describes his galleries to his visitors: "Within one square a thousand heads are laid / So close that all of heads the room seems made / . . . And here and there, whilst with obsequious ears / Thronged heaps do listen, a cutpurse thrusts and leers / With hawk's eyes for his prey" (1.2.19–27). With characteristic wit, Middleton punctuates the static image of theatrical unity with a figure of mobility, startling his audience in the midst of compliment with a menacing insertion. But this is more a theatrical moment than an urban one; although *Roaring Girl* is one of Middleton's most urban plays in terms of its setting and description (there are approximately forty urban locations named in the play), this crowded scene – presented as portraits lining the arcades of a rich man's mansion – is kept separate from that world.

Instead, Middleton typically conveys urban density through a kind of synecdoche, part for whole, in which the small numbers of figures who inhabit the play are imagined to multiply across the urban landscape. In *The Phoenix*, for example, the mercenary interactions between the unnamed Knight and Jeweler's Wife, who call each other "Pleasure" and "Revenue," are intended to capture an entire range of social relations between gentry and citizens, reiterated throughout the entire city from this single example. Towards the close of the play, the title character (a Duke's son in disguise, secretly surveying the corruptions of his father's city) attacks the Jeweler's Wife for her promiscuous behavior as one "For whose close lusts the plague never leaves the city," adding, "Now few but are by their wives' copies free, / And brought to such a head that now we see / City and suburbs wear one livery" (15.231, 240–2). Repentant and fearful of punishment, the Wife replies, "Let me have pardon, I beseech your grace, and I'll peach 'em all, all the close women that are; and upon my knowledge there's above five thousand within the walls and the liberties" (248–51). The extent of the city's sexual depravity is registered through the duplication of the "close lusts" of the Wife's body, now open for inspection; we are less to imagine that she truly knows five thousand "close women" than that there is some kind of iterative affinity between the body we see and all those that we imagine, occupying the untold corners and secret rooms of the metropolis. A similarly gendered understanding of the city is found in *The Patient Man and the Honest Whore*, where Hippolito attacks Bellafront for her prostitution in terms that invoke crowded urban space:

> For your body,
> It's like the common shore, that still receives
> All the town's filth. The sin of many men
> Is within you; and thus much, I suppose,
> That if all your committers stood in rank,
> They'd make a lane, in which your shame might dwell,
> And with their spaces reach from hence to hell.
>
> (6.376–82)

The idea of city as whore is ancient, of course, and a model that stands in direct contrast to the "reverend mother" of *Truth*, but Middleton invests the commonplace with an unusual spatiality. As "the common shore," the city sewer, Bellafront is an urban node, a conduit for city movement much like the places of entertainment (taverns, promenades, and playhouses) that dot the plays; she contains the city, and the city passes through her, marking out its streets with the "spaces" created by their physical bodies.

In both of these examples, bodies onstage connote bodies offstage, in a kind of corporeal reflection that evokes an embodied city. But to imagine Middleton's theatre as a discrete microcosm of its larger urban world, with a clear boundary between the two, is to mistake the dangerous fluidity of the metonymic connections between stage and city. This fluidity is strongly suggested by the opening scene of *Five Gallants*, which implicitly turns to the theatre audience for its register of signification. In this extraordinary scene, the pawnbroker Frip reads the current plague bill aloud in order to determine whether he should accept or refuse the clothing brought to be pawned:

What parish is your pawn, my friend? [*Reading from the bill*] St Bride's: five; St Dunstan's: none; St Clement's: three. Three at Clement's! Away with your pawn, sir; your parish is infected. I will neither purchase the plague for six pence in the pound and a groat bill-money, nor venture my stock into contagious parishes. (1.1.43–9)

Like Bellafront's body, Primero's pawnshop is a kind of urban conduit: the gathering and passage of clothes through his shop suggests the dense interrelations of human contact. Primero's cruel quarantine seeks to restrict urban mobility to formal commodities, to keep "stock" separate from infection. However, as the play makes clear, his trade is itself a kind of disease on the city, a virulent deforming of human relations; his servant's declaration that "the pox sits at meat and meal with him" (1.1.5) suggests both Frip's fear of the plague and his connection to it. The plague, of course, is the preeminent urban disease, associated with both depopulation and overpopulation throughout the period.[4] *Five Gallants* is a play that brings the plague unusually close to home. Ben Jonson's *The Alchemist* is often described as an aggressive manifestation of the plague in an urban play, but it has nothing on Middleton's actual recitation of a plague bill, counting deaths in various parishes. How would a theatregoer from St. Clement's parish feel as the name was recited – and what about those sitting next to him? The tally of parishes links population and urban location, portraying the spread of the disease through the populations of London. And if Frip's house is constantly under danger of the plague due to its intimate contact with the rest of the city, so too is the crowded location where Frip's house is being presented: Middleton's theatre is not merely a representation of Error's thronged city, but one of its principal intersections.

NOTES

1. On the opposition between these two ubiquitous representations of London, see Manley, *Literature and Culture*, especially Chapter 3.
2. See Orlin, *Locating Privacy*. On early modern London's changing social and cultural makeup, see also (among others) Manley, *Literature and Culture*; Archer, *Pursuit of Stability*; Rappaport, *Worlds Within Worlds*; Finlay, *Population and Metropolis*; I. Munro, *Figure of the Crowd*; Howard, *Theater of a City*; Griffiths and Jenner (eds.), *Londinopolis*; Merritt (ed.), *Imagining Early Modern London*; and Griffiths, *Lost Londons*, as well as Seaver, "Middleton's London".
3. Figures taken from Orlin, *Locating Privacy*, p. 156.
4. See, for example, Middleton and Dekker's discussion of the plague in *News from Gravesend*.

## CHAPTER 5

# Domestic life in Jacobean London

## Catherine Richardson

Many of Middleton's plays explore London domestic life – this essay focuses on two, *A Chaste Maid in Cheapside* and *Women Beware Women*. As a supposedly controllable space in which deeds can in theory be performed in private, the household offers an essential location for the action of both comedy and tragedy. But early modern domestic life was not only a key dramatic trope; it was also an essential political concept. The household was the principal social unit, the one around which social life was organized. The householder was responsible for the public and private behavior of those in his care, and that responsibility underpinned communal law and order. As it mirrored the authority of a monarch in his kingdom, so the position gave access to political power in the neighborhood: "In London only householders served in local office, received parish poor relief and paid local taxation," and most of them were men (Boulton, *Neighbourhood*, p. 102). But the more impressive that household, the greater the authority of its head. In a growing metropolis, the complex relationships between wealth and authority were worked out through material display – the size of the house and objects with which it was filled embodied the householder's standing within the local community.

During Middleton's lifetime London's housing stock was on the whole old, and it bore the marks of many alterations. The redistribution of land after the Reformation had fundamentally altered the townscape of central London, freeing up large complexes of buildings for domestic use. Holy Trinity Priory Aldgate, for instance, became home to a large house called the Ivy Chamber, built at the crossing between the transepts of the old priory church; to small tenements in the sides of the choir whose "fireplaces, ovens and privies were grafted on to the Romanesque walls and arches"; and to the workshops of a delftware pottery run by refugees from the Low Countries in its precincts (Schofield, *Building*, p. 148; Peck, "Building," p. 305).

These properties were not planned from scratch, but rather adapted to the space and building materials available. Businesses, their workers and clients tended to congregate in the same localities. Their properties rubbed up against one another – rich and poor, worker and gentleman sharing party walls and parts of entranceways; production sharing a monastic precinct with consumption. While Middleton was writing, this kind of domestic life was drawing to a close. Timber buildings with their jetties almost meeting across narrow streets were going out of fashion; the ordered symmetries of classical designs were taking shape in Whitehall and Greenwich, and the urban planning of large squares like Covent Garden began a few years after Middleton's death. In the first decades of the seventeenth century, however, the distinctive organization of domestic life in London streets kept different social groups and material processes in close contact.

Domestic life was very diverse in these differently sized houses. Properties were often subdivided. Some were occupied by multiple tenants with shared kitchens; some properties had no kitchens, much less an oven in which to bake. For many Londoners, then, working, eating, and sleeping were activities that were carried on in separate locations, and this challenges modern understanding of what "home" means (Pennell, "Victualling," p. 230). But for others still the commercial pressures of the city meant that their house was also their business premises. It is this type of house in which the Yellowhammers of *Chaste Maid* live and work. Yellowhammer is a goldsmith; Whorehound arrives just as a customer is having a chain weighed; and the two conversations about wives and value become entangled. If we investigate this kind of property as it was lived in by contemporary Londoners, we can explore how Middleton uses a recognizable material culture on the stage. In 1622 an inventory of the goods of Robert Manne, citizen, was taken in Walbrooke Ward just off Cheapside.[1] His business was mercery and haberdashery, and over £800 worth of wares was held in his shop and two warehouses. He had many yards of black and colored calicoes, of taffeta sarcenettes, of velvet and its cheaper cousin refusado, of white, London dye, and damask cypress, of rich and ordinary taffeta, of satin, fustian, and narrow perpetuanas. In small wares he had over thirty different kinds of hatbands, costing from a penny each to a few shillings for embroidered ones, silk and other stays (bodices), feathers, ribbons, galloon and purled parchment lace, bugle (beaded) buttons, and hairbrushes.

These lists of subtly different goods embody the range and variety of the consumer culture through which households were provisioned and their inhabitants dressed – different versions of the same item suited different pockets and styles, and the diversity of colors and textures stimulated demand. Manne's inventory mentions fabrics whose names suggest origins in the Levant, France, Flanders, Milan, Utrecht, and China. Londoners' desire for novelty made theirs a very open material community, fed by diversity from England's provinces and abroad. Into the port of London came linens, silks, calicoes, and threads; metalwares; wine and brandy, fruit, pepper, sugar, tobacco; raw materials like flax, hemp, wool, dyestuffs, and timber (B. Dietz, "Overseas," p. 124). Their presence in the city created a theatre audience familiar with goods whether or not they owned them.

Manne owed money to men involved in the cloth trades and their associated processes such as dying and boxmaking, which were among the almost three-fifths of London occupations involved in the production of goods. Being familiar with household objects meant producing as well as consuming them. Middleton's plays fall naturally into a metaphorical language of production to explore human nature and sexuality. "As there is no woman made without a flaw," says Yellowhammer, "Your purest lawns have frays, and cambrics bracks." And Maudline replies, "But 'tis a husband solders up all cracks"(1.1.36–8). Relations between men and women are translated into processes of making and remaking, in a language replete with technical terms.

A contemporary sensitivity to the material variety which London offered comes across strongly in Middleton's plays – a visceral sense of the appetites and the ready possibility of their indulgence. There is a common meta-phorical strand of something approaching gluttony: As Livia says in *Women Beware*, men taste "many sundry dishes . . . And if we [women] lick a finger then sometimes, / We are not to blame" (1.2.40–5). Later on in the play, kissing Isabella, the Ward is in raptures: "O, most delicious scent! Methinks it tasted as if a man had stepped into a comfit-maker's shop to let a cart go by all the while I kissed her" (3.3.61–3). Relationships become cupidinous – men desire women and this gives women "value"; as a result they become elided with household goods. The relentlessly dim Tim explains to his tutor in *Chaste Maid* that his sister has eloped, shouting, "Thieves, thieves! My sister's stol'n! Some thief hath got her: / O, how miraculously did my father's plate 'scape! / 'Twas all left out" (4.4.1–3). To him, silverware and sisters might well appeal to the same kind of thieves.

The variety of goods with which Manne's house was furnished places him socially. His widow slept in a featherbed, on a standing bedstead sur-rounded with curtains and a valance. A truckle bed suggests that a servant slept in the room with her, and several chairs and five low stools were provided for the entertainment of visitors, the latter for sitting around the bed. A court cupboard and three chests held her belongings. Among the most valuable were her domestic fabrics: needlework cushions and a green cupboard cloth with a silk fringe (see Figure 5.1). This was not an especially

Figure 5.1 Long cushion cover, probably for a wooden bench. Silk velvet, embroidered with silk and metal thread, depicting flowers and insects, England, c. 1600. Such objects were a source of considerable domestic pride.

fine room by the standards of London merchants, some of whom owned Persian carpets, Venice chests, Russian leather chairs, and china dishes – the fruits of their overseas trade.[2] Across the town on The Strand, the Earl of Arundel was displaying a collection of pictures and marbles within his house (Peck, "Building," pp. 281–3). Nevertheless, Mistress Manne's chamber shows typical indications of a market in domestic plenty: the needlework cushions and fringed cloths are indicative of an environment enriched with non-essential processes and trimmings.

These goods were significant possessions – with so few items in the domestic interior they showed status clearly and succinctly. They were, therefore, we might presume, the source of considerable pride. But they were also assets, flexible enough to be translated into cash in times of need. Henslowe's pawnbroking accounts include some household goods, among which domestic fabrics were by far the most common: "articles of bedlinen, sheets, rugs, curtains, napkins and tablecloths" were pledged considerably more frequently than furniture (Boulton, *Neighbourhood*, p. 90). Those additional fabric items which signified enhanced wealth and status could, in other words, be cashed in during times of austerity, and were therefore the tipping point between enough and a little luxury.

Because small differences between objects signaled social position so clearly, Middleton is able to use things as a way of talking about people's status. So Yellowhammer mentions the day his wife sent their son "the silver spoon to eat his broth in the hall amongst the gentlemen commoners" (1.1.57–8). The spoon is shorthand for the material differences between gentlemen and tradesmen here, but also a way of talking very precisely about the edge – the competitiveness and the lack of understanding – between these two groups. Discussing such differences explicitly would be hard – they are below the surface of what we are to understand the Yellowhammers know about themselves. Such objects both pinpoint and puncture their social pretensions from their own mouths. A more vicious version of the same technique is used in *Women Beware*, as Leantio approaches the lodgings of his former wife, now the Duke's lover. He judges her advancement materially: "She's simply now advanced. I took her out / Of no such window, I remember, first; / That was a great deal lower, and less carved" (4.1.43–5). The carved window is the first in a series of objects the couple use to taunt one another about how their altered status was achieved.

As this focus on the window as boundary suggests, the household was the center of private life within the very public context of the city. Manne's house had a "back garret" and a chamber over the inner warehouse, which suggests that the latter was a part of the house, perhaps behind the shop. Different qualities of space were available at front and back – the relative security and permeability of rooms were measured in relation to the street. These sensitivities were echoed on the stage where they become associated with the householder's control over his female family members. Yellowhammer makes the connection in 3.1 as he states that he will "lock up this baggage [his daughter] / As carefully as my gold: she shall see / As little sun, if a close room or so / Can keep her from the light on't" (41–4). The household appears to offer the possibility of reserving goods and people from the public areas of exchange, but in drama this is a dangerous fantasy. Although Moll was "kept / Under a double lock" (4.4.2–3), the conventions of comedy allow her to make her escape. In *Women Beware* Leantio's attempts to keep his wife from prying eyes is similarly unsuccessful. He tries to lock his "life's best," indeed its only, "treasure" in a place "At the end of the dark parlour ... / So artificially contrived for a conveyance / No search could ever find it" (3.1.243–5) – a room dark because without windows, buried in the center of the house. Middleton uses the household as a controllable space to explore the gendered nature of notions of private property within the acquisitive city.

The relationship between carefully described objects and spaces creates strongly realized domestic interiors in many of Middleton's plays. Livia's house is at the center of *Women Beware*, acting as a space for entrapment and a context for illicit sexuality. The relationship between Bianca and the Duke is brought into being within an elaborate metaphor of elite aesthetic experience: "The gentlewoman, / Being a stranger, would take more delight / To see your rooms and pictures" (2.2.270), Guardiano remarks. "Here, take these keys. / Show her the monument too – and that's a thing / Everyone sees not" (275–7), Livia replies. Later, he says that he, "to prepare her stomach by degrees / To Cupid's feast ... showed her naked pictures by the way" (400–2), and Bianca, commenting that her "eye ne'er met with fairer ornaments" (310), is told that "a better piece / Yet than all these" is to come. The Duke, in other words, is positioned as the centerpiece of elite aesthetics – the final surprise in a collection of erotica, astounding because he demands that she be participant in rather than audience to his sexuality. Bianca, in a statement rich with irony, says she has been taken from place to place "so fashionably" (453), pointing up the connections between the art objects which define the highest fashion and a new set of immoral behaviors to which they have apparently become allied.

This experience of the house as a kind of aesthetic ravishment which shades into physical violation – one which Leantio is also offered by Livia in 3.2 – changes Bianca. "I'm sure she's strangely altered," the Mother says, pondering on the contrast between "great cheer at my lady's / And such

Figure 5.2 English silver gilt embossed and chased ewer, design based on a 1531 Italian print by Agostino Veneziano showing an antique Roman object. These ewers were among the most impressive and expensive pieces of domestic silverware. London, 1583–4.

mean fare at home" (3.1.5–7) as the possible source of her discontent. And Bianca herself articulates her fallen state through domestic objects – her immediate focus is on the "defects" of her husband's house:

> Why is there not a cushion-cloth of drawn-work,
> Or some fair cut-work pinned up in my bedchamber,
> A silver and gilt casting-bottle hung by't?
>
> (19–21)

She offers to spare her family the expense of "a silver basin and ewer," but points out, "Never a green silk quilt is there i'th'house, mother, / To cast upon my bed?" (27–8) (see Figure 5.2). These precisely described objects differentiate the domestic lives of the gentry and aristocracy and the citizenry of London. Bianca's sinful sexual awakening, then, is negotiated through a newly aggressive articulation of the stuff of the household, and adultery awakens a peremptory desire for intricately "wrought" and therefore expensive things – moral inferiority sharpens her social superiority.

*Chaste Maid* considers the more productive aspects of sexuality through its articulation of processes of making. Allwit, whose status as a father is radically compromised, states that children "are pretty foolish things, put to making in minutes; / I ne'er stand long about 'em" (2.3.31–2) – unlike many of the play's more expensive objects they are easily "knocked out," and for Touchwood Senior this is the source of some regret: "Some only can get riches and no children, / We only can get children and no riches" (2.1.11–12). Childbearing is given a prominent material context: Allwit describes Whorehound's provisions for his wife thus:

> A lady lies not in like her; there's her embossings.
> Embroid'rings, spanglings, and I know not what,
> As if she lay with all the gaudy-shops
> In Gresham's Burse about her
>
> (1.2.32–5)

This "accessorized" chamber provides the context for a performance of Whorehound's plenty after the birth in *Chaste Maid*: "*A bed thrust out upon the stage*, Allwit's Wife *in it*," as the stage direction at 3.2 reads. He enters with two silver spoons and a "fair high standing-cup" (3.2.43), expensive christening gifts, "To the love of the babe" (3.2.40), and he has also provided the food and drink for the Gossips. Opening up one's house for entertainment converted "wealth into a form of social capital," and the curiously public, socially competitive intimacy of this scene is palpable (Boulton, *Neighbourhood*, p. 138). Being invited inside encouraged indulgence in others' plenty, as Allwit points out (ironically as the plenty is not his): "Now out comes all the tasselled handkerchiefs, / They are spread abroad between their knees already" (3.2.51–2) to receive the sweetmeats. The move is reminiscent of the Mother's assertion in *Women Beware* on her way to Livia's banquet that "I'll step but up and fetch two handkerchiefs / To pocket up some sweetmeats, and o'ertake thee" (3.1.267–8). The provision of hospitality which was an essential element of higher status within London's small communities made the household a curiously permeable place where material plenty could be compared and then taken outside.

The scene offers a superbly realized household space which functions both mimetically and metaphorically. The Gossips are given low stools partly as a satire on the false humility of Puritans, but also because such stools were used to turn private chambers into public spaces, as we have seen in Manne's inventory. Long before the end of the event the women, who have "no consciences at sweetmeats," have "culled out / All the long plums" (3.2.62–4); the desire for the drink "in plate" – in the silver vessels for the christening – has given way to the need for chamber pots. The perfections of hospitable show have become the detritus of consumption. When the curtains around the bed are drawn Allwit picks over the possibly pissed-upon furniture, confiding in Davy, "Fair needlework stools cost nothing with them," and exclaiming, "Look how they have laid them, / E'en as they lie themselves, with their heels up!" (3.2.198–200). The strong sense of an interior space is given by the amount of furniture on stage, but also by his pointing out, "How hot they have made the rooms with their thick bums! / Dost not feel it, Davy?"; "Monstrous strong, sir" (3.2.193–4) is the reply. The realism of this tangible atmosphere has work to do; it is not an end in itself. In *Women Beware* Bianca, finally ridding herself of Leantio, says:

> I'll have this sauciness
> Soon banished from these lodgings, and the rooms
> Perfumed well after the corrupt air it leaves.
> His breath has made me almost sick, in troth.
>
> (4.1.107–10)

The heat, smell, and bodily fluids which visitors leave behind them and the revulsion caused, comic or otherwise, gets to the heart of domestic life in the city. Inviting people inside articulates divisions between social groups, and those divisions, symbolized by the objects wealth produces, were magnified and clarified in the socially mixed communities of Middleton's London.

NOTES

1. London Metropolitan Archives CLA/002/02 roll 2. My thanks to David Mitchell for sharing his work on these inventories.
2. E.g. John Williams, London Metropolitan Archives CLA/002/02 roll 7.

## CHAPTER 6

# Life and death in Middleton's London

### Elizabeth Lane Furdell

Thomas Middleton lived his days in London, a city of about 200,000 in 1600. Born in the heart of the old walled city in 1580, he spent some time at The Queen's College, Oxford, but returned home without a degree by 1601. His theatrical successes ultimately enabled him to afford property in Newington, Surrey, near active playhouses on the Bankside, but his association with London persists. Its citizens were not so urbane in Middleton's era to belittle chatter about criminals, immigrants, neighbors, lawsuits, robberies, and illnesses. Health issues in particular occupied much discussion among the population and became fodder for writers. Enjoying a long and vigorous life in Middleton's London required both a robust constitution and good luck. Harvest failures in the English countryside caused famine in the cities. The ruined crops of 1596 produced starvation the following year throughout London, although the city had resources to ameliorate the food shortages common to other parts of the country. Civic leaders arranged for the importation of grain during the worst of the crisis; nonetheless, parish registers in the city show an increase in burials that year in rich and poor neighborhoods alike.[1]

As if dearth did not generate sufficient challenge to Londoners, periodic bouts of plague bedeviled the growing metropolis during the reigns of Elizabeth I and James I. Established after an outbreak in 1592, the Bills of Mortality gave authorities and inhabitants information about increases or decreases in the number of city deaths. After an epidemic in 1603 that killed over 25,000 citizens, including the family of Middleton's sister, parish clerks weekly collected and published the information, which also contained christenings and causes of deaths. More burials than baptisms took place during Middleton's lifetime. Indeed, fewer than half of London-born children survived to a marriageable age, and immigrant youths were especially defenseless against infection, despite the fact that the city had a set of plague protocols, five hospitals, and a pesthouse at St. Giles Cripplegate. The Bills of Mortality chart the number of deaths attributable to various diseases and show spikes in fatalities several times during Middleton's era that dwarf those of the famine year. Authorities labeled these deaths from plague, but in reality they may have been due to any similar contagion like typhus, a "New Disease" carried by human body lice. Pestilence further affected the playwright, shuttering London theatres for almost a year from May 1603 to April 1604.

With stages closed, Middleton collaborated with Thomas Dekker on plague pamphlets. In *News from Gravesend: Sent to Nobody* (1604), he voiced concern about specific citizens while Dekker, the principal author, fretted over the effects on the community as a whole. What if there were metaphysical origins of pestilence, as Dekker assumed? What if England were being punished by a wrathful God incensed at the licentiousness of its citizenry? Or could evil have spawned the deadly plagues that ravaged London? In *The Meeting of Gallants at an Ordinary* (1604), Middleton, this time taking the lead, portrays London in the grip of plague, its horrors manifest. In a debate among War, Famine and Pestilence, "the cowards of hell," Pestilence boasts to War that it can triumph in carnage: "I slay forty thousand in one battle ... Their groins sore pierced with pestilential shot" (3–46). Later in the work, tales about the cause of the scourge, some quite sardonic, are told at a tavern, in due course emphasizing the arbitrary nature of the contagion. Speculating about the origin of epidemics could lead a writer into trouble with civil and religious authorities, especially since James I, a very superstitious Scotsman interested in demons, had recently ascended the throne. Middleton afforded an antidote to Dekker's pessimism, comparing the pesthouse to a private playhouse. Given the frequency of plague infestations and their lethality, perhaps it is not surprising that Middleton felt the need to bestow "black humor" on his beleaguered fellow citizens during their darkest hours (Chakravorty, *Society*, p. 38).

Londoners, like all residents of the two kingdoms governed by the Stuarts, could surely use Middleton's satirical resilience after the death in November 1612 of the popular heir to the throne, 18-year-old Prince Henry. After an illness of just two weeks, Henry died of typhoid fever, a disease not then identified, leading to considerable speculation, including a faint hint of foul play. The usual source of typhoid fever is contamination in water or from the unwashed hands of food servers, but Londoners helped spread the rumor that royal physicians, in particular Jacobean court doctor Theodore Turquet de Mayerne, caused the "putrefaction" to spread throughout the prince's body by purging the sick young man with rhubarb and senna (Furdell, *Royal Doctors*, p. 111). An autopsy exculpated Mayerne and all the others who had attended Henry. Investiture of the remaining royal son,

Prince Charles, took place in 1616, partly in Chelsea and partly at Whitehall, and Middleton wrote *Civitatis Amor* for the occasion. A personification of London speaks out for peace and hope under the Stuarts.

Just as the city government provided bread during times of scarcity, it also offered its denizens circuses in the form of civic entertainments. In 1620 Middleton was named City Chronologer of London, a salaried office responsible for annual pageants in October inaugurating a new Lord Mayor. He had worked on earlier municipal shows. His impressive debut in 1613 with *The Triumphs of Truth*, a paean to the New River project, saluted the mayoralty of Thomas Myddleton and the contributions to the water project of Hugh Myddleton, neither a relation (see Ceri Sullivan's essay in this volume, p. 83). The Fleet River, which emptied into the Thames at Blackfriars, had become an unsanitary ditch along which no reputable people would live. Instead, prisons like Newgate and Ludgate lined its banks. The Fleet functioned as an industrial dump for the city's tanners, dyers, and butchers. Despite the fact that London's poor used wells and privies along its margins, most knew the importance of fresh water to the preservation of their community, and the New River project brought clean, potable water to them from Hertfordshire. Chartered by King James in 1604, the engineering development faced objections from landowners who worried about flooding or who fretted that roads to London might be disrupted by lead-lined wooden aqueducts. When Hugh Myddleton ran short of funds to finish the endeavor, the king provided half of the expenses for a 50 percent share in the New River Company, and water began flowing to the capital in September 1613.

Though Middleton continued as City Chronologer, in 1624 he ran afoul of the national government over the mocking content of his play, *A Game at Chess*, which satirized the major domestic and foreign policy crises of King James's final years. The hubbub over the play led to banning its production after nine performances as well as the temporary closing of all London theatres and the arrest of Middleton. No new Middleton play appeared after this one. His final civic program in 1626, *The Triumphs of Health and Prosperity*, reveals the author's concern for a diminishing of English exceptionalism. The brief show began and ended with a rainbow to demonstrate London's resilience after the plague of 1625, when no festivity had been held. Several tableaux within the pageant remind the new mayor and citizens alike of the challenges and opportunities in the city's renewal.

Besides bouts of plague, Londoners suffered through the appearance of new diseases and the relentlessness of familiar ones. Syphilis arrived in Britain at the end of the fifteenth century, likely transplanted from the New World to the Old by Tudor explorers, but Englishmen dubbed the new malady, for which they had no immunities, "The French Pox." Ague, the age-old seasonal fevers that afflicted all of marshy England, proved resistant to various treatments during Middleton's lifetime. Contemporary documents refer repeatedly to the sweating sickness or "English sweate," which disappeared after 1551 but still haunted the dreams of many; its cause remains stubbornly obscure to us today, although hantavirus or relapsing fever seem like possible culprits. Smallpox nearly killed Queen Elizabeth in 1562, but many of her subjects were not as lucky as she and did not recover from its onslaught. Not surprisingly, with such widespread concern for disease and dying, anatomical and iatric words made their way into the English vocabulary, into poetry, sermons and stories; dramatists in particular could splash stages and pages with blood and other fluids from the interior body.

Londoners, like threatened humans everywhere, searched for reasons behind their health miseries. Competing claims for medicine versus religion as methods of preventing sickness confused Middleton's contemporaries and appeared in his plays (Peterson, "Performing Arts," p. 5; Belling, "Infectious Rape," p. 116). So did allusions to cases Londoners recognized, like the Mary Grove-Elizabeth Jackson episode Middleton drew on for an examination of hysteria. Grove, a teenager, developed frightening symptoms that ranged from sore throat to blindness in 1602 after a shouting confrontation that included curses from the elderly Jackson. The old woman was accused of witchcraft by Grove, whose home became a kind of theatre as physicians tried to relieve her illness; her parents even brought in the illustrious Dr. Thomas Moundford from the College of Physicians, an expert on melancholy, to try to rid her of her agony. Finally, puritan preachers "dispossessed" her of her demons (MacDonald, "Introduction," pp. x–xiii). In *The Revenger's Tragedy*, Middleton confronted the conundrum of a mother who behaved in anything but a motherly fashion. Was she afflicted with a legitimate medical disorder or had the devil possessed her? The woman's exorcism and ultimate contrition confirmed the notion of demonic possession for theatregoers. In the same play, Middleton references bloodletting as a cure for overheated passions.

Likewise, Middleton "ripped from the headlines" thinly disguised references to poisons, prompting his audience to ponder the fine line between medicinals and potions for health and those for homicide. Poisons inhabit Middleton's plays, from the tainted skull in *Revenger* (1606) to a character "deadly as the basilisk" in *The Changeling* (1622) and the realization by Beatrice-Joanna in the same play that toxins can cure if prescribed wisely. Poisons obsessed Londoners of Middleton's era and he reflected their fears back to them on stage. The most notorious murder case of Jacobean

London was the horrific poisoning of poet Thomas Overbury, an Oxford classmate of Middleton's. Ultimately tied to a prominent couple, Robert Carr, Earl of Somerset, and his wife Frances Howard, Overbury's agonizing death became the talk of the town. (See Alastair Bellany's essay in this volume for details, p. 117.)

The Lieutenant of the Tower, Gervase Elwes; Anne Turner, widow of a Catholic physician; the jailer Richard Weston; and James Franklin, an apothecary, all hanged for their part in the crime. Mrs. Turner, having consulted London's infamous sorcerer Simon Forman on romantic matters, had connived with Weston and the Somersets to administer sulfuric acid to Overbury in his food. In 1616 the Somersets were tried and convicted of the murder, sentenced to die for the crime, but pardoned by King James in 1624 after rendering financial restitution to His Majesty. Only Frances admitted her guilt. Lord Chief Justice Edward Coke, who had presided over various trials in the Overbury affair, mounted a purge of cunning men and self-styled wizards dabbling on the fringe of medicine. Middleton exploited the theme of corrupt courtiers and slow death by toxin in his 1616 tragicomedy, *The Witch*. The plot involves black magic devised by several witches to prevent an inappropriate marriage from being consummated and to effect wasting sickness in the intended target; it contains a scene in which a husband complains of impotence with his bride, something the third Earl of Essex, Frances Howard's unwanted first husband, had done at his divorce proceedings. *The Witch* not only reminded Middleton's audience of the Somersets and the Overbury case, it also underscored the connection between medicine, magic, and mystery.

At this moment of physical and moral challenge to their fellow citizens, medical men bickered over what theories of healing to follow, further exacerbating public doubt. Physicians educated at Oxford and Cambridge in the Elizabethan and Jacobean periods overwhelmingly embraced the ideology of the ancient physician Galen, who posited a humoral analysis of sickness and health that required balancing the body's blood, phlegm, yellow and black bile in order to maintain or restore well-being. Highly individualized diagnoses often required "heroic" measures, such as bleeding or purging, and frequently accompanied astrological assessments of the optimum time to administer such treatments. By the middle of the sixteenth century, a serious challenge to Galenism emerged in the chemical medicine of Swiss maverick Paracelsus and his largely Protestant followers. Asserting that disease came from external forces and not from within the body, Paracelsus urged experimentation, patient observation, and the search for the specific causes of ailments affecting whole groups of sufferers. He advocated the use of poisons to treat poisons, insisting that the proper dosage made them remedies. As his teachings became part of the medical curriculum of continental universities, English and Scottish students matriculating away from home came to embrace Paracelsianism and brought the theoretical controversy back to Britain and the College of Physicians in London. Thomas Mouffet led the charge, representing a cultural shift away from humoralism and towards alchemical medicine. Among those who tried to establish a compromise between the two camps stood the eminent Dr. Mayerne. Through Mayerne's influence, the London Pharmacopoeia of 1618 reflected equilibrium, albeit temporary, between credentialed Galenist doctors from Oxbridge and Paracelsian reformers from continental universities.

Middleton demonstrated an awareness of the theoretical issues dividing medicine and hinted at his preference for the Galenic tradition. The heroine Jane in his 1616 tragicomedy *A Fair Quarrel*, co-written with William Rowley, derisively calls the physician a Paracelsian. Not only is the corrupt doctor lacking in traditional medical principles, he lacks moral authority as well. When he tries to blackmail Jane into bed, she dares him to defame her. Her character's disdain for a degreed physician echoes growing public antagonism towards formal medicine, disrespect exacerbated by a flood of vernacular medical literature like John Gerard's *Herball* (1597). This work and others aimed at providing an alternative source of information for laymen and women saddled with the responsibility of providing care for their families and households (Slack, "Mirrors of Health," pp. 237–73). Most Londoners could not have afforded the fees of any physician, Galenist or Paracelsian, but patronized the traditional healers, midwives, and charlatans who largely relied on their interpretation of Galen's teachings supplemented with their own, mostly innocuous concoctions and a dollop of self-taught astrology. Preventive measures for them would incorporate charms, amulets, and rituals.

Besides the dispute over theory, a struggle for jurisdictional authority rent the fabric of London medicine. Henry VIII had chartered the College of Physicians in 1518 and given it licensing authority. The learned doctors subscribed to clearly differentiated medical ranks based on function and tried mightily to enforce a prohibition on unsanctioned practices. Only licensed physicians could legally identify illness and stipulate remedies, which were then prepared by apothecaries and administered by surgeons, both of whom physicians regarded as mere tradesmen. Indeed, apothecaries usually had shops where a variety of merchandise from treacle to tobacco could be purchased by the public. While apothecaries and surgeons held credentials from their respective guilds, many of these men tried to extend their services beyond merely assisting university-educated doctors to diagnosing and prescribing on their own. Other "irregular" practitioners, like unauthorized healers and quacksalvers, midwives, and wise women, had no legitimate business in medicine at all in the view of the elite physicians, and the College's *Annals* from Middleton's time reveal implacable pursuit of any violation of the Fellows' prerogatives. Learned doctors deliberately undermined public confidence in iatric itinerants and ridiculed the theatricality of quack medicine (Katritzky, *Women*, p. 133). Middleton knew of these status and gender tensions within the medical community and exploited them in his plays. In partnership again with Dekker, he featured a Mistress Gallipot (the word gallipot means a druggist's glazed mixing vessel) as a foolish tobacconist's wife with a roving eye in *The Roaring Girl*, a 1611 theatrical production based on a notorious cross-dressing virago of the day, Mary Frith; the drama attempted to persuade the audience that the thief "Moll Cutpurse" was more admirable than Mistress Gallipot. To underscore this preference, Mary Firth may have appeared in person on stage in the play (Kahn, *Middleton*, p. 721).

By the 1620s politics had entered the iatric fray as Paracelsians attacked not just the theoretical claims of traditionalists, but their professional domination as well. Many proponents of the new medicine charged that learned physicians greedily tried to monopolize health care despite challenges from more democratic, more affordable practitioners like surgeons and apothecaries. However, once again Middleton tips his hat to the elite College of Physicians and derides its challengers by putting ridiculously pretentious words in the mouth of the surgeon in *Quarrel*, performed at court at the peak of Mayerne's medical influence. Middleton may have embraced puritan theology, but there is little linking his plays to more egalitarian access to medicine. Nevertheless, he did mean to engage "in direct colloquy with his audience, intending a candid and topical commentary to be recognized" (Corrigan, "Crisis Literature," p. 287). He intended to foster discussion on illness, the nature of medicine, and who should practice it. Thomas Middleton died in the summer of 1627 at the age of 47, having created a cutting picture of tragicomic London life in plays that seem as relevant in the twenty-first century as in his own. Perhaps it is ultimately true that "all meaningful theatre is like the plague," for it makes us look inward and see ourselves as we are (Artaud, *Theatre*, p. 22).

NOTE

1. Appleby, *Famine*, pp. 137–9. London does not appear to have suffered greatly from another famine in 1623 that devastated the north of England.

## CHAPTER 7

# The city's money

## Aaron Kitch

In one of his experiments with living small, the Roman stoic Lucius Seneca recounts a journey in which he travels in what he calls "rustic style," accompanied by only a few servants. He consumes a lunch requiring only an hour to prepare and rides in a carriage driven by a shoeless driver (Seneca, *Letters*, p. 48). Such reduced circumstances prompt the philosopher to raise some fundamental questions about wealth: Do good Romans, for example, praise poverty and fear wealth? Do riches necessarily corrupt the mind? Should the Roman senate pass a law abolishing money all together? Seneca's responses to these questions – that wealth does affect human desire but that we should temper our passion for money rather than proscribe laws against it – anticipate Middleton's own fascination with wealth and its vicissitudes. Middleton follows Seneca (whom he likely translated as a schoolboy) in linking wealth and the political imaginary in some of his civic pageants, but goes further than the classical philosopher in exploring the shaping influence of wealth on human sexuality and psychology in his city comedies.

As Swapan Chakravorty suggests, many of Middleton's city comedies "establish the drive for money and sex as the motor of human behavior at all levels." These drives help shape what Chakravorty calls, following Jean-François Lyotard, a "libidinal economy" (*Society*, p. 44) in which, for example, Mrs Allwit's sexualized longing for pickled cucumbers (1.2.7) in *A Chaste Maid in Cheapside* symbolizes her desire to buy luxury goods at the Royal Exchange (1.2.35). Elsewhere, sex and money are inversely related; as Quomodo observes in *Michaelmas Term*, "to get riches and children too, / 'Tis more than one man can do" (4.1.37–8). The citizen-merchant Gallipot complains in *The Roaring Girl* that "We venture lives / For wealth, but must do more to keep our wives" (6.152–3). Money and its circulation – made, lost, stolen, lent, and invested – shape plot, character, and setting in Middleton's works to an extraordinary degree. Even those characters like Candido in *The Patient Man and the Honest Whore*, who claims to transcend the trade by which he earns his living, cannot avoid the language and logic of economics: though he elevates himself above the dishonest gallants who know the price of all, Candido nonetheless defines his own virtue as a wealthy "stock" fit for a "monarch" (15.532–3). At the same time, Middleton defines wealth as fundamental to the establishing of political order in his civic entertainments. It is not unusual, for example, to find a character describing his love for King James I in *The Whole Royal and Magnificent Entertainment* (1604) in "leaves of purest gold" (346). Writing for some of London's powerful trading guilds and celebrating the annual election of a London citizen to the office of Lord Mayor, Middleton explores the implications of global trade on the civic space of London. His pageants represent the power of wealth to shape social order and build communal bonds.

The London that Middleton depicts in many of his works is defined by the pursuit of wealth, pleasure, and prestige. The citizen plays of Dekker and the city comedies of Jonson are in some ways equally attuned to the material operations of civic commerce, but Dekker tends to glorify civic labor while Jonson employs the corrective morality of classical comedy. Middleton's city comedies are more open-ended, cynical, and unsettling in their implications. Middleton's usurers, prodigals, courtesans, and conniving gallants inhabit a society that resembles capitalist societies like our own to the degree that quotidian life becomes subject to impersonal market forces. "No man shall have bread, fire, flesh, or drink without credit or ready money," asserts the narrator of Middleton's mock-almanac *Plato's Cap* (284–5). Several scholars have addressed the way that early modern commercial theatres could serve as new forums for staging the effects on human behavior and society (see Agnew, *Worlds Apart*; Bruster, *Drama and the Market*; Leinwand, *Theatre*). The boom-and-bust cycle of England's export of woolen cloth created new demographic patterns in the sixteenth century and generated new questions about the function of wealth on public and private life. Economic reformers like Thomas Gresham and Thomas Misselden advised monarchs like Elizabeth I and James I on strategies for harnessing commerce in the service of the English state, one with imperial ambitions (Wood, *Political Economy*; C. H. Wilson, "Trade," p. 495). Inflation, population increase in London, currency devaluation, the influx of Spanish gold from the Americas, and a spike in law suits over failed credit contracts all combined to create new opportunity and uncertainty.

One way that Middleton responds to this world is to stage commerce in terms of human relations. In *Roaring Girl*, for example, Middleton and

Dekker examine key rituals of early modern commerce through the shop-keepers who sell tobacco, feathers, and other popular luxury items to socially mobile gentlemen. Middleton uses this "real" economic activity as a foil for his broader examination of the commodification of human desire. Sebastian Wengrave promises his betrothed, Mary Fitzallard, that he will "owe" his "affection" to her even as he will "spend" his "counterfeit passion" on Moll Cutpurse, the eponymous roaring girl (1.104–5). Sebastian's counterfeit passion for Moll leads his father to assent to his marriage to Mary, despite her small dowry. This fake investment of libidinal energy in the cross-dressed Moll reproduces the logic of interchangeability at work in a full market economy. In a parallel plot, the gallant Laxton (who "lacks" a "stone" or testicle) hopes to win money from the hapless Gallipot as compensation for his sexual impotence. The complicit Mistress Gallipot constructs a fiction about a precontracted marriage to Laxton that itself proves profitable. These fictions are successful to the degree that they can be believed by others, linking them to the institution of the theatre itself.

The "roarer" Moll Cutpurse, whom Middleton based on the historical Mary Frith, both embraces and disowns aspects of the material world, as captured by her song in scene 8:

> I dream there is a mistress,
>     And she lays out the money;
> She goes unto her sisters,
>     She never comes at any.
> She says she went to th'Burse for patterns;
>     You shall find her at St. Kathern's,
> And comes home with never a penny.
>
> (8.103–9)

The song unites the profit-based economy of prostitution with the ideal of poverty associated with Christian asceticism. Like a "mistress" who can be either a housewife or a sexual servant, the "sisters" can refer either to nuns or prostitutes. The mistress "lays out the money" either because she gives her possessions to charity or because she wants to look over her earnings; she returns home "with never a penny" either because she has been making the rounds among the inhabitants of this notoriously impoverished neighbor-hood or because the money she has earned through prostitution has been stolen or confiscated by her bawd.

The ambivalence of the song mirrors Moll's ambivalent status in the play. Far from picking the pockets of gentlemen, as her nefarious reputation would suggest, she refuses the counterfeit coin and gold watch that

Alexander Wengrave and his spy Trapdoor use to trap her. She helps Sebastian and Mary achieve their heterosexual coupling, exposing as false the assumption of Sir Alexander that "deep spendings" will "draw her that's most chaste to a man's bosom" (2.227–8). But her presence also inspires the sale of tobacco that is used to purchase sex, which is then used to buy luxury trinkets. This pattern of substitution through exchange follows the logic of the commodity defined by Marx, in which real relations between humans are transformed by virtue of their "exchange value" into abstractions that become personified in the public realm of the marketplace (Forman, "Marked Angels," p. 1533). And yet the setting of the play, with its focus on the small exchange of petty goods, remains precapitalist. This fictional substitution designed by Sebastian – in which Moll is a red herring for Mary – conquers the explicitly economic machinations of Laxton, with their violent consequences ("I'll now tear money from thy throat," yells Mistress Gallipot at one point [9.286]).

*Michaelmas* explores a similar dynamic, even as the predatory economic fictions of the draper Quomodo and his sidekicks Shortyard and Falselight suggest corruption at the heart of the London wool trade. Quomodo manipulates the trust and status anxiety of the Essex gentleman Richard Easy during a London dice game, tricking Easy into mortgaging his lands in exchange for unmarketable and moth-eaten cloth. This jest reveals the failure of traditional notions of aristocratic "credit" based on personal relations (Shortyard impersonates the friend of one of Easy's Essex neighbors) in the face of extreme financial pressure. *Michaelmas* revels in Quomodo's plotting, which is a main source of the play's comedy. Like Moll, Shortyard denies the strict economic desires he represents elsewhere when he says, "Hang money! Good jests are worth silver at all times" ("They're worth gold," is Easy's ironic rejoinder) (3.1.285–7). Having secured Easy's lands, Quomodo embodies this endorsement by pursuing yet another jest – faking his own death. In a classic example of the deceiver deceived, Shortyard tries to cheat Quomodo's son out of his inheritance, revealing land to be as insecure a commodity as the false cloth that Quomodo uses to secure it. Even Quomodo's own identity can evaporate in the trial scene, where the Judge convicts him of being a "counterfeit" because he does not confess to being as deceptive as he is (5.3.25).

*Chaste Maid* likewise links commercial exchange and the substitutability of commodified passion with the circulation of profitable fictions. The play demystifies family relations as essentially economic, but this materializing gesture is dependent on several fictions, including that the Welsh prostitute accompanying Sir Walter Whorehound is really his niece from Wales

whom Tim Yellowhammer will marry (Altieri, "Against Moralizing,"
p. 176). The Allwit family is, broadly speaking, a fiction sustained by the
wealth of Whorehound, who pays Jack Allwit in exchange for the privilege
of sleeping with his wife and fathering his children. In lieu of jealousy,
Allwit expresses his joy because of the relationship, taking Whorehound's
gold and remaining free of the "affliction" of those unknowing cuckolds
who work hard to feed their wives for the pleasure of other men (1.2.47).

   *Chaste Maid* also portrays wealth in relation to female fertility, a natural
"treasure" that is appropriated by men in marriage. Sexual reproduction
becomes in the play a commodity to be bought and sold like any other,
symbolized by the way that Touchwood Senior offers his services to the
infertile Kixes in exchange for gold. At the same time Maud Yellowhammer
resorts to faking her own death in order to elope with Touchwood Junior, a
failed effort to escape from the play's relentless materializations of human
value (her mother calls her a "jewel" as she yanks her by the hair [4.4.27]
while her brother refers to her skin as "white money" [5.2.17]). This fiction is
believable and allows Maud to marry her lover, but it is also suggests that
even death does not free one from the commercial forces that structure
kinship relations and shape character in early modern London.

   Middleton's city comedies are thus firmly rooted in the economic
realities of early modern London, even as they shape these realities with
satire, Roman comedy, and English cony-catching pamphlets. These comedies associate hoarding of wealth with an entrenched and moribund landed
class that is at risk of being supplanted by a more progressive class of urban
tricksters – tricksters who capitalize on their superior position within urban
credit economies that depend increasingly on fictional impersonation as a
means of establishing trust and generating commerce. Thus the classic
paternal "blocking" figures of attic comedy take on new economic meaning
in Middleton. For example, both Pecunius Lucre and his dissolute nephew
Theodorus Witgood are arrivistes in *A Trick to Catch the Old One*, but
Lucre's usury and fetishism of landed property are aligned with an outmoded economic approach, whereas Witgood's strategy of inventing a
fiction that he wills into reality in order to earn wealth becomes its own
credit economy. Instead of trading his unsecured inheritance for wine and
women, Witgood uses his power of theatrical improvisation to achieve
wealth. This acquisition of land, wealth, and status requires more than
legal chicanery – it also depends on habits of speech, dress, and behavior
that accompany the new social status. Such habits are part and parcel of a
new economy of credit in which contracts between fictional persona sustain
commercial relations (Muldrew, *Economy of Obligation*). In an era before

the development of formal systems for assessing risk, but when traditional notions of reputation, honesty, and honor were challenged as guarantees of creditworthiness, the concept of "character" itself was subject to redefinition (Kitch, "Character of Credit").

In this sense, then, wealth in the city comedies is primarily a vehicle of aggressive self-interest, even if the financial trickery of characters like Follywit and Witgood leads ultimately to a redistribution of money through marriage. By contrast, Middleton's civic pageants portray wealth as a key feature of public life: money may be a threat to the integrity of civic office in the form of bribes, but, when it is well managed, it can also help to establish social harmony and civic virtue. Consequently, Middleton's pageants celebrating the annual election of a new Lord Mayor of London every October 29 both praise and critique the values of the guilds and the ascendant merchant class they helped support. In *The Triumphs of Truth* (1613), for instance, the character of London appears dressed as an elderly matron wrapped in luxurious silk to warn the new Lord Mayor to "disdain all titles / Purchased with coin, of honour take thou hold / By thy desert, let others buy't with gold" (177–9). The figure of Honour delivers a similar message at the conclusion of *The Triumphs of Honour and Virtue* (1622) when he warns the new Lord Mayor against "making friends / Of Mammon's heaps, got by unrighteous ends" (298–9). "Mammon" here indicates the false god of riches from the New Testament, particularly Matthew 6:24, as an index of illegitimate mercantile gain. A more positive icon of wealth is the figure of Liberality, who appears with the figure of London near the end of *Truth*, her head "circled with a wreath of gold" (535). Liberality personifies the moderation of civic wealth that embraces abundance without falling prey to the dangers of prodigality. It is a virtue enacted by the very production of the civic pageant: the printed text of the pageant emphasizes the liberality of the performance of *Truth*, what Middleton himself calls the "generous and noble freeness of cost and liberality" on behalf of the Grocers, who sponsored the celebration that year (59–60). Such liberality is a measure of the honor and prestige of the guild itself. The figure of Error, by contrast, represents precise knowledge of the price of things, convenient for those who need to follow the "markets" or measure bribes (284).

*Truth* thus links the "bounty" of its own entertainment, which was consumed for free by London's citizens, with religion, knowledge, chastity, and charity (608–10). The pageant also dramatizes the arrival of the King of Moors, who praises English merchants and factors for their "religious conversation" that has led to his conversion to the "true Christian faith"

(436, 440). Middleton draws on a tradition of Moors who appeared in sixteenth-century midsummer shows, but also glances at the prestige of the Grocers, who joined forces with the East India Company as agents of international commerce (Barbour, *Before Orientalism*, p. 89). In this way, Middleton's sophisticated economic language invests the conventional allegorical content of his pageant with new meaning. By celebrating liberality in symbolic ways, he aligns the civic pageant with the courtly masque, an even more extravagant spectacle that justified its expense in terms of the king's munificence. But it is the power and prestige of London commerce rather than the glory of the monarch that is celebrated in pageants like *The Triumphs of Honour and Industry* (1617), which represents Traffic and Industry as sisters linked with love and glorifies a pageant of nations bound together by "virtue of Traffic" (100). This traffic binds diverse nations in "harmonious peace" (84) in *Industry*, an international version of the ideal of brotherhood that defines the code of honor for London's guilds. As opposed to the masques of Ben Jonson at the royal court of King James, such ideals are not taken for granted in Middleton. The Lord Mayor, as opposed to the monarch at the ideological center of the court masque, must first be led through the Castle of Fame and match "reward" with "justice," attaining honor in his profession.

In his civic pageants and in his paean to James's pacifism, *The Peacemaker* (1618), Middleton defends London's wealthiest merchants against criticism that they were draining England of valuable currency and flooding the English market with unnecessary imports. His pageants suggest, by contrast, that strong trade will lead to peace abroad and political stability at home. Middleton's civic works thus praise wealth not for its material value but as a vehicle for achieving ideals like honor, liberality, and trustworthiness. These sustaining fictions, much different in origin and effect from those promulgated by tricksters like Witgood and Follywit, share nevertheless in Middleton's extraordinary faith in the power of theatrical forms to construct new realities capable of propelling new social identities. Where wealth in the city comedies works generally as a self-interested prize whose acquisition tends to dissolve communal bonds, the orderly control of commerce in the civic pageants becomes a key element of political order for an expanding English nation.

CHAPTER 8

# Trade, work, and workers

## Natasha Korda

Trade, work, and workers in Middleton's London were largely regulated by
the urban guilds or livery companies. The livery companies were central to
the economic life of the city because it was through them that artisans
earned the right to practice particular crafts or trades as "freemen" or
citizens. Although this right was typically earned by serving an apprenticeship to a master crafts- or tradesman, it could also be obtained through
patrimony (by sons of freemen when they turned 21 and paid a fee),
redemption (the payment of a large fee in lieu of serving an apprenticeship),
or translation (whereby a freeman might transfer from one company to
another after paying a fee). Livery companies collected fees for every
important step in the occupational lives of their members, in addition to
charging "quarterage" (a quarterly tax for the privilege of membership) and
levying fines for disobeying company ordinances. The "freedom" that came
with citizenship thus entailed financial obligation as well as privilege,
constraint as well as license. The wealth accrued by the livery companies
afforded freemen a corporate identity and culture, social prestige (signified
through their livery, pageants, feasts, halls, and so on) and economic
assistance in the form of charity, pensions, and loans (see Rappaport,
*Worlds Within Worlds*, pp. 195–200).

Yet the livery companies' internal stability and external control over
London's workforce loosened during Middleton's lifetime, as they began
to break "away from the purpose for which they were originally founded,
and were taking part in pursuits and industries alien to their primary
functions" (A. H. Johnson, *Drapers*, vol. II, p. 174). The larger, more
established livery companies experienced increased internal division
between the mercantile interests of their liverymen (the elite of the company, who were often far removed from the practice of their crafts) and the
industrial concerns of their yeomanry (less prosperous, manufacturing small
masters and journeymen) (Unwin, *Gilds and Companies*, pp. 224, 226; see
also Unwin, *Industrial Organization*, pp. 41–69, 103; Archer, *Pursuit of*

*Stability*, pp. 100–1). This loosening of the guild system likewise occurred partly as a result of London's population growth (and the resulting pressure of external competition from non-citizen, migrant laborers) and partly as a result of internal competition from crafts- and tradesmen who had earned their freedom in one trade but were practicing another (A. H. Johnson, *Drapers*, vol. II, p. 63; see also Kellet, "Breakdown"; Fisher, "Experiments"; Kramer, *English Craft Gilds*, p. 138). The latter phenomenon took on unprecedented proportions in the late sixteenth century, when guildsmen began to take advantage of a custom of London whereby "every Citizen and Freeman" who had "been an Apprentice in London unto any trade by the space of seven years," could "lawfully and well relinquish that trade and exercise any other trade at his will and pleasure" (Tawney and Power [eds.], *Tudor Economic Documents*, vol. I, pp. 378–83). Originally intended to apply only to those engaged in wholesaling, rather than in production and retailing, by the later sixteenth century the custom was invoked by crafts-men all over London as justification for the pursuit of trades other than those for which they had served apprenticeships (Archer, *Pursuit of Stability*, pp. 114–15).[1] As a result of this practice, by the early seventeenth century "the trades and companies within the city were almost inextricably tangled" (Thrupp, *Bakers*, p. 64). Although the degree of control livery companies were able to exercise over the crafts and trades consequently diminished, they nonetheless retained their status and privileges within the walled city as a result of their wealth and landed property, as well as their control over entrance to the freedom and citizenship of the city and over election to government offices (A. H. Johnson, *Drapers*, pp. 175–6, 240).

Outside the walled city, however, the livery companies' control over trade, work, and workers was made increasingly difficult by their limited ability to enforce labor standards and market regulations there (Archer, *Pursuit of Stability*, pp. 225–6, 234; D. J. Johnson, *Southwark*, pp. 313, 315; Kellet, "Breakdown," pp. 381–2). By some estimates, London's population nearly trebled during the second half of the sixteenth century, fueled largely by the exponential increase in immigration to the city's rapidly expanding extramural parishes and suburbs (Finlay, *Population and Metropolis*, p. 51). Informal commerce flourished in the suburbs as increasing numbers of impoverished migrants – including "foreigners" from the countryside, "aliens" or "strangers" from other lands, and women – took up occupations outside of guild control, swelling the ranks of non-citizen laborers. This informal workforce engaged in a host of disorderly commercial practices frowned upon by the livery companies, from unlawful gaming and unli-censed alehouse-keeping to street-hawking, pawnbroking, and usury.

It is no accident that the success of the commercial theatre in England coincided with the loosening of the guild system and expansion of the informal economy, nor that the theatres were located in the very same suburbs and liberties of London in which such unregulated commerce thrived. For the professional playing companies and the entrepreneurs who backed them took maximum advantage of the flexible forms of trade found in the informal sector (Agnew, *Worlds Apart*, p. 54). Many of those involved in the professional theatre – including actors, playwrights, and managers – were livery company members who had earned their freedom and then opted to leave these traditional occupational backgrounds (Kathman, "Grocers," p. 3).[2] Certain aspects of the older economic structures were imported into the new profession of playing, such as the apprenticeship system. Yet there were important differences between the playing companies and the livery companies, for the players had "no central organization, no court system, and no regulations that governed all of them … and [they] certainly did not have the social prestige of the ancient guilds, like the Goldsmiths or the Mercers" (Streitberger, "Personnel and Professionalization," p. 347). By retaining structural aspects of the livery-company system in their new economic ventures, however, the professional players "subtly … relat[ed] the work of acting to the crafts and professions, and thereby implicitly la[id] claim to their rights and privileges" (Orgel, *Impersonations*, p. 65). The commercial playing companies were in this sense transitional economic formations that retained certain residual structures of the guilds, while at the same time assuming the emergent form of innovative capital ventures, such as the joint-stock trading companies. Situated between the formal and informal sectors of the market economy, they enjoyed a hybrid status that allowed them to take opportunistic advantage of both.

The shifting economic landscape of Middleton's London provides a useful framework within which to understand his "work" as a dramatist – both his choice to pursue the career of playwright and the corpus of work he subsequently produced. The forays of freemen and their families into new trades associated with the rise of capitalism, including those associated with the commercial theatre, and the potential gains of such commerce as well as its risks, profoundly shaped the events of the playwright's early life. Although he was born into privilege, with a clear path to citizenship – his father was a prosperous freeman (and gentleman) of the Worshipful Company of Tilers and Bricklayers (*Middleton*, p. 29) – Middleton chose not to pursue his father's trade, nor that of his stepfather, Thomas Harvey, who was a "Cittizen and grocer of London" (Christian, "Family History,"

p. 495).[3] Yet we can see the loosening of the guild system at play in the occupational lives of his father and stepfather, and it may be that their economic decisions helped to pave Middleton's path to the commercial theatres. One such decision did so quite literally: in 1577, several years before Middleton was born, his father William purchased a fifty-year lease on grounds adjoining the Curtain theatre in Shoreditch "where now comenlye the Playes be played," and converted a dairy house there into tenements for which he received "a greate yearlie rent." The Curtain tenements helped to support Middleton's family after his father's death and brought him into proximity with the commercial theatres. When he later sold his half-share in this and other leases inherited from his father to his brother-in-law, Allen Waterer, in 1600, Middleton used the money to help fund his Oxford education (Eccles, "Thomas Middleton," pp. 518, 526).

If William Middleton's investment in new construction in the expanding metropolis exemplified the potential profits to be made by such ventures, Thomas Harvey's foray into capitalist (ad)venture demonstrated its risks. A member of the prosperous Grocers' Company, which had strong ties to the joint-stock overseas trading companies, Harvey became chief merchant for Sir Walter Ralegh's colony at Roanoke, and invested not only "the greatest parte of his owne Wealth which he had vppon the same [voyage] but also borrowed Diuers somes of money of others for his better expedic[i]on therein" (Christian, "Family History," pp. 491–2, n. 12). Yet his plan "to descrye & fynde out the Commodytyes of the same Country" ultimately failed when, "the successe of the same voiadge not fallinge out so prosperously as was expected," Harvey ended up "in very miserable Case," having "spent or lost whatsoeuer" he had invested (Eccles, "Thomas Middleton," p. 519). Returning to London in this impecunious state in 1586, he set his sights on the newly widowed, prosperous leaseholder Anne Middleton, whose properties would ordinarily have been conveyed to him when they married, in accordance with the common law of coverture. Under this law, a wife could not own property in her own name, sue or be sued, or make contracts on her own behalf, and her husband took possession of whatever property was hers prior to her marriage. Men who were fortunate enough to marry wealthy heiresses or widows therefore had access to free capital with which to pay off their debts, purchase lands, or start a business.

Yet Anne demonstrated her own economic ingenuity prior to her marriage by setting up a legal trust to protect her marital property. Her plan was to rent the Curtain house and property "to tennauntes at her Will & to receave the renttes & profyttes therof comynge to her owne vse for the mayten[an]ce & relieffe of herself . . . & her children," and to safeguard her children's inheritance (Christian, "Family History," p. 494). Trusts of this kind were increasingly used by women during the period to circumvent the law of coverture (Erickson, *Women and Property*, pp. 103–13). Needless to say, husbands did not always relinquish their proprietary rights in their wives' property without a fight; indeed, when hard-pressed by creditors they frequently resorted to violence in attempting to regain possession of it (Hunt, *Middling Sort*, pp. 160–1). When Anne refused to hand over her property held in trust after their marriage, Harvey "grewe into great Colloure" (i.e. choler) and lodged a complaint with the Lord Mayor. Anne was not intimidated, however, and once again showed considerable legal and financial savvy by having herself arrested for not delivering the portions to which her children were entitled. Knowing that under coverture her own legal identity was "covered" by her husband, and that he was therefore responsible for her debts, she thereby forced Harvey to deliver her children's portions to the Lord Mayor's Court in cash. In 1587 Harvey was granted a loan of £50 for two years by the Grocers' Company, but this seems not to have restored him to solvency (Seaver, "Middleton's London," p. 68). Over the next fifteen years, husband and wife continued to fight in and out of court over Anne's and her children's assets. Harvey was imprisoned several times for his debts, and once in 1595 for attempting to poison Anne (Eccles, "Thomas Middleton," pp. 520–2). In 1600, he filed two lawsuits aimed at recovering all the family properties and was eventually successful. In 1601 Thomas Middleton claimed from the City of London the £25 that had been held for him since his father's death. With Harvey's legal victory over his mother, however, this was all that remained of Middleton's inheritance. Although Middleton claimed the status of a "gentleman," he was thus nonetheless forced to work for a living. It is around this time that we find him "in London daylie accompaninge the players" (Phialas, "Early Contact," p. 192).

Although it is certainly true that "the world of tradesmen and guildsmen was one Middleton knew well and at first hand" from his upbringing (Seaver, "Middleton's London," p. 68), this world was, as we have seen, rapidly changing and riven with tensions from without and within during the playwright's lifetime. His plays register these tensions: they are thus populated not only by an array of citizen crafts- and tradesmen (including goldsmiths, apothecaries, mercers, linen- and woolen-drapers, tailors, tanners, weavers, fellmongers, glovers, barber-surgeons, braziers, vintners, scriveners, and their journeymen and apprentices), but also by a new workforce of non-citizen tradespeople (usurers, pawnbrokers, perfumers, tobacco-men, feather-sellers, and Dutch merchants), unemployed and impoverished city-dwellers (hospital boys, poor fellows, cheaters, and bed-lamites), working women (shopkeepers, tirewomen, merchant's wives, itinerant vendors, nurses, bawds, and prostitutes) and highly sought-after wealthy heiresses and widows whose capital, as Anne Middleton's life so poignantly demonstrates, was in high demand in the new economy.

Middleton and Dekker's *The Patient Man and the Honest Whore* (1604), for example, juxtaposes the formal and informal economies of the city, gendering the former as masculine and the latter as feminine. The eponymous "patient man" is Candido, a wealthy citizen and linen-draper, who represents a nostalgic ideal of civic stability among tradesmen, a stability that was perceived to be in decline in Middleton's time. Nothing moves Candido to anger, not even extravagant losses in trade. He seeks nothing but "calm order" (5.190) in his home and shop. As his name suggests, Candido is an "honest-dealing" (5.60) tradesman, whose wares are of a "true weave ... far from falsehood" (5.61). Yet the play makes clear just how rare Candido's stability is, as all who surround him are enraged by his patience and seek, futilely, to rile him. In contemporary London, the play implies, the imperturbable citizen-tradesman is thus as much an oxymoron as the "honest whore." The immutability of Candido's humor is opposed in the play to the fickleness of female desire (instanced by the sudden conversion of Bellafront the whore and the erratic temperament of Candido's wife Viola, who is as vexatious as he is impassive), and to the economic instability of his brother-in-law Fustigo, an impecunious venturer not unlike Thomas Harvey, who is "moved and moved again" (2.78) in his sea travels. The play likewise registers contemporary civic instability and tension within the guild system, which Candido's character aims to deflect, when his apprentices take up their clubs and beat Fustigo (7.152), recalling the apprentice riots that threatened the stability of Middleton's London in the 1590s.

The positive potential of the economic transformations Middleton witnessed during his lifetime is perhaps most fully imagined in his Lord Mayor's pageants. In *The Triumphs of Honour and Industry*, sponsored by the Grocers' Company in 1617, for example, the allegorical figures of "Industry" and "Traffic or Merchandise" sit side-by-side atop an "illustrious chariot" (54–5): "Industry hold[s] a golden ball in her hand, upon which stands a Cupid, signifying that Industry gets both wealth and love, and, with her associate Traffic or Merchandise, who holds a globe in her hand, knits love and peace amongst all nations" (57–61). No trace of intracompany strife between mercantile liverymen and industrial yeomen, nor of the risks of global commerce, remains in this harmonious image of commerce and industry united.

The dark underside of these transformations comes to light perhaps most vividly in his city comedies, which reveal the multifarious market abuses of the metropolis, practiced by citizens and non-citizens alike. Thus, in *A Chaste Maid in Cheapside* (1613) the city's wares are shown to be as imperfect as its wives: "there is no woman made without a flaw," Yellowhammer the Goldsmith acknowledges, "Your purest lawns have frays, and cambrics bracks" (1.1.36–7). Deceitful trading practices are likewise the subject of satire in Middleton's pamphlets, such as *The Owl's Almanac* (1618), which contains mock prognostications for the "fundamental trades" (1454) of the city (including the mercers, grocers, drapers, fishmongers, goldsmiths, skinners, tailors, haberdashers, salters, ironmongers, vintners, clothworkers, dyers, brewers, leathersellers, pewterers, barber-surgeons, armourers, bakers, chandlers, girdlers, cutlers, butchers, saddlers, carpenters, shoe-makers, and painters). In each case, the good fortune foretold for the company is grounded in skullduggery, as when it is predicted that the draper's "yard is like to be as short as ever it was, and you shall have many days as dark as twilight" (1566–8).

Although Middleton never earned the freedom, in certain respects he modeled his professional life on the newly flexible forms of trade that surrounded him, writing in a variety of genres and for no fewer than seven playing companies. In so doing, he "exploit[ed] the varied artistic opportunities offered by different casts, theatres, audiences," and took advantage of "the rivalry between companies, getting a higher price for his product by offering to sell it to a competitor" (G. Taylor, "Lives and Afterlives," p. 42). Yet unlike contemporary journeymen who worked for wages, Middleton had no master. In this respect he resembled the young gallants or single women who live by their wits in his plays, such as his "honest whore," who lives "in bonds to no man" and thus is "free for any man" (6.309, 311). Perhaps we may glimpse in the independence of Moll in *The Roaring Girl* (1611) the imagined freedom Middleton saw foreclosed when his mother chose to remarry, and sought to recapture through his own work as a playwright: "I have the head now of myself . . . marriage is but a chopping and changing, where a maiden loses one head, and has a worse i' th' place" (4.44–7).

NOTES

1. Examples of the growing numbers of freemen taking advantage of this custom abound. During Elizabeth's reign, members of the Drapers' Company were pursuing occupations as diverse as embroiderer, upholsterer, felt-maker, silk-weaver, wine-seller, grocer, apothecary, barber-surgeon, smith, gunner,

pewterer, salter, woadmonger, painter-stainer, printer, bookbinder, bookseller, and stationer (A. H. Johnson, *Drapers*, p. 165).

2. Theatre people are known to have been freemen of the following companies: Merchant Taylors (8), Innholders (1), Drapers (16), Goldsmiths (15), Fishmongers (3), Apothecaries (4), Grocers (11), Joiners (1), Bricklayers (2), Farriers (3), Mercers (4), Vintners (3), Weavers (3), Pewterers (2), Scriveners (1), Barber-Surgeons (2), Stationers (1), Brewers (1), Haberdashers (3), Ironmongers (1), Saddlers (1). Most were freed through servitude, although some were freed through patrimony and a few through redemption (Kathman, "Grocers," pp. 47–9.

3. Nor did he decide to earn his freedom as a bricklayer or grocer while pursuing a life in the theatre, as did Ben Jonson and John Heminges, respectively (Kathman, "Grocers," pp. 47–8).

## CHAPTER 9

# Supplying the city

Ceri Sullivan

In the spring of 1613, Thomas Middleton worked on natural resources in three productions for the summer and autumn: the city comedy *A Chaste Maid in Cheapside*; *The Manner of His Lordship's Entertainment*, which celebrated the opening of a major new water supply for London by the Welsh engineer, Hugh Myddelton; and *The Triumphs of Truth*, a pageant for the installation of the latter's brother, Sir Thomas Myddelton, as the new Lord Mayor. The Grocers' Company commissioned the pageant for Sir Thomas in February; the New River (as the watercourse was called) reached its reservoir at Clerkenwell in April, and the composition of *Chaste Maid* is usually dated to the end of Lent. Their performances were also close together, since the comedy was probably acted between Easter and August 1613, the New River opened on September 29, and the mayoral pageant took place on October 29. As was the custom, *Truth* was published when it was performed so copies could be sent to influential people, but – unusually – it was reprinted two years after the event, with *His Lordship's Entertainment*.

Supplying London with basic commodities – cheese, corn, hemp, fish, and so on – in the quantities demanded by what its inhabitants saw as a megalopolis (over 200,000 consumers) was both a headache for city fathers and an opportunity for entrepreneurs. This was even more so when utilities, such as sewage and transport, were in question. These often demanded new technologies, new pricing structures, and new financing arrangements to cope with supply on a permanent basis over a large area in high volume. Such projects are highly visible and carry big social penalties if they go wrong. Middleton's three productions celebrate the success of his patrons in carrying through the risky, cutting-edge, communal enterprise of bringing piped water to London. He shows how large cities need their talented immigrants, even in a credit crunch.

Increasing demand had already produced a number of capital-intensive schemes.[1] In 1581, a 500-year lease of the first arch of London Bridge was granted to Peter Morris, a Dutch or German engineer, for a pumping machine to supply water direct to private houses in the city, using pipes laid in the streets. In 1594, Sir Bevis Bulmer set up a pump at Broken Wharf to supply the west of the city (like Hugh Myddelton, Bulmer was an expert in precious metals mining, which gave him insight into hydraulics and financial capital as well as a welcome at court). John Darge's scheme to supply water from Fogswell pond by lead pipes (a project absorbed by the New River scheme in 1614) brought him £60 each year. William Hardin ("'Pipe-pilgrimages'") argues that *His Lordship's Entertainment* captures the moment when water became a commodity, under the control of a mercantile elite. In truth, London already realized that water was an economic as well as a natural resource. Domestic users paid a cob (a water-bearer) to carry standard 3-gallon tankards from public conduits, though the water itself was free, and the city charged for water for trade purposes. Both Bulwer and Myddelton charged for water not by unit cost but by a lease of time. Myddleton's water was expensive, though: a lease of twenty-one years cost 20 shillings for connection, and a 5 shilling quarterly rent, when the average labourer earned a shilling a day.

None of these early projects was on a grand enough scale to cope with London's burgeoning size, and engineers began to think about streams arising at the edge of the London basin, such as where the gravel overlying a chalk substratum petered out at Chadwell, near Ware, and at Amwell, near Hertford. Getting the paperwork done and finance raised to start the New River took seven years of wearisome parliamentary and city council lobbying, not to mention negotiating with reluctant owners of land to be compulsorily purchased. On March 28, 1609, London's governing body, the common council, deputed Hugh Myddelton to exercise its powers, impatiently stipulating that physical work should finish by the very tight deadline of spring 1613.

In the first phase of work, from August 1609 to January 1610, the Cut, as it was known, grew briskly, engaging up to 130 laborers at a time. Many were countrymen of Myddelton: "Davie Gryffethe" and "Rees Uphughes" (who together carried the shelter for the surveyor's level), "Howell Joahns" (who started as a ganger in 1611, but by 1613 had risen to be in charge of the cistern house), Morgan and Griffeth Evans, Thomas Davies, John Hughes, William Jones, Davie Roberts, Morgan and Huw Williams, Thomas Edwards, Thomas Griffeths, John Lewis, Davie Price, and Robert Howell are some of the Welsh employees recorded in the disbursement books. The canal was cut at 10 feet wide and about 4 feet deep, and followed a winding course of nearly 39 miles into the reservoir. Trenches were sunk to 30 feet, aqueducts raised to 23 feet. Even when work started, the legal challenges were not over. Obstructive landowners, using a parliamentary bill, stopped the work in January 1610, forcing Myddelton to apply for an extension of time from the city. The king had taken an interest when the canal passed through the grounds of his palace at Theobalds, and in August 1612 agreed to pay half the capital costs of the work in return for half the annual profits and half the enterprise (though he was to take no part in management). Work started again in November 1611; on April 10, 1613 the trench reached the Mantells at Clerkenwell, where the Round Pond (later to be called the New River Head) was to be made. The project was not yet finished. Nearly as much was spent on local distribution as on bringing the stream to London (£18,525 up to James's entry into the scheme, and about £17,000 between January 1612 and December 1614, on the purchase of elm, boring the trunks, and laying the pipes). Distribution to public conduits and private houses started shortly after the opening, with the domestic supply turned on in each area two or three days a week by perambulating turn-cocks. Inspection and fining procedures were put in place to check water being run to waste and to stop people selling it on, but there were still frequent complaints about private quills (that is, small pipes) – authorized or not – that reduced the public supply.

*The Manner of His Lordship's Entertainment upon Michaelmas Day Last, being the Day of [Sir Thomas Myddelton's] Election, at that Most Famous and Admired Work of the Running Stream, from Amwell-head unto the Cesterne at Islington* was acted on September 29, the day of the mayoral election – the brothers came as a package. A personification of Perfection welcomed assembled city dignitaries (the then Lord Mayor, Sir John Swinnerton; the mayor-elect, Thomas; the City Recorder, Sir Henry Montague; and many aldermen) to a mount erected in front of the Round Pond. Drums and trumpets sounded, as over sixty laborers, in green caps and carrying symbols of their trades, marched two or three times round the cistern and then presented themselves before the mount. Hugh Myddelton was praised for conquering malice, envy, and rumor, through an unstinting supply of money, engineering ability, and strength over the years. The principal workers were presented: the mathematician (Edward Pond), the master of timberwork (William Parnell), the clerk (William Lewyn), the pipe-borer (Richard Parkes), the pavier (Thomas Horne). At the words "flow forth," the stream was let into the cistern, "drums and trumpets giving it triumphant welcomes" (*Middleton*, p. 962), followed by a peal of ordnance.

For Hugh's elder brother, Thomas, 1613 was a similarly gratifying year, being the culmination of a steady and lucrative rise through the ranks of the

Grocers' Company. He had been made free of the company in 1582, admitted to the livery in 1592 (when he joined three others as surveyors of the customs in all ports outside London), and appointed Assistant to the Grocers in 1611 (the position normally taken by someone in line for the wardenship). Signs of his increasing wealth were not confined to London, since in 1595 he bought the lordship of Chirk Castle, Denbighshire. Success in civic government followed these mercantile accolades: after ten years as an alderman and city sheriff he was elected Lord Mayor. When he took the oath of office on October 29, 1613 he appointed his namesake to write the pageant that accompanied the religious and civic rites. *Truth* was billed in the printed description as "a solemnity unparalleled for cost, art, and magnificence" (*Middleton*, p. 968); it cost £1094, about the same amount as the second Globe. At the Guildhall, Myddelton was welcomed by London, who warned him against selling offices and invited him to keep the "king's chamber," London, fit for his majesty (*Middleton*, p. 970). On his return, he was met at Baynard's Castle wharf by Truth's Angel and Zeal, who foretold Error's mists would try to engulf him. At St. Paul's Chain, Error and Envy urged him to use the opportunities of the position. At Paul's Churchyard, Myddelton viewed five Spice Isles, whose Moorish king praised the success of merchants as missionaries in his lands – but Error broke in again. The pageant moved along Cheapside to the Little Conduit, where London's Triumphant Mount was attacked by Error's disciples, namely Barbarism, Ignorance, Impudence, and Falsehood. Though wafted away by Truth, at Cheap Cross, the Standard, and other unnamed locations on the way to the feast at Guildhall and on the return to St. Paul's, Error repeatedly fell over the Mount. At Leadenhall, though London and Time rejoiced over the new Lord Mayor, Truth bluntly told him he would always be under surveillance.

By 1613, the pageant genre had standard features, particularly London's submission to the king, praise for the civic good works of merchants, and personified virtues. Middleton struck two new – and not altogether complimentary – notes (Bromham, "*Triumphs of Truth*"). First, Myddelton is again and again warned against nepotism and knowing "the worth of every office to a hair" (*Middleton*, p. 971). Second, Error makes constant challenges, and is only rebutted by promises that the mayoral behavior would be watched carefully: before, "his follies were not spread, / Or his corruptions;" now, "they're clearly read / E'en by the eyes of all men ... / There is no hiding of thy actions now" (*Middleton*, p. 976).

Hugh and Thomas bore watching, as part of a Welsh hegemony in London in 1613. Their father, Richard Myddelton, governor of Denbigh castle, had nine sons and seven daughters. The first son, Richard, a London merchant before he retired to Wrexham, had eleven children. Three of these were also London merchants, two adventuring in their uncle's New River Company when it incorporated in 1619. The Denbigh governor's third son, William, was a trader to London from the Netherlands. The fifth and eighth sons, Charles and Fulke, were traders in London, before becoming governor of Denbigh castle and the high sheriff of Denbighshire respectively. The sixth son, Hugh, was a member of the Goldsmiths' Company, an alderman and MP for Denbigh, and the father of seven sons and eight daughters. He was the king's goldsmith, lending him large sums out of the fabulous profits of his lead and silver mines in Cardiganshire (by 1609 reputed to be making him £2,000 p.a.). The seventh son, Robert, a London merchant and skinner, had shares in the Virginia, East Indies, and Northwest Passage companies, and was MP for Weymouth and London. The ninth son, Peter, followed his brothers and became a London merchant. As this roll call suggests, there was an overwhelming number of overachieving Myddeltons who arrived from North Wales to finance and manage the capital's markets, water supply, and civic affairs; who took care to strengthen links with the crown; and who then retired to the Principality to take up public roles and send the next generation down south.

In *Truth* and *His Lordship's Entertainment*, then, though London formally acknowledged what it owed the Myddeltons, it did so with some caveats: Hugh's water was expensive and affected the public supply; Thomas needed watching to ensure city offices and decisions (including who worked on and profited from the New River project) were not subject to undue influence by the Welsh. However, *Chaste Maid* turns these London irritations on their head, by making great play with its Welsh references.

Here is a Sir Walter Whorehound down from North Wales, with his Brecknock (Breconshire) mistress and his kinsman, Davy Dahumma. "I bring thee up to turn thee into gold" (1.1.5107), he declares confidently to "the Welsh Gentlewoman" (she has no other name). This "pure Welsh virgin" (1.1.111) brings with her some two thousand runts and nineteen mountains (4.1.94). The strangers cause some bewilderment among the Londoners when they speak and sing in Welsh (or is it Hebrew, wonders Tim), from the first "Duw cato chwi" (1.1.102) to a complete scene in Welsh and Cambridge Latin (4.1.100–33). When Tim guards his sister, Moll, before she is to be married off, he considers borrowing the sword of "Harry the Fifth" (the Welsh Tudor) from "him that keeps the monuments" (4.4.49–50) at Westminster Abbey (himself a Welshman, David Owen). The mere mention of Wales – of course – prompts sheep references from the cockneys. Touchwood Junior thinks Sir Walter has "brought up his ewe-mutton to find / A ram at London" (1.1.144–5), his brother keeps "of purpose two or three gulls in pickle / To eat such mutton with" (2.1.81–2), and Tim consoles himself with the "true saying: 'There's nothing tastes so sweet / As your Welsh mutton'" (4.1.159–60). The inference that the Myddeltons are one subject of *Chaste Maid* is strengthened when the family's puritan allegiances are remembered.

Everyone – not just the women – drinks, seeps, flows, and spurts. The paired fertility symbols, Touchwood Senior and Sir Walter (or "Water," as the name was pronounced in the period), match each other in turning water into gold in equally fertile improvisations. The Country Maid announces Touchwood Senior's talents: "There's a gentleman ... / has got / Nine children by one water that he useth" (2.1.178–80). She reassures Sir Oliver that Touchwood Senior is such a vigorous projector that "he'll undertake / Using that water, within fifteen year / For all your wealth, to make you a poor man, / You shall so swarm with children" (2.1.185–8). Touchwood Senior confides to the audience that the medicine he offers Lady and Sir Oliver Kix is a "little vial of / Almond-milk ... [costing] threepence" (3.3.89–90). Yet, married as he is to a lady who asks indignantly "can any woman have a greater cut?" (2.1.138), Sir Oliver is willing to pay fabulous sums for this most expensive water ever: forty marks a spoonful (2.1.143), or even £500 a pint (2.1.193). He ends with the offer of £1,000 for an effective dose, even though it drains him of civic benevolence ("'Tis but 'bating so many good works / In the erecting of bridewells and spittlehouses," 2.1.145–6) – though this is knocked down to £400 when he finally pays up (3.3.125). Touchwood Senior insists Sir Oliver rides to Ware (the Cut's head spring) to feel the water's benefits. This is a triumphant success, and Sir Oliver rejoices that "as our joy grows, / We must remember still from whence it flows / Or else we prove ungrateful multipliers" (5.3.2–4). Similarly, Sir Walter (whose lodging "o'looks / The waterhouse" [1.2.29–30], and has a view of pageants at the "Pissing-Conduit" [3.2.182]) would swop his Welsh connection for a London goldsmith's position, and is in the market for Moll Yellowhammer (even though she dances like a "plumber's daughter" [1.1.20]). Lady Kix makes Sir Walter himself into a pregnant sponge, when she urges Sir Oliver to pay for Touchwood Senior's waters with a snappish

> 'Tis our dry barrenness puffs up Sir Walter;
> None gets by your not-getting but that knight;
> He's made by th'means, and fats his fortunes shortly
> In a great dowry with a goldsmith's daughter.
>
> (2.1.156–9)

Touchwood Senior, too, takes in as well as letting go, gloomily admitting to "every year a child, and some years two – / Besides drinkings abroad" (2.1.15–6). Such a fluid presentation of masculinity runs counter to much city comedy, in foregrounding productivity over lust, semen over sex. Sir Walter and Touchwood Senior look on with naive, helpless pride at their irrepressible golden showers that can make barrenness itself moist; "shake the golden fruit into her lap; / About it, before she weep herself to a dry ground," as Touchwood Junior instructs his brother (3.3.11–2).

Commentary on the comedy has hitherto tended towards the gloomily improving in tone, castigating it either for supporting a cash nexus based in economic individualism, or for fearing women as sexually, verbally, and physically incontinent (see Chakravorty, *Society*, pp. 96–106; G. Harris, "'This is not a pipe'"; Paster, "Leaky Vessels"). Yet if the play is read with both public entertainments in mind, its interests in money, sex, and water have a more local, literal, and positive value. What with expensive male Welsh water and London goldsmiths, private streams, and children every-where, the play calls out to be looked at in terms of the Myddeltons' activities. Contrary to the standard reduction of city comedy, no one here has to choose between economic activity and sex. *Chaste Maid* rebuts traditional complaints about trade putting ownership above use, and offers instead a vision where abundance comes from harnessing immigrant talents and natural resources on a communal basis.

NOTE

1. Fuller details of the New River project are in C. Sullivan, "Middleton's View of Public Utility."

CHAPTER 10

# Celebrating the city

### Karen Newman

Civic celebration in the Renaissance has a long history that can be traced to the triumphal entries held in honor of Roman military victories. Powerfully depicted in Mantegna's well-known series of paintings, the "Triumphs of Caesar," (now at Hampton Court), and witnessed in the early modern built environment by the survival of Roman triumphal arches in various locations throughout Europe and north Africa, in the later Middle Ages the triumph metamorphosed into the related phenomenon of the royal entry that marked a monarch's or his consort's entrance into a capital or other city, or his or her accession to the throne. Entries consisted of an ordered procession by the lavishly costumed royal household through richly decorated city streets lined with civic dignitaries and the public. Beginning with relatively minor officials and liveried servingmen and ending with the nobility and finally the royal family, such processions mirrored the social hierarchy under royal authority.[1] Particularly important entries came to be accompanied by street pageants that punctuated the processional route and were mounted by the city, its guilds, or other corporate groups. Throughout Europe from at least the thirteenth century, rituals and entertainments of various kinds were mounted by cities to celebrate accession, coronation, dynastic weddings and births, royal visits, and military victories.

In the mercantile cities of the Low Countries, civic pageants and festivities celebrated guilds and their trades as well as religious holidays, and are said to have been the prototypes for London's civic pageantry (Fairholt, *Lord Mayor's Pageants*, part I, p. ix). The most important of such civic celebrations in Thomas Middleton's day were the Lord Mayor's shows, often dubbed "Triumphs," thus trading on the humanist prestige of the Roman triumph. Held annually on October 29 to celebrate the election of the city's Lord Mayor, the shows were commissioned by the city's guilds to honor a duly elected member. In the course of his career Middleton wrote seven Lord Mayor's shows as well as other forms of civic entertainment; apparently following on his petition to the Court of Aldermen and their review of his services to the city, in 1620 he was appointed first City Chronologer, charged with collecting and setting down "all memorable acts of this City and occurrences thereof, and for such other employments as this Court shall have occasion to use him in."[2]

Middleton's life (b.1580, d.1627) spanned a period in which the city of London grew exponentially: scholars calculate that its population may have more than quadrupled between 1550 and 1650, from over 80,000 to some 400,000 or more.[3] Demographic urbanization represents an important material definition of cities, but scholars of urbanization also study what is sometimes called the "urbanization of society."[4] Rapid growth, population concentration, and the development of extensive, coordinated activities, including a centralized state with its attendant bureaucracy and large-scale markets, fostered an unprecedented concentration of both financial and cultural capital and promoted distinctive urban behaviors, social geographies, and new forms of social exchange in early modern London.[5] Though some form of inaugural ceremony had celebrated the installation of London's mayor as early as the twelfth century, the inaugural shows accompanied by pageants with scripts written by leading dramatists date from the 1540s. They marked not only the expansion of civic power that accompanied London's dynamic growth and the decline of religious ceremony following the Reformation, but also what Lawrence Manley has termed the "theatricalization of London's traditional civic ceremonies." Such "theatricalization" developed in tandem with the rise of the public theatre and with the "general inflation of ceremony that was part of the 'imaginative refeudalization' of culture throughout sixteenth-century Europe."[6] As London grew and its merchant elite gained wealth and power, the city companies commissioned new and increasingly elaborate forms of display to celebrate that power.

Middleton's earliest contribution to civic celebration seems to have been a speech for the figure of Zeal in the sixth of the eight pageants along James I's coronation procession route through the city in 1604. The text that survives is an amalgamation of work by Dekker, Jonson, and Stephen Harrison; we know of Middleton's contribution from an acknowledgment by Dekker at the end of the speech: "If there be any glory to be won by writing these lines, I do bestow it (as his due) on Thomas Middleton in whose brain they were begotten" (2182–4). Middleton's Zeal offers hyperbolic praise of the king and his power to unify the kingdom and to ensure peace, justice, and harmony. Whereas Ben Jonson famously disdained the populace and in his welcome for James at the Fenchurch Street arch spurned its "grounded judgements," Middleton concludes Zeal's speech by emphasizing the city's populace and the role of "all estates" in praising and welcoming the new king (see Figure 10.1). Throughout Middleton's

Figure 10.1 Londinium. *The arch's of triumph erected in honor of the high and mighty prince.*
*Iames.* (London, *c.* 1613).

career writing and organizing the mayoral shows, he foregrounds London's citizens and their mercantile interests, not just those of the king and court.

Though we cannot trace with any certainty Middleton's activities in the public theatre between 1610 and 1620, as R. C. Bald pointed out more than a generation ago, we can follow his "civic employments" throughout the decade and well into the 1620s ("Civic Employments," p. 65). One of his earliest projects was an entertainment, now lost, in honor of the marriage of the Earl and Countess of Somerset commissioned by the Lord Mayor and aldermen, and apparently performed at the Merchant Taylors' in January 1613. But Middleton may already have been at work on his first Lord Mayor's show, *The Triumphs of Truth*, commissioned by the Grocers and paid for, as was customary, by a levy on members of the company, to celebrate the election of their compatriot Sir Thomas Myddelton (no relation) as Lord Mayor in 1613. As indicated in the introductory matter to the pageant text, the show was

> Directed, written, and redeemed into form, from
> the ignorance of some former times, and
> their common writer, by Thomas Middleton.
>
> (*Middleton*, p. 968)

As these lines attest, and as evidence from the company's accounts witnesses, Middleton had responsibility for the execution as well as the conception and writing of the show. From this extant text and other contemporary evidence, we can only surmise something of the dramatic event itself.[7] From the Grocers' Court Books we know that the company carried out a review of needed pennants, banners, and other decorations in February 1613. Anthony Munday, Middleton, and others submitted proposals for the pageant, and records indicate that Munday received £149 for his "device," which included provision for apparel, hiring players, and arranging the transportation, while Middleton received £40 "for the ordering overseeing and writing of the whole Device."[8] An "artificer" received another £310 to provide fireworks and to build and paint the pageant sets that included a ship, chariots, several islands, and a "Triumphant Mount" set up near the Little Conduit in Cheapside, where the allegorical figure of London drove away the darkness, caused by Error, shrouding the mount. In one pageant, a King of Moors appeared with his queen to admit that though he once "in days of error did ... run" (431) pursuing false religion, through the power of English merchants "to convert infidels" (442) he has been "brought to the true Christian faith" (440).

Middleton's pageants often witness London's expanding mercantile interests around the world (the Grocers and the East India Company had a
number of overlapping members during the early decades of the seventeenth
century). *Truth* ends with a battle between Truth and Error presented as a
psychomachian struggle for the Lord Mayor's soul. As David Bergeron has
observed, "London exists in at least two ways in the pageant: as present reality
and as representation," as an allegorized "fictionalized, female character," a
"reverend mother" on whose head sit "steeples and turrets," and as the very
space in which the show itself takes place (*Middleton*, p. 966). At the
staggering sum of £1,300, it was apparently the costliest of the Lord
Mayor's shows. As Middleton instructs in the pageant's opening lines:

Search all chronicles, histories, records, in what language or letter soever; let the
inquisitive man waste the dear treasures of his time and eyesight, he shall conclude
his life only in this certainty, that there is no subject upon earth received in the
place of his government with the like state and magnificence as is the Lord Mayor
of the City of London. (*Middleton*, p. 968)

It is hard not to hear in this vaunt not only civic pride, but an assertion of
civic power and competition with monarchical authority and its attendant
ceremonies.

John Stow's 1598 *Survey of London* offers a contemporary account of the
election process and its attendant rituals. Elected on Michaelmas Day
(September 29), the new Lord Mayor took office a month later. On the
morning of October 29, aldermen accompanied the Lord Mayor to the seat
of city government, Guildhall; from there, the entire company boarded
barges that took them up to Westminster where the Lord Mayor took the
oath of office. In *Truth*, Middleton describes the mayor and his entourage
returning downriver to Baynard's Castle, from there on to St. Paul's, then
to Cheapside, back to Guildhall, again to St. Paul's for services before
ending for dinner at the Lord Mayor's home. Along the route, the company
encountered speeches and various tableaux. Whereas the royal entries began
at the Tower and moved west through the City towards Westminster, the
Lord Mayor's procession moved from west to east, from court to city. The
movement to Westminster for the administering of the oath of office, and
then back again, to Guildhall and the City, mirrors the continuing struggle
between monarchical power and city authority throughout the late sixteenth and seventeenth centuries, a struggle in which Middleton played an
ongoing part.

Following *Truth*, Middleton wrote a series of inaugural shows as well as
other entertainments for which he was paid handsomely. In 1616 he oversaw

*Civitatis Amor*, an "entertainment by water" commissioned by the city to celebrate the installation of Charles as Prince of Wales following the death of Prince Henry. Middleton's pageants take up the conventional themes of the inaugural shows: encomiums to London and its worthies, to the incoming Lord Mayor, and to the company from which he comes. Some sort of chariot, a host of allegorical personages, and a "landscape effect" such as "the Five Islands, the continent of India, a Wilderness, a Beautiful Hill, and London's Triumphant Mount" were regularly featured (Bald, "Civic Employments," p. 74). At least one pageant along the route usually made reference to the company financing the show: the Continent of India, for example, celebrated the Grocers' Company's trade with the east; the Golden Fleece and Jason complimented the Drapers; a Wilderness with Orpheus and wild beasts sporting fur honored the Skinners. Middleton worked with a variety of artisans in mounting the shows, most notably Garret Christmas, a "carver," as he is termed in the accounts, with whom he worked on a number of his civic projects and whom he describes as "a man excellent in his art, and faithful in his performances" (Bald, "Civic Employments," p. 73).

A well-known account of Middleton's 1617 pageant, *The Triumphs of Honour and Industry*, again commissioned by the Grocers, provides a rich, if highly biased, picture of the churning urban crowd and the excitement offered by the inaugural shows:

Looking below us onto the street we saw a huge mass of people, surging like the sea, moving here and there in search of places to watch or rest – which proved impossible because of the constant press of newcomers. It was a chaotic mixture: dotards; insolent youths and children, especially of that race of apprentices I mentioned earlier; beribboned serving wenches; lower class women with their children in their arms: all were there to see the beautiful show. We saw few [coaches] about, and fewer horsemen ... because the insolence of the crowd is extreme.[9]

Orazio Busino, chaplain to the Venetian ambassador, here reveals his condescension towards the London crowd with its mix of persons: old and young, women and children, servants and apprentices, and, according to him, its lack of persons of status and wealth as marked by their form of transport – "few coaches" and "fewer horsemen."

In the conclusion to *Postmodernism, or, the Cultural Logic of Late Capitalism*, Fredric Jameson reflects on the materialist dimension of demography and the "radical cultural effects" of what he terms the "enlargement of the peopled universe" associated with urbanization and globalization: "the more other people we recognize, even within the mind, the more peculiarly

precarious becomes the status of our own hitherto unique and 'incompara-
ble' consciousness of 'self'" (pp. 359, 358).[10] In seventeenth-century London,
the city's inhabitants confronted a "horror of multiplicity": as Busino
observes, "Foreigners in London are little liked, not to say hated," and he
describes a brawl along the pageant route in which the London crowd set
upon a gentleman believed to be connected with the Spanish embassy
(*Middleton*, p. 1267).[11] Here both foreignness and status or degree would
seem to have incited the London mob. Scholars of early modern England
have often detailed the fearful responses of monarchy and municipal govern-
ments to the demographic explosion that swept London in this period, the
futile attempts to prevent migration to the capital, the riots against foreign
workers, legislation that sought to govern the theatre, housing, traffic, filth,
and crime. The new space of the metropolis, the relentless saturation of what
had been only recently empty and open spaces, the promiscuous encounters
of the urban pedestrian, and the need to reduce spatial barriers and provide
access to newly developing market spaces breached status boundaries and
generated profound anxiety about order and place.

Yet Middleton's Lord Mayor's shows celebrate the very burgeoning multitude of persons that troubled some of its inhabitants and its city government.
*Industry* ends with a Pageant of Nations representing the "several nations
where commerce abounds." Kate Levin has noted the mix of fear and
admiration towards foreign nations, particularly Spain and France, in the
London of the first decades of the seventeenth century: the English feared
Catholicism and invasion by a second Armada. Middleton, as she observes,
capitalized on such attitudes in his pageant – Busino describes the Spanish
representative of the Pageant of Nations as "kissing his hands right and left,
but especially to the Spanish Ambassador, who was a short distance from us,
in such a wise as to elicit roars of laughter from the multitude" (Levin (trans.
and annotated), "Busino's Eyewitness Account," *Middleton*, p. 1253). Here
Middleton implies that the Lord Mayor and London's merchant elite warrant
diplomatic greetings as surely as the king. Middleton's mayoral shows helped
to produce a distinctive urban discursive space in which persons of different
status and degree mixed, in which foreigners and Londoners mingled, and in
which the commerce of "nations" and the globe would soon make London
the world city they celebrated.

NOTES

1. See Smuts, *Middleton*, pp. 219–23. On royal entries and their impact on popular
   opinion in Tudor and Stuart England, see also Smuts, "Public Ceremony."

2. On Middleton's appointment as City Chronologer and the evidence of subsequent payments made to him, see Bald, "Civic Employments," pp. 66–7, 76–7. Middleton's London records seem to have been extant into the eighteenth century (p. 68). See also Manley, *Middleton*, p. 1399.

3. On the English population explosion in this period, see Wrigley and Schofield, *Population History*, who estimate an increase in population of some 66 percent, from 3 million to just over 5 million between 1550 and 1650; and Finlay, *Population and Metropolis*. More recently, see Harding, "Population of London."

4. See especially Wirth, "Urbanism," and Pahl (ed.), *Urban Sociology*. See also Tilly's longer definition of urbanization in *The Vendée*, pp. 16–20.

5. Though the full effects of the so-called financial revolution in England would not be felt until the late seventeenth and eighteenth centuries, there was already a *concentration* of financial capital in London. See Dickson, *Financial Revolution*, and Neal, *Financial Capitalism*.

6. Manley, *Literature and Culture*, p. 212. On the "refeudalization" of early modern culture and ceremony, see Yates, "Elizabethan Chivalry," pp. 4–25 and Strong, *Art and Power*, p. 19, both cited in Manley. On the link between the medieval midsummer shows and the inaugural shows, see Wickham, *Early English Stages*, vol. III, p. 56.

7. On pageant texts as commemorative books and their relation to the inaugural shows and "textual performance," see Bergeron, "Stuart Civic Pageants."

8. *Middleton*, p. 965. If we bear in mind that in the early seventeenth century, a playwright might get £12 for a play, that Thomkis received £20 for one play in 1615, roughly contemporaneous with Middleton's inaugural shows, and Brome a little less than £20 per play in the 1630s, we get some idea of the importance of the mayoral shows as compared with the public theatre. Thanks to David Kastan for corroborating this point. See McMillin, "Professional Playwriting," pp. 225–38.

9. "Orazio Busino's Eyewitness Account" of *The Triumphs of Honour and Industry*, translated and annotated by Kate D. Levin, *Middleton*, p. 1266. I have amended the anachronism "carriages" to "coaches."

10. On the impact of urbanization on populations, see Davis, "Urbanization."

11. Busino's account reveals in particular a prejudice against the Spanish.

## CHAPTER 11

# *Violence in the city*

## *Jennifer Low*

For some time, critical work on the city comedies of Middleton and Jonson has linked the dramas with the "cony-catching pamphlets" of such writers as Thomas Harman, Thomas Dekker, and Robert Greene. These pamphlets describe a criminal underworld in which cheaters and criminals established a secret society of the underclass, complete with its own tricks and its own vocabulary. These texts – and the dramas that draw upon them – have offered the erroneous impression that thieves and vagrants were responsible for much of the violence in early modern London. In fact, neither vagrants nor petty criminals were responsible for much violent crime in early modern London, if we can believe J. A. Sharpe's examination of court records (*Crime in Early Modern England*). The cony-catching pamphlets of Thomas Harman and Thomas Dekker may provide an index to the fears of the middling sort, but their tales of a criminal underworld were fictions. Evidence suggests instead that the group most inclined to violence was the aristocracy.

The commonest kinds of urban violence in Middleton's time were in fact brawls and duels, and these phenomena – particularly duels – were far more common among the gentle sort (ironically) than among working men or vagrants. Yet urban violence in Middleton's dramas tends to appear in conjunction with canting, the secret language of confidence tricksters. The consistent correlation suggests that the dramatists perceived a link between fighting and canting. The link derived from the elaborate formulas that gentlemen used to initiate their violence – ritualistic language that Middleton and his collaborators seem to mock by emphasizing its similarity to the secret language supposedly developed by criminal elements to conceal their crimes. The verbal codes of the duello are repeatedly characterized in Middleton's dramas as a set of technical terms that merely indicate the speaker's membership in an elite group of people in the know.

During the early modern period, much of the violence in crowded urban areas was still structured by the remnants of the feudal system. The opening scenes of *Romeo and Juliet* and *'Tis Pity She's a Whore* probably give a fairly accurate impression of how family feuds were maintained. Plays such as these transposed English manners to Italian settings, giving later audiences the impression that such brawls were not common in Britain. But the armed servitors of English lords were all too eager to prove their loyalty by insulting the menservants of rival families or responding to insults with "a word and a blow." The relatively new sport of fencing, which rose to prominence in London in the 1580s, changed the equation in a number of ways. A practice initially restricted to members of the aristocracy, fencing and the more lethal duel were imitated by rebellious members of the proto-bourgeoisie. The popularity of fencing was heightened by its portrayal on the public stage, often by actors with skill in mimicry of gesture and body language.

During the fourteenth and fifteenth centuries, the crown had been dependent on the nobility in time of war for supplying an army drawn from their bands of armed servants. These enormous retinues, whose first loyalty was to their lord, were a danger to the authority of the crown during times of peace. In their pursuit of power or preeminence, warlike noblemen had no qualms about lawless behavior. Once a quarrel between families had been initiated, bands of armed men might attack other bands on sight or prepare ambushes for individual noblemen on the opposing side. Noblemen could use their retinue, essentially, as hired bullies. Little could be done to restrain such behavior. Lawrence Stone comments that "the fields about the City [of London] and even the main arterial roads were continual scenes of upper-class violence. Bloody brawls and even pitched battles occurred in Fleet Street and the Strand, and little protection could be offered by the authorities until hours or days after the affair was over" (*Crisis*, p. 231). Such behavior even took place at court occasionally, though the Marshal's Court responded with greater severity to those brawls.

Throughout the sixteenth century, courts of law worked to bring this kind of riot under control. Brawling in London was treated with more severity than in the country, though few noblemen were actually punished for their casual violence. The feuds, after all, indicated the power of the noblemen involved, and the courts stopped short of any discipline that might seriously affront the families involved. Retainers, however, were punished for hotheadedness and the instigation of violence, and noblemen, over the course of the century, were encouraged to take their quarrels to court rather than to the streets.

Tudor policy in the sixteenth century consistently encouraged members of the aristocracy to trim their retinues. Historians aver that the rise of humanism also helped to tame aristocratic lawlessness and lack of discipline. This, combined with long periods of peace during Elizabeth's reign, taught the aristocracy to see their role as counselors on the Ciceronian model, serving in government and at court rather than leading troops to war. These cultural forces reinforced various royal policies that had been created during the first half of the sixteenth century to diminish the latitude of the powers of the aristocracy.

The lifetime of Thomas Middleton saw substantial change in how aristocratic violence was most often manifested. The introduction of the rapier in England prompted a craze for dueling among the aristocracy, and the popularity of the weapon soon rose among those lower on the social scale, as they imitated their social superiors. Paradoxically, the rise of the duel actually aided in limiting aristocratic violence. The early modern duel itself owed its existence to improved techniques in steel-forging, for the duel originated in the creation of the rapier. The rapier, or épée, was developed in Spain or Italy in the second half of the sixteenth century; its blade is much thinner than that of the sword and is designed for thrusting rather than for cutting or slashing. Until its development, sword-fighting was less a matter of technique than of endurance. Even swords designed for use with one hand could not be manipulated with finesse: heavy and cumbersome, they tired the user, who needed great strength to continue a fight to the finish. Shakespeare's description of the fight between Mortimer and Glendower offers a fairly accurate impression of the sheer effort involved in swordfighting: "In single opposition, hand to hand, / He [Mortimer] did confound the best part of an hour / In changing hardiment with great Glendower. / Three times they breathed and three times did they drink / Upon agreement, of swift Severn's flood" (*1 Henry IV*, 1.3.98–102).

The rapier, in contrast, was such a light weapon that it could be worn at one's belt with ordinary clothes and used easily. Footwork and warding rather than a shield or armor enabled the fencer to avoid injury, and consequently the victory in a match was determined by skill rather than strength. Yet the capital boasted only a few fencing schools and the fees were prohibitively high for all but the wealthiest men. Thus, the use of the weapon carried some social cachet – at first, at least.

Middleton himself attacked the basis of the duel when he wrote *The Peacemaker* in 1618. A work whose title page gives the impression that James I was the author, this pamphlet reinforces the rhetorical moves initiated by Tudor policy, commenting that "[w]hen every man will be the master of his own revenge, presuming to give law to themselves, and in rage, to right their own wrongs, at which time the sword is extorted out of the hand of magistracy, contrary to the sacred ordinance of the Almighty" (ll. 377–81). These words uphold the authority of civil law, which the nobility often saw as irrelevant to their own. But Middleton also attempts to redefine the concept of honor, arguing first that men of true fortitude distinguish whether or not the grounds of a quarrel are worthy. He goes on to address the question of posthumous fame: "Perhaps because some have said that fame hath a perpetuity, thou hasten'st to lose thy soul to provide for thy name. How much thou deceivest thyself! Why, it is no more than the echo of a glory, for as an echo no longer resounds than it is fed with a voice, no longer does fame sound forth man's praises than it is supplied and cherished with deservings" (ll. 544–50).

In beautifully structured prose, Middleton develops the most effective arguments he can against this aspect of aristocratic privilege. But neither the best rhetoric nor the most authoritarian peacemaker could defeat "the haughty *challenge*, the curious *duel*, or the blood-thirsty *revenge*" (*Peacemaker*, ll. 675–6). The aristocracy of England were too deeply engaged in maintaining their honor to disregard wanton insults from those challenging their pride of place.

Though dueling was something of a plague in its own right, the custom of the duel was good for the commonweal in comparison to the feuding that preceded it. As an aristocratic custom, it could not be practiced by men of lowly status; as a ritual, it was hedged round with detailed procedures that prevented impetuous action. The duel limited combat to the principals involved and promised quick resolution of the quarrel, thus preventing long, drawn-out feuds among the extended family of great houses.

For the gentry and aristocracy, the duel substituted for military exploits as a performance of honor that enabled them to prove their own worth by public means. The dramatic potential of the duel was enhanced by the ritual formulas required to challenge a man to combat, and these formulas themselves may have provided some outlet for angry feelings. As Stone asseverates, "Violence in word or deed was thus regulated, codified, restricted, sterilized" (*Crisis*, p. 244; see also McCoy, *Rites of Knighthood*, p. 58). These formulas are detailed in *Vincentio Saviolo His Practise*, where the fencing-master-turned-author begins by explaining that injuries to be resolved by the duel may involve either verbal or physical insults ("by wordes or deedes"):

Caius sayth to Seius that hee is a traitour: unto which Seius aunswereth by giving the lie: whereuppon ensueth, that the charge of the Combat falleth on Caius, because hee is to maintaine what hee sayd, and therefore to challenge Seius. Now when an injurie is offered by deede, then do they proceed in this manner. Caius

striketh Seius, giveth him a boxe on the eare ... Wherewith Seius offended, saith
unto Caius, that ... he hath abused him, or some such manner of saying.
Whereunto Caius aunswereth, Thou lyest: whereby Seius is forced to challenge
Caius, and to compell him to fight, to maintaine the injurie which hee had offered
him. (Saviolo, *His Practise*, sig. R4r)

It was inevitable that the duel should have been represented onstage. For the
dramatist, the rules of the dialogue proved an irresistible target to
embroider, satirize, and weave into extravagant plots.

I have argued elsewhere that while the rapier may have been a fashion
accessory desired by both gentlemen and other sorts of men, the codes of
dueling practice were likely to evoke amusement from the middling sort (see
Low, *Manhood and the Duel*, pp. 93–118). Among the playwrights who were
Middleton's contemporaries, only Chapman glorifies dueling, characteriz-
ing a combat in Homeric terms in *Bussy d'Ambois*. Middleton himself made
the duel of honor the center of *A Fair Quarrel* (1616), a drama co-written
with William Rowley that satirized dueling codes. (See Figure 11.1.)

The subject of *Quarrel* is the code of honor and the overly nice ethical
sensibility of Captain Ager, a young military man, who "gives the lie" to
another soldier, thereby challenging him to the duel after being called "son
of a whore." Ager's mother, who fears for her son's safety, tries to prevent
the duel by insisting that she was once false to her husband, "betray'd to a
most sinful hour / By a corrupted soul I put in trust once, / A kinswoman"
(2.1.183–5). On receipt of this piece of misinformation, Ager feels he can
only retract his challenge, since he no longer believes that the insult is a lie.
Ager gives up the fight, though he is stung by the comments of his
incredulous seconds. But when his disgusted combatant walks off the
field commenting that Ager is "a base submissive coward," the frustrated
young captain is overjoyed. Ager calls back his opponent, exclaiming, "Oh,
heaven has pitied my excessive patience, / And sent me a cause. Now I have
a cause! / A coward I was never" (3.1.113–15). Ager wins the duel, naturally,
and becomes reconciled with his opponent after the man experiences death-
bed remorse for the gratuitous insult.

What is interesting about the play is the explicit connection between
ritualized verbal challenges and nonsense words, possibly part of Middleton
and Rowley's attempts to collaborate effectively. In one of the subplots, a
typically bumptious country squire, the Cornish gentleman Chough, joins a
"roaring school" where he smokes a pipe and learns insults appropriate to
provoke a challenge to the duel. "I say thy mother is a callicut, a panagron, a
duplar, and a sindicus," says the Usher (4.1.130). The terms, which sound
like the mangled names of polyhedrons, recall the references to geometry in

Figure 11.1 Title page of *A Faire Quarrell* (London, 1617).

fencing manuals but are clearly intended to evoke laughter. Later, a doctor's obscure diagnosis of Ager's wounded opponent rounds off the play's implication that all specialized vocabularies are nonsense, used simply to exclude the uninitiated. Overall, however, *Quarrel* plays both ends against the middle: the duels enacted onstage are clearly intended to draw fanciers of combat to the play, while the witty dialogue disparaging the codes of honor would have amused both those who aspired to be gentlemen and those who despised such precise and finical codes.

*The Roaring Girl* (1611), another collaborative venture (this one by Middleton and Dekker), includes two duels, both fought by the play's title character, the roaring girl Moll Cutpurse. Given the play's notoriety among readers of early modern drama today, we may not fully recognize how odd the term "roaring girl" would have sounded. A roaring boy, of course, was a prodigal, a young gentleman who spent his time and his substance in fashionable pursuits – including, of course, fencing in the Italian style. Roaring itself, according to Overbury's character "A Roaring Boy," involves the sending of challenges – "by worde of mouth: for he protests (as hee is a Gentleman and a brother of the Sword) hee can neyther write nor reade," but Overbury identifies the roaring boy as well by copious drinking, smoking the newfangled tobacco weed, gambling, and the propensity to cheat men new to town (Overbury, *Overburian Characters*, p. 58). The concept of a roaring *girl* is shocking not only because of Moll's masculine attire but because her behavior itself is loose and unwomanly: her pipe smoking, viol playing, free wandering about the city, and easy acquaintance with men of all ranks indicates to the male characters her extraordinary immodesty: perversity if not actual prostitution.

The reputation of the actual Moll Frith was not as spotless as that of Middleton and Dekker's creation, but the playwrights seem to have created their urban Britomart with an end in mind. The roaring girl fights first with a man who has slandered her, and later with a roaring boy tellingly called Laxton ("Lack-stone") who has tried to buy sexual favors from her. When he objects incredulously to dueling with a woman, she explains that her goal is "To teach thy base thoughts manners! Thou'rt one of those / That thinks each woman thy fond flexible whore: / If she but cast a liberal eye on thee … then she's quite gone" (5.72–6). Certainly, Moll is depicted according to the norms of the time as unnatural, but she descends from the classical tradition of Amazons and androgynes. Moll uses the duel as a didactic tool, attempting both literally and figuratively to teach gossipy gallants a lesson. She rails against the power of slander, specifically that of male slander of virtuous women. Interrogating the woman's position, this play treats the duel of honor as a truth test, harking back to the judicial duel of the medieval period. Combat is a recurrent theme in the play's imagery, used to describe the astute man's rhetorical strategies and verbal manipulation of others.

Moll's duel with Laxton answers with deeds the aspersions he has cast on many women, including Moll herself. She enforces her victory by preparing to kill Laxton once he has yielded; not until he abjects himself, begging for his life as he would from a male duelist, does she agree to spare his life, acting as befits a young gentleman. In treating Laxton so harshly, Moll is trying to teach him respect. Revealing that her masculinity goes beyond her men's clothes, Moll shows him that a woman may manifest as much power to harm men as men themselves have: as he uses traditionally female tools in slandering women's virtue, she turns the tables by using masculine force upon him.

These dramas, though urban in setting, should not be read as realistic representations of urban phenomena. They offer an ironic, sometimes lighthearted, view of urban violence that suggests we should regard dueling as quaint, the codes of honor as irrational. What we see in the plays may be either the conscious decision to conform to the genre's requirements or an indication that Middleton himself could not sympathize with the aristocratic code of honor, a code that disrupted the civil order and that Francis Bacon described as "a kind of wild justice." History, however, takes the long view: though the duel did indeed challenge the primacy of civil law, its popularity was a salutary change from the brawls that had resulted from quarrels among noble families. Despite the documented proliferation of duels, many more fights were certainly avoided because the formulas of the challenge ensured that cooler blood had time to prevail.

## CHAPTER 12

# Middleton and the law

## Subha Mukherji

Unlike many of his contemporaries, Middleton's evident familiarity with the law did not come about through a stint at the Inns of Court. In fact his Oxford education had to be compromised so that he could come to London and help with his family's ongoing legal wrangles, centered mainly on his mother Anne's second husband Thomas Harvey's attempts to take possession of the family property, and her fierce attempt to protect it for the benefit of her daughter Avis and son Thomas. Avis's husband, Allen Waterer, however, turned out to be more of a predator than a protector, and Thomas had "to come from Oxenforde to helpe his mother Anne Harvie when her husbonde was at Sea whereby he thinketh he lost his Fellowshipp at Oxenforde," as a deponent at the Court of Requests states. Another says that "for nowe he remaynethe heare in London daylie accompaninge the players" (PRO, *Requests* 2/224/19, February 8, 1601). A robustly litigious London around 1600 provided his route into the geographically and culturally adjacent theatrical London.

In the early works, law is one of the most visible faces of the viciously predatory city. In the judicially framed prose narrative *The Nightingale and the Ant* (1604), expanded for printing into *Father Hubburd's Tales*, the narrator is the ant, a figure of industry and diligence; his sympathy is with the figure of the ploughman, representing "rural fortunes" (708), whose voice he takes on: "I was sometimes ... a brow-melting husbandman." "Philomel" is the judge who, suspecting the ant to be a spy, catches him in her beak.

> But yet her mercy was above her heat.
> She did not – as a many silken men
> Called by much wealth, small wit, to judgement's seat –
> Condemn at random. But she pitied then
> When she might spoil

(55–9)

This equitable "Justice" is unlike her human counterparts. Both her audition and the ant's presentation offer a gentler version of the snarling satire of law and lawyers, alongside other undoers of the old agrarian order, that abounds in Middleton's early comedies. But the dialogue also touches on Middleton's deeper concerns with natural justice and mercy. And it brings the law and the writer's art into an ambiguous configuration. The ant as ploughman belongs to the older order where emblems and signs were the currency, as opposed to the lawyers, mercers, and scriveners who dealt in the written word. Called upon, with other husbandmen, to witness the mortgage of his lord's estate by his profligate young heir in London, and mocked by lawyers for their illiteracy, he has the last laugh:

I took the pen first of the lawyer, and turning it arsy-versy like no instrument for a ploughman, our youngster and the rest of the faction burst into laughter at the simplicity of my fingering. But I, not so simple as they laughed me for, drew the picture of a knavish emblem, which was *A Plough with the Heels Upward*, signifying thereby that the world was turned upside down since the decease of my old landlord (429–37)

Another ploughman surprises the city slickers with another emblem, "for they little dreamed that we ploughmen could have so much satire in us as to bite our young landlord by the elbow" (450–2). But then the narrator laments the corruption of the young gentleman, "caught . . . in the net of the law" (459–60) – and the ways of the Inns. The delicate satiric description of the crush in the lawyers' chambers, with mercers, merchants, and law books crammed in together, is, however, brutally disrupted as the lawyer's word "'fines' went off with such a powder" that the ploughmen, unable to withstand (or pay) it, are turned into country ants again (701–6). Law thus becomes an upstart economy symbolized by its textuality – still possible to discredit, but increasingly undeniable in its social impact.

The power of the word, here aligned with urban energy and its rapacious agent, the lawyer, is nevertheless what shapes Middleton's tale. This is not radically different from the paradox of his dramatic satires of the law, related in turn to the paradoxical combination of proximity and rivalry between law and rhetoric that goes back to Justinian. The cultural and commercial collusion between the two cultures underpins much of it, the legal world being inseparable from the urban life that Middleton shows up and feeds off, especially in the early plays written for the boys' companies. Quomodo in the satirical city comedy *Michaelmas Term* (1604–6), played by Paul's Children a couple of years before Barry's *Ram Alley*, also turning on legal roguery in London, testily addresses the spectators as "all you students at Inns of

Cozenage" (2.3.486), while relying on the private theatre audience's share of
Innsmen for the detailed legal realism to work. Not that there was a shortage
of law students at the public playhouses on the south bank: already in 1592,
"gentlemen of . . . the Innes of Courte" are listed by Nashe among those who
spent money at these theatres (Gurr, *Shakespearean Stage*, p. 200). The diary
of Edward Heath, a young student at the Inner Temple between 1626 and
1631, shows that he spent more money on playgoing than on lawbooks, and
more time at the theatre than at Westminster (BL MS Egerton 2983). But the
so-called private theatres were specially known for their repertory of satirical
comedies about law and lawyers, and their legal audience. One of the earliest
records of a Blackfriars audience comes from an Inn-of-Court student: Henry
Fitzgeoffrey in *Satyres and Satirical Epigrams* (1617).

Law, then, was not simply like the "villainous law-worm" Tangle
"[diving] into countrymen's causes" (*The Phoenix*, 4.44–5, 171–2); it was
also the business that brought increasing numbers of the nobility as well as
the landed gentry into London, generating the productive interface on
which city comedy thrived – "manna" and "marrow" not only to Tangle
(4.116) but to Middleton himself; part of the buzz and addiction of comic
London. Besides, the country occasionally has its answer to the city, as in
the figure of the country justice Falso who tricks Phoenix. Middleton's
"law" straddles country and city, extending to constables and churchwar-
dens, and spreading across ecclesiastical, criminal, civil, and equity juris-
dictions. Not unsurprisingly, given his own involvement in debt litigation
with John Knapp in 1600, and with Robert Keysar (Manager of the
Children of the Revels) in 1609, actions for debt feature prominently
(Phialas, "Early Contact," p. 190; Hillebrand, "*Viper's Brood*"). The ubiquitous presence of the rich widow theme in his plays – *Phoenix*, *A Mad
World, My Masters*, *A Trick to Catch the Old One*, *A Chaste Maid in
Cheapside*, to name but a few – had grounding in personal experience too.
Anne Middleton's preemptive legal conveyance during her brief widowhood, and before marrying Harvey, sought to ensure that the property was
in trust with three Inner Temple members until it could revert to her
children. Precisely this practice is at play in *The Widow* (1616), where
Valeria conveys her riches to Justice Martino to thwart hungry suitors,
while in *The Lady's Tragedy* (1611) it structures feelings, as the Tyrant likens
the life of the defiantly chaste Lady who has escaped his lust through suicide
to "a widow's state made o'er in policy / To defeat [him]" (4.2.48–9). In the
comedies, courtesans looking for a good catch pretend to be rich widows.
Middleton is also aware of the legal and financial power widowhood gives
women – no longer *femmes covert* but able to own property and litigate

in their own right, especially in canon law and equity courts. Like many real-life female litigants adopting a strategically helpless rhetoric to preempt anxieties about litigating women, Valeria protests, "I'm but a woman, / And, alas, ignorant in law businesses," but she is in fact as experienced and canny legally as she is sexually (*Widow*, 2.1.52–3). At the same time, widows are shown to be easy targets for gallants, gentlemen, and knights; some of Middleton's peers and collaborators were brought to Star Chamber for making a play – the now lost "Keep the Widow Waking" – out of a salacious court case around the entrapment of a rich widow into marriage, with the help of law tricks (Mukherji, *Law*, pp. 186–92). The ambiguities of marriage law underpin several Middleton plays: when the Niece in *Phoenix* calls Fidelio her "vowed husband" (9.65), but her lecherous uncle Falso enlists Tangle's help to prevent their marriage (her father's will makes her dowry conditional upon Falso's consent), what is at issue is the duality in early modern law whereby a private de praesenti contract was canonically valid but not fully licit and ineligible for property rights at common law – the root of Claudio and Juliet's predicament in *Measure for Measure*, which Middleton adapted in 1621.

*Phoenix* may seem an extreme example of Middleton's legal satire, with the term-trotting pettifogger Tangle's law-Latin and lists of writs and "*sursurraras*" (4.123) driving him insane. It is not until the law in his veins is purged by bloodletting that his madness is cured, and he regains conscience, truth, and compassion: "Now I've least law, I hope I have most grace" (15.347). The evil of law is connected here, almost theologically, with its written words – "no more shall thou in paper quarrel" (15.327) – a mordant sequel to the ant-ploughman's alternative script trumping the lawyer's pen. The sixteenth century saw a significant shift from manuscript and oral assimilation to print, with the proliferation of legal commentaries, yearbooks, and handbooks, to make the memorially accretive common law easier to learn. But ironically, the sheer unwieldy bulk of the printed material, combined with its hermetic discourse, could be potentially counterproductive and liable to a travesty of the "common erudition" that defined common law, owing to piecemeal use by legal middlemen – the law being unavailable to all in a single authoritative book (Ives, "Later Year Books," pp. 67–9; Baker (ed.), *Reports*, vol. 11, pp. 160–3). Let a Tangle loose on Coke's *Commentaries on Littleton*, and you might get what we have here – focusing the potential for absurdity within the written culture of law, burgeoning but unmonitored in its translation into wider application from the "collective mind of the profession" (Baker, *Introduction*, 172). But this is also the play with Phoenix's earnest paean to "thou angel . . . sober Law"

(4.200–30), and a display, in the final trial, of the saving justice of benev-
olent absolutism, as the disguised Phoenix reveals his identity after watching
over his father's kingdom, to save both it and him from treason. The point
of Phoenix's encomium, as well as of the play, is the vast difference between
"true justice" (4.220) and its corruption in practice: "abuse" has "deformed"
law (4.205). Tangle, after all, is one of those hangers-on of the law who
populated the fringes of legal London – like *Ram Alley*'s Throat, or Lurdo in
John Day's *Law Tricks* (1604). Like the unassimilable Dampit in *Trick*,
he is a barretor – "a common wrangler, that setteth men at ods, and is
himselfe . . . at brawle with one or other" (Cowell, *Interpreter*, sig. I3v). But
Tangle's rapture on law as he knows it (4.115–24) is as resonant as Phoenix's
praise of its abstract principles.

A more troubling, conceptually engaged yet hyper-resolved treatment
of law occurs in *An/The Old Law, Or a New Way to Please You*, a play
Middleton wrote with Rowley and possibly Heywood (*c.* 1618). The ostensible referent is the chilling new law of Epire, propounded by its Duke, by
which all old men and women are to be put to death after they cease to be
useful to state and family:

> Our law is fourscore years, because we judge
> Dotage complete then, as unfruitfulness
> In women at threescore.
>
> (2.1.14–16)

But this "old law" negatively evokes *the* old law – the Old Testament with
its commandments, the fifth of which was to "honor thy father and thy
mother." Epire's "old law" turns out to "please" those who violate that
commandment: young courtiers like Simonides who cannot wait to see
their parents dead so that they can inherit and take over, and young wives
like Eugenia who plan their second marriage in impatient anticipation of
their husbands' termination. The noble Cleanthes and his wife Hippolita,
by contrast, try to save Cleanthes's father Leonides by disobeying the edict,
giving Leonides out to be dead and hiding him away – until he is found and
taken. The "law" then, to start with, seems aligned with tyranny and
tragedy, while its disobedience, which would politically and legally count
as treason, is what we are drawn to sympathize with. Antigona, the doomed
Creon's wife, pleads on the ground that

> His very household laws prescribed at home by him
> Are able to conform seven Christian kingdoms
> They are so wise and virtuous.
>
> (2.1.101–3)

Simonides dismissively comments that the poor man "bought a table indeed, / Only to learn to die by't" (2.1.119–20), evoking not only the written word of law on a tablet but more specifically "the first and second Table" – the ten commandments of Exodus (20:12) – which James I so vociferously declared it a sin to disobey (*His Maiesties Speach*). The ideological problem signaled by the axis of audience sympathies is the analogy between filial and political allegiance that James explicitly set up in talking about the true law of monarchies, an analogy present throughout the play: "The King towards his people is rightly compared to a father of children" ("Trew Law," p. 272). To "rise up against" a lawful monarch is as "monstrous and unnaturall" as for children to "put hand into" their father, and no wickedness by the king could justify such rebellion. By this logic, Cleanthes's defiance of monarchical law is culpable. Yet, the Duke, in ordering his subjects to sacrifice their natural parents, is going against the patriarchal function James advocated in *Basilikon Doron*, whereby the king should be "as their naturall father and kindly Master" (p. 218). As the parricidal Simonides reminds Cleanthes, "none can be / A good son and a bad subject; for, if princes / Be called the peoples' fathers, then the subjects / Are all his sons, and he that flouts the prince / Doth disobey his father" (5.1.197–201). The logic by which he accuses Cleanthes of "treason in the height of degree" (5.1.208) would be entirely recognizable to the play's Jacobean audiences. James drew on the Scriptures, "the fundamental Lawes of our owne Kingdome" and "the law of Nature" to assert the absolute and divine prerogative of kings ("Trew Law," p. 261). This triangulation further problematizes the apparent polarities of *Old Law*. The assumed coincidence of the law of God, the law of nature and the law of man ("Trew Law," p. 72) is shown to be liable to fracture in an absolutist monarchy, when human law, supposedly mimetic of divine law, commands unnatural actions. The closeness of monarchically imposed statutes to "tyranny" is meanwhile addressed by the condemned Creon (1.1.235–51). The non-congruence between natural law and positive law is clear in the First Lawyer's impatient response to Cleanthes: "You understand a conscience, but not law" (1.1.101).

What cuts through the knot and saves the day within the dramatic fiction is the law of genre. The "Old Law" turns out to have been a ruse, to be replaced by a new law (New Testament?) – also "inscribed" on a "table" (5.1.288) – which reverses the judicial hierarchy. The Duke reveals, in a lastminute tragicomic twist, that the "Old Law" was a trial of virtue, and produces, to amazing music, all the old men taken away to be killed and given out to be dead. The case is altered as these men and Cleanthes are now made judges of "disobedience and unnatural blood" (291). Yet this resolution, including forgiveness, does not just provide a new law to "please"; it is also a comment on tragicomedy being a fantasy of reconciliation – not only among characters but between contradictory components of legal ideology in an absolutist monarchy, which can only be harmonized through a slippage from the law of the State to the law of a genre which Guarini, the Renaissance theorist of tragicomedy, defined as being premised on "the danger, not the death." But the danger – of death and of anarchy and tyranny – communicates itself too vividly in the action for the containing structure to seem inartificial. "Nature," meanwhile, asserts its dark possibilities: perhaps, unlike Hooker's natural law which was meant to be both self-evident and rational (*Works*, vol. 1, pp. 233–4, 228–9), the instinct displayed by the majority of Epireans, including the entertaining Clown, are expressive of a "nature" that the Duke had some inkling of and has unleashed, like Shakespeare's Vincentio, into an interregnum of radically alternative law. The definition of "common law" itself, which the play might seem to be upholding, gets irredeemably complicated. We notice, too, that among the wives who, for entertaining suitors in their husbands' lifetime, are now righteously proscribed from "[marrying] within ten years after" (5.1.325–6) is Eugenia, a 19-year-old married to the 79-year-old Lisander.

Issues of gender are intimated most intriguingly, though, in the First Lawyer's metaphor where the anatomizing agency normally ascribed to law is displaced on to lawyers – the law itself becomes the object of dissection, a female body thrown about and eviscerated by male professionals:

> Sir, we have canvassed it from top to toe,
> Turned it upside down, threw her on the side,
> Nay, opened and dissected all her entrails,
> Yet can find none
>
> (1.1.297–300)

This gendered dig into law's entrails, however, is also a comment on the violence inherent in the abuse of law, seen here in the lawyers' (faked) attempt to devise "wrested sense" (1.1.293) to preserve Creon.

The overarching frame of a false trial conducted by the Duke is intrinsic to the tragicomic plot, though less articulately about the ethics of emotion than such a device is in, say, Shakespeare's *Cymbeline* or Massinger's *The Picture*, or, later, Ford's *The Lady's Trial*. But shades of a critique of the fictive use of law are here, too: witness Antigona's protest, "Can you play and sport with sorrow, sir?" when Creon jokes about the "Old Law" – with implications for the larger sporting with anguish that the Duke's edict entails. This impulse, rarely associated with Middleton or indeed Rowley,[1] but evidently part of a generic tendency that is increasingly self-conscious after Shakespeare, finds an uncommonly psychological treatment in the subplot of *The Lady's Tragedy*, where Anselmus's wife is put to "trial," at his insistence, by his reluctant friend Votarius, since Anslemus insists on having her virtue proved through the test of temptation. His only ground for doubt is the "wild seed / Suspicion sows" (1.2.153–4). Both Votarius and the wife succumb and are eventually betrayed. It is normally tragicomedy that isolates the epistemic impulse behind needless "trying," thereby questioning the rationality of suspicion. Suspicion, as Barbara Shapiro has shown ("Rhetoric," pp. 59–62), had become a "legal category" by the mid seventeenth century, a sufficient basis for pre-trial arrest and examination, and had, ironically, been established by the mid sixteenth century as a rational ground to replace the irrational proofs (such as ordeal) that were officially abolished by canon lawyers in the thirteenth century. Based on the notion of *felix culpa*, tragicomedy licenses torment and provides an ideal form for such trials in a political-legal context. Here, though, it is adopted by tragedy, with the result that make-belief becomes real and the tragic potential of the plot erupts into destruction.

Middleton's engagement with the law, then, is not only informed with the nitty-gritty of jurisdictional procedure and extra-jurisdictional practice, but alive to its productivity at the facetious, philosophical, and affective levels at once. Further, he deploys its resources with a sharp sense of both public interest and the affinities between aspects of law and specific genres: witness his translation of the sensational 1605 case around Walter Calverley's murder of his children and attempted murder of his wife, closely following the pamphlet account, *Two Most Unnatural and Bloody Murders* (1605), into the hard-hitting *A Yorkshire Tragedy* (1605–6[?]). This domestic tragedy is a world apart in tone from his city comedies, as well as from the serious questioning of justice in the tragedies and tragicomedies. Alertness to literary and commercial contexts is united also in the central scenes (5–10) of *Timon of Athens* (1605) with Timon's creditors, interwoven with the trial where Alcibiades pleads for his guilty friend. Among Middleton's contributions to this collaboration, they show that "debt" for Middleton was not just a repository for satire, but connected legal maneuvers with deeper concerns of ethics, usury, and justice that were being hotly debated from the 1570s to the 1630s, in the context of Puritan praise of thrift. But through it all, one hears the "the dizzy murmur of the law" (*Phoenix*, 12.39), even when it is faint.

NOTE

1. But Heywood's *A Fair Maid of the West* plays with this theme.

# PART II

# The national and international context

## CHAPTER 13

# The court

## Alastair Bellany

> Say to the court it glowes
> And shines like rotten woode
> Say to the church it showes
> whats good, yet doth no good
> If Courte or Church replye
> Give Courte & Church the lye.
>
> Sir Walter Ralegh, 'The Lie', *c.* 1595
> (Bellany and McRae [eds.], "Early Stuart Libels," A3)

> But, great man,
> Every sin thou commit'st shows like a flame
> Upon a mountain: 'tis seen far about.
> And with a big wind made of popular breath
> The sparkles fly through cities; here one takes,
> Another catches there, and in short time
> Waste all to cinders.
>
> (*Women Beware Women*, 4.1.208–14)

Languishing in personal disgrace, chilled by Elizabeth I's seemingly unrelenting disapproval, Walter Ralegh had every reason to be bitter. But his pithy, disillusioned dismissal of the royal court – as a place that shines and glows, not like gold, not like the sun, but like the sickly sheen of decaying wood – perfectly captures the two faces of the court in the later Elizabethan and early Stuart imagination.

In theory contemporaries had every reason to think the royal court might shine like the sun, for it was the spectacular center of much of the kingdom's political life. It occupied multiple physical sites – several royal palaces near London, an administrative complex in Westminster, and the mansions of the great nobility both nearby and in the countryside. And it played multiple interlocking roles. At its core, the court comprised the monarch and the royal household (and, under James I, the households of his queen and eldest son). But it was also the center of national political, financial, and legal administration and their accompanying bureaucracies. It was a vital point of contact between the monarchy and its more powerful subjects, a gathering place for the noble, the ambitious, and the powerful. It was a center of conspicuous consumption and display, and of artistic production and performance, much of which expressed and legitimated the authority of the monarch and the nobility. The court was also the fount of patronage, dispensing the reward and office that sustained the nation's political elite and formed the sinews that connected and moved an often unwieldy body politic (see, for example, Peck, *Court Patronage*; Peck (ed.), *Mental World*).

In principle, the court was also supposed to be a center of conspicuous morality. When James VI of Scotland became king of England in 1603, his arrival was marked by the publication of *Basilikon Doron*, his meditations on the duties of kingship written a few years earlier for his eldest son, Henry. The treatise was a statement of intent, offering his new subjects an authoritative vision of moral kingship. Kings, James wrote, should provide an image of virtue for their subjects to emulate, serving as "bright lampes of godlinesse and vertue ... going in and out before their people" to light their way. But not only the monarch had to set an example of a "vertuous life"; his "Court and companie," too, had to project an exemplary "love of vertue, and hatred of vice." Awestruck subjects would be only too quick to emulate a wicked courtier's ill example; and so, James urged, "make your Court and companie to bee a patterne of godlinesse and all honest vertues, to all the rest of the people" (*Basilikon Doron*, 148–9, 166–70; Bellany, *Politics*, pp. 1–24).

James's vision of the court as an exemplar of virtue was matched by a much darker set of inherited expectations about court life's inherent immorality. At court, corruption ruled, as the ceaseless competition for access, favor, reward, and power spawned deceit, dissimulation, and crime. At court, ruthless and ambitious men pursued private gain, not the common weal. At court, virtuous counsel was disrupted by faction, poisoned by envy, and drowned out by flattery. At court, the spectacular culture of display bred only luxury, effeminacy, and lust. By the time of James's accession, these venerable stereotypes of courtly degeneracy seemed especially pertinent to a host of disillusioned observers. Catholic polemicists had long lamented the court's corruption, attacking both the overweening murderous ambition of the queen's favorite Leicester and the far more effective power grab of William and Robert Cecil. Other Elizabethans turned to Tacitus, whose depictions of courtly decadence under Roman imperial tyranny seemed eerily contemporary. On the stage, elements of this late Elizabethan discontent found voice in Shakespeare's stunning portrait of Denmark's "rotten" court and in Jonson's fusion of Catholic and Tacitean disaffection in *Sejanus*, his portrayal of a Tiberian Rome where courtly lust and murder, dissimulation and surveillance were all symptoms of a political culture poisoned by tyranny (Bellany, *Politics*, pp. 1–24; Smuts, "Court-Centred Politics"; Worden, "Ben Jonson"; P. Lake, "Ben Jonson").

For all James's protestations about virtue, his own court became indelibly associated with scandalous immorality. The sheer volume of political news increased rapidly in the early seventeenth century, with a variety of media forms circulating in a virtually unpoliced literary underground, spreading effectively uncensored and highly damaging images of the court to a geographically broad and socially variegated public. Among these media, one genre in particular was associated with the proliferation of scandalous images of the early Stuart court: the verse libel. These libels, virtually all of them anonymous, circulated beneath and beyond the range of the censor, primarily in manuscript copies that might be posted in public spaces, passed around dinner tables, sung aloud or recited in the streets, sold by scriveners, or, most often, passed among and between networks of friends or kin. Verse libels were transcribed into newsletters, collected into poetical miscellanies, or copied into commonplace books of political news. These libels – over 300 of which survive for the early Stuart era – reflected and projected an image of the court as an exemplar of transgressive morality, corrupt religion, and poisoned politics. Libels mocked and attacked the courtly elite, tarnishing their reputations and connecting them to an array of sexual, fiscal, moral, and political corruptions (Bellany and McRae (eds.), "Early Stuart Libels"; Cust, "News and Politics"; Bellany, "Railing Rhymes Revisited"; McRae, *Literature*). Major clusters of these poems appeared in the wake of great courtiers' deaths: the first significant Jacobean outpouring, for instance, followed the 1612 death of James's chief minister, Robert Cecil, Earl of Salisbury, and depicted him as a fiscally corrupt, low-born, syphilitic crookback, an agent of tyrannical misgovernment whose animal cunning had destroyed better-born, more virtuous men (Croft, "Reputation"; Bellany and McRae (eds.), "Early Stuart Libels," D).

Libels also targeted royal favorites – the young men whom James controversially raised to positions of great rank and power. From the beginning of the reign, James showered favored courtiers like Philip Herbert or James Hay with rewards, and allowed them much-coveted privileged access to the royal person. But the exercise of royal favoritism soon acquired a more significant political dimension. The young Scot Robert Carr had first caught James's eye in 1607, and for a while was content to translate royal favor into much the same kind of rewards and access others had enjoyed. By late 1610, however, Carr's political ambitions had broadened. Created Viscount Rochester in 1611 and Earl of Somerset two years later, Carr transformed the role of Jacobean favorite from boon companion to central participant in the political, factional, ceremonial, and administrative life of the court. As Carr's power and perceived influence increased, rival factions of courtiers maneuvered either to woo him to their cause or to displace him in the king's affections. Late in 1614, thanks to the efforts of powerful courtiers discontented with Carr, a rival favorite emerged. Unlike Carr, George Villiers was English, the handsome younger son of a decayed gentry family, who had acquired an eye-catching courtly veneer in France. Although James may have briefly contemplated a system of dual favorites, balancing rival factions and nationalities, the heated competition between Carr and Villiers triggered a sequence of events that led to Carr's ruin, and to the establishment of Villiers – later Earl, Marquis, and, finally, Duke of Buckingham – as supreme royal favorite who would wield political power far greater than Carr's had ever been (Bellany, *Politics*, Chapter 1; Lockyer, *Buckingham*).

Favoritism raised uncomfortable questions about the king's government (see especially Perry, *Literature and Favoritism*). On what grounds did the favorite hold authority? What social or moral qualities did he possess, and did they fit him to wield power? Did the favorite's failings, perceived or real, imply something troubling about the king? Did favoritism produce a dangerous monopoly of access that could isolate the monarch from an appropriately broad range of counsel? Would the concentration of power, reward, and office in one individual inevitably create dangerous currents of ambition, pride, and envy that could destabilize the court? Would the king rule his favorite, or might the favorite rule the king? The problem of the favorite, and all these troubling questions, loomed over the Jacobean court, and over early Stuart politics and political culture more generally, for two decades.

Torrents of libelous verse attacked both great favorites, and the careers of Carr and Villiers played central roles in the evolution of images of court scandal and corruption. Indeed it was a court scandal of unprecedented scale and publicity that destroyed Carr. Carr's political ascent had been stage-managed by his friend Sir Thomas Overbury, who acted as adviser, intelligencer, and agent, brokering alliances between Carr and several powerful and ambitious English courtiers. In 1613, however, Overbury and Carr had quarreled after the favorite began an illicit relationship with Frances Howard, the unhappy wife of the 3rd Earl of Essex. The liaison with Frances Howard drew Carr into the orbit of the Howard court faction, and away from men and policies that Overbury had cultivated. When Overbury attempted to thwart the relationship, Carr and the Howards engineered his imprisonment in the Tower. As Overbury lingered in prison, Frances Howard sued in ecclesiastical court to nullify her marriage to Essex on the grounds of non-consummation. If successful, the suit would allow her to marry Carr, cementing an alliance that would give a perhaps unstoppable momentum to the controversial pro-Spanish, anti-parliamentary policies favored by the great Howard nobles, the Earls of Northampton and Suffolk. The imprisoned Overbury was powerless to intervene, and, by the end of the summer of 1613, he was apparently willing to bow to the new political realities in order to secure his release. After several delays, Frances Howard was finally granted her nullity suit in late September 1613. Numerous libels attacked the nullity as a sham that gave official license to a wicked woman's whorish lusts, but Frances Howard was finally free to marry Carr (Bellany, *Politics*, Chapter 1; Lindley, *Trials*; Bellany and McRae (eds.), "Early Stuart Libels," F).

Overbury, however, did not live to see the nullity granted: he died in the Tower about ten days before the final decision. At the time, his death was attributed to natural causes, but, in the autumn of 1615, in the midst of the bitter court struggle between Carr and Villiers, a plausible allegation surfaced that Overbury had been poisoned. His keeper in the Tower, Richard Weston, was arrested, and Weston's confessions led to a number of alleged co-conspirators on the fringes of the court and then, quickly and inexorably, to the plot's alleged ringleaders: Frances Howard and Robert Carr. Although the evidence against Carr was much weaker than that against his wife, the Overbury murder scandal of 1615–16 ruined him. In May 1616, Carr and his wife stood trial for murder; both were convicted, and although their lives (unlike the lives of their humbler accomplices) were spared, they spent several years in prison.

The Overbury scandal crystallized a horrifying image of court corruption. The crowds who packed the murder trials and gathered to witness the executions of the condemned heard fantastic stories of lust, betrayal, and murder; of ambitious men and ungoverned women; of witchcraft and poison; of pride and dissimulation; of popery, treason, and political assassination. These stories reached yet larger audiences in manuscript trial reports, in newsletters, in fevered talk and rumor, in printed broadsides and pamphlets, and in the bitter verse libels that scourged the favorite and his countess while implicating the king in their sins (Bellany, *Politics*, Chapters 3–5; Bellany and McRae (eds.), "Early Stuart Libels," H). "Ah! The court, the court," lamented Frances Howard's confidante Anne

Turner, who paid for her part in Overbury's death with her neck. "God bless the King and send him better servants about him, for there is no religion in the most of them, but malice, pride, whoredom, swearing, and rejoicing in the fall of others. It is so wicked a place as I wonder the earth did not open and swallow it up" (National Archives, London, State Papers Domestic, James I, s p 14/83/21).

His lawyers portrayed James as an agent of moral reformation whose prosecution of Overbury's murderers made him the living embodiment of divine justice. Tendentious as this claim might have seemed in 1615–16, it was further undermined by a succession of widely publicized new scandals. Lord Treasurer Suffolk, Frances Howard's father, who had narrowly survived the Overbury affair, was brought down in 1618 on charges of grotesque fiscal corruption. The king's secretary, Sir Thomas Lake, was ruined in a tawdry scandal involving his wife, his daughter, a disputed inheritance, and allegations of sexual transgression and attempted poisoning (Bellany, *Politics*, pp. 252–4). And scandalous allegations and libelous assaults continued to dog the new favorite, George Villiers. Throughout the 1620s, libelers depicted him in a variety of transgressive guises: a dangerously ambitious "upstart" stealing office and reward from the true nobility; a Hispanophile crypto-papist and a debauched Ganymede; a patron of witches and whores; a heartless poisoner and effeminate traitor (Bellany and McRae (eds.), "Early Stuart Libels," L, N–P). His relationship with James stirred anxiety and suspicion. Some libelers suggested the king was literally bewitched, while others fretted the enchantment was sexual, that the handsome Villiers had seduced James and persuaded him to surrender government of the realm to a base, inexperienced, and morally corrupt youth (Bellany and McRae (eds.), "Early Stuart Libels," L; Young, *James VI and I*).

Thus libels and scandals figured the Jacobean court as a sink of corruption, a place where monarch and courtier alike were ruled by passion; where lust, greed, and ambition triumphed; where base men and unruly women slipped the bonds of patriarchal authority; where favorites dabbled in magic and demonic witchcraft, and succumbed to the lures of Antichristian Rome; where the culture of display manifested only a deadly pride; and where poison – the most frightening, the most foreign, and the most courtly of murderous techniques – was king.

These scandalous images of the early Stuart court surely worked upon the imaginations of dramatists, playgoers, and readers. Fictional dramas of court scandal, set on foreign shores, did not have to mimic English events precisely, and we do not have to read them as coded accounts of contemporary events with a direct correspondence between real and fictional characters and action. But the stage did provide yet another public space in which to wrestle with the implications of court corruption, and playwrights could generate dramatic and political energy from public knowledge of contemporary scandal and from the libelous discourse that fueled that knowledge. The destructive power of princely lust in Middleton's *Women Beware* surely resonated with theatregoers who had witnessed the Overbury affair, or who worried that a king enamored of a favorite had allowed his physical desires to rule his political reason. The murderous Beatrice-Joanna in *The Changeling,* who uses an assassin to prevent one marriage in order to make another, cannot be reduced to a thinly disguised Frances Howard, but her dramatic power is built on Frances Howard's scandalous reputation, just as *The Witch* undoubtedly draws energy from the peculiar histories of courtly witchcraft and impotence revealed during the Essex nullity and the Overbury affair (Malcolmson, "As Tame"; Lancashire, "*The Witch*").

The libelous discourse of court scandal and corrupt favoritism also helps us to appreciate some of the complex political work performed by Middleton's greatest commercial success, 1624's *A Game at Chess* (see, especially, Cogswell, "Thomas Middleton"). In Middleton's play, the Machiavellian Black Knight, a thinly disguised version of the Spanish ambassador Gondomar, dreams of penetrating the English court, of sexual, political, and religious seduction. From at least the time of the Overbury scandal, verse libels had registered real anxiety that this kind of popish and foreign seduction of the court had already occurred. By the early 1620s, the perceived presence of popery at court seemed to some observers to explain why the crown pursued a Spanish alliance and failed to defend James's daughter and the beleaguered Protestants of Bohemia and the Palatinate. For the libelers, the most dangerous member of the Spanish faction – the falsehearted, "Jesuited" courtiers – was the favorite Villiers. A notorious 1623 libel, "The King's Five Senses," conjured an especially potent image of a popishly corrupted court, with Villiers at its immoral center. Like Middleton's play, the libel suggestively yoked Hispaniolized popery to sexual corruption. The king, the libeler feared, was surrounded by seductive temptations: by "Spanish treaties" undermining the gospel; by the "Cand[i]ed poyson'd baites / Of Jesuites and their deceipts"; by the "damned perfumes" of "Mirrhe and frankinsense" burning on "altars built to Gods unknowne"; and by the "beardlesse Chinn" and "moyst palme" of "a Ganimede" – the favorite – "Whose whoreish breath hath power to lead" the king "which way it list" (Bellany and McRae (eds.), "Early Stuart Libels," L8).

But by 1624, in the libels as well as in Middleton's play, these fears had been reworked and revised. The yoked popish and sexual threat remained, but now it was cornered and contained by virtuous English courtiers. In Middleton's play, the "Jesuited" English are expelled, and the White Duke, Villiers, devises the cunning stratagem that unmasks Spanish machinations. Villiers and Prince Charles face the sensual lures, religious and sexual, of the Black House (Catholic Spain), but they do not succumb; they only feign moral corruption to fool their enemies. The play thus finesses the sexual allegations that had dogged Villiers: when the White Duke confesses to lust, he does so to deceive the Spanish, and it is Olivares, the Spanish favorite, who is labeled Ganymede.

Villiers' transformation from popish Ganymede to patriot hero represented a remarkable shift, present not only in Middleton's play and the anti-Spanish pamphlets usually cited as its sources, but also in verse libels penned during 1624. When Spanish ambassadors trying to halt the march to war brought James serious allegations against his newly bellicose favorite, the libelers rushed to defend their erstwhile victim: Villiers was now figured as Spain's "terror and dread" (Bellany and McRae (eds.), "Early Stuart Libels," O11), and compared to the martyred Ralegh. "Let not that head," one libeler beseeched James,

> satisfy the thirst
> Of Morish pride? Which was the very first
> of all thy favourites? Er'e undertooke
> His Countryes Cause and thus did overlooke
> Spanish Deceiveings. For he hath done more
> Then twenty of thy favourites before.

Villiers was no longer among the "Jesuited Englishe drunke with Popery / What veiw your Country with a Spanish eye." If James would let him, he would be another "brave Scipio" to "sacke proud Spayne" (Bellany and McRae (eds.), "Early Stuart Libels," O12).

Much to his own consternation, Villiers's stint as patriot hero, in the libels and on stage, was short-lived. By 1625 libelers had resumed their attacks; by 1626 those attacks were beginning to acquire an unprecedented new intensity. The disturbing specter of the corrupt royal favorite, wielding power over the weak new king, Charles I, and the decadent court with apparent impunity, was inextricably intertwined with the political crisis of the later 1620s – mounting friction between king and Parliament; anger, confusion, and social dislocation in the wake of embarrassing military defeats; and heightened religious and constitutional anxieties. The virtually demonic favorite who haunted contemporary imaginations was a fantasy figure. But fantasy fed fear, fear fed hatred, and hatred fed violence (Bellany, "Murder"). In August 1628 an assassin's knife cut George Villiers down. His death ended the era of the great royal favorite at the English court and, after a last astonishing outburst of verse celebrating the murder, also ended the first great age of libelous politics (Bellany and McRae (eds.), "Early Stuart Libels," P). Charles I worked hard to fashion his court as a model of order and virtue, and to a significant extent he succeeded (see, for example, K. Sharpe, *Personal Rule*). But although the court's reputation recovered, a great deal of damage had already been done: a decade and a half of scandal and libelous allegation had revealed and deepened political fault lines that reopened to calamitous effect in the later 1630s. In the civil war and revolution that followed, the memory of court scandals and court favorites would play new, and even more damaging, political roles.

## CHAPTER 14

# States and their pawns: English political tensions from the Armada to the Thirty Years War

## Thomas Cogswell

Extraordinary circumstances in 1624 allowed Thomas Middleton to abandon a playwright's customary caution about even mentioning contemporary politics and to explain that, for once, his audience

> shall see the men in order set,
> States and their pawns, when both the sides are met;
> The houses well distinguished
>
> (*A Game at Chess: A Later Form*, Prologue, 3–5)

He was as good as his word; *Game* knowingly alluded to many current events, and among them one bulked large. At first, Middleton only referred to it as "the great monarchal business" (2.1.167), but eventually he explained the "masterpiece of play" was "T'entrap the White Knight and with false allurements / Entice him to the Black House" (4.2.77–9). The White Knight, however, had his own plot against the Black House to "prevent their rank insinuation . . . / [and] strike 'em grov'ling" (4.4.2–4). His sidekick, the White Duke, agreed to help but rather nervously warned

> Sir, all the gins, traps, and alluring snares
> The devil has been at work since '88 on
> Are laid for the great hope of this game only.
>
> (4.4.5–7)

As the White House eventually triumphed over its Black opponents, the audience witnessed a retrospective on the various diabolical "gins, traps, and alluring snares" which had threatened England "since '88." This essay will briefly sketch this high-stakes conflict between "States and their pawns" from the Armada to the Thirty Years War.

England emerged from the Middle Ages as a *dominium politicum et regale* in which the monarch was subject to law that the monarch and Parliament approved. Chief among the parliamentary privileges was its exclusive control over "extraordinary" taxation. Monarchs ordinarily were expected to "live within their own," financing both the state and their entourage from their estates and various fiscal perquisites. In wartime, however, Parliament was expected to approve an "extraordinary" supply of money as well as subsequent grants if the conflict continued. But as the costs of warfare skyrocketed, this common late medieval arrangement frequently came under stress as rulers experimented with less restrictive alternatives. As early as 1525, Henry VIII and Wolsey tried to launch the Amicable Grant, an extra-parliamentary levy, only to abandon it in the face of opposition. Similar efforts would have been inevitable if the plunder of the English monasteries had not produced a substantial windfall. Only late in Elizabeth's reign after the crown had sold off the bulk of the monastic estates did severe financial nightmares again haunt the Exchequer officials. The queen responded by enthusiastically embracing parsimony in titles, rewards, and expenditures, but even ruthless cheese-paring could not satisfy the voracious fiscal demands of the long Anglo-Spanish conflict, 1584–1604 (Sommerville, *Royalists and Patriots*, pp. 55–104; Hoskins, *Age of Plunder*).

The Armada war proved Elizabeth's defining moment; no one forgot when she appeared in armor at Tilbury, vowing to fight and die beside her troops. Yet the war that fashioned the image of Gloriana also tarnished it. With increasingly poor grace, Parliament approved £1.5 million in new taxes, and the wartime polarization ended any moderation towards English Catholics, several hundred of whom were eviscerated by her executioners. Meanwhile she found herself bankrolling the Dutch Republic and Henri IV of France while struggling to fend off Spanish attempts to depose her. Unfortunately for Elizabeth, Philip II soon discovered that for a modest investment of troops and money in Ireland, he could nearly force her into bankruptcy as she tried to maintain her grip on the island. As wartime expenditures outstripped even generous parliamentary subsidies, money came to obsess her ministers. Consequently, her heir inherited the apparently perpetual war against Spain and her debts of £400,000 (Hammer, *Elizabeth's Wars*; F. Dietz, *Public Finance*, pp. 49–99).

James I promptly made not only peace with Spain but also a full-on Anglo-Spanish *entente* his geopolitical hallmark. Trade between the two countries boomed, and a remarkable number of Protestant Englishmen not only developed a taste for Spanish tobacco, but also learned Spanish and even visited the country (see Trudi L. Darby in this volume, p. 144). Thus by the early 1620s the Spanish ambassador and Middleton's Black Knight, the conde de Gondomar, was well attuned to James and his state precisely because the king had long fervently embraced the Anglo-Spanish *rapprochement* (Carter, "Gondomar"). James's moral commitment to peace also paid a handsome dividend, of course, for it allowed him to slash military spending to the bone. His economy drive, however, did not include the court. Unlike Elizabeth, he was a family man with a wife, two sons, and a daughter, all of whom needed to maintain a certain dignity and grandeur, and his comparative penury in Scotland encouraged him to live large in England. As he showered clothing, jewels, land, and houses on his courtiers, his family, and himself, his weary financial officers focused on revenue enhancement rather than on any serious economic retrenchment at court, and his advocacy of the "divine right of kings" led them to ponder how best to loosen, if not end, the parliamentary grip on taxation. Early in his reign, James decided that the easiest way to do so was to impose or to increase existing import duties, which had not been revised in decades. This move immediately generated controversy. Although the royal judges not surprisingly found for the crown in Bate's Case (1606), many Parliament men continued to think impositions illegal without parliamentary authorization. In 1610, they pondered the possibility of the Great Contract, a deal in which they would have granted an annual tax in return for the abolition of impositions and other "feudal" levies, but the proposal eventually collapsed after protracted wrangling (Willson, *King James*, pp. 159–270). Hence early on two troubling issues emerged to darken the popular mood – James's lifestyle and his fondness for non-parliamentary fiscal experiments.

Lord Burghley's son, the Earl of Salisbury, generally kept royal expenditures within moderate bonds, but his death in 1612 left the Exchequer to the Earl of Suffolk, whose fondness for conspicuous consumption rivaled that of James himself. Extravagance consequently came to define the 1610s. At his daughter's wedding in 1613, James and his family appeared wearing jewels worth £900,000, well over twice the crown's ordinary income. Suffolk himself poured money into building Audley End, a truly palatial country house which James humorously observed was too grand for a king but might do for a Lord Treasurer. Although James and his ministers repeatedly tried to argue otherwise, a majority in the Commons persisted in the belief that no extraordinary supply was necessary, and aside from a generous grant in 1606, they declined to underwrite the regime. Frustrated by their intransigence, James did not summon Parliament between 1610 and 1621 save for a few weeks in 1614. While undeniably unfortunate, this nadir in relations between crown and Parliament had no real impact – at least as long as the country remained at peace, which was exactly where Rex Pacificus wanted to keep it. Instead of further pleas to Parliament, James sold off anything of value; he settled a Dutch debt of £618,000 for £200,000 in ready cash; he auctioned off titles; and when sales flagged, he even invented a new one to flog, that of baronet. Nevertheless, notwithstanding a wave of patents and monopolies that washed over the realm and the (mercifully brief) attempt to alter the traditional pattern of the all-important Anglo-Dutch wool trade, the royal debt steadily climbed, reaching nearly £1,000,000 at the end of the decade (F. Dietz, *Public Finance*, vol. 1, pp. 100–81; Prestwich, *Cranfield*, pp. 1–198; Stone, *Crisis*, pp. 65–128).

Along with the display of wealth came suspect morals, as James surrounded himself with lithe young men like Robert Carr, later the Earl of Somerset, and George Villiers, later the Earl, Marquis, and eventually Duke, of Buckingham. Londoners followed suit and began to experiment too, and in 1620 there was a series of sensational tracts denouncing reportedly rampant transvestitism in the metropolis. Londoners and country gentlemen alike were of two minds. Many personally benefited from the orgy of consumerism during the long Jacobean peace, making money from courtiers and acquiring new titles and lands. But doubts grew nonetheless about the moral and sexual decadence oozing out of Whitehall, doubts which many godly ministers played on with their sermons. Proof positive of the moral squalor came with Sir Thomas Overbury's death; in 1616–17, Somerset's wife was convicted of arranging for his poisoning in order to cover up the unsavory details of her lurid divorce. Even more eye-opening was the denouement; James ultimately intervened and reduced her death sentence to house arrest while permitting her accomplices to be marched off to the gallows. Meanwhile, in 1618, James's quip about Audley End lost its humor as he learned of Suffolk's systematic embezzlement of the Exchequer, in part to finance the largest private house in the country. These scandals only cleared the way for Buckingham to assume more control of Whitehall, placing his clients in important offices and marrying members of his extensive clan into the aristocracy. For many, this succession of unedifying episodes served to confirm the view that "all England was like a merry Christmas and him [Buckingham], the Lord of Misrule" (Folger Shakespeare Library, V.a. 439, fol. 41; Bellany, *Politics*, pp. 1–180; Young, *James VI and I*; Lockyer, *Buckingham*, pp. 3–24).

The party ended in 1618 as imperial representatives sailed out of a window in Prague down to a pile of manure. James then had to confront his worst fear, as he was quickly being pulled into a major war. The Bohemians, who traditionally elected their king, had picked a Hapsburg prince, Ferdinand II,

but after he failed to maintain a promised religious toleration, the Bohemian
nobility deposed him and instead elected Frederick V, the Elector of the
Palatinate, whose wife was Elizabeth, James's daughter. These events in
central Europe began a tangled conflict which eventually sprawled across
the continent and lasted thirty years, shaking England, along with many
other European states, to the core and opening up dangerous political fault
lines (G. Parker, *Thirty Years War*, pp. 2–60).

Rejecting calls for further religious reformation, instead James had followed
a moderate Calvinist course between Rome and Geneva, a policy that irritated
some but enraged few. Puritans unhappy with his famous equation of "no
bishop, no king" found solace in his appointment of George Abbot, a good
Calvinist, as Archbishop of Canterbury in 1610. Likewise, after their nearly
explosive 1605 response to his accession, the English Catholics quickly discovered that between James's closet Catholic queen and his hispanophilia,
they had much to grumble about but little to fear. A major central European
conflict centering on religion, however, made religious moderation hard to
maintain. Arrayed against the Protestants were not only the papacy, but also
the House of Austria with far-flung possessions in Spain and Portugal, the
Netherlands, Naples, Sicily and Milan, Austria and Hungary, to say nothing
of Central and South America and the Philippines; the King of Spain infor-
mally directed this conglomerate, which silver mines in Mexico and Bolivia
financed. Protestant hopes were soon dashed in 1620 when Ferdinand drove
Frederick out of Bohemia and began its forced recatholicization. English
concerns then shifted to the Palatinate, beset by Hapsburg armies. Here
dynastic and religious concerns intertwined. Elizabeth and her children
might inherit the British throne; indeed her grandson, George of Hanover,
eventually did so in 1714. Moreover, Heidelberg, Frederick's capital, was a
prominent Calvinist intellectual center. Consequently, calls for military intervention rose in England. While some favored dispatching an English army
up the Rhine, most were uneasy at that option's expense and the efficacy; it
cost too much and played to the Spaniards' strength, their professional army.
Instead most English advocates of intervention plumped for a "diversi-
onary" naval war along Elizabethan lines. By patrolling the Atlantic and the
Caribbean, English ships, it was imagined, would prey on Spanish shipping
and intercept the flow of silver, thus neatly kneecapping the celebrated Spanish
military juggernaut while bringing peace to the Empire and Frederick back
to the Palatinate. Better still, rich Spanish prizes would help defray some, if
not all, of the naval expenses. Variants on this strategy could be followed in
several tracts and heard in the 1621 Parliament (Fincham, "Prelacy"; Cogswell,
*Revolution*, pp. 6–54; W. B. Patterson, *King James*, pp. 293–338).

Yet James thought otherwise. He carefully limited his quarrel to Ferdinand II and the Catholic League but not to Philip of Spain. Seconding his discriminating constitutional sense was the realization that in a straightforward war, the Catholics would have the larger battalions. Therefore, although he sent a token English force in 1620 to secure the Palatinate, he focused on negotiating a settlement, the centerpiece of which would be the marriage of his heir, Prince Charles, to the Spanish Infanta. Further sweetening this plan was the thought of the Infanta's massive dowry, which would relieve James's more pressing financial woes and further postpone any reckoning with Parliament. Although long discussed, an Anglo-Spanish marriage had never advanced very far because neither side could resolve the fate of the English Catholics, Spain insisting on their formal toleration and James offering only de facto favor. But as the continental crisis bid fair to engulf England, James reopened the negotiations, hopeful that a creative solution would emerge to the Catholic question and confident that the Anglo-Spanish marriage in turn would lead to a mutually satisfactory solution to the future of the Palatinate. The Spaniards embraced the idea, setting English diplomats and Gondomar to work and couriers galloping across the continent.

Progress, however, proved slow, and as months passed without any definitive resolution, James's subjects became increasingly restive. Eager to assist Frederick and Elizabeth, the Parliament men in 1621 proved surprisingly accommodating, and instead of waiting until the end of the session as was customary, they immediately passed a subsidy bill for over £200,000. James was delighted; their bellicosity only strengthened his negotiating position with the Spaniards. His happiness grew further still in June when they pledged their financial support in any future conflict. Again, he sought to extract full diplomatic value from their resolution. But later in the year, after misinterpreting ambiguous signals from court, Parliament advised against the Spanish match, and James, anxious to preserve the Anglo-Spanish entente, dissolved the session, thus preserving his prerogative and his comparative poverty. Without Parliament's support, any English military threat was simply unbelievable; hence James could only hope for the best and play along. Towards that end, he formally suspended in 1622 the penal laws, providing a de facto toleration. Meanwhile Catholics became increasingly prominent at court and across the country; indeed Buckingham's mother and wife, among others, openly converted to Rome. At the same time, the continental situation deteriorated. By 1621 steady Hapsburg military pressure had whittled Frederick's grip down to three Palatine towns. In response, James finally unleashed his fleet, dispatching a squadron into the Mediterranean where, to the dismay of many of his subjects, English seaman acted against North African pirate bases rather than Spain itself. In fact, since the freebooters captured Spanish and English merchants alike, James was actually doing the Spaniards a favor (Cogswell, "Phaeton's Chariot"; Hebb, *Piracy*).

As the Anglo-Spanish negotiations seemed to be achieving nothing, except neutralizing England, contemporaries began to wonder if the Hapsburgs were not simply lulling James to sleep while they crushed his son-in-law; indeed one anonymous tract even asked the Defender of the Faith which faith he was defending. This context provided the somber political overtones to the 1620 polemical battle over cross-dressing, for some whispered that James's passivity was simply part of the systematic feminization of English society by "Queen James." Whispering was particularly endemic among the godly, and some ministers boldly spoke against James's policy, as Dr. Hakewill did at court in 1621, for example, preaching on the passage, "Arise Lord and be revenged of thy Enemyes" (Folger Shakespeare Library, X.d. 502/10). In response, the "conformist" ministers (many of them future Arminians), court authors like Ben Jonson, and English Catholics launched attacks on puritan disobedience while they hymned the blessings of peace (Butler, *Stuart Court Masque*, pp. 239–75).

Over the winter of 1622–3, the crisis reached its height. Then the Hapsburg troops finally stormed Heidelberg and Mannheim, killing dozens of Englishmen, and such was their strength that James agreed to withdraw his troops from the last of Frederick's Palatine towns. Testy diplomatic exchanges followed, but saber-rattling soon gave way to renewed marriage talks, and early in 1623 Charles and Buckingham donned false beards and set out for Madrid. The news generated an emotional tsunami in England, matched only by the 1588 Armada. The prospect of the heir apparent alone in Spain, surrounded by cunning Catholic clerics and Buckingham, whose own religion was deeply suspect, horrified many contemporaries who assumed that the Spanish match – and England's recatholicization – were inevitable. Only God seemed able to prevent catastrophe, and in an astonishing development, He apparently did, for late in 1623, Charles returned without the Infanta. Although James still talked about the marriage taking place at some future date, Charles pointedly did not. Meanwhile Buckingham, long regarded as *the* moral cancer infecting the body politic, underwent a dramatic transformation. In February 1624 he told the Parliament men how the trip to Madrid had all been a ploy to get the Spaniards to reveal their juggling. The match, he explained, had been intended simply to immobilize England, for Philip would never have married his sister to Charles, at least not until he converted to Rome. Having exposed their ruse by playing a double game, the favorite then urged the Parliament men to work with the Prince to help ease James into the continental war. They readily agreed. Consequently, the 1624 session witnessed a remarkable return to the Elizabethan norm. The Commons voted a generous extraordinary supply of almost £300,000, which allowed England to move onto a war footing, repairing coastal and Irish defenses, refitting the fleet and sending 6,000 troops to the hard-pressed Dutch Republic. Furthermore, acting on Parliament's emphatic advice, James finally broke off the Anglo-Spanish marriage talks, and he enforced the penal laws against the Catholics, banishing all Jesuits and priests from the island on pain of death. With the country apparently reverting to Elizabethan form, launching a war against Spain, with godly ministers and Parliament men at last cooperating with the government, the populace hailed Charles as the parliamentary prince and Buckingham as the people's favorite (Cogswell, *Revolution*, pp. 135–262; Redworth, *Prince and Infanta*).

To be sure, the widespread joy over the "blessed revolution" of 1623–4 and over England's abrupt exit from the Spanish orbit proved short-lived. With the colossal military failures of the Mansfelt and Wimbledon expeditions in 1625, with Buckingham's descent on the Île de Ré in 1627, and with bitter rows erupting over Catholics, Arminians, and a new extra-parliamentary levy, Charles's relations with Parliament promptly disintegrated. In 1628 a disgruntled lieutenant assassinated Buckingham, and in the following year the return of impositions to political center stage prompted Charles to withdraw from the war, embarking instead on his "Personal Rule" without Parliament from 1629 to 1640 (Russell, *Parliaments*, pp. 204–415; Cogswell, "John Felton"). We know that events would shortly overwhelm the much delayed English entry into the Thirty Years War. Nevertheless there is no gainsaying the wild enthusiasm in the summer of 1624 after Middleton's White Knight and White Duke had outfoxed the wily Gondomar and broken the Black House's viselike grip on England. Bitter divisions would soon rend the newly reunited English polity, but that fact only underscores the poignancy of the play's ending when Middleton sent out the pawn of the White Queen, a character clearly resembling Elizabeth of Bohemia, to salute the audience as "true friends of the White House and cause, / Which she hopes most of this assembly draws." The White Queen, the pawn reported, set little value on the damage done by the Hapsburgs and their allies since "Her White friends' hands will build up fair again" (Epilogue, 3–4, 10). And for nine days, crowds packed the Globe to watch this daring play which put modern "States and their pawns" on stage and allowed the audience to see "check-mate given to virtue's foes" (Prologue, 4–8) as Charles and Buckingham thwarted the Spaniards' "great monarchal business."

## CHAPTER 15

# Religious identities

## Ian W. Archer

Thomas Middleton's religious identity has proved elusive. In a book of 1980 Margot Heinemann identified him as a puritan dramatist. That claim rests to a large extent on his stage sensation, *A Game at Chess* (1624), which plugs into the virulent antipopery characteristic of what she labels the "parliamentary puritans" associated with the Earl of Pembroke and other alleged opponents of the Duke of Buckingham. Middleton was also perhaps unusually close to the city fathers, writing his first script for the Lord Mayor's show in 1613 and another six between 1617 and 1626, and accepting a new office, that of City Chronologer, from 1620. Although the annals on which he fitfully worked are not extant, we know from a summary of their contents that they were far more than standard civic annals, but touched on events of national importance seen through the lens of the patriots. Moreover, the university-educated Middleton was comfortable penning theological tracts. He was the author of a Calvinist treatise, *The Two Gates of Salvation* (1609), republished in 1620 as *The Marriage of the Old and New Testament* with a dedication to two London merchants who Heinemann identifies as Puritans. Heinemann's case did not find favor among historians, who in their revisionist fervor were busily rejecting the notion of a parliamentary puritan party at the same time as she was inscribing Middleton in the puritan pantheon. Against the evidence of Middleton's godly sympathies can be placed his participation in the theatrical construction of Puritanism, and Heinemann had considerable difficulty in explaining away these satirical passages (Chakravorty, *Society*, pp. 9–13; Bawcutt, "A Puritan Dramatist?"). The controversy reflects disagreement over the way we should use labels of religious identity, as well as the real fluidity of religious positions in Jacobean London.

Middleton's drama undoubtedly drew upon, fashioned, and reinforced popular stereotypes of Puritanism. The punctiliousness of the godly over ceremonies is associated with sectarianism: children should be "well kersened i' the right way / Without idolatry or superstition, / After the pure manner of

Amsterdam" (*A Chaste Maid in Cheapside*, 3.2.3–5). Puritans are consistently presented as arch-hypocrites, professing spirituality, but prone to greed, lechery, and drunkenness, and affecting a hollow lowliness that masks self-ishness. In *Chaste Maid* (1613) the puritan gossips at the christening gorge themselves on comfits, and they are so besotted with alcohol (the spirit, as they punningly refer to it constantly) that they bepiss themselves. In *The Puritan Widow* (1606) their charity is exposed as a sham: "Sooner charity from the devil than good from a puritan … Thou … givst me charitable faces, which indeed is but a fashion in you all that are puritans" (1.4.55–107). The recently deceased husband of Widow Plus was fashioned by the godly as a model of charitable virtue, but in fact "he got his wealth with a hard gripe … / He would eat fools and ignorant heirs clean up, / And had his drink from many a poor man's brow" (2.1.189, 192–3). Like Jonson, Middleton constantly mocked the forms of godly self-identification, "the faithful … the sisters … the brethren" and mercilessly sent up the speech rhythms of everyday godly discourse: "children are blessings if they be got with zeal / By the brethren, as I have five at home"; one should be "well mettled, like the faithful, to endure … / Tribulation here and raise up seed" (*Chaste Maid*, 3.2.16–35).

Middleton's naming of two characters after outposts of London Puritanism, Nicholas St Antlings (St. Antholins) and Simon St Mary Overies (as St. Saviour Southwark was sometimes known) so outraged the godly clergy that he was unusually singled out for criticism in William Crashaw's antitheatrical diatribe at St. Paul's Cross in 1608:

Two hypocrites must be brought forth; and how they shall be described but by these names, Nicholas S. Antlings and Simon S. Maryoveries. Thus hypocrisy, a child of Hell must bear the names of two Churches of God, and two wherein God's name is called on publicly every day in the year, and in one of them his blessed word preached every day (an example scarce matchable in the world): yet these two, wherein God's name is thus glorified, and our Church and State honoured, shall be by these miscreants thus dishonoured, and that not on the stage only, but even in print. (*Sermon*, p. 170)

Middleton exacted his own revenge in *Hengist, King of Kent* (1616–20), where Oliver the Puritan (interestingly, in the context of a national depression in the cloth trade figured as a traitor to the national economy through his weaving of fustian) not only has his loom broken by patriotic English weavers, but is also made to endure the performance of a play: "sure the only way / To execute a Puritan is seeing of a play" (5.1.180–1).

Patrick Collinson has drawn attention to the way in which literary representations such as these shaped popular understandings of what a

Puritan was. Puritanism had its origins in religious polemic, entering common discourse as a term of abuse in the anti-Martinist agitation of 1589–90 (Collinson, "The Theatre"; Lake and Questier, *Antichrist's Lewd Hat*). In claiming that the theatre "constructed" Puritanism, Collinson has sometimes been represented as suggesting that Puritanism did not really exist, but there must have been some substance to it for the stereotypes to have resonated. Nevertheless, because of the term's polemical uses, it does become more difficult to define what exactly a Puritan was. We can no longer identify Puritans with a belief in Calvinism, because that was the dominant orthodoxy until the Arminian theological coup of the 1620s. Thus Middleton's exploration of the Calvinist theology of double predestination in the biblical typological treatise *Two Gates* cannot be taken as proof positive of puritan commitment. Nor can we identify Puritans with hostility to bishops and support for a Presbyterian system of church government, because that seems to have been a minority position, and one very much in abeyance in James's reign.

But there does seem to have been a puritan bottom line in a skeptical attitude towards elements of the prayer book ceremonies: the use of the sign of the cross in the baptismal service and the ring in the marriage service. It is true that Puritans might show themselves willing to compromise on these issues. When James insisted on subscription to the notion that the prayer book contained nothing contrary to the Word of God, many buckled, but an uneasy truce prevailed where evangelically sympathetic bishops did not press for full observance with the prayer book, merely a token compliance. That truce held so long as the establishment remained committed to an antipopish agenda and shared a Calvinist platform with its godly critics.

We can also identify a puritan culture, a system of religious practices and forms of godly sociability, which provided the raw material which rendered the antipuritan satire plausible. When the Kent minister Josias Nichols came to describe Puritanism in 1602 it was as "the people [who] do hear sermons, talk of the scriptures, [and] sing psalms together in private houses etc." (*Plea*, p. 12). Puritans placed the Word of God as revealed in the scriptures and interpreted by God's ministers at the heart of their religious experience. At one level this was an intensely communal experience; they might walk together to church singing psalms; at the sermon itself they would be leafing through their Bibles to locate the passages the preacher was referring to, while others would be jotting down notes of the main points as an aid to possible discussion in household groups. But Puritans were also intensely introspective, for the central problem of their faith was the question of assurance: if works availed nothing in the predestinarian scheme, how did one know that one was saved? For this reason, the puritan conscience was subject to constant self-examination, best captured in the voluminous notebooks of the godly London turner Nehemiah Wallington, who scrutinized every occurrence for evidence of God's providence, and who imposed on himself and his household a godly discipline through which he might gain assurance (Seaver, *Wallington's World*). This was Calvinist predestinarianism in practice – experimental predestinarianism, as it has been called. By placing predestination at the center of their understanding of their relationship with God, the godly were committed to working out its implications in their daily lives. This set them apart from their more conformist neighbours who paid lip service to the doctrine, the so-called credal predestinarians (Lake, "Calvinism," pp. 32–76).

What was the nature of the religious culture of the capital in which Middleton grew up and worked? Although historians of this period sometimes write in terms of evangelical failure, their evidence tends to come from rural England. Ministers coming up from the provinces to preach in the capital were rather more impressed: "Oh London, London, excellent things are spoken of thee thou city of God," exclaimed the Kent preacher Thomas Jackson in 1609, marveling at "the very ark of the presence of God above all other places of this land" (*Convert's Happiness*, pp. 30–5). With almost all benefices served by graduates, and with one-third of livings in the hands of doctors of divinity by 1600, the London clergy were the best educated in the kingdom. Steady investment by the laity ensured that there was an extraordinary profusion of sermons. By 1600 forty-four parishes boasted lectureships. In the 1620s the figure had risen to fifty-nine, over half the total number of parishes. At the center of the capital's religious life were the weekly set-piece sermons at St. Paul's Cross, held in the presence of the civic elite, but attracting a wide audience from across the capital. Pious Londoners could shop around this ecclesiastical supermarket to hear the most popular preachers of the day, "sermon gadding," as it was called. In an imagined conversation recorded in 1589, one Londoner remarked of his local preacher that his ministry was always "dead and without spirit in mine ears," but in Southwark more edifying fare was to be found: "O sir, if you had heard this other man, you would have said there had been a great difference. And for my part, I desire to hear those by whom I am most edified" (*Sophronistes*, p. 19). Visitors to the capital "thought not their business fully ended" until they had heard the star turn William Gouge at St. Anne Blackfriars (Clarke, *Eminent Divines*, p. 105). Of the London preacher Nathaniel Culverwell, we hear that "he preached the love of God so sweetly that my heart melted to hear him" (Rogers, *Obel*, p. 412).

In one remarkable week the turner Nehemiah Wallington clocked up no fewer than nineteen sermons. Londoners were not passive receptacles: laymen played an active role in the theological spats that took part among the godly; theological disputes were conducted before lay audiences; contending ministers might mobilize laymen through gossip; and sometimes disputes were initiated by the enquiries of laypeople.

But we should not necessarily move from recognizing the vibrancy of London's religious culture to labeling that culture "puritan." The label has perhaps been applied too readily: we encounter "puritan parishes" (St. Stephen Coleman Street, St. Antholins, St. Anne Blackfriars) or "puritan companies" (the Haberdashers), even broadly defined "puritan elites." For want of direct evidence on confessional allegiances, historians argue from behavior; if people behaved in puritan ways, then they must have been puritan. But there is plenty of room for dispute about what those forms of puritan behavior actually were, and syllogistic forms of argument abound: Puritans opposed theatre, London's aldermen opposed theatre, therefore London's aldermen were Puritans. It is all too easy to move from a recognition that Middleton had patrons in the city elite to the assumption that they must have been puritan. We need a more nuanced account of religious allegiances within the elite. There undoubtedly was a core of hard-liner anticeremonialists, some of them Presbyterian fellow travelers, at Guildhall, but they were a minority, balanced by evangelical conformists, and by some who may have been tempted by what has become known as avant-garde conformity, rebalancing the relationship between preaching and sacraments in the economy of salvation (Hickman, "Religious Belief"; Archer, "London and the Theatre").

So what of Middleton's allegedly puritan patrons? The Lord Mayor for whom he wrote his first pageant, *The Triumphs of Truth*, in 1613, his namesake Sir Thomas Myddleton, fits the bill. Not only did Myddleton participate in godly projects such as the translation of the Bible into Welsh, but he was also one of the group of city bigwigs who backed the controversial benefaction of the widow Sarah Venables to support silenced nonconformist clergy, a bequest that was contested in the law courts (Tyacke, *English Protestantism*, pp. 114–15, 122–3). But with the mercer Richard Fishborne and his business partner, the merchant taylor John Browne, the dedicatees of Middleton's tract, *The Marriage of the Old and New Testament* (1620), we are on less firm ground. We know little about Browne, but Fishborne certainly "behaved" in a godly way that might suggest puritan credentials. His charitable bequests reveal a man extremely concerned for the provision of a preaching ministry. He left endowments to support weekly sermons, a parish lectureship, and various charities. The Mercers were also entrusted with £2,000 to purchase impropriations to ensure that parishes could support a learned minister, "such as shall be well known to be honest, discreet, and learned men fearing God and painful in their ministry that by their life and doctrine they may win many souls in Christ Jesus." Fishborne was aware of the possible tensions in the triangulated relationship of parishioners, beneficed minister, and lecturer. At St. Bartholomew Exchange he recommended that the parson be given the lecturer's stipend as a salary enhancement, but that if the parishioners did not "like of him" they might elect someone else. If the lecturer was unacceptable to the parson then the bequest would be in abeyance. Perhaps here Fishbourne was acknowledging the kind of conflicts that the Laudian ascendancy exacerbated, but he clearly enjoyed good relations with the parson, John Grant, and with the current St. Bartholomew's lecturer, Humphrey Peake. Puritans they were not. Peake was a royal chaplain about to be foisted on St. Martin-in-the-Fields by the Bishop of London; Grant was a conformist who was sequestered from his living in the civil war. Fishborne left bequests to other clergy who seem to have been conformist (National Archives, London, PROB 11/245, fos. 461r–4v). Nathaniel Shute, rector of St. Mildred Poultry, celebrated Fishborne as a "natural son of the Church of England" in his funeral sermon, and pointedly remarked that he was "none of the peripatetic professors, who have a walking religion, from one Church to another, and from their own ordinary pastor to a worse" (*Corona*, pp. 28, 42).

The evangelical conformist position was tenable because so many elements of the prayer book service had been detoxified of their popish associations in the context of the sustained preaching of the Gospel, and the greater security of the religious settlement under a male monarch with heirs. Indeed many of those of evangelical sympathies were prepared to put their weight behind the campaign for the beautification of the capital's churches, giving money for projects like the new stained-glass windows in St. Stephen Walbrook. Religious imagery was less contentious in the 1610s than it had been in the 1560s and than it was to become in the 1630s as Laud's campaign tarred previously acceptable practices once more with the popish brush (Merritt, "Church-Building"). In 1622 Middleton himself wrote verses to celebrate the consecration of the church of St. James, Duke Place, presided over by the Calvinist Archbishop Abbot. He testifies to the support of key members of the city elite: "Barkham the worthy . . . Generous Hamersley, and Campbell the grave" (Lord Mayor Sir Edward Barkham and Aldermen Hugh Hamersley and James Campbell), who had worked "From ruins to redeem this house of prayer" ("The Temple of St James," 5–22).

In James's reign the broad acceptance of Calvinist orthodoxy and the militant anticatholic stance taken by the ecclesiastical establishment served to foster Protestant unity. Evangelical conformists like George Downham, rector of St. Margaret Lothbury from 1596 to 1601, could combine virulent antipopery with the defense of *jure divino* episcopacy and the friendship of Archbishop Bancroft, hammer of the Puritans (*Oxford Dictionary of National Biography* [*ODNB*]). Indeed Puritanism could be seen to be as much of a threat to that unity as Catholicism. James I was fond of these parallels, warning his son in the widely circulated *Basilikon Doron* (1599) to beware of "both the extremities": "as well as ye repress the vain Puritan, so not to suffer proud Papal bishops" (*Political Writings*, p. 27). Oliver Ormerod's 1605 pamphlet *The Picture of a Puritan* presents Puritanism and popery as closely related. Sampson Price, rector of Allhallows the Great, in his Paul's Cross sermon of 1613, *England's Warning by Laodicea's Lukewarmness*, lashed out at atheists, papists, and Puritans as subverters of the Church (*ODNB*). Thomas Adams, who could deliver as good a Paul's Cross jeremiad as any Puritan, nevertheless supported kneeling at communion, and attacked the "fond scrupulosity of those who demanded rigid conformity to the primitive times, as if the spouse of Christ might not wear a lace or a border for which she could not plead prescription" (*ODNB*). As Donna Hamilton has argued, Middleton was stressing the equivalence of Puritanism and Catholicism in *Puritan*. In the conjuring scene held in the Puritan Widow Plus's household he "mocks Catholic practices, associates Puritans with Catholic practices, and constructs Puritan households as places inhabited by extremists" (*Middleton*, p. 511).

Antipopery was the cement that held otherwise conflicting Protestant views together. Catholicism, as Peter Lake has demonstrated, was constructed as an antireligion, the inversion of all that was truly Christian, fostering idolatry, feeding off the ignorance and credulity of the people, and presided over by the Pope who was literally understood as the Antichrist (Lake, "Anti-Popery"). Antipopery had entered the bloodstream, its themes nurtured at a popular level through commemorations of the providential deliverances of Elizabeth's accession and the defeat of the Armada. The invocation of the specter of popery, the notion that by splitting Protestant unity Puritans could open the door to the Romish wolves, was a potent deterrent to religious agitation.

But the Jacobean religious truce between competing versions of the Church of England was a fragile one. From the 1590s onwards some clerics, among them prominent London ministers, were developing an alternative vision that was much more sacramentally oriented. At St. Giles Cripplegate in the 1590s, Lancelot Andrewes was preaching doctrines which called into question elements of Calvinist orthodoxy (Fincham and Tyacke, *Altars Restored*, p. 86). James enjoyed the preaching of some of these figures, but their more controversial views were by and large kept out of print and the hierarchy remained firmly Calvinist. With the outbreak of the Thirty Years War and the foreign policy dilemmas it posed, the cracks in the facade of Protestant unity became ever more apparent. James did not share the confessional interpretation of the war held by his godly subjects and pursued the controversial strategy of seeking diplomatic leverage with the Hapsburgs through a Spanish marriage for his son Prince Charles.

Such a policy offended broad swaths of Protestant opinion. It is not surprising to find puritan troublemakers like John Everard launching attacks on the cruelty and tyranny of the Spanish from the vantage point of Paul's Cross in February 1621, but many more moderate voices joined in the storm of vituperation (McClure (ed.), *Letters*, pp. 350, 449, 451). James issued repeated proclamations against "lavish and licentious speeches in matters of state" (Larkin and Hughes (eds.), *Royal Proclamations*, vol. 1, pp. 495–6, 519–21), and his ecclesiastical patronage began to swing towards the more pliant Arminian sympathizing clergy, some of whom doubted the identification of Pope and Antichrist.

Middleton's *Game* tapped into the same deep vein of antipopish sentiment. Through the demonic character of the Black Knight, a thinly veiled caricature of Count Gondomar, the former Spanish ambassador, he presents Spain's ambitions for a universal monarchy, "that great work / Called the possession of the world" (3.1.85–6). Among Middleton's sources was the tract by the minister Thomas Scott, *Vox Populi, or Newes from Spain* (1620), a brilliant spoof purporting to be Gondomar's report to the council of state in Spain on how he had subverted the English government. Scott's work had been so inflammatory that he had to seek exile in the Dutch Republic, but by the time Middleton wrote, the wheel had turned. The so-called "blessed revolution" in England's foreign policy saw Buckingham and Charles performing a volte-face in the wake of the collapse of the marriage negotiations in Madrid. The fact that they now shared the priorities of the Earl of Pembroke makes Heinemann's classification of the play as puritan opposition drama untenable; the play is likely to have had some encouragement from elements at the court (Cogswell, "Thomas Middleton").

This formulation does not quite capture the radical force of Middleton's intervention. It is true that a number of literary productions sponsored within the court articulated a militant anti-Spanish view in 1623–4, but none plugged into the discourses of popular antipopery in quite the way that Middleton did (Limon, *Dangerous Matter*, pp. 98–129). In presenting the struggle as a cosmic battle between black and white, Truth and Error, he was presenting the binary view of Catholicism as the antireligion. While the actions of the white pieces are guided by the Christian God, the black pieces are doing the Devil's work. The dastardly designs of the Jesuits (with whom the Black House is consistently associated) on the White Queen's Pawn, a figure "Of truth and goodness never yet deflow'red" (aka the Church of England, [Induction, 10]), and the plot of the Black Knight to secure the conversion of the White Knight (aka Prince Charles) are thwarted; the black pieces are dispatched to the "hell-bag." This confessional view of the conflict was not shared by Buckingham and Charles, who were now negotiating for a French Catholic marriage as part of their strategy for building an anti-Hapsburg coalition.

Middleton may have joined in the theatrical satire of Puritanism, but the changing circumstances of the 1620s meant that his broadly Protestant world view was coming into collision with an establishment that was in the process of redrawing the boundaries. An opportunity was provided in 1624 for a brief conjunction between different groups in a common anti-Spanish enterprise, but the alliance was highly contingent and would collapse within a year, as Charles's Arminian proclivities became clear. It became a standard complaint of evangelical Protestants that the Arminian faction was redefining the Protestant mainstream as puritan. When Middleton republished his Calvinist religious tract in 1620 and again in 1627, it carried rather different implications from 1609, identifying him with the group that was in the process of being labelled puritan (Ferrell, *Middleton*, p. 682).

## CHAPTER 16

# The obsession with Spain

## Trudi L. Darby

In the 1620s Thomas Middleton wrote three plays with Spanish themes: *The Changeling*, *The Spanish Gypsy* (both collaborative works), and *A Game at Chess*, his own work and one of the most notorious plays of the decade. Middleton's interest in Spain was not unique: most of his contemporary playwrights brought Spanish subjects into their work at some time and several borrowed plot material from Spanish fiction (Darby and Samson, "Jacobean Stage," pp. 206–22). This chapter will set Middleton in the context of the Jacobean obsession with Spain.

Spain was the enemy – or at least, it had been until 1604 when in his first major foreign policy action as King of England, James I signed the Treaty of London which ended the war between England and Spain. The two countries had been at war since the 1570s and had become bogged down in conflicts by proxy, as England supported rebels against Spain in the Netherlands and Spain supported rebels against England in Ireland. By the end of Elizabeth I's reign, both sides were ready for peace. As Thomas Cogswell writes, "Elizabeth's greatest victory was simply holding her own against Philip II of Spain, and for this limited victory, the old queen paid an almost prohibitive price" (Cogswell, *Revolution*, p. 12).

James's personal motto was "blessed are the peacemakers." Peace with Catholic Spain was a cornerstone of his foreign policy until the last year of his reign, but it was always controversial, with a strong group at court and in Parliament favoring active support of Europe's Protestant states. Leaders of this group in the second decade of James's reign included the Lord Chamberlain, William Herbert Earl of Pembroke. Pembroke and his brother Philip were the dedicatees in 1623 of the Shakespeare First Folio, and among their other connections in the theatre was the playwright Philip Massinger, whose father had been a steward in the Pembroke household (*ODNB*; Nicolson, *Arcadia*, pp. 162–90). Pembroke seems to have had a hand in the staging of *Game*.

James's aim was to avoid war by maintaining a balance between the Protestant and Catholic powers of Europe.[1] His daughter, Elizabeth, was married in 1613 to a Protestant leader, the Elector Frederick V of the Palatine, and the following ten years were spent in attempting to negotiate a balancing marriage alliance between James's heir, Charles, and the Infanta María Ana of Spain. The Spanish Match, as this policy became known, was encouraged by Spain's ambassador in London from 1613 to 1618, Diego de Sarmiento, later created Count Gondomar, the title by which he was usually known in London. Gondomar served a second period as ambassador from 1620 to 1622. He was particularly close to James's queen consort, Anna of Denmark, while his influence on James was both suspected and feared.

By the time Middleton began his series of three Spanish plays in 1622, opinion had split into distinct pro- and anti-Spanish parties. The hispanophiles, led by Prince Charles and the royal favorite Buckingham, supported James's peacemaking, but found their policy increasingly unpopular as Charles's sister Elizabeth and her husband became embroiled in conflict with the Austrian Hapsburgs, cousins of the Spanish royal family. The anti-Spanish party favored war with the Hapsburgs, and when James called a Parliament in 1621 they held the majority position. Members of the Spanish party were suspected of Catholic sympathies: indeed, Buckingham's mother converted to Catholicism. Those of the pro-war party tended to be vigorous in their support of Protestantism, and Middleton's sympathies seem to have been with this latter group, from whom his patrons were drawn (Heinemann, *Puritanism*, pp. 258–82).

Spain was a topic of great interest, both to those who supported the Spanish Match and to those who opposed it. The booksellers who clustered around St. Paul's Churchyard sold increasing numbers of translations from the Spanish, ranging from practical texts such as *The Art of Navigation* through romances such as *Amadís de Gaule* to Cervantes's *Don Quixote*. Cervantes's novels evidently circulated among playwrights, even before the first translation of *Don Quixote* appeared in 1612, and John Fletcher in particular was mining Cervantes's stories for plot material from 1613 onwards (Samson, "Cervantes and Fletcher," pp. 223–9). For the rest of his life – he died in 1625 – Fletcher turned to Cervantes for inspiration for his plays, extracting themes and stories from Cervantes's collection of short stories *Las novelas ejemplares* (*The Exemplary Novels*, 1613) and from his last prose fiction *Los trabajos de Persiles y Sigismunda* (*The Travails of Persiles and Sigismunda*, 1617), translated into English by an anonymous translator in 1619. It is likely that Fletcher had at least a reading knowledge of Spanish and was able to read his sources in the original language (Darby,

"Cervantes," p. 23). Middleton similarly was able to read Cervantes (G. Taylor, "Lives and Afterlives," p. 34), and other literary speakers of Spanish included Ben Jonson and John Donne. Teaching Spanish was a fruitful business: Paterson and Samson's database[2] identifies thirty-one editions of Anglo-Spanish dictionaries published in London between 1500 and 1640, of which five were published in 1623. The best-known of the dictionaries, Minsheu's *Dictionary in Spanish and English* (1599), was reprinted three times in 1623, along with his *Spanish Grammar*. According to Jonson's *The Masque of Owls* (1626), the failure of the Spanish Match was an economic disaster for would-be teachers of Spanish who now had "not a scholar to teach" (Cogswell, *Revolution*, p. 270).

Within London, Spain was not just of cultural interest but a subject of political excitement. Gondomar's unpopularity with Londoners was legendary. As late as 1659 John Rowland wrote that, "Gondomar is yet fresh in the memory of many men who knew him when he lay leiger here from the King of *Spain* . . . it had been better for our nation if that politick *Spaniard* had never trod upon *English* ground" (Rowland, *Choice Narrative*, p. iv). The context here must be remembered: the "Powder Plot" of 1605 to murder the royal family and the English Parliament was the work of Catholics, who were synonymous with Spain in popular discourse. Had it succeeded, the Plot would have been the first peacetime atrocity to have been carried out on English soil. Its very novelty was terrifying. In 1620 Thomas Scott, an anti-Spanish polemicist based in the Netherlands, published *Vox Populi* in which he demonstrated the evils of Spanish government. The pamphlet struck a chord with readers in London: copies circulated in manuscript with scribes competing for contracts to produce them by the dozen (Love, *Culture and Commerce*, p. 97). *Changeling*, with its claustrophobic atmosphere of moral degeneration in a Spanish fortress, must have caught precisely this morbid fear of Spain.

In 1623 Prince Charles and Buckingham added to the tension by traveling incognito to Madrid. Impatient of the intricacies of diplomacy, Charles attempted to woo his Infanta in person, thus effectively making himself a hostage in the court of Philip IV. In London, this trip was met with incredulity at Charles's foolhardiness, as Glyn Redworth's anecdote about King James's jester encapsulates: "When Archie the Fool had first heard about the Prince's trip to Spain he put his jester's cap on James's head. The King asked, but what if Charles comes back safely? In that case, cried the Fool, I will put my hat on the king of Spain's head instead" (*Prince and Infanta*, p. 100).

In practice, Charles's romantic visit quickly turned sour as it became obvious that the Spaniards would not agree to a marriage without religious toleration for English Catholics, which for political reasons it was impossible for James and Charles to grant. Buckingham took offense at his treatment by Olivares, Philip's favorite (Redworth, *Prince and Infanta*, p. 132), and the visit descended into a diplomatic embarrassment. Charles's greatest acquisition in Madrid was not a bride but an art collection enriched by some gems from Philip IV's own holdings (Brotton, *Sale*, pp. 78–108). Charles and Buckingham landed back in England on 5 October 1623, to scenes of wild rejoicing that he was both safe and unmarried. As John Taylor wrote, "The ioyfull newes of his happy returne, filled the whole Kingdome with excessiue ioy . . . the City of *London* in expression of their louing duties, haue spared for no cost, either generall or particular" (*Welcome*, A4ᵛ).

Meanwhile, Middleton had been working with William Rowley and others on *Gypsy*, which drew on two of Cervantes's *Exemplary Novels*: *The Little Gypsy Girl* and *The Power of Blood*. The play was performed for Charles at Whitehall in November 1623, and mixes local Spanish color – the romantic life of the gypsy band – with a story about a vicious rape redeemed by marriage. Perhaps Charles enjoyed a tourist's memories of Spain's exotic southern culture from the safety of his rooms in autumnal London. But whatever they thought of the play, Charles and Buckingham were now as anti-Spain as they had previously been pro-Spain, and over the winter months that followed they worked on persuading James to go to war with the Hapsburgs. Throughout 1624 preachers gave bellicose sermons that would have been banned a year earlier and anti-Spanish pamphlets openly appeared on the booksellers' stalls. Thomas Scott produced *The Second Part of Vox Populi*, in which he showed Gondomar explaining to a council of Spanish dignitaries his stratagems for ruining England. Dedicated to James's daughter and son-in-law, "The High and Mighty Princes, Frederick and Elizabeth, by the Grace of God, King and Queen of Bohemia, Princes Palatine of the Rhine etc," it left its readers in no doubt of what to expect. The title page was engraved with a portrait of Gondomar himself, and two other engravings in the text showed the council of Spaniards and a conclave of Jesuits. Gondomar himself is described as "appearing in the likeness of Machiavelli," while behind Gondomar in the portrait appear his "chair of ease," a reference to the anal fistula from which he reputedly suffered, and his sedan chair. Both items would appear as props in the staging of Middleton's *Game* in August 1624.

Londoners knew Gondomar. They recognized his portrait in print and they would recognize him when Middleton put him on stage. Although by far the biggest city in England, the population of London in 1624 was still sufficiently small for gossip to travel rapidly by word of mouth. There was even a local Exchange for gossip: Paul's Walk. The nave of St. Paul's Cathedral, on the western side of the walled City, was the meeting place for those who wanted to know what was happening: "Certainly, for the first few decades of the [seventeenth] century, news was still primarily an oral commodity, and its emporium was the nave of St Paul's cathedral" (Love, *Culture and Commerce*, p. 193). Outside the doors of St. Paul's, in the churchyard around St. Paul's Cross where sermons were given and public announcements were made, was the center of the book trade. Here booksellers had their stalls and the title pages of topical works would be on display. Peter Blayney estimates that at the beginning of the seventeenth century there were twenty-eight booksellers cheek-by-jowl in the churchyard (*Bookshops*, p. 76), and other major booksellers had premises nearby in Fleet Street to the west, and further east within the City. Charles's adventure in Spain and his safe return were the subject of, by one estimate, "a minimum of 25 per cent of all publications in 1623" (Wikeley, "*Honor Conceal'd*," p. 189). News traveled orally through the watermen carrying fares on the Thames, at the bottom of the hill to the south of St. Paul's: they were "evermore telling strange news, most commonly lies" (Capp, *World*, p. 8). And finally, news circulated in manuscript. By the early 1620s there was a sophisticated production system for regular newsletters about significant events in London, including detailed reports of the debates in Parliament on the Spanish Match. Subscribers chose whether to receive a short or long newsletter and whether to receive it weekly or more frequently; the compiler of the newsletter employed scribes to make and dispatch multiple copies (Love, *Culture and Commerce*, pp. 9–22). Thus genuine news, gossip, innuendo, and fabrications alike circulated quickly within the square mile of the City and beyond.

The culmination of this frenzy of interest in Spanish matters was Thomas Middleton's *Game* of 1624. On one level the play is an allegory of good and evil represented by a chess game, but the actors playing the pieces clearly impersonated James (White King), Charles (White Knight), Buckingham (White Duke), Philip IV (Black King), and Gondomar (the villainous Black Knight). With six surviving manuscript texts and two printed editions, we have more contemporary copies of this play than of any other from the period.[3] Middleton's source here was *The Second Part of Vox Populi*. Not only do the Black pieces act out some of the deceits that Scott attributes to Gondomar and to the Jesuits, but the printed quartos also have title-page illustrations that clearly derive from the engravings in Scott's pamphlet (Astington, "Visual Texts," pp. 239–45). The play is an open attack on Philip IV and, especially, on Gondomar, even though the ambassador had been back in Spain for two years by the time the play appeared. The players – the King's Men, the company patronized by James himself – must have realized that they were taking a risk in staging the play and gave it an unprecedented run of nine consecutive performances, to make as much profit as they could as quickly as possible. Yet, when questioned, the players were able to produce a license to act the play issued on 12 June by the Master of the Revels, Henry Herbert (Bentley, *Jacobean and Caroline Stage*, vol. 1, p. 104).

The question of how Herbert came to license such a contentious performance has puzzled scholars (Heinemann, *Puritanism*, pp. 151–71; Limon, *Dangerous Matter*, pp. 118–21). That the risk was considered worth taking reflects a number of factors. First, the play was an allegory. Herbert could claim that the text as he saw it was innocuous and he did not know that the players would impersonate Gondomar (see Janet Clare's essay in this volume, p. 176). Second, the play was staged in August, when the king and Privy Council were away from London. Third, as we have seen, Spain was still in the news, so the performances played to packed houses. Fourth, the players relied on support from within James's circle. Master of the Revels Herbert was a cousin of Lord Chamberlain Herbert, the theatre-loving Earl of Pembroke who was part of the anti-Spanish faction. More importantly, the Duke of Buckingham and Charles were known to be now in sympathy with the sentiments implicit in the play and might be supposed to welcome overt support for their current policy of war with Spain. The script flatters Charles by casting him as White Knight, who finally outwits Black Knight (Gondomar) and claims "checkmate by discovery." And finally, we should not overlook the fact that the play's mockery of Gondomar must simply have been funny, in a way that it is impossible to understand at this distance in time. Satire is always dangerous – its edge is part of its humor. Here, Middleton allowed the audience to confront its enemies and to defeat them. He took away the fear of Spain and Gondomar by laughing at them.

The King's Men were literally "the King's servants." In 1604, for example, when he had several ambassadors visiting at once and not enough courtiers, James had employed them to wait on the Spanish delegation who were negotiating the Treaty of London (Barroll, *Politics*, pp. 49–59); and when James died in 1625, they were given an allowance for mourning clothes and walked in his funeral procession. For the king's own players to be so critical of Spain demonstrated how far attitudes had changed since Charles and Buckingham set out for Madrid in 1623. Although Gondomar's replacement as ambassador complained to James and the play was closed down, less effort was made to punish the players than might have been expected. The Council made an investigation and the Lord Chamberlain wrote to the King's Men to prohibit them from playing, but they were in business again after a few days.

A warrant was issued for Middleton's arrest and his son stood surety for him, but we have no evidence that the playwright suffered any penalty (Bentley, *Jacobean and Caroline Stage*, vol. 1, pp. 11–12). On the contrary, in 1625, when Charles became king, Middleton was commissioned to write a pageant to celebrate his entry into London.[4] Middleton not only retained his post of City Chronologer, but in 1626 the Drapers' Company commissioned him to write the inaugural pageant for the new Lord Mayor. *The Triumphs of Health and Prosperity* was Middleton's last work.

Of Middleton's Spanish plays, *Changeling* remained in repertory until the 1660s and is now acknowledged as one of the greatest plays of its age. *Gypsy* was given a private performance before the heir to the throne and *Game* made Middleton a household name in London. The obsession with Spain had served Middleton well.

### NOTES

1. For analysis of the politics of this period, see Cogswell, *Revolution* and Thomas Cogswell's essay in this volume, p. 126; Heinemann, *Puritanism*; and P. H. Wilson, *Europe's Tragedy*, esp. pp. 116–67.
2. Hosted at http://ems.kcl.ac.uk
3. For a full discussion of the extraordinary complexities of this play, see Taylor, *Companion*, pp. 712–911 and *Middleton*, pp. 1773–9, 1825–9.
4. The Entry was canceled because of plague (Taylor, *Middleton*, pp. 1898–1900).

# PART III

# *The theatrical context*

## CHAPTER 17

# The social cartography of Middleton's theatres

### Andrew Gurr

To make sense of Middleton's plays we need to "place" the companies and playhouses he wrote for and their distinct social allegiances. From 1602 onwards this exceptional Londoner wrote for a uniquely wide range of amphitheatres and so-called "private" indoor theatres, some nearly thirty years old, others new. The kinds of audience who attended these different venues need identifying, if only to indicate the complexity of Middleton's own attitude towards his society. Born as he was in the center of the city, we might well ask why he chose to move his entire family away from London a mile south of the Thames for the last seventeen years of his life.

Middleton's own social allegiance was not so obviously to the gentry as birth and his early city comedies for the boys' companies might suggest. His first plays were for the Admiral's Men, one of the two designated duopoly companies in London. They were famous for, among other plays about the city, Dekker's *The Shoemaker's Holiday*. That play, staged in 1599 at the Rose, celebrated the lowest of London's social levels, handicraft apprentices. It has a scene in which a group of shoemakers armed with cudgels outface a party of gentry armed with the standard gentry gear, their swords. Such allegiance was the expectation in the company where Middleton's writing career started. Through the rich period that followed, however, he soon started to diversify.

The year 1602, after Middleton was first noted as "accompaninge the players," was an excellent year for youngsters keen on writing plays. The eight-year-old Privy Council order restricting the London companies to only two, the Lord Chamberlain's and the Lord Admiral's, had lost its power by 1600 under the pressure of audience demand and entrepreneurial enterprise, so that by then as many as six companies, two of them made up of boy players, were in London demanding fresh plays. London had a massive appetite for new material, since each playhouse had to promise something fresh every afternoon. Moreover, with the renewed boys' companies staging plays at venues inside the city, the different types of playhouse in use created divisions among the social groups that went to particular types of playhouse and playing company. Middleton's first plays were written for the companies using outdoor playhouses under Philip Henslowe, who was then running two companies, the Admiral's at the Fortune and Worcester's at the ageing Rose. Worcester's was the first company of adult players besides the original duopoly to succeed in getting a foothold in London. It prospered, becoming Queen Anne's Men at the end of 1603 and having the Red Bull built for it in 1604. This rapid enlargement in the number of playing companies meant not only that the demand for new plays more than doubled in this decade, when the new king gave playgoing his personal cachet by making himself and his family patrons of all the companies with a foothold inside London, but also that the makeup of audiences for plays became more diverse. Soon the new range of distinct audience types began to feature in the plays. Middleton stood at the heart of this growth, and his plays reflect this diversification. Through the following twenty years, as Scott McMillin has noted, "No playwright of his time had his work performed on a greater variety of London stages" (*Middleton*, p. 77).

His life shows equally diverse signs of his social allegiance in London. Born in 1580 in the parish of St. Lawrence Jewry near Cheapside in the center of London, son of a bricklayer with gentry origins, Middleton had gentry status and went to study at The Queen's College, Oxford in 1598. His first writing, though, was for the citizen-loyal Admiral's Men. While working for them he met and married Maria, the sister of Thomas Marbeck, an Admiral's player and musician. Their son Edward was born in 1604. By then he was writing plays for the Paul's boys' company. For them he produced the satirical *The Phoenix, A Mad World, My Masters, Michaelmas Term, Your Five Gallants, A Trick to Catch the Old One,* and *The Puritan Widow.* All these can be classed as "city comedies," based on contemporary London life and characters, and normally owing more social allegiance to the younger gentry of the court and the Inns of Court than to the citizens. The boys' company plays reflected London life and the running conflict between young gentry and citizens, especially the wives and daughters of the more affluent merchants. Since most of the city comedy plots were based on penniless gentry trying to get love or money and preferably both, chiefly by seducing fools, mostly female citizens, the allegiance and appeal the boys' company expected of its audiences was upper-class rather than the lower-class allegiance marked most clearly at the outdoor theatres used by the Admiral's Men.

Yet just how precise it is to include the plays written for the boys' companies in the category known as "city comedies," and exactly where the main targets for Middleton's wit were to be found among London's complex social divisions and groups of playgoers, are matters for considerable debate. Throughout the years of the boys' companies, which expired during the long plague closure of 1608–9, Middleton continued writing for companies playing at the outdoor theatres, with their much broader social allegiance. Writing with Dekker in 1604 for the Fortune he produced *The Patient Man and the Honest Whore*, and then, after a few plays for the King's Men at the Globe, still in collaboration with Dekker he wrote *The Roaring Girl* for the Fortune company in 1611. By himself for the same company he wrote his own distinctive version of the city comedies, *No Wit/Help like a Woman's*, in which a loyal wife outwits every male and female in the play. While writing for both sides of the social fence, however, in 1609 he moved his family well outside the city to the then-remote suburb of Newington Butts, a mile south of the river, where between 1575 and 1595 a playhouse that Henslowe took an interest in had been in occasional use. This change of residence seems to have accompanied a switch in the subjects of his plays. By 1613, once his celebrated collaboration with William Rowley began, he diverged into writing *A Chaste Maid in Cheapside*, again a city comedy like *No Wit*, this time for the Lady Elizabeth's Men, Rowley's company, at the Swan, another outdoor playhouse. Both these plays made heroes of the citizen women whom the city comedies usually made into gullible victims of gentry enterprise.

In his last years he renewed his versatility by writing for what seems to have been his final venue, Christopher Beeston's new Cockpit, the first playhouse to rival the Blackfriars as an exclusive indoor venue. For the Cockpit he most likely produced what are now regarded as his most celebrated plays: *The Changeling* (1622, with Rowley) and probably *Women Beware Women*, whose date is uncertain. Most likely these were written along with *The Spanish Gypsy* (again with Rowley) for the Lady Elizabeth's Men, a company that changed its patron and its playhouses several times, using the old Swan, the even older Curtain, and the Red Bull as their outdoor playhouses, but also for some time the new indoor venue the Cockpit. In 1616 and after, still with Rowley, he may have written *A Fair Quarrel* and *An/The Old Law* for the company that Rowley then led, Prince Charles's Men, when it was caught in a process of switching between the indoor and outdoor playhouses under the general management of Christopher Beeston, who ran both the Red Bull and from 1616 the Cockpit.

Through much of this twenty-year writing career Middleton also produced entertainments for the court and the city. Consequently any particular allegiance he might have had in the wide social range of London's society is difficult to identify, if only because from at least 1613 he was regularly writing shows and "Triumphs" for civic dignitaries, particularly the annual Lord Mayor's show. In 1620 his appointment as City Chronologer brought him a regular income and committed him to continue the mayoral and other pageants he had been writing since 1613.

His initial playwriting for the Admiral's continued intermittently for a good ten years, and plays for the other outdoor playhouses went on much longer. Thus his early shift to Paul's Boys at the tiny playhouse nestling on the flanks of the cathedral was a radical switch, and we can only speculate about why he found them such an attractive alternative to the adult players. The two boys' companies did have freedoms that the adult companies lacked. *Phoenix* was among the first of the "city comedies" staged for the wealthier section of London's playgoers. Having a far smaller capacity for audiences than the outdoor venues, the indoor boys' companies charged a lot more for admission and consequently played to much more "select" audiences. Their writers expected the great majority of their audiences to be people of leisure. The indoor playhouses gave their richest clients closest proximity to the stage, sitting them in boxes flanking the stage or on stools on the stage itself, whereas the outdoor venues allowed those who paid least to stand round the flanks of the stage. In his commendatory verse for Fletcher's *Faithful Shepherdess*, a play written in 1608 or so for the boys at Blackfriars, Ben Jonson wrote that the main indoor audience in that playhouse comprised

> *Gamster, Captaine, Knight, Knights man,*
> *Lady,* or *Pusill,* that weares maske or fan,
> *Velvet,* or *Taffeta* cap, rank'd in the darke
> With the shops *Foreman* or some such *brave sparke*
> That may judge for his sixe-pence.

Gamblers, soldiers, gentry and their servants, ladies and rich whores, the usual indoor patrons, could share their places with the head of a handicraft shop. Anyone of such a low rank would pay only the minimal price at Blackfriars, because sixpence was half a day's wage, getting him nothing more than a seat in the top gallery furthest from the stage. It cost five times that much to sit in a box alongside the stage. Such an exclusive position was thirty times the price of standing alongside the stage at the Globe, Fortune, or Red Bull. The year 1600, when the Privy Council's duopoly collapsed and boys' companies reopened at indoor venues, was the first time prices came to determine the character of different playhouse audiences.

The audience range that Middleton wrote his plays for was hugely varied. The social range of Jacobean London's playgoers was vast, and each segment of society maintained its own traditions, each with its own kinds of dress and behavior. Laborers wore wool, usually with leather jerkins; house servants dressed in blue; the gentry wore swords; and ladies often went outdoors veiled or masked to protect their white complexions. They flaunted velvets and silks, while the citizenry wore linen and wool. Courtiers wore shades of scarlet. Officially, gold ornaments were worn only by the nobility, as the Sumptuary Laws, which King James abolished in 1604, had demanded. Such distinctive attire continued in use to declare social status.

At the outdoor amphitheatres such as the Rose, the Fortune, the Red Bull, and the Globe, the social range was extreme, locations inside them mainly fixed by price differentials. People from the lowest social level could stand in the yard – in 1621 John Taylor wrote of how "a beggar with his many" could watch a play from the yard, "all in for one penny" (Gurr, *Playgoing*, p. 280). At the other extreme, in 1636 the Lord Chamberlain, Philip Earl of Pembroke, quarreled with King Charles's cousin the Duke of Lennox over the key to a privileged box at the Blackfriars (Gurr, *Playgoing*, p. 293). On the whole, citizens and artisans, including apprentices in the yard surrounding the stage, dominated the outdoor audiences, while the indoor venues were ruled by law students and other gentry, who, officially, were supposed to live off the money from their lands, so never took employment. Nashe called such idle gentry "afternoon's men," a euphemism for drunkards who never got out of bed before noon.

In 1615 social difference between the indoor and outdoor playhouses began to affect the thinking of the Master of the Revels when he was choosing plays to entertain the court through the long Christmas season. From then on his orders to the companies at the Fortune, Red Bull, and other outdoor playhouses to perform for the court came to an end. The King's Men continued to dominate court performances because by then its use of the indoor Blackfriars had shown it to be easily the most socially favored company in London. The reason for the Master rejecting outdoor plays must have related to the title increasingly (and derisively) given to the Fortune and the Red Bull as "citizen playhouses." Under James the city and the court kept their distance from one another. Middleton's attempts in his mayoral pageants from 1620 onwards to emphasize the need for cooperation between king and city contain some intricate reflections on that distance.

Changing conditions in playing through these years suggest that some of the reasons why Middleton made his shifts from one playhouse to another were quite practical. By 1607 the boys at Paul's playhouse had closed, and the Blackfriars company was in serious trouble for its audacious satires. The former duopoly companies, the King's Men at the Globe and the Prince's at the Fortune, were a safer bet. Later Middleton wrote indifferently for indoor and outdoor venues for reasons that may reflect his chosen company's varying fortunes with their playhouses rather than any particular social allegiance. Just as the King's Men's plays shifted seasonally from indoor to outdoor and back, so Middleton's plays depended for their venues on whatever resource the company he sold his plays to could secure for itself. His later plays for the King's Men might equally be staged at the outdoor Globe or the indoor Blackfriars, and similarly his long alliance with the clown Will Rowley and his company meant that their plays switched unpredictably between outdoor and indoor playhouses. Once Christopher Beeston got the Cockpit into use he had his own reasons for using his control of the Red Bull along with his indoor venue to switch companies from one to the other.

Besides his exceptional coverage of the full range of playhouse venues in Jacobean London, Middleton developed a powerful commitment to both court and civic celebrations. Over the years six of his plays appeared at court, starting with two of his boys' company comedies, *Phoenix* and *Trick*, both of them staged for the king before 1608. After the boys' company years, through the next decade King James saw the Prince's Men's play *No Wit*, and the Lady Elizabeth's *Quarrel*. In the 1620s Prince Charles saw *Changeling* and, in his anti-Spanish phase, *Gypsy*. All the plays chosen for the court, bar *Changeling*, were comedies. Of Middleton's civic entertainments, some were composed for members of the nobility, although most of the fourteen pageants for which scripts survive were for the City.

His first direct involvement in the annual civic entertainments was two scripts for the brothers Hugh and Thomas Myddleton. One was for Hugh Myddelton's Michaelmas pageant celebrating his great work of rechanneling London's rivers and building the 40-mile New River canal in 1613. The celebration was held at the new cistern in Islington. On the same day Hugh Myddelton's brother Thomas, the playwright's namesake, was elected the next Lord Mayor. In his matching pageant for Thomas, called *The Triumphs of Truth*, Middleton developed the kind of celebration scripted in previous years by Anthony Munday, another poet from the Henslowe group, who had collaborated with Middleton but who under King James wrote nothing more for the stage, creating only each year's mayoral pageants. At the end of *Truth* Middleton acknowledged Munday's continuing contributions to the mayoral shows.

Middleton's next contribution to civic events was to lay out the London script for the investiture of Charles as Prince of Wales in 1616, which he called *Civitatis Amor*. From then on he largely took over from Munday as the chief writer for the mayoral pageants. Between 1602 and 1616 Munday had scripted nine. Middleton wrote one for each new Lord Mayor in 1617, 1619, 1621, 1622, and 1623 (with Munday), and produced his last mayoral pageant, after a break probably caused by the upsets over *A Game at Chess*, in 1626, a year before his death. As the printed text of each asserted, they were "performed through the city" each year on October 29, the Festival of St. Simon and St. Jude. The mayor's traditional route went by water from Westminster, where he took his mayoral oath, to Baynard's Castle on the north bank of the Thames below Fleet Street where he disembarked, and then up Ludgate Hill to St. Paul's and along Cheapside to the Guildhall. The prescribed devices and speeches scripted by Middleton were set at intervals along the way.

Such a diverse range of writing presses us to ask just where in this complex and competitive situation between citizens and gentry, city and court, did Middleton hold his own allegiance. The very complexity of his identifiable stances suggests that he was far too acute to take sides readily. He was never an overt radical. We should perhaps keep in mind Linda Woodbridge's point about the "overwhelming conservatism of Renaissance satire, whose targets were not obnoxious authority or repressive convention but fops, usurers, outlandishly dressed women, smokers, lying travelers – those who failed to conform to repressive convention. Paradoxically, early modern organized rebelliousness was a tool of social continuity. In its triumph, the younger generation ultimately became indistinguishable from the generation it supplanted" (*Scythe*, pp. 212–13). That may or may not apply to Middleton himself. His versatility must reflect his personal outlook. His class loyalties were complex, but he was always careful to hold back from the kind of partisan sympathies that Dekker exploited in *The Shoemaker's Holiday*. He had his own allegiances – for instance, he seems to have held consistently to a much higher view of the role of women in London's society than most of his peers – but in the end they were well concealed.

CHAPTER 18

# *The boys' plays and the boy players*

## David Kathman

Thomas Middleton first made his name in the theatre by writing comedies for the Children of Paul's, one of the two boys' acting companies that became immensely popular in London in the first decade of the seventeenth century. Middleton wrote five plays for Paul's between 1603 and 1607 – *The Phoenix, Michaelmas Term, A Trick to Catch the Old One, A Mad World, My Masters*, and *The Puritan Widow* – and several of his plays were later performed by other boys' companies, notably *Your Five Gallants* by the rival Blackfriars Boys. While Middleton did collaborate on several plays for other companies during this period, the comedies he wrote for Paul's are among his most popular plays to this day, and among the most popular examples of London "city comedies."

While these plays can still be enjoyed today without any knowledge of their origins, it is significant that they were written for companies of boys, rather than adults. The Elizabethan and early Jacobean boys' companies were notorious for the topicality and scathing satire that eventually contributed to their downfall, and the fact that Middleton cut his dramatic teeth in this environment was to influence the rest of his career. To modern observers, these companies, in which boys played all the adult roles, including highly sexualized ones, may seem exotic and unusual. Even so, knowing something about the boys who performed in these companies and the conditions under which they worked is helpful for a full understanding of Middleton's early dramatic output.

### EARLY HISTORY OF THE BOYS' COMPANIES

The boy actors for whom Middleton wrote in the early seventeenth century were maintaining a dramatic tradition going back more than a century. English choirboys had sometimes been used for singing parts in medieval drama, and in the late middle ages there is occasional evidence of grammar school boys and choirboys putting on plays. Such performances became much more common in the sixteenth century, with the Children of the Chapel Royal and the choristers of St. Paul's being most prominent. In the middle of the century, the dramatic activities of both companies became more regular, the Chapel Children under Richard Edwards and William Hunnis, the Paul's choristers under Sebastian Westcott (Hillebrand, *Child Actors*). Other boys' companies became popular too, such as those of Westminster School and Windsor Chapel; between 1564 and 1576 more than forty plays were performed at court by companies of boys (Gurr, *Shakespearian Playing Companies*, pp. 227–9).

A major turning point came in the mid 1570s, when the boys of Paul's and the Chapel Royal both began performing regularly in London for paying customers, ostensibly as rehearsals for their court performances. This was part of a commercial explosion that also resulted in the building of three open-air playhouses – the Theatre, the Curtain, and Newington Butts – and the conversion of four London inns into part-time playhouses, all within about two years. By December 1575, Sebastian Westcott had converted a room in the almonry on the south side of St. Paul's Cathedral into a playhouse, and the boys were performing there for "great gain."[1] In August 1576 Richard Farrant, former master of the Windsor Chapel boys and now deputy master of the Chapel Royal boys, leased several rooms in the Blackfriars compound in the southwest corner of London and converted them into an indoor playhouse in which the Chapel boys were soon performing. In 1578 "the children of her majesty's chapel" and "the children of Paul's" were among six playing companies allowed by the Privy Council (Berry [ed.], "Playhouses," p. 310).

These early commercial boys' companies were popular, but a combination of external and internal factors eventually led to their downfall. Richard Farrant and Sebastian Westcott died in 1580 and 1582 respectively, leading to several years when the Paul's and Chapel boys merged under the patronage of the Earl of Oxford. This combined company played at court in 1584–5 under the leadership of Henry Evans and Oxford's secretary John Lyly, but they lost the Blackfriars playhouse in 1584 in a dispute over the lease. Subsequently they performed at Paul's for several more years under the leadership of choirmaster Thomas Giles, with Lyly as their most important playwright. Lyly had become famous for his highly stylized prose work *Euphues* (1578), and in the 1580s he wrote numerous plays for the boys' companies, including *Campaspe, Sapho and Phao, Gallathea*, and *Endymion*. These were mainly romantic comedies that included allegorical flattery of Queen Elizabeth, but also satirical portraits (real or perceived) of other court figures (Gair, *Children of Paul's*, p. 109). In 1589 Lyly was one of several

writers hired by the government to counter the satirical Puritan pamphlet-
eer Martin Marprelate, and the same year Paul's Boys put on plays attacking
Martin. The ensuing controversy, presaging the later troubles of the
Jacobean children's companies, probably contributed to the Paul's playhouse being shut down around 1590.

## THE LATER BOYS' COMPANIES

After nearly a decade of suppression, the commercial boys' companies
returned in 1599, when Paul's Boys again began performing plays for the
paying public in the same space as before. They did so under a newly
appointed Master of the Choristers, Edward Pearce, with the financial back-
ing of the Earl of Derby (Berry, "Playhouses," p. 307). A year later the Chapel
Children also began performing for the public again, in a hall in the
Blackfriars complex that adjoined their earlier playhouse but was much larger.
This hall was owned by the famous actor Richard Burbage, whose father
James had tried unsuccessfully to make it the new playhouse of the Lord
Chamberlain's Men. On September 2, 1600, Burbage leased the hall to Henry
Evans, who had briefly held the lease on the earlier Blackfriars playhouse, and
who was backing the new company along with Nathaniel Giles, Master of the
Chapel Children, and John Robinson (Berry, "Playhouses," pp. 501–30).

The boys in these newly commercialized companies were typically
between 10 and 13 years old, somewhat younger than the 13- to 21-year-
old apprentices who played female roles in the adult companies (Kathman,
"Shakespeare's Boy Actors," pp. 222–3). Some of them became quite well
known, such as Salamon Pavy and Nathan Field of the Chapel boys, and
their companies became fierce rivals to the adult companies, including the
Chamberlain's Men of Shakespeare and Burbage. There was considerable
pressure to find talented boys, especially as both companies became more
commercial and drifted away from their origins as groups of choirboys. In
December 1600, Henry Evans and Nathaniel Giles kidnapped 13-year-old
Thomas Clifton to act in their Blackfriars playhouse, even though he could
not sing or read music. A lawsuit by the boy's father, Henry Clifton,
eventually forced Evans to give up control of the company in 1602, and in
early 1604 the company's connection with the Chapel Royal was broken
when King James issued a new patent (not including Nathaniel Giles) that
called them the Children of the Queen's Revels. Nothing exactly comparable happened to Paul's Boys, but by 1603 Edward Pearce had partnered
with a speculator, Thomas Woodford, who acted as the company's business
agent. Both companies went through various managers and investors over

the next several years (M. Shapiro, *Children*, pp. 18–29). In 1607 a new company of boys with no pretense of being choirboys, the Children of the King's Revels, started performing in a new playhouse in Whitefriars.

This commercialization and competition, along with the banning of prose and verse satire in 1599, led the boys' companies to become increasingly topical and satirical in their plays. They are referred to in *Hamlet* as an "eyrie of children" who "so be-rattle the common stages (for so they call them) that many wearing rapiers are afraid of goose-quills."[2] The boys' companies were key players in the so-called "War of the Theatres" between Ben Jonson, John Marston, and Thomas Dekker in 1599–1601; Jonson's *Cynthia's Revels* and *Poetaster* were performed by the Blackfriars Boys, while Marston's *Jack Drum's Entertainment* and (probably) *What You Will*, and Dekker's *Satiromastix*, were performed by Paul's Boys.[3] In early 1603 George Chapman was sued for writing a now-lost play for Paul's Boys, "The Old Joiner of Aldgate," a thinly disguised depiction of a real-life scandal over a rich heiress. While most Paul's and Blackfriars plays were not so directly topical, those companies did become known for their satirical city comedies. These took place in contemporary London among the citizen and professional classes, were full of local allusions, and took satirical jabs at common city types such as grasping lawyers and jealous old citizens.

This satirical bent eventually got the new boys' companies in trouble and led to their downfall, just as with the earlier incarnation of Paul's Boys. After James came to the throne, the Blackfriars Boys repeatedly clashed with members of his court. In late 1604 or early 1605 they performed Samuel Daniel's *Philotas*, which caused Daniel to be hauled before the Privy Council to explain the play's obvious parallels to the Essex Rebellion, still a sensitive subject. Later in 1605, they performed Chapman, Jonson, and Marston's *Eastward Ho!*, whose jokes about Scottish courtiers caused Jonson and Chapman to be imprisoned, followed in early 1606 by John Day's *Isle of Gulls*, which further mocked the Scots. In March 1608 James finally shut down the Blackfriars company after they performed another Scots-mocking play and Chapman's *The Conspiracy of Charles, Duke of Biron*, which depicted the Queen of France being slapped by the king's mistress. In August of that year the Blackfriars playhouse was taken over by the King's Men. Paul's Boys had avoided much conflict with the court, but Middleton's *Puritan* (1606) fiercely mocked Puritans as hypocrites and was attacked by William Crashaw in a Paul's Cross sermon in February 1608 (see Ian W. Archer's essay in this volume, p. 135). The company may have already been defunct by then (the last record of a specific performance is in June 1606), but in any case there is no sign of them after 1608.

The Jacobean boys' companies did have a last gasp of popularity after the long plague closure of 1608–9, when a new version of the Children of the Queen's Revels, including former Blackfriars star Nathan Field, took over the Whitefriars playhouse of the now defunct King's Revels boys. This company played at court numerous times, but it appears to have been a "children's" company in name only, since Field and other colleagues such as William Barkstead were in their early twenties. In 1613 they merged with Lady Elizabeth's Men, another youth-oriented company, but after 1616 separate versions of the Revels company and Lady Elizabeth's traveled around England performing under various patents.

## MIDDLETON'S PLAYS FOR THE BOYS' COMPANIES

As noted above, Middleton was one of the leading writers of city comedies for the boys' companies, mostly Paul's. The plays he wrote for these companies include some prototypical examples of London city comedy, illustrating most of the common tropes that such plays parodied, such as the prodigal gallant trying to recover his fortune from a greedy relative, or the high-born person in disguise. Looking at these plays in chronological order allows for a good overview of the development and evolution of city comedies, and also helps put Middleton's later career into context.[4]

The first play that Middleton wrote for Paul's, *Phoenix*, can be considered a sort of proto-city comedy. Although it is nominally set in Ferrara and the characters have Italian names, those characters behave very much like Londoners in the first year of King James's reign, when the play was written. The admirable lead character, the Phoenix, is a fairly transparent representation of James, but there is also much pointed satire, mainly at the expense of lawyers and other professional types who formed the core audience for Paul's. Various unsavory characters abuse the legal system and address each other in legal jargon, and a major subplot involves the Captain literally selling his wife in a reductio ad absurdum of merchant greed and the commodification of women. The play's disguised-nobleman plot has obvious similarities to Shakespeare's *Measure for Measure* (written around the same time and later revised by Middleton), but it was also a common device in Jacobean boys' plays such as Marston's *The Malcontent*, Lording Barry's *The Family of Love*, and Middleton's own *Five Gallants*.[5]

Middleton's next three plays for Paul's were *Michaelmas*, *Trick*, and *Mad World*, written between 1604 and 1606. These plays exhibit many similarities and are among the best, most popular examples of London city comedy. They are set in London (except for part of *Mad World* set in a country house) and satirize various city types, ranging from highborn gallants to underworld denizens. Their main plots are parodic variants on the fable of the prodigal son, which had been a staple of sixteenth-century morality-type plays.[6] All three plays involve prodigal heroes (Easy in *Michaelmas*, Witgood in *Trick*, Follywit in *Mad World*) who temporarily lose their estate to an older foil but eventually regain it. In the first two plays this main foil is an unscrupulous enemy (the merchant Quomodo in *Michaelmas*, Witgood's uncle Lucre in *Trick*), while in *Mad World* he is Follywit's genial grandfather Sir Bounteous Progress, himself something of a prodigal spendthrift. These plays especially parody the morality play conventions of repentance; Witgood and Jane in *Trick* and Penitent Brothel in *Mad World* appear to repent their sins at the end, but they do so in an ironic and cynical way. In *Michaelmas* and *Trick*, Easy's and Witgood's wooing of their older adversaries' women provides some Oedipal overtones, but these illicit couples lack much romantic spark and remain physically separated, illustrating how much romance had become subordinated to satire in the Jacobean children's companies. At the end of *Mad World*, Follywit discovers that his new wife is not only a courtesan, but his grandfather's former mistress; however, after his grandfather gives the couple a thousand marks, Follywit replies, "Tut, give me gold, it makes amends for vice" (5.2.311), illustrating the cynical attitude of these plays towards money and sex.

Middleton's final city comedy for Paul's, *Puritan*, differs from the others in that the main object of his satire is religion, specifically puritan non-conformists. The play was written in the wake of the 1605 Gunpowder Plot and the subsequent Oath of Conformity, which required Catholics to swear allegiance to the king. This environment was hostile both to Catholics and to Puritans, who thought the English Church should move further away from Catholicism. Middleton satirized Puritans through his title character and her servants Nicholas St Antlings and Simon St Mary Overies (named after notoriously puritan London parishes), depicting them as hypocrites engaged in Catholic-like practices (Hamilton, *Middleton*, pp. 509–13). As noted above, this play attracted the hostility of William Crashaw, who preached against it in February 1608, soon after it was printed.[7] It may have been one of the last plays performed at Paul's; in any case, Middleton's follow-up city comedy, *Five Gallants* (1607), was written for the Blackfriars boys' company. Its plot involves the unmasking of five false gallants representing satiric portraits of various types, and is a good example of the obsession with hidden identities found in city comedies by Middleton and others.

The heyday of the Jacobean boys' companies was soon over, but Middleton wrote one more comedy that could be considered a boys' company play. *A Chaste Maid in Cheapside* (1613) was written for Lady Elizabeth's Men shortly after they had merged with the Children of the Queen's Revels to form a single company of young men. It is an intricately plotted city comedy, arguably one of the last of the genre, in which nearly everybody except the virginal title character is an object of sharp satire. By this time, however, the stage satire of the previous decade had fallen out of fashion in favor of more romantic themes, exemplified by Shakespeare's late plays and by Beaumont and Fletcher. Middleton did write or coauthor several more comedies, some of them set in London, that feature such familiar plot elements as the prodigal son story. However, they are oriented less towards satire and more towards Fletcherian romance and sentimentality than his earlier city comedies; in fact, Middleton and Rowley's *Wit at Several Weapons* was printed in the 1647 Beaumont and Fletcher folio and long attributed to that duo (*Middleton*, p. 980; *Companion*, pp. 375–7). Despite this shift, Middleton remained very capable of biting satire to the end of his career, as shown by his last play, *A Game at Chess*. Middleton's city comedies for Paul's and Blackfriars are no longer quite as central as they used to be to his reputation as a playwright, but it is not much of an exaggeration to say that they were among the most important influences on the rest of his career.

## NOTES

1. Gair, *Children of Paul's*, argued that the playhouse was in the cloisters of the cathedral's chapter house, but Bowers, "Playhouse of the Choristers of Paul's," and Berry, "Where Was the Playhouse?" independently and convincingly argued that it was in the almoner's house immediately to the west, though they differed over the exact location of the playhouse within this building.
2. Shakespeare, *Hamlet*, P. Edwards (ed.), 2.2.315–18. This passage appears only in the First Folio version of the play, but the 1603 First Quarto includes a shorter section alluding to the boy players.
3. Some scholars, such as Knutson in *Playing Companies*, have argued that the War of the Theatres was largely a marketing ploy and much less contentious than historians have generally assumed; however, Bednarz, *Poets' War*, argued that the "war" involved real philosophical differences.
4. Other boys' company plays not discussed here (such as *Blurt Master Constable*) have been attributed to Middleton in the past, but here only the boys' plays included in the Oxford *Middleton* are considered, as I take these attributions to be correct.
5. *The Family of Love* used to be commonly attributed to Middleton, but G. Taylor, Mulholland, and Jackson ("Thomas Middleton") argue convincingly

for Barry's authorship. Cathcart argues that Barry was revising an earlier version of the play by John Marston (*Marston*, pp. 79–140).

6. Such parodies were extremely popular in the first decade of the seventeenth century, in Paul's and Blackfriars plays such as *Eastward Ho!* and *The Knight of the Burning Pestle*, and in adult company plays such as *The London Prodigal*; see M. Shapiro, *Children*, pp. 120–7.

7. For more on *Puritan*, see Andrew Gordon's essay in this volume, p. 37.

## CHAPTER 19

# The adult companies and the dynamics of commerce

## Roslyn L. Knutson

When Thomas Middleton began to write for the stage in the late spring of 1602, he served an apprenticeship of sorts with the Admiral's Men at the Fortune and Worcester's Men at the Rose, after which he sold his work to the Children of Paul's at the playhouse on the grounds of St. Paul's Cathedral. By 1606, however, he was writing again for the adult companies, though not exclusively; and he would continue that business relationship throughout his career. This professional arc – from men's companies with large outdoor playhouses, to a boys' company in a small indoor theatre, to the men's again – challenges the scholarly truism that the so-called elite venues and their dramatists were aesthetically and financially superior to the so-called citizen playhouses with their comparatively down-market fare. The smart money, accordingly, would tell Middleton to stay with the elite venues, but he did not do that. Consequently, his plays offer a perspective on the commercial dynamic of the adult companies, specifically the alleged binary division of audiences into "citizen" and "elite." The contention here is that Middleton complemented his sassy boys' company style of city comedy with "retro" features of offerings from the 1590s, and as a result his contributions to the men's repertories from 1606 onwards resist classification as up- or down-market, as elite or citizen fare.

Considered objectively, the adult companies offered a novice playwright distinct advantages. They had a voracious appetite for new plays to fill their calendar of five or six performances per week. In the book of accounts kept by Philip Henslowe (familiarly known as *Henslowe's Diary*), the Admiral's Men at the Rose from mid 1594 into 1597 performed thirty-five plays a year on average, about twenty of which were new; from 1598 to 1603, they laid out cash for completed scripts as well as piecework for additions to existing plays at the rate of two or three a month throughout the year. The adult companies also offered the opportunity to collaborate with experienced writers. The initial records of Middleton as dramatist in *Henslowe's Diary* on May 22 and 29, 1602 show him joining the team of Anthony Munday, Michael Drayton, John Webster, and Thomas Dekker on a script for the Admiral's Men at the Fortune called "Caesar's Fall" (Henslowe, *Diary*, pp. 201–2).[1] Middleton would work with these men again in the years ahead, and by learning the art of collaboration early, he positioned himself to acquire new partners such as William Shakespeare and William Rowley. Through an association with Henslowe in 1602–3, Middleton had the chance to write for two companies simultaneously. By October he had begun a project for Worcester's Men for a play unnamed (Henslowe, *Diary*, p. 217); in November he had finished "Randall, Earl of Chester" for the Admiral's Men (Henslowe, *Diary*, pp. 205–6). Towards the end of his career, Middleton would team up with William Rowley and Worcester's dramatist, Thomas Heywood, to write *An/The Old Law* for Prince Charles's (I) Men, which was newly under the management of Christopher Beeston, himself an alumnus of the 1602–3 company of Worcester's Men. The adult companies toured more consistently than did the boys', and they had more invitations to perform at court.[2] By working for the men's companies, Middleton was therefore challenged to design scripts for multiple venues and diverse audiences.[3]

Despite these advantages, scholars have traditionally considered employment by the men's companies after 1600 as second-rate unless the company was the Chamberlain's/King's Men. Several biases underlie this opinion. One is the preference for the company that acquired Shakespeare as house dramatist. Theatre historians used to promote Shakespeare not only for the quality of his work but also for his eschewal of collaboration. Built into this privileging was the belief that most other dramatists lived hand-to-mouth, shopping themselves indiscriminately to partners and companies for repertory fillers that were soon discontinued and forgotten. Another bias was for indoor playhouses and their allegedly elite audiences, access to which the King's Men gained by acquiring the Blackfriars Playhouse in 1608. In contrast, the other men's companies in London after 1603 had no indoor site until the Phoenix (alias Cockpit) was built in 1617. A third bias concerns the repertory. Quite simply, any dramatic formula Shakespeare did not choose was considered inferior. Thus companies were assumed to be pandering to audiences of the middling sort when they acquired scripts featuring biblical narratives, hagiographies from John Foxe's *Book of Martyrs*, or moralities on the middle-class virtues of thrift and marital fidelity.

The long-standing disdain for adult companies and their repertories is evident in Andrew Gurr's comparison of the Admiral's Men (who became the Prince Henry's Men in 1603) with Shakespeare's company: "by the end of their long life the Admiral's company catered chiefly for the mass of 'citizen' playgoers at the cheaper outdoor playhouses, whereas their opposites, the King's Men, fed and chiefly lived off the richer playgoers at the indoor Blackfriars" (*Shakespeare's Opposites*, p. 4). Recently, however, scholars have begun to rehabilitate those citizen playhouses. Lucy Munro points out that distinctions "were not as fixed as some would have liked, and companies, dramatists and actors swapped between playhouses throughout" the early decades of the seventeenth century ("Governing," p. 101). Questioning the opinion that the Globe slipped to a poor second after Blackfriars was acquired, I have argued that "the King's Men had two playhouses, both alike in quality" during Middleton's career ("Two Playhouses," p. 116). Much of what John Astington says about playing at the Red Bull is applicable to the Fortune, namely that the adult companies were "competitive players in a market" ("Playing the Man," p. 132), and that their plays were seen not only in London by "rowdy apprentices" but also at court by present and future rulers of England (p. 131).

Middleton's plays further rehabilitate the adult companies and their multiple venues by appealing to a broad spectrum of playgoers. An example is *No Wit/Help Like a Woman's*; or, *The Almanac*, which Prince Henry's Men played at the Fortune *c.* 1611. In this play, Middleton updated several comedic conventions and expanded the traditional festival ending into theatrical spectacle. John Jowett observes that the play "anticipates Restoration comedy" (*Middleton*, p. 779) in part by the promotion of the female characters such as Mistress Low-water beyond the models of Portia, Rosalind, and Viola, who are the enterprising, cross-dressing rescuers of comedic endings in Shakespeare's plays, 1596–1602. Mistress Low-water, in contrast, drives her financial and matrimonial plots from the outset. Further anticipating comedic trends, Middleton turned mismatches in gender identity into a harsher cultural interrogation of "incest and female homoeroticism" (Jowett, *Middleton*, p. 780). Consequently, his male characters are relatively marginalized. One exception is Savourwit, a manservant whose double entendres recall the verbal sparring of the boys' company comedies. Savourwit coarsens the romantic matches of the play and the comedic teleology of begetting to "a chopping girl with a plump buttock [who] / Will hoist a farthingale ... / And call a man between eleven and twelve / To take part of a piece of mutton with her" (250–3). Another is Weatherwise, one of the many suitors of the widow, Lady Goldenfleece. Weatherwise is a throwback to the humors characters of the 1590s. His personality disorder is to interpret all occasions by his ever-present almanac, as evident in the scenes he controls: the banquet, the wedding masque, and the epilogue. The banquet is laid out according to the signs of the zodiac, and each participant is seated accordingly. Weatherwise means for the device to reward him with "the widow's plumb-tree" (4.89); but she instead becomes enamored with Mistress Low-water, who is disguised as a young gallant. The final scene of the play is an extravagant masque in which the widow's disappointed suitors take the parts of Air, Fire, Water, and Earth. Jowett points to the use in the Revels Accounts of the play's subtitle, *The Almanac*, and suggests that the performance given by Prince Henry's Men on December 29, 1611 "highlighted Weatherwise" and his two set-piece scenes ("Middleton's *No Wit*," p. 194). By making a case for the humor character's spectacles as the most memorable features of the court performance, Jowett identifies "retro" devices supposedly catering to the citizenry as ones that appealed additionally to the elite.

Like *No Wit*, Middleton and Rowley's *A Fair Quarrel* was performed at citizen and elite venues; and by its success at both, it challenges arbitrary distinctions in audience taste. As a property of Prince Charles's (I) Men and Christopher Beeston, the play would have been performed outdoors at the Red Bull and indoors at the Phoenix (Cockpit). According to the title pages of both issues of its 1617 quarto, *Quarrel* was also performed at court "before the King" (*Companion*, p. 633). At least two aspects of the play account for its appeal across class lines. One is its handling of familial issues. As Suzanne Gossett has pointed out, *Quarrel* continues a theatrical interrogation of sibling dynamics begun in the domestic relations plays at the turn of the seventeenth century, including *A Woman Killed with Kindness* and *Measure for Measure*. In this category *Quarrel* "is unusually explicit about power relations between brothers and sisters, traces these relations through several social strata, and does not finally attempt to contain or deny all of the tensions released" (Gossett, "Sibling Power," 444). Those strata include the aristocracy (Lady Ager and her son); the military (the Colonel and his sister); and trade (the physician and his sister). Citing the sibling dynamics of the Ralph Verney family and that of the 3rd Duke of Buckingham (Edward Stafford), Gossett demonstrates that a brother's power was problematic for Jacobean citizenry and elite alike. A second pattern cutting across class boundaries – quarreling – is evoked by the title of the play, which had special resonance in the 1590s playhouse world. A play now lost entitled "Hot Anger Soon Cold" was written by Ben Jonson, Henry Porter, and Thomas Dekker for the Admiral's Men in August 1598. Within a month (September 22), Jonson would kill a fellow player in a duel (Gabriel Spencer, who had himself killed a man in a street fight in 1596).

Porter would be killed in less than a year (June 1599) in a duel with a fellow playwright (John Day). In Middleton and Rowley's *Quarrel* the hot anger is mitigated somewhat by its military context, but the chief roarer is a civilian, Chough, whose braggadocio diminishes his status as gentry. The second issue of the 1617 quarto advertises new scenes of "M$^r$ *Chaughs* . . . Roaring" (*Companion*, p. 633), and it would be tempting to see in the additions an appeal to an audience of rowdies. However, similarly debased aristocratic roarers such as Sir John Falstaff were hugely popular among elite audiences, and noblemen such as the Earl of Oxford were as given to hot anger as their social inferiors (see Jennifer Low's essay in this volume, p. 98).

Middleton wrote for the King's Men from *A Yorkshire Tragedy* (probably 1605) to *Anything for a Quiet Life* (1621). The expectation raised by scholars' division of playhouses into "citizen" and "elite," coupled with a hierarchy among companies that elevates the King's Men, is that Middleton's plays post-1608 would cater to that company's classier playhouse, the Blackfriars. However, the range of popular generic formulas in his contributions to the repertory suggests that Middleton had diverse audiences in mind. Those formulas include tragedies of true crime (*Yorkshire*) and revenge (*The Revenger's Tragedy, The Lady's Tragedy*); comedies of the "problem" and city variety (*More Dissemblers Besides Women, The Widow, Quiet Life*); pre-Norman chronicle history (*Macbeth, Hengist, King of Kent*); classical history (*Timon of Athens*); tragicomedy (*The Witch*), and the sui generis *A Game at Chess*. Furthermore, the textual and printing history of Middleton's plays for the King's Men provides no substantive support for the argument that he was writing primarily for audiences at the Blackfriars. The manuscript of *Witch* carries a subtitle specifying performance at Blackfriars; however, the date of the manuscript is 1624–5, nearly ten years after the debut of the play (Ioppolo, *Dramatists*, p. 147). The assignment to Blackfriars does not therefore necessarily locate the play's initial or intended venue. Three quartos of Middleton's plays for the King's Men carry title-page advertisements of the Blackfriars: *Widow, Hengist,* and *Quiet Life.* In each case, however, the editions appeared some thirty years or more after the opening runs of the plays and thus cannot be trusted as evidence of their initial or intended venues.

In order to argue that any given play acquired by the King's Men was designed specifically for the Globe or Blackfriars, scholars often turn to aspects of staging for evidence. A noisy, flashy stage moment is labeled "spectacle," a term that for Andrew Gurr raises images of "massed battles with drum and trumpet-calls, . . . [and] devils with fireworks" designed to thrill the masses at citizen playhouses (*Shakespearian Playing Companies*, p. 132). However, as Lucy Munro points out, "[s]pectacle is not necessarily unsophisticated in its use" ("Governing," p. 102). Middleton's *Witch* illustrates the point, with its "spectacular staging needs" that according to Marion O'Connor were "particularly well served by the theatrical resources . . . at the Blackfriars" (*Middleton*, p. 1128). In comparison, Gary Taylor sees the Middleton-enhanced *Macbeth*, which was either a repertorial companion or replacement in 1616 for *Witch*, to "have been a theatrical highlight at the Globe *or* Blackfriars" (*Middleton*, p. 1168 [emphasis added]). It seems likely that the *Macbeth* of 1606, as well as that of 1611, is lost; it is thus impossible to know how comparatively barren its witches' scenes were.[4] But a few common denominators between *Witch* and Middleton's additions to *Macbeth* show the resemblance of spectacle in plays with more than one venue. For example, in the 1616 *Macbeth*, Middleton retained the songs and presumably the dances from 3.3 and 5.3 of *Witch*, dropping the character of Firestone (Hecate's saucy son). The talking, singing, dancing, flying cat was carried over in these scenes, but his introduction as a product of Hecate's conjuring in 1.2, fiddle in hand, was omitted. Middleton dropped the lurid cooking scene in *Witch* (1.2), with its stage properties of serpents, snakes, and chrisom babe to be boiled for its flight-enhancing fat. Other missing elements include Firestone's darkly humorous banter, Hecate's conveniently impressive trance at the entry of a client (Sebastian), and the sub-motif of her sexual desire for a second client (Almachildes). Perhaps Middleton decided that the busy, brothel-like kitchen of *Witch* detracted from the motif of prophecy in *Macbeth*, or undermined the political dimension of pre-Norman Scotland history. But the result of his alterations to the Shakespearean *Macbeth* for a revival in 1616 was a considerable enhancement of the witches' scenes, though they still fell far short of the spectacular staging in his own *Witch*.

*Hengist, King of Kent*; or, *The Mayor of Queenborough*, which the King's Men acquired some time between 1616 and 1620, is considered "one of the most popular plays of the Jacobean and Caroline eras" (Ioppolo, *Middleton*, p. 1448). Like Middleton's contributions to adult company repertories generally, *Hengist* is a mix of retro and nouveau theatrical devices appealing to citizen and elite audiences alike. Several prominent features make it seem much more old-fashioned than its placement late in the chronology of Middleton's plays would suggest: the use of a presenter (the chronicler, Raynulph Higden); the focus on ancient British history in the story of Vortiger and the consequences for the kingdom of his inviting aid from Saxon invaders; complex dumb shows of both the iconographic and battlefield kind; a royal villainess; and a richly contrasting clown plot with its homespun economic problems and play-within-a-play. But *Hengist* also illustrates relatively recent theatrical agendas. The women of the play in their militant virginity (Castiza) or promiscuity (Roxena) are Jacobean, not Elizabethan. The wanton *and* murderous Roxena is also an extended topical allusion to the aristocratic subject of a recent political scandal (Frances Howard). The mayor of Queenborough is not merely a bumptious petty official but a vehicle for a "complex condemnation of the economic crisis" facing the cloth trade (Ioppolo, *Middleton*, p. 1449). Additionally, *Hengist* meshes sophisticated blank verse with malaprop-laced prose. In its double ending it balances the mayor's banquet (and its play-within-a-play that deteriorates into a food fight) with a fiery battle in which the disinherited Christian brothers win back the kingdom from the pagan usurpers.

By the time Middleton died in 1627, the theatrical landscape had changed significantly. Fewer adult companies were able to maintain a successful business year round, and boys' companies existed as extensions of the men's enterprises (i.e., Beeston's Boys). The playgoing habits of two Englishmen provide insight into the contrast between the late Elizabethan and early Caroline playhouse worlds. Edward Pudsey, a gentleman from Derbyshire, lived in London around 1600 and attended plays frequently; in his late twenties at the time (he married in 1605), Pudsey copied lines from many of these into his commonplace book, including excerpts of *The Patient Man and the Honest Whore*, by Middleton and Dekker. The salient feature of these notations for issues of audience class at the outset of Middleton's career is that they show Pudsey attending performances by adult and children's companies at the prominent outdoor and indoor playhouses without apparent favoritism. Sir Humphrey Mildmay, in comparison, attended indoor playhouses primarily but not exclusively, according to notations in his diary, which he began in 1633 at age 40 (he had married in 1616). These notations do not include a Middleton play, some number of which would have been available in reruns. The conclusion to draw is not that Pudsey liked Middleton's plays and Mildmay did not, for any reasons of content designed to appeal to specific audiences. Rather, the variables in the evidence of playgoing – age, marital status, class, personal taste – are too complex to support the reductive binary of "citizen" and "elite" for playhouses, playgoers, and repertories. A better measure of commercial dynamics in the Jacobean period than the assessment of audience taste by theatrical venue is the multipurpose appeal of Middleton's plays.

NOTES

1. The title "Two Shapes" in the May 29 entry is presumably a variant entry for "Caesar's Fall."

2. Middleton profited from one such performance in December 1602 when he was paid 5 shillings to write a prologue and epilogue "for the playe of bacon for the corte" (Henslowe, *Diary*, p. 207).

3. I rely heavily and gratefully on "Middleton's Theatres" by Scott McMillin for the view of the playhouse world in 1602 (pp. 74–87).

4. Taylor suggests that the pre-1616 *Macbeth* text "was much less impressive" in its dramatization of the occult than the text included in the 1623 Folio (*Middleton*, p. 1166).

CHAPTER 20

# *The theatre and political control*
## Janet Clare

By the time Middleton began to write for the stage in the early 1600s he had already brushed with censorship. Among the satirical works called in and publicly burnt in what has become known as the Bishop's Ban of 1599 was Middleton's *Microcynicon: Six Snarling Satires*, written when he was 19 (McCabe, *Satire*). These six "snarling satires," like those of John Marston and Joseph Hall, were directed at vice and social abuse, and his targets were generalized and anonymized: the usurer, the cheat, the sodomite, the prodigal. In the Epilogue to *Microcynicon* Middleton refers allusively to the raven that was once white and is now black, suggesting both social degeneration and the infection of writer and reader through immersion in satire (*Middleton*, p. 1984). Presumably it was the infectious nature of satire that concerned both the Privy Council and the ecclesiastical licensers for the press. As with most extreme acts of censorship, the bonfire of satires and the concurrent restrictions on the writing of history were tied more into the political moment. One of the repercussions of the clampdown on the print circulation of verse satire was its channeling into the theatre.

In his early comedies written for Paul's Boys, Middleton is as much the satirist as the dramatist: his targets were the new middle classes, the upwardly mobile, tricksters and fraudsters, and those who managed to live easily with their consciences. Unlike the case of his contemporaries Marston and Jonson, there is no evidence, documentary or textual, that Middleton's early satirical city comedies, which were performed in the intimate surroundings of the Paul's playhouse, attracted the censorship of the Master of the Revels. The procedures of early Jacobean censorship seem to have been in a state of flux and their operation was erratic, by turns lenient and reactionary (Clare, *Dramatic Censorship*, pp. 119–72). One of the most well-known cases is that of *Eastward Ho!*, written in 1605 by a triumvirate of satirists, Jonson, Marston, and Chapman, for the Children of the Queen's Revels. It is worth citing the case because some of the details correspond to the later reaction to *A Game at Chess*. The plays of the Queen's Revels, as detailed in the patent granted to the company, were to be licensed by the poet and coterie dramatist Samuel Daniel, a procedure which deviated from the well-established Elizabethan practice of licensing for performance by the Master of the Revels. *Eastward Ho!*, however, was not licensed by anyone. Later Chapman was to plead disingenuously that the dramatists considered there was nothing in the play likely to give offense and in any case the Lord Chamberlain was then away from London. Even if the text had been perused it is possible that it would not have invited censorship. Though the play included a few lines satirizing the king's knighting and privileging of fellow Scots, these are not particularly conspicuous when the text is read, but when a line such as, "I ken the man weel, hee's one of my thirty pound knights" is delivered on stage with a Scottish accent, the satire of the king would have been pronounced. An informer, a Scotsman, reported the performance to James, who reacted accordingly. For their indiscretions Jonson and Chapman were imprisoned (Marston fled the city) and were only released after numerous letters of appeal, including ones written to the king, the Earls of Pembroke, Suffolk, and Salisbury, and Lucy, Countess of Bedford. A succession of other satirical plays led to the Children of the Queen's Revels being stripped of royal patronage and to a tightening of censorship, a development which also seems evident in the manuscript of Middleton's *The Lady's Tragedy*.

It was when Middleton chose to make topical political comment in *Lady*, *The Witch*, and – notoriously – *Game* that his work became subject to censorship and suppression. The inferences about censorship drawn from bibliographical history are quite distinct; the three cases reveal different patterns in the operation of censorship. *Lady* exists in the form of a manuscript that shows the censor's interventions and playhouse markings. *Witch* exists only as a presentation transcript, while the most scandalous of the three, *Game*, exists in multiple copies and manuscript transcripts.

In 1611 a play without title came to the Revels Office and was censored and licensed by George Buc, who had succeeded Edmund Tilney as Master the previous year. Buc had been Tilney's deputy, and in this position he seems to have appropriated the right to license plays for publication, with the effect that earlier separate practices in relation to press censorship and theatrical censorship (press censorship being in the hands of ecclesiastics or their deputies; theatrical censorship closer to the court in the hands of the Master of the Revels) began to coalesce so that all play censorship was controlled by the Master of the Revels. In practice, a play which bore the license of the Master of the Revels could be entered in the Stationers' Register for publication.

Buc's imprimatur is seen on the final page: "This second maiden's tragedy (for it hath no name inscribed) may with the reformations be acted publicly. 31 October 1611." Buc's allusion to the text, arising, it can be reasonably conjectured, from his recent perusal of *The Maid's Tragedy*, has given modern editors a title for the play. The Oxford *Middleton* editors have confidently attributed it to Middleton and retitled the play *The Lady's Tragedy*.[1] In the play corruption is endemic; courtiers support a usurper, simply known as the Tyrant, and only at the end do they resist and depose the Tyrant and reinstate the rightful ruler, Govianus. In the meantime, the Lady, who is the beloved of Govianus, has killed herself, rather than be raped by the Tyrant.

While Buc's interventions are not as considerable as those of Tilney in the manuscript *Sir Thomas More*, his hand can nevertheless be seen throughout the playbook, particularly evident in critiques of the court and constructions of court politics. He has deleted oaths in compliance with the 1606 *Act to Restrain Abuses of Players*, by which it was forbidden to name God, Christ, the Holy Ghost, or the Trinity on the stage. Most notable in this manuscript is the deletion of the Catholic oath "By the mass," which would have been explicable in a play located in Italy. Other deletions are political. When Helvetius, the Lady's father, tries to put pressure on his daughter to succumb to the Tyrant, he cynically derides sexual morality: "Talk like a courtier, girl, not like a fool." Buc has made a cross in the margin, deleted the word "courtier" and replaced it with "woman" (2.1.69). The censor has thus turned an anti-court comment into a misogynist one. At the point where the Lady declares that she would rather commit suicide than be sexually coerced by the Tyrant, she declares that she "scorns death / As much as great men fear it" (3.1.160–1). Buc has made a marginal cross and interlined "some" before "great men." Govianus's grief is conveyed in an ironic observation: "'Twas a strange trick of her. Few of your ladies / In ord'nary will believe it; they abhor it. / They'll sooner kill themselves with lust, than for it" (3.1.220–1). There is heavy scoring through of the lines and marginal crosses in pencil and ink indicating Buc's disapproval of this allusion to rampant female sexuality in high places.

The area of censorship of specific interest is revealed in the scene depicting the uprising against and the murder of the Tyrant. Regicide as the ultimate response to oppression was a contentious ideological and legal issue. In endorsing the Tyrant's assassination, *Lady* is politically provocative and Buc's hand is in evidence in muting the impact. When the Tyrant calls out "Your King is poisoned," Buc has deleted the exclamation and replaced it with "I am poisoned" (5.2.68). In the Tyrant's desperate threat to devise a grotesque death for Govianus as a traitor, Middleton makes a contemporary allusion. Govianus's death will be "beyond the Frenchmen's tortures" (5.2.141–2): this Buc has changed to "extremest tortures." To understand the rationale of this censorship, we need to put it into context. Henri IV of France had been assassinated the previous year, and even by contemporary standards his murderer had suffered an appalling death. James I, who lived in perpetual fear of assassination, had immediately ordered that any publications about French affairs should be prohibited (Clare, *Dramatic Censorship*, p. 174). In the play, an audience applauds both the death of the Tyrant and the courtiers for changing their allegiance to Govianus. From the perspective of the state censor, however, a scene depicting the murder of a king on stage was alarming enough without evoking contemporary resonances.

From Buc's "reformations" inferences can be made about mid Jacobean censorship. More specifically, however, we see in Middleton a dramatist not quite knowing how far he can go in essaying critiques of the court and its corrupt sexuality, arguably testing the waters and attempting to extend parameters. Like *The Revenger's Tragedy* the play stands out for its depiction of sexual depravity in a rotten court, but in *Lady* the satirist's disgust at the ruler's abuse of power and the familiar vices of the court – sexual coercion, sycophancy, and nepotism – is articulated in more measured, less lurid terms. The latter is a more dangerous play in so far as Govianus is first the displaced ruler, then the assassin, and finally the king.

Topicality seems to have something to do with the obscure fate of *Witch*, a play that Middleton wrote for the King's Men at the Blackfriars, according to Marion O'Connor in mid 1616 (*Middleton*, p. 1124). The play survives only in Ralph Crane's transcript, which contains Middleton's dedication to Thomas Holmes. In its allusions to the provenance of the play, the dedication is cryptic, as dedications recording circumstances lost to us often are.[2] Middleton tells Holmes that with much difficulty he has recovered the text of his play and that the play was an "ignorantly ill fated labour." Tying together the fate of the play with the legal condemnation of witchcraft, Middleton adds, "Witches are (ipso facto) by the Law condemned, and that only, I think, hath made her lie so-long, in an imprisoned obscurity." The interpolation of rather conventional witchcraft scenes of spell-making and conjurings seems, on its own, unlikely as the cause of either the play's theatrical failure or its absolute condemnation. This has prompted considerable speculation that the play – unwittingly or otherwise – came a little too close to court politics and scandal (Lancashire, "*The Witch*"). One of the plot lines of *Witch* has a thwarted suitor, Sebastian, contriving, through the charms of the witches, the impotence of Antonio, who, during Sebastian's absence, has married Isabella, to whom Sebastian was formerly betrothed. This scenario takes from or coincidently refracts certain details of the most often cited sexual scandal of the Jacobean court, that of Frances Howard. On the grounds that her first husband, the Earl of Essex, was impotent, Frances Howard obtained a divorce so that she could marry the king's favorite, Robert Carr. Essex claimed that he was impotent only with Howard and that this was caused by supernatural impediment.[3] Certainly there is an uncanny resemblance between the Howard/Carr intrigue and the dramatic intrigue of *Witch*, just as the virginity test in *The Changeling* brings to mind the physical examination of Frances Howard before the divorce. Frances Howard and Robert Carr were married with the king's blessing. While there was no doubt a prurient appetite for plays that configured the salacious affair, in the light of the court eminence of the protagonists the King's Men may well have been obliged to "imprison" Middleton's play in obscurity.

Hardly anything is known about *Witch*. The same can hardly be said of Middleton's last play, *Game*, which offers not only the best documented account of early modern theatrical censorship, but the fullest record of the production of any play in the period. (Contemporary references are reproduced in *Companion*, pp. 865–73.) Though quite peripheral to his design, Middleton had previously used the metaphor of a chess game in *Women Beware Women*. In *Game*, however, the whole play is structured on the strategies and maneuvers of a game between the rival Black and White Houses, with the characters identified simply by the pieces on the board. Under cover of this artifice Middleton is at his most audaciously topical. The game in which the White House defeats the Black House and puts the pieces/protagonists into the "bag," represented on stage as a hellmouth, discredited the foreign policy of the previous year.[4] As one observer noted, by means of the allegory "the whole Spanish business is ripped up to the quick" (*Companion*, p. 869). Peace with Spain had been one of the achievements of James's foreign policy. The treaty of London of 1604 had brought to a close the thirty-year-old Anglo-Hispanic hostilities, and throughout James's reign the possibilities of cementing the relationship through a marriage alliance were explored. In March 1623 James's son Charles and his favorite Buckingham, encouraged by the former Spanish ambassador Gondomar, journeyed incognito to Madrid in the confidence that such a surprise arrival and romantic quest would force the hand of the Spanish and that Charles would thus win the Infanta. The venture was naive in its calculation that Philip IV would agree to an interfaith marriage without demanding substantial concessions for English Catholics. Charles and Buckingham were treated with great hospitality and exposed to all the splendor of the Hapsburg court, but it was quite clear that in the absence of Charles agreeing to convert to Catholicism there could be no marriage contract. In October 1623 Charles and Buckingham returned to England without the Infanta. Although the whole venture had been a fiasco, Charles was at the height of his popularity, further enhanced when he and Buckingham put themselves at the head of the anti-Spanish war party.

The following year Middleton wrote *Game*, a play that is as much anti-Catholic, or more precisely anti-Jesuitical, as it is anti-Spanish. The attempt to ensnare the White Knight and the White Duke (Charles and Buckingham) is represented as part of a grand design for world domination. In asides and soliloquies the Black Knight (equated with Gondomar), in league with the Father General, congratulates himself on pushing forward "the business of the universal monarchy" (*Game: A Later Form*, 1.1.244). There are allusions to such measures as James being persuaded to release imprisoned priests and Jesuits during the marriage negotiations (3.1.90–5). In its allegory and abstractions, evoking English Protestantism threatened by European Catholicism, *Game* is closer to a morality drama than it is to Middleton's psychologically probing tragedies or to the material world of his comedies. One reason, although not the only one, why *Game* was licensed by Henry Herbert, the comparatively inexperienced successor to George Buc, was that the play's interventions in national and international affairs were apparently depersonalized and consistently coded. That is, until the play was performed.

It was the performance of the play that caused it to be both an immediate commercial success and, in the eyes of the Spanish, a national insult. Gondomar suffered from an anal fistula and rode in a special chair (a "chair of ease"). John Chamberlain, in a letter to Dudley Carleton on August 21, 1624, referred to Middleton's play not as *A Game at Chess* but "our famous play of Gondomar," and describes how Gondomar was counterfeited "to the life, with all his graces and faces" and that the actor had a discarded or replica costume ("a cast sute of his apparel for the purpose") and rode in his litter. But, adds Chamberlain, even more seriously the actors had played "somebody else," whom we can infer to be James as the White King (*Companion*, p. 870). There was, needless to say, a tacit understanding that the reigning monarch was not represented on the stage.

*Game* was literally a nine-day wonder. The title page of the first quarto, published the year after its performance, draws attention to an unprecedented nine-day run at the Globe. The playhouse was apparently packed out. Chamberlain makes a specific reference to the social, economic, and professional diversity of the audience, "old and young, rich and poor, masters and servants, papists and puritans" (*Companion*, p. 870), revealing how the play had tapped in to an inveterate bias against Spain and Catholicism. The run came to an end because of the interventions of the Spanish ambassador, who complained to James of the "dishonourable fashion" in which the King of Spain, Gondomar, and James himself had been represented on a public stage (*Companion*, p. 868). The play flouted international etiquette. While Charles and Buckingham had been in Madrid, to forestall possible conflicts a decree ordered that "no one should dare to say any word to them [Charles and Buckingham] which could offend them," under threat of severe punishment (Cano, "Entertainments," p. 71). Yet here was Middleton writing an anti-Spanish play in which the actors impersonated the Spanish king and dignitaries. Following Spanish intervention the Privy Council was instructed to investigate the licensing of the play. The players produced "an orriginal and perfect Coppie . . . allowed by Sr *Henry Herbert*" and affirmed that they had acted the text as licensed (*Companion*, p. 870). The book was sent to the king, who took the next step of asking the Privy Council who was responsible for the "personnatinge of *Gondemar*" (*Companion*, p. 871). Quite clearly the aim was not to punish Middleton or the company, beyond token recrimination, but to mollify the Spanish. Following the investigations into licensing and performance, Pembroke, the Lord Chamberlain, instructed the Council to "take such Course" with the actors "as might give best satisfacion to y^e Spanish Ambassadour" and preserve the honour of the King of Spain and his ministers. The company was forbidden to play, but only for a few days; *Game* was "antiquated and sylenced," yet published illicitly the following year (*Companion*, p. 871). If the inscription on one of the play manuscripts is to be believed, Middleton was imprisoned in the Fleet and released following a witty verse petition to the king (*Middleton*, p. 1895; *Companion*, p. 873).

Understandably, *Game* has excited considerable attention as a case study of Jacobean censorship. It has even been described as an example of non-censorship. How did the play come to pass the censor? Like a number of other Jacobean satires, but far more audaciously, the satirical thrust was activated in performance and consequently the play incurred post-performance censorship. Whatever Hispanophobia Herbert might have detected in the text, it would, in the light of the discredited foreign policy, have seemed non-controversial and certainly consonant with national feeling. It was this clever articulation of national fervor that effectively brought Middleton's stage career to an end.

NOTES

1. The editor, Julia Briggs, presents parallel texts: the censored/revised version and the manuscript text ignoring censorial and playhouse interventions.
2. See, for example, Chapman's dedication of his *Byron* plays in 1608 to Thomas Walsingham, and Thomas Walkley's address to the reader in the 1622 edition of *Philaster*.
3. The fullest treatment of Howard's divorce and the two trials is in Lindley, *Trials*.
4. Much has been written on the aborted Spanish match. See, for example, the essays in Samson, *The Spanish Match*.

## CHAPTER 21

# Music on the Jacobean stage

## Linda Phyllis Austern

> There [in the theatre] set they abroche straunge consortes of melody,
> to tickle the eare; costly apparel, to flatter the sight; effeminate gesture,
> to ravish the sence; and wanton speache, to whet desire too [*sic*]
> inordinate lust.
>
> Stephen Gosson, The Schoole of Abuse (1579)

Music in the English theatres of Middleton's era belonged to a tradition of
sensuous live performance, along with costume, rhetorical gesture, the
sound of actors' voices, strategic lighting in the enclosed private theatres,
and the smell of the gunpowder used for verisimilitude in scenes of hunting,
battle, and state ceremony. As early seventeenth-century plays, masques,
triumphs, pageants, and other multimedia entertainments were committed
to writing before or after performance, they were encoded entirely in
words. To a reader, a direction for music may feel like an interruption of
the text. To an audience, the actual sound would be integral to the flow of
the action and its meaning. More than merely "to tickle the eare," music as
indicated in the plays of Middleton and his contemporaries is an essential
aspect of each work, used for as many purposes as in the modern cinema. The
music and musical effects that are often described or indicated by words
are absolutely vital to the full impact and understanding of Jacobean drama.[1]

As with modern film scores, Jacobean theatre music was assembled for
each play from a mix of new and preexisting pieces. Due to its independent
materiality and the conventional use of concrete verbal descriptors for
certain of its elements, music at least partially supersedes what has been
called the free-floating aspect of performance for which a script or playbook
remains inadequate (Orgel, "Book of the Play," p. 52; see also Gurr, "New
Theatre Historicism," p. 71; and Stern, "Re-Patching," pp. 156–7). It was
transmitted independently from the dramatic text, primarily as part of a
vibrant oral tradition, but also through a more specialized form of notation
for a more limited market. During this period, music was not collected

specifically for or from the theatre in manuscript or in print. Songs, dances, and ballad tunes used in plays were incidentally included in anthologies assembled mostly for amateur domestic performance or as pedagogical aids (Austern, "Thomas Ravenscroft," pp. 238–40; Chan, *Theatre of Ben Jonson*, pp. 20–34; Duffin, *Shakespeare's Songbook*, pp. 23–38; Duckles, "Music for the Lyrics," p. 118; G. Taylor and Sabol *et al.*, "Middleton, Music, and Dance," pp. 121–2), much as one can currently purchase numerous arrangements of show tunes or download multiple versions of songs included in a cinematic soundtrack. Many songs and instrumental pieces floated freely in and out of dramatic works as performed and printed. Some originated from, or were perhaps subsumed by, the oral repertory of popular song and dance. Others were probably maintained by the musicians employed by theatre companies, court, and the city of London, from which they could easily pass from work to work (Austern, *Children's Drama*, p. 24; Chan, *Theatre of Ben Jonson*, pp. 32–3; Cutts, "Hecate-Scene," pp. 201–2; Cutts, "Masque and Stage Music," pp. 185–8; Cutts, "Original Music," p. 204; Seligmann, "Functions of Song," pp. 258–61; Stern, "Re-Patching," pp. 158–9).

On the page of any Jacobean play, masque, pageant, or other similar work, texted song has been rendered indistinguishable from spoken verse. A reader or editor may be left to intuit that the insertion into the dialogue of a brief poem that is general in subject, impersonal in tone, and predictable in meter and versification indicates a song (Jorgens, "Matters of Manner and Music," p. 239; Stern, "Re-Patching," pp. 156–7). Such a poem may be more clearly headed "*Song*" (as in *The Patient Man and the Honest Whore*, scene 9, opening), even if divided dialogically between characters and particularly appropriate to the given situation (as in *The Nice Valour* 5.1.44–78). It may simply follow a stage direction, spoken cue, or description that a particular character sings, such as "*Enter Audrey, who spins by the curtains and sings*" (*A Trick to Catch the Old One* 4.5.1). It may be omitted altogether in favor of such a direction as "*A song to the organs*" (*A Mad World, My Masters* 2.1.171), or more simply "*the song*" (as in *Your Five Gallants* 2.1.120 ), or even inferred from surrounding dialogue (as in *Mad World* 4.1.62 ff.). Likewise, the time to complete a dance, a dumb show, a choreographed entrance or procession, or other instrumental work has been compressed to the seconds required to read dialogic cues or a short description.

The Jacobean theatre or other space for multimedia entertainment was a realm in which the acoustic, the aesthetic, performance practices, and well-established metaphors of music were brought seamlessly together. For a society on the cusp between primary orality and literacy, drama, masque, and pageantry joined with balladry and other forms of strophic song to provide narrative entertainment and didactic reinforcement of key cultural tenets. Whether for speech or music, in the theatre or any other space, early modern individuals were trained to practice a kind of active, engaged audition that was believed to closely entangle the bodies and souls of speaker or musician and listener (Bloom, *Voice in Motion*, pp. 112–13; Rooley, *Performance*, pp. 9, 13–14). The theatre was an acoustically live space, as much an instrument for the production and reception of sound as a frame for visual spectacle (Bloom, *Voice in Motion*, p. 7; Folkerth, *Sound of Shakespeare*, pp. 17–18; Smith, *Acoustic World*, pp. 206–8). Physical conditions of Elizabethan and Jacobean theatrical architecture, whether the semi-open public playing space or the fully enclosed private one, enabled the sound of all sorts of the era's musical instruments, from the airy softness of the recorder through the plucked-string lute to the sustained reedy resonance of the hautbois or shawm and the strident combination of drum and trumpet (Long, *Shakespeare's Use*, pp. 16–31; Smith, *Acoustic World*, pp. 208–22) (see Figure 21.1). Jacobean commentator Thomas Gainesford lists "song" and "musicke" among the conventional abilities of an actor (*Rich Cabinet*, p. 118). Documentary evidence indicates that several of the most celebrated London players from Middleton's youth were known for musical skills; at least one company for which he wrote, the Lord Admiral's Men, maintained quite a collection of the sorts of instruments used in the era's plays (Holman, *Four and Twenty Fiddlers*, pp. 138–9).

The significance of music on stage was based on cultural practice, intellectual beliefs about the art, and theatrical tradition. Jacobean stage works invariably feature music where strong passions or other unseen forces are at work, at the margins between the ordinary and the extraordinary, the passage between life and death, or where particular kinds of music or instruments might help to characterize individuals. As remains the case in our own era of electric guitar, jazz saxophone, classical piano, and karaoke, an individual's musical training and choice of what to perform where, when, and before whom provide clues about identity and self-fashioning. To participate in music within a Jacobean play is to also perform gender, profession, social status, and sometimes nationality. Characters may do so in adherence or opposition to cultural norms.

The plethora of surviving music books and self-tutorial manuals from Middleton's era clarify that the ability to sing, dance, and perform on soft-sounding instruments that were played in a seated position (such as lute, viol, or virginals) were considered necessary skills, or at least social graces, for well-to-do men and women. When Maudline asks at the beginning of *A Chaste Maid in Cheapside* whether her daughter has practiced her virginals, an expensive instrument played by the era's gentry and nobility as well as

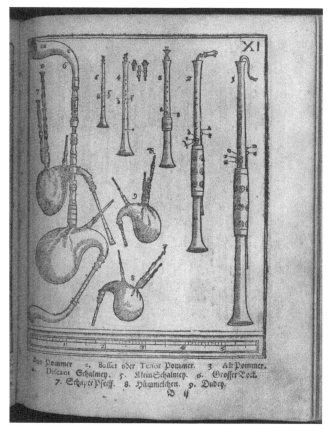

Figure 21.1 Shawms (hautbois), loud reed instruments played by professional musicians, shown with bagpipes. From Michael Praetorius, *Theatrum instrumentorum* (Wolfenbuttel, 1620).

children of successful merchants, her ambitions become clear (1.1.1–2) (see Figure 21.2). With the exception of dance, however, musical skill among the leisured classes was not to be displayed in public or before an audience of any but the most familiar. Paid or commanded performances, along with louder instruments and those requiring a standing posture (such as violin, brass, and some wind instruments as played in this era), were deemed the province of professionals, servants, soldiers, or oral entertainers. The patronage of domestic music and participation in masques and other entertainments were prerogatives of privileged Jacobeans as well as of their reflections on stage.

Well-bred women in particular were admonished not to play instruments or sing secular songs in front of men to whom they were not related by

Figure 21.2 Young woman playing the virginals. From the frontispiece to
*Parthenia or The Maydenhead* (London, 1613[?]).

blood or marriage, or to perform on instruments that distorted their bodies
or drew direct attention to their sexuality. Conversely, where women's
sexuality could be bought, sold, or traded, or where sanity or status have
been lost, there is music on display. The song that opens *More Dissemblers
Besides Women* proclaims the Duchess's status as both noble and properly
chaste as much by its performance in her private space as by its text (1.1.1–6).
In contrast, the Welsh Gentlewoman of *Chaste Maid* is all too willing to

Figure 21.3 Three sizes of viols (violas da gamba), bowed stringed instruments held upright between the performer's legs, favored by socially elite amateur musicians and shown here with similar instruments. From Michael Praetorius, *Theatrum instrumentorum* (Wolfenbuttel, 1620).

sing a bawdy song before an audience of admirers, which further character-izes her nationality and status (4.1.160–93). And true to their profession, the courtesans of *Five Gallants* are introduced as singers and instrumentalists, and even run a sham music school (2.1.35–53). On the other hand, when Moll sings and plays the viol dressed as a man among her male companions in *The Roaring Girl*, she is appropriating the musical privileges of affluent men (8.76–129). (See figures 21.3 and 21.4.)

Figure 21.4 Modern viola da gambist Mary Springfels, founding director of the Newberry Consort, prepares to play her bass viol in concert; note the smaller treble viol to her right.

To early modern thinkers, sound was of the same airy substance as the human soul and other spirit entities, able to enter through the ear, penetrate to the heart, and infect the entire somatic system through the blood (Finney, *Musical Backgrounds*, pp. 119–22; Smith, *Acoustic World*, pp. 98–9; Tomlinson, *Music in Renaissance Magic*, pp. 105–15). Significantly, the ear, particularly linked to memory and learning in early modern thought (Smith, *Acoustic World*, p. 110), is the one human sense receptor that cannot close or withdraw itself from direct stimulus without removal of the entire body, rendering an audience member a completely willing participant in any acoustic phenomenon. Music was considered the primary object of the sense of hearing, the most complex, artificial, and delicately manipulable of the aural arts due to its range of vocal and instrumental timbres and simultaneous capacities for harmony and melody. It spoke directly to the seat of the passions, shared between human beings and animals. Music was the very essence of eros, sacred and profane, defined as "a science of love matters occupied in harmony and rhythmos" (Morley, *Plaine and Easie*, p. 195). Perhaps more importantly, in a web of significance extending backwards through the Middle Ages to Greek and Roman antiquity, sounding music evoked the unheard order of the natural and celestial realms, the body politic, human physical or moral integrity, and the working of unseen forces divine or demonic (Folkerth, *Sound of Shakespeare*, p. 18; Gouk, "Music, Melancholy," pp. 173–4; Gouk, *Music, Science*, pp. 95–111; Hollander, "Musica Mundana," pp. 58–65; Tomlinson, *Music in Renaissance Magic*, pp. 131–3).

Verbal references to the art and its affective capacities stood in for these properties. For Lactantio at the beginning of *Dissemblers*, for instance, the appearance of Aurelia is "soul's music" in contrast to the audible song from the Duchess's offstage lodging (1.1.1–7). In a more extended usage, *The Phoenix* closes with the (re-)establishment of harmony in the generic tradition of mainstream Elizabethan and Jacobean comedy. The concluding lines of the play, spoken by the morally upright Prince Phoenix after he emerges unscathed from the political corruption around him, refer to the reflection of heavenly concord into his court and kingdom: "when all hearts are tuned to honour's strings / There is no music to the choir of kings" (15.349–50). Immediately beforehand, the previously corrupt Tangle, having been quite literally purged of his bad blood and appropriately medicated for renewal, reminds the audience of the metaphorical connection between musical harmony and the health of both human body and body politic: "I begin to feel / I have a conscience now, truth in my words, / Compassion in my heart, and, above all / In my blood peace's music. Use me how you can, / You shall find me an honest, quiet man" (15.341–5). The efficacy of his cure, its effect on his vital spirits, is rendered tangible through the reference to the unheard music in his blood, as is the restoration of social and political harmony through Phoenix's choice of words. No textual description is given of any sounding music at this point, although it was conventional for Elizabethan and Jacobean plays to conclude with a musical performance (Orgel, "Foreword"). As the spoken text gave way to post-play music, heard or unheard, a sense of harmony prevails and the physical and metaphysical aspects of music and its power echo each other.

More common in the Middleton canon, however, is the failure of such conventional expectations, or even an ironic juxtaposition of sounding harmony with a tableau of mayhem and destruction (see Sutherland, *Masques*, p. 90 and Seligmann, *Functions of Song*, pp. 48, 53–5). In such cases, audience attention is drawn not to the infinite reflection between physically sounding music and its metaphysical extension into unseen realms of concord and agreement. Instead, Middleton tends to shatter these expectations and emphasize the stark contrast between music as heard and as metaphor for order. In many of his works, skepticism replaces the age-old notion that harmony binds together all things, and that it can be captured from higher realms through music or its extension into measured dance. Sometimes music is only mundane entertainment that reveals something lacking in its patron or participants. In *Mad World*, for example, the extravagant Sir Bounteous Progress shows off to a sham "lord" not only his impressive collection of musical instruments; he also displays the abilities of his "musicians in ordinary," the domestic staff retained to provide music for their employer, along with a feast brought in to a choreographed entrance (2.1.156–70). Here, music is an aspect of sensory excess and conspicuous consumption, reflecting the multiple levels of deception, desire, and folly that dominate the play. Sir Bounteous's fine taste enables him to recognize and command fine music, but neither his larcenous grandson nor his own shortcomings. And unlike the masque as practiced at court or in many of the era's other comedies, the one that concludes *Five Gallants* pointedly does not reinforce the cosmic, political, or social order of the ruling class. Nor does it emphasize the upstanding moral qualities of its participants through appropriate allegorical roles. Instead, it exposes theft and the falsity of the play's wrongdoers and social climbers, including the cross-dressed courtesans who are neither ladies nor women (5.2.1–74).

Music that ends in silence and the stillness of death often draws attention to a lack of concentric harmony from the world of human action through a broken body politic to distant, uncaring celestial spheres. This is particularly true in tragedies in which vengeance takes place to a stylized show of music and movement before the final lines. The concluding scene of *The Revenger's Tragedy* (5.3), for example, begins with a dumb show accompanied by "*sounding music*" and continues through the sensual excesses of a banquet and the appearance of a blazing star. These lead in turn to paired masques of revengers and murderers who sequentially dispense and discover death with measured steps to dance music that is itself disrupted by the sound of thunder (5.3.40). These carefully planned and performed juxtapositions of harmony and horror, of passions gone wild but enacted to ordered musical accompaniment and disordered nature, conclude more than seventy-five lines from the end of the work. The play terminates not with music but in the silence of "death on death," a bloodletting that is never analogized to higher harmony as seven corpses lie upon the stage. Throughout the work, it is only the symbolically named Vindice who refers to the metaphorical capacities of music. At the midpoint of the play (3.5), in a scene that foreshadows the spectacular denouement, Vindice and Hippolito sadistically murder the Duke to the "loud-" and "loud'st music" that accompanies another banquet and a display of erotic excess.[2] After Hippolito acknowledges paradoxically that the music had enabled their bloody deeds, Vindice inverts the usual reference to the art as metaphor for a healthy body politic reflected both in celestial order and the state's divinely empowered head: "'Tis state in music for a duke to bleed" (3.5.221). Later, Vindice renders himself into a wire-strung "instrument that speaks / Merry things sadly" in order to play "some strain of melancholy" (4.2.27–30). It is a further irony that, by the time the play was produced, music was so widely acknowledged to be a homeopathic cure for melancholy that instrumental pieces circulated commercially for the purpose (Holman, *Dowland*, pp. 50–2). Middleton also upends the same convention in *Chaste Maid*, where Moll's desperate song appears to end her life instead of her melancholy illness (5.2.33–48).

Jacobean audiences expected spectacular music in conjunction with supernatural phenomena and the arts of magic on stage, particularly the topsy-turvy, disordered female world of witchcraft. With their tuneful songs, antisocial dances, and showy use of machinery, stage witches bore little relation to presumed practitioners of *maleficia* outside of the theatre or masquing hall. Their function was to entertain (Purkiss, *Witch in History*, pp. 199, 207–10). And some of that entertainment value enabled witches' song-and-dance routines to acquire an independent life, lifted as modules from one work to another, such as the song shared between *The Witch* (3.3.39–72) and *Macbeth* (3.5.34–73), and the dances whose music and choreography may have been used in both of those as well as Jonson's *Masque of Queens* (Ewbank, *Middleton*, p. 1167). The main purpose of the relevant scenes is clearly to showcase the singing, "straunge consortes of melody," "costlie apparel," sense-ravishing gesture, and flying machines for which theatres were famed. However, as is seen in *Witch*, many of the conventional circumstances for music are brought together in such moments of liminality between the tangible and intangible, masculine and feminine, and the workings of spirits within a vortex of human passion and desire. Musically, "Come Away Hecate" helps to underscore the developing narrative with its paradoxical offbeat rhythms, alternation between disjunct and dance-like motion, and bright major-key tonality

(Henze, "Invisible Collaborations," pp. 78–9; Seligmann, "Functions of Song," pp. 167–71).[3] In the inverted world of this play, those who openly practice evil are rendered jolly and entertaining through music, and the more mundane human characters are truly dangerous.

NOTES

1. An indispensible resource for understanding musical references and terminology in early modern English drama, including allusions that might not be readily identifiable as musical to non-specialist readers, is C. R. Wilson and M. Calore, *Music in Shakespeare*. The most thorough modern collection of Elizabethan and Jacobean music for the early modern English theatre is Duffin, *Shakespeare's Songbook*, which presents performable versions of all texted songs included or referred to in the complete Shakespeare canon, many of which also appear in the works of such other of the era's playwrights as Middleton. Extant settings of music from Middleton's plays are given in modern editions in G. Taylor and Sabol *et al.*, "Middleton, Music and Dance," pp. 137–73. In addition to the set of audio compact discs that accompany Duffin, *Shakespeare's Songbook*, a particularly useful set of recordings of Jacobean (and Caroline) theatre music is "Hark! Hark! The Lark: Music for Shakespeare's Company" (London: Hyperion, 1997).

2. "Loud music" in the theatre literally meant the use of such "outdoor" or noisy brass, reed, and percussion instruments as trumpet, cornett, hoboy, shawm, or drum. But it also implied coarseness in certain contexts, of which this is clearly an example; see C. R. Wilson and M. Calore, *Music in Shakespeare*, p. 247.

3. A modern score of this song, plus the other from *Witch* and the Witches Dances likely shared between this play, *Macbeth*, and the anti-masque to Jonson's *Masque of Queens*, are available in Cutts, *La musique de scène*, pp. 7–16. Historically informed performances of "Come Away Hecate" and both Witches Dances are available on the audio CD *Shakespeare's Music* (Dorian Recordings, 2000).

# PART IV

# *The context and conditions of authorship*

## CHAPTER 22

# Middleton and "modern use": case studies in the language of A Chaste Maid in Cheapside

## Sylvia Adamson (with Hannah Kirby, Laurence Peacock, and Elizabeth Pearl)[1]

### INTRODUCTION

There is as yet no full-length study of Middleton's language, but incidental comments by his literary analysts suggest a critical consensus that he "celebrates 'modern use' . . . [His] language is more immediately intelligible to twenty-first-century readers, less encumbered with classical allusions or obsolete linguistic forms, than the writing of any of his contemporaries" (G. Taylor, "Lives and Afterlives," p. 33). On this view, his affinity is less with Jonson and Dekker than with their Restoration descendants, such as Wycherley, and his language is a harbinger of the naturalistic plain style that was to become dominant in the later seventeenth century – a style taking perspicuity rather than "copia" as its rhetorical ideal, and the conversation rather than the oration as its rhetorical model (Adamson, "Literary Language"). His comedies, in particular, seem to anticipate the Royal Society's preference for "the language of Artizans . . . and Merchants, before that of Wits and Scholars."[2] In *A Chaste Maid in Cheapside*, certainly, the "scholars" are pedants or fools and the "wits" concentrate on turning the plot rather than turning a sentence. No one is linguistically "witty" in the style of Mercutio or Touchstone, and the play's moral monsters, Yellowhammer and Allwit, though symbolically named, use language that resists the symbolic extension that Jonson accords to Volpone's similar predatory avarice. As Tomlinson notes (cited in Barber's edition of Middleton, *Chaste Maid*, p. 5), "the verse lingers over clothes, furnishings, possessions so cheap and ordinary they cannot possibly stand for anything beyond their own limited and worldly significance" – a comment that casts Middleton as a forerunner of the technique of documentary realism that Barthes identified in the language of the nineteenth-century novel (*Language*, pp. 141–8).

In this essay, we revisit the question of Middleton's modernity, as we investigate three aspects of the play's language: its use of sociolinguistic varieties, puns, and second person pronouns.

## MIDDLETON'S LANGUAGE VARIETIES

Inheriting from classical rhetoric a division of style into three basic
types (a high or grand style, a middle style, and a plain or low style), the
Renaissance reinterpreted the model for literary application by mapping
it on to generic, social, and affective coordinates (so that the grand style,
for instance, was associated with tragedy, with nobly born protagonists,
and with the power of moving) (Adamson, "Grand Style" ). But in his
introductory epistle to the published version of *The Roaring Girl* (1611),
Middleton mocks the grand style of his Elizabethan predecessors and
the latinate vocabulary that was one of its distinguishing features: "huge
bombasted plays, quilted with mighty words to lean purpose" (*Middleton*,
p. 726), and in the invocatory Latin preface to his tragic poem, *The
Ghost of Lucrece*, he puns on his name (Thomas Medius ... Tonus) to
identify himself as a naturally "middle-toned" man (*Middleton*, p. 1989).
Traditionally, the middle style was the one that decorum prescribed for
lovers and merchants, which in theory made it a suitable vehicle for
plays such as *Chaste Maid*. But given the increasing size and complexity
of early modern London society, the middle style fitted "the middling
sort" as comfortably as a straitjacket. Hence, those attempting to write
a modern realistic city comedy found themselves impelled by the same
need to catalogue the varieties of London types as the contemporary
writers of "character books," such as Overbury, Earle, and Webster. The
difference is that dramatists faced the requirement, as character writers
did not, to find appropriate speech forms for their characters that would
go beyond the blueprints for the three styles provided by classical or
vernacular rhetoric manuals. This requirement was at once liberating
(it accounts for the fresh, transcriptional quality ascribed to Middleton
by critics from Hazlitt onwards) and problematic. As I have argued
elsewhere (Adamson, "Varieties"), in order to differentiate language
varieties and make them recognizable, writers typically rely on a set of
stereotypical features. But this carries the danger that the target variety is
recognized not only *by* stereotype but *as* stereotype. Its representation has
an affinity with caricature and most readily serves the purpose of satire.
The Jacobean city dramatists in general embrace this purpose. Jonson in
particular makes a virtue of necessity and hyperbolizes the stereotype: in
his rendition of "the alchemist" or "the Puritan," rant and cant apoth-
eosize into a new kind of grand style of their own. Middleton, by
contrast, seeks a more middle-toned way of anatomizing the cries of
London.

## Language varieties and satire in A Chaste Maid in Cheapside *(by Laurence Peacock)*

The massive expansion and diversification of London's population during Middleton's lifetime is documented elsewhere in this volume (see essays by Ian Munro and Karen Newman, pp. 45 and 90). Middleton's plays attest to another indication of the city's new metropolitan status, the number and copresence of different languages. Rogues and scholars, lords and ladies, merchants, Puritans and lawyers jostle together in his city streets, all speaking with their own distinctive styles and, in some cases, different languages altogether. These differing linguistic styles conform to David Crystal's definition of a language variety as "any system of linguistic expression whose use is governed by situational variables," where the "situational variables" in question are the speaker's class, profession, and, frequently, location (*Dictionary*, p. 324).

Thus *Chaste Maid* begins with a linguistic geography lesson. No sooner has Maudline used the word "error" than her husband, Yellowhammer, comments:

> Errors? Nay, the city cannot hold you, wife,
> But you must needs fetch words from Westminster
>
> (1.1.27–8)

"Fetched" from the Westminster law courts, the French-derived word *error* fails to pass the city goldsmith's border control. Yellowhammer draws definite dividing lines between the French-speaking lawyers (the law courts being the final bastion of non-anglicized French in early modern England) and the English-speaking city.[3] Nor is French the only language to intrude upon the opening scene. The letter that arrives from the Yellowhammers' son, Tim, is written in the language of the universities, Latin. This new addition is also unwelcomed by Yellowhammer, who declares that his son, like the city itself perhaps, has "grown too verbal" (1.1.68). The need for a proper translation prompts further sociolinguistic distinctions:

MAUDLINE: Go to my cousin, then, at Inns of Court.
YELLOWHAMMER: Fie, they are all for French; they speak no Latin.
MAUDLINE: The parson then will do it.
YELLOWHAMMER:                         Nay, he disclaims it,
    Calls Latin 'papistry'; he will not deal with it.

> (1.1.96–9)

Such rigid distinctions are undercut by a level of irony that blurs the boundaries Yellowhammer attempts to construct, in as much as "disclaim" is one of the French legal terms that he has just denounced.[4] Similarly, the parson, invoked by Maudline as a speaker sufficiently well educated to understand Latin, rejects it as the language of Catholicism – but using a Latin-derived term of abuse: "papistry."

Language varies along class as well as religious lines. A nicely illustrative moment occurs in the opening scene when Sir Walter Whorehound is introduced to Yellowhammer's daughter, Moll:

SIR WALTER: Why, how now, pretty mistress? Now I have caught you.
    What, can you injure so your time to stray
    Thus from your faithful servant?
YELLOWHAMMER: Pish, stop your words, good knight – 'twill make her
        blush else –
    Which sound too high for the daughters of the freedom.
    'Honour' and 'faithful servant'! They are compliments
    For the worthies of Whitehall or Greenwich;
    E'en plain, sufficient, subsidy words serves us, sir.

                                                    (1.1.126–33)

Again, Yellowhammer displays a keen awareness of the geographical and social boundaries of certain linguistic forms. In this instance, it is Sir Walter's use of terms such as "honour" and "faithful servant" that marks his language as that of a "brave court-spirit" (1.1.124) and hence "too high" for use in the "freedom" or city. Yellowhammer's profession of "plain ... words," however, is somewhat undermined, first by the considerably less plain words that dress it out ("sufficient," "subsidy"), and then by his subtle appropriation of the language of the court in his very next line. Referring to Sir Walter's whore (whom he thinks to be a landed Welsh gentlewoman), he asks, "And is this gentlewoman your worthy niece?" (1.1.134). Yellowhammer's "worthy" here echoes his earlier phrase "the worthies of Whitehall, or Greenwich" as his initial proclamation of linguistic inferiority (no doubt designed to be satisfying to Sir Walter's ears) is followed by an equally flattering switch to courtly vocabulary when describing his son's prospective wife.

With such sharp, at times even stereotypical sociolinguistic distinctions, Middleton's characters become easy targets for satire. Nowhere is this more clear than in his unflattering depiction of the Puritans. In addition to what were presumably appropriately plain costumes, the "faithful" (3.2.16) are also instantly recognizable by their specific vocabulary: "children of the spirit" (2.4.15), "pure," "tribulation," "brethren," "antichristian," and "the wellspring of discipline" (3.2.5, 17, 48, 90, 171). When Allwit expresses his contempt for the godly, then, he does so by echoing their distinctive vocabulary:

FIRST PURITAN: *Verily*, thanks, sir.
ALLWIT:                              *Verily*, you are an ass, forsooth
                                                            (2.3.22)

In 3.2, Middleton expresses his own contempt, when he makes one of his now not-so-pure Puritans pun on the literal and theological senses of "fall." After too little temperance and too much wine, the suggestively named Mistress Underman drunkenly stumbles and justifies herself by saying: "'Tis but the common affliction of the faithful; We must embrace our falls" (3.2.174–5).

Perhaps more so than the Puritans, the scholars of *Chaste Maid* also see their linguistic identities twisted back upon themselves. Knowledge of Latin, the "international language of education," in Middleton's staged and real worlds, instantly marked out those schooled in the humanist curriculum (Görlach, *Early Modern English*, p. 36). Although himself an Oxford alumnus, Middleton parodies the vogue among the educated for Latinizing their native English. The Tutor's line "I give great *approbation* to your *conclusion*" (4.1.82), by which he means "yes," for instance, exposes learning as preciosity.[5]

Tim Yellowhammer's self-conscious attempt to present himself as a mature scholar newly returned from Cambridge also invokes Latin and is equally destined for failure. Indignant at being patronized by his mother – "Served like a child, / When I have answered under bachelor!" (3.2.133–4) – Tim demands to be called by his new university name, "'Tim'? Hark you: 'Timotheus,' Mother, 'Timotheus'" (3.2.155), and demonstrates his newfound wisdom by disputing with his Tutor in Latin. Act four, for instance, opens with a set-piece debate over whether or not a fool is an "*animal rationale*." The Latin exchange follows the structure of logical disputations. Ironically, however, for all Tim's confidence that "By logic I'll prove anything" (4.1.40), his argument here (that a fool is "as reasonable a creature as myself" [4.1.36–7]) is proved true by events, when he is fooled into marrying "Sir Walter's whore." The irony (and with it a satirical victory for the uneducated city over the learned universities) is further compounded by the fact that in the earlier disputation scene Maudline's contribution provides an unheeded warning for her son:

TIM: Why, what's a fool, mother? . . .
MAUDLINE: Why, one that's married before he has wit.
                                                            (4.1.32–3)

Educated but not wise, and puritan but not pure, Middleton's linguistic varieties allow him to mark out his characters for recognition and ridicule alike.

MIDDLETON'S PUNS

From the classics, from the Bible, and from medieval morality plays, Renaissance writers inherited a literary convention (which for some was also a theological belief) that names tell the truth about the people or things they signify. This was the basis both for the use of revelatory names (such as Jonson's Epicure Mammon or Surly) and for the practice of "heuristic" punning, in which a similarity in the names of things reveals a likeness in the things themselves, however dissimilar they may appear. Revelatory names are largely confined to comedy, but heuristic puns occur more widely; their appearance in "serious" genres, such as sermon, tragedy, and religious poetry, is a distinctive feature of Renaissance style. George Herbert exemplifies the form in his sonnet, *The Sonne* (1633), when he congratulates the English language for giving "one onely name / To parents issue and the sunnes bright starre" (5–6) because this "demonstrates" the double nature of Christ, who is truly the "sonne of man" in both senses (14).[6]

But Herbert's poem exposes a problem with the theory it expounds. If the sun=son pun is language-specific (it does not occur in French, for instance) its "truth" can hardly be universal. The problem is compounded when we recognize (as Middleton does in *Chaste Maid*) that the English language itself is not a homogeneous whole, but a collection of different varieties, each of which may have its special vocabulary and its specialized meanings.

This perception forms the basis of what we might call "the varietal pun," a distinctive strand in the Renaissance's repertoire of wordplay, which depends on a word shifting its meaning in different contexts and for members of different social groups. In the following exchange in *Chaste Maid*, for example, Touchwood Senior uses "nail" as a technical term of measurement (two and a half inches), while the Wench (an indignant mother) interprets it as a reference to her child's fingernails.

TOUCHWOOD SENIOR:                                    . . .excuse me
  Of this half yard of flesh [i.e. the baby], in which I think it wants
  A nail or two.
WENCH:           No, thou shalt find, villain,
  It hath right shape and all the nails it should have.
(2.1.83–6)

Such misunderstandings prefigure John Locke's finding that the word "gold" for instance, will *necessarily* carry different meanings for, say, the child, the alchemist, and the goldsmith. In Locke's view, which would predominate for the next two centuries, the word–meaning relation is not intrinsic and universal, but arbitrary, localized, and contingent, and puns are a source of confusion rather than insight.[7]

### Cheapside unsignified: naming and punning in A Chaste Maid in Cheapside *(by Hannah Kirby)*

Punning is troublesome within the world of Middleton's Cheapside. In *Chaste Maid*, his portrayal of language's duplicity suggests a more wary attitude to the practice than Herbert's. Middleton presents a society riddled with vice and exploitative dishonesty, in which all inward turmoil is expressed and masked at once, as Allwit's jealousy and parsimony combine in his comment that Whorehound "not only keeps [= 'enjoys sexual possession of'] my wife, but a keeps [= 'financially maintains'] me" (1.2.17). Behind almost every signifier, the signified constantly shifts, allowing no statement to remain stable, so that language becomes unreliable and communication is seriously obstructed. When Whorehound first returns to the Allwits' house, for example, he jealously enquires whether Mrs Allwit has been "entertain[ing] ... strangers in my absence" (1.2.85–6). Hearing the servant begin the reply, "no living creature entered" (1.2.91), Whorehound latches onto the pun on *entered* (= "entered the house" and "sexually entered") so strongly as to ignore even its negation: he focuses on the innuendo without even its immediate context. Everything that the servant actually asserts is ignored and the verb "to enter" retains a meaning (to both Whorehound and the audience) that is distinct from and dominates the one that the speaker really intended.

Middleton's use of the pun here retains (in Locke's terms) the *wit* of words with one form but two concurrent meanings that characterized the puns of the Renaissance (e.g. sonne = "heavenly body" and "male offspring"), but Whorehound's single-mindedness suggests a contrast between two contradictory meanings that rather aligns Middleton with the practices of the later seventeenth century and what Locke called *judgment*.[8] *Judgment* in punning focuses on the poignancy of contrast. Allwit's "keeps" arguably retains concurrent meanings, as do Touchwood Senior's uses of the words "gear" (= "business" and "male genitalia") and "ware" (= "goods" and "women") (2.1.17, 100).[9] However, examples of *judgment* in punning are more rife in *Chaste Maid* than one might expect: if Maudline was "quick" with her dance teacher in her youth she could really only have been pregnant *or* light-footed (1.1.10); the "bout" threatened or promised to Touchwood Senior could only be legal *or* sexual (2.1.76–7). In shifting from concurrence to contradiction in the pun's duality, and in allowing puns (albeit comically) to disrupt the progress of the plot and the communication of the characters, Middleton demonstrates uneasiness that seems to anticipate the later seventeenth century's growing distrust of double meanings in favor of single and perspicuous relationships between form and meaning (Adamson, "Literary Language," pp. 568, 600).

Middleton queries the place of any truth in a world saturated with constant resignification, implying that *nothing* means what it ought to. References to Lent might seem to offer monitory contrasts to the excesses of Cheapside's inhabitants. But Lent is practiced only in name, as even its official Promoters are corrupt, lustful, and gluttonous, subverting the season's traditional significance, as Allwit predicts:

> This Lent will fat the whoresons up with sweetbreads,
> And lard their whores with lamb-stones; what their golls
> Can clutch goes presently to their Molls and Dolls
>
> (2.2.67–9)

The infection even spreads to Middleton's central romantic plotline. Touchwood Junior equivocates when he commissions Yellowhammer to craft Moll's wedding ring with the truthful but misleading inscription, "Love that's wise / Blinds parents' eyes" (1.1.202–3), and when he attempts to justify his own underhandedness, "Rather than the gain should fall to a stranger, / 'Twas honesty in me to enrich my father" (1.1.171–2). When feeling sincere emotion, both he and Moll reject speech entirely: he finds that his "joy wants utterance," and she declares herself "silent with delight" (5.4.48–9).

Middleton's attitude to language is best seen, however, in his strategies of naming, where again he appears precocious. Anne Barton suggests that, between 1603 and 1621, Middleton moved "away from morally defining names in the direction of a more neutral and quietly suggestive nomenclature," which left his characters more open to interpretation (*Names*, p. 78). In *Chaste Maid* Middleton's naming of characters, like his punning, is in a transitional state. Sometimes we *are* confronted with the literally apt (Yellowhammer hammers gold), or the undisputed (Whorehound hounds after whores), but we also encounter the enigmatic: how far is Allwit simply a "wit-all" [= "contented cuckold"], and how far made all-powerful by his wits? In what proportions are the Touchwood brothers hopeful, irascible, or passionate? (see *OED*, "touchwood"). In the case of Moll, the name is apparently fallacious (she is clearly *not* one of the "molls and dolls" referred to in Allwit's rhyme). And many characters have no name at all, notably the "Welsh gentlewoman" (aka "Sir Walter's whore"), who is left to "prove" her nature after the play closes.

It is true that Moll's or Touchwood Junior's names may raise morally apposite queries about their conduct (is Touchwood's courtship motivated purely by incendiary passion or partly by Yellowhammer's wealth? does Moll's defiance of her parents align her with the lawless Moll Cutpurse?), but this is not the same kind of ambiguity as the destructive shiftiness of constant punning. Rather, it presents options between which the reader is free to choose. Like Middleton's transition towards *judgment* in puns, it grants his audience respect, conceding that they are able to consider the subtleties of a text and its characters for themselves.

## MIDDLETON'S PRONOUNS OF ADDRESS

By 1600, in the view of many linguistic historians, *you* had become the default form for second person singular address, leaving *thou* as a form with special significances, whether of affection (*thou pretty rogue*) or contempt (*thou villain*). More extremely, it has sometimes been claimed that *thou* had largely fallen out of use in colloquial speech and that these affective uses were retained only as a convention of drama. Even if this is the case, older writers and playgoers would certainly recall the earlier sixteenth-century use of the *you-thou* pair as a signal of social power relations, where *you* was the pronoun of address used by subordinate or self-subordinating speakers and *thou* was spoken by those with power or authority within domestic or social relationships. And it is worth noting that some non-literary texts of the seventeenth century testify to the ongoing power of *thou* to demote the mighty, whether spoken by the Attorney General in the trial of Sir Walter Ralegh ("All that he did was by *thy* instigation, *thou* Viper; for I *thou thee*, *thou* Traitor") or by the accused in the many trials of the Quaker, George Fox (who persistently offended magistrates by calling them "thou" and refusing to doff his hat).[10]

In the absence of recordings of actual speech from the period, we can only speculate on how far Jacobean dramatists reflect or lag behind the state of the language. Statistics compiled by Hugh Craig for ninety-four dramatists of the period 1580–1642 show that *thou*, *thee*, and *thy* are three of the top ten items falling in frequency over time ("Grammatical modality," p. 39). But while *you* may be gaining in ascendancy, the *thou* forms remain in

Middleton's repertoire, even in the relative social realism of his city comedies, and retain their potency as an instrument in the power games of the protagonists and the satiric purposes of the dramatist.

### Intimate insolence: the art of thou-ing in A Chaste Maid in Cheapside *(by Elizabeth Pearl)*

Middleton, like Shakespeare, uses both the *you*-forms of the second person singular pronoun (*you, ye, your, yours*) and the *thou*-forms (*thou, thee, thy, thine*). *Thou*, the declining form in the language and the less frequent choice for Middleton, predominates in *The Wisdom of Solomon Paraphrased, Ghost, Civitatis Amor*, and *The Triumphs of Love and Antiquity*, where it appears to be used to lend the language a patina of antiquity.

In Middleton's dramatic dialogue, interactions between *you* and *thou* options are more complex. Two fine examples in *Chaste Maid* involve the kinsmen, Sir Oliver Kix and Sir Walter Whorehound. Both are aristocratic characters, who would traditionally be expected to use the *thou* of a social superior and to receive a respectful *you* from family and subordinates. They are indeed the most frequent users of *thou*-forms in the play, but their usages are significantly different. Sir Walter expends most of his twenty-seven *thou*-forms in a stream of abuse against his former mistress and her pander-husband. Sir Oliver's *thou*-forms are exclusively directed towards his wife and mark fluctuations of feeling in their tempestuous marriage.

Sir Walter's first greeting of Allwit invokes the *thou*-form (by using its specialized verb ending, *-st*) and immediately introduces its ambiguities:

SIR WALTER: How dost, Jack?
ALLWIT:                              Proud of *your* worship's health, sir.
SIR WALTER: How does *your* wife?

                                        (1.2.69–70)

Coupled with the familiar "Jack" (rather than *John*), Sir Walter's "How dost" could be the greeting of an intimate equal. But since this is the combination that he elsewhere uses to children ("how dost, Nick?" at 1.2.115) and servants (1.1.139), we could equally infer that he is verbally putting Allwit in his (subordinate) place. Allwit's reply makes it quite clear that we are concerned here with relations of power rather than solidarity. His use of the *you*-form is exaggeratedly formal (amplifying "you" into "your worship"). Servants in the same scene address Sir Walter simply as "sir" (1.2.86, 89, 92) and Allwit later adopts this lesser formality (1.2.98). We may read Sir Walter's switch to reciprocal *you* in his response to Allwit as comically ironic; a wealthy aristocratic lover acknowledging a dependent cuckold as his social equal. By act five, the tables turn as Sir Walter realizes that this pseudo-equality has become a moral reality. His moral decline has taken him from adultery to (apparent) homicide and he returns home as a wounded fugitive.

Greeting Allwit once again, he is somewhat less polite:

SIR WALTER: Touch me not, villain! My wound aches at *thee*,
    *Thou* poison to my heart!

(5.1.13–14)

Sir Walter equates his physical injury with spiritual damages. His physical rejection of the previously intimate Allwits ("touch me not") is reinforced with vehement *thou*-ing. This time he ignores Allwit's placatory "your worship" (5.1.16, 18) and he jeeringly echoes but refuses to reciprocate Mrs Allwit's respectful *you* of polite concern.

WIFE: How is't with *you*, sir?
SIR WALTER:               Not as with *you*,
    *Thou* loathsome strumpet!

(5.1.34–5)

Twenty of Sir Walter's twenty-seven *thou*-forms cluster in this scene and mark it as a moment of high emotion and melodramatic comedy; counterpointed with the persistent politeness of the Allwits' address forms, Sir Walter's *thou*-ing seems to parody the language of tragic intensity.

The Kixes' dialogues may offer a more realistic representation of contemporary usage; they are beautifully constructed, pivoting on the emotional nuances of pronoun-switching. Middleton's thematic ironies of power reversal are microcosmically captured in the couple's volatile *thou*-ing. On their first appearance, Sir Oliver begins with the *thou* of intimacy, marked as polite by the addition of "pray thee" (2.1.133) and affectionate by the addition of "sweet wife" (2.1.120, 126, 137), but he is soon provoked into the *thou* of anger/contempt (foregrounded, as in the case of Sir Walter, by the close-coupling of two *thou*-forms together): "hang *thee*, *thou* hast had too many" (2.1.150). This prompts Lady Kix to reciprocate:

LADY:                         *Thou* li'st, brevity!
SIR OLIVER: O, horrible! Dar'st *thou* call me 'brevity'?
    Dar'st *thou* be so short with me?
LADY:                    *Thou* deservest worse . . .
SIR OLIVER:            Talk not on't, pray *thee*;
    *Thou*'lt make me play the woman and weep too.

(2.1.150–5)

Breaching the traditional asymmetry of husband–wife address, which prescribes that wives use respectful *you* to their husbands, Lady Kix's angry
*thou*s appear emasculating, reiterating her husband's impotence on a verbal
level. When he acknowledges his weakness, Lady Kix, having gained the
upper hand, reverts to the *you*-form in a calmer passage of factual discourse
(2.1.156–61).

The Kixes' dialogues are much like sporting events, each phrase a cut or
parry in the match. Intimacy and insolence turn on a single breath. When
they next enter together, Sir Oliver is again *thou*-ing his wife, but this time it
is clearly the *thou* of aggressive accusation: "*Thou* liest, barrenness! ... 'Tis
*thy* fault ... *Thine*; 'tis *thou* art barren" (3.3.40, 48, 49). And this time it is
Lady Kix who plays the woman and weeps. Her tears recall Sir Oliver from
abusive to affectionate *thou*-ing and she regains her ascendancy by adopting
the traditional *you* of wifely self-subordination:

SIR OLIVER: *Thou* art nothing of a woman.
LADY:                                      Would I were less than nothing! [*She*] *weeps*
SIR OLIVER: Nay, pri*thee*, what dost mean?
LADY:                                      I cannot please *you*.
SIR OLIVER: I'faith, *thou* art a good soul; he lies that says it;
  [*Kissing her*]
  Buss, buss, pretty rogue.

                                                          (3.3.83–6)

Marital harmony is restored – until Lady Kix subverts a wifely "you" with a
reproach: "had *you* been ought, husband, / It had been done ere this time"
(3.3.94–5), which prompts a new bout of reciprocal, vituperative *thou*-ing
(3.3.96–8).


                          CONCLUSION

All three of our case studies find Middleton presenting a Janus-faced
ambivalence towards "modern use" in language. His representation of
varieties pushes towards a new social realism, but one limited by the
technique of stereotyping and the genre of satire – although characters
such as Yellowhammer and Allwit are on the verge of escaping from stereotype by their conscious manipulation of the language(s) around them. In
pronoun usage, while Middleton attests to the contemporary decline of
*thou* (particularly in his representations of citizen language), he still relies on
it to underwrite the sincerity of the mutual affection between Moll and
Touchwood Junior (1.1.150; 3.1.47) or to reveal the depth of Allwit's

contempt for Sir Walter (2.2.56). His multiple puns, similarly, pull in two directions. While his characters wrestle with momentary and generally misleading coincidences of sound (never more so than when Maudline triumphantly "translates" Tim's Latin "parentibus" into English "pair of boots" at 1.1.71), below the level of their consciousnesses, the dramatist himself seems to be reaching back towards the serious puns of Renaissance tragedy, which encapsulate and synthesize a play's central concerns. Barber notes the recurrent and reverberative puns that cut across the characters' individual scripts. The pun on *flesh* (e.g. 1.1.7, 1.2.105, 2.1.107–8, 2.1.84), reinforced by the more specific pun on *mutton* (= "meat" and "whore," e.g. 2.1.82, 4.1.160), "links meat with sex and both with general carnality" (Barber's edition of Middleton, *Chaste Maid*, p. 7). The pun on *get* (= "be-get" and "acquire money") is even more important. Re-echoing within and between speakers (e.g. 1.2.19, 1.2.123, 2.1.11–12, 2.1.157, 2.2.174–6, 2.3.27–30, 3.3.62), it sounds the keynote for all four separate plots of *Chaste Maid* as they play variations on a single theme, that traditional ideals of procreation, family relationships, and natural inheritance are transmuted by the commercial values and imperatives of Cheapside.[11]

NOTES

1. This essay emerged from a graduate seminar, *Language, Rhetoric and Style in the English Renaissance*, organized by Sylvia Adamson at the University of Sheffield in 2008–9; individual case studies were contributed by seminar participants, as indicated in the text; the essay's design and its linking narrative were contributed by Adamson, who also edited the whole.

2. Reported by Thomas Sprat in his *History of the Royal Society* (1667); excerpted in Görlach, *Early Modern English*, pp. 257–60.

3. For the uses of French in early modern England, see Görlach, *Early Modern English*, pp. 167–8.

4. All etymologies and definitions in this essay are from *OED online* edn.

5. For a full discussion of "Inkhornism", see Barber, *Early Modern English*, pp. 81–90.

6. For names in comedy, see Barton, *Names*; for puns in tragedy and sermons, see Read, "Puns"; for changes in practice during the period, see Adamson, "Literary Language," pp. 554–6, 608–13.

7. See Locke, *Human Understanding*, Book 3, especially Chapters VI, IX, X.

8. For Locke's distinction between "wit" and "judgment," see *Human Understanding*, Book 2, Chapter XI, § 2.

9. See "gear," *n.*, 5.b and 11.c, and "ware," *n.*[3], 1.a and 4.b (or 4.c), in *OED online* edn.

10. For fuller discussion of the relation between "you" and "thou" in this period, see Barber, *Early Modern English*, pp. 208–13, "'You and 'Thou'"; Hope,

"Second person,"; Wales, "'Thou' and 'You'". Relevant excerpts from Fox's journal are given in Görlach, *Early Modern English*, pp. 375–6.

11. See Levin, "Four Plots," for the play's plot structure; Ricks, "Moral and Poetic Structure" and "Word-Play" examine the interrelations between puns and plots in Middleton's tragedies.

CHAPTER 23

# Collaboration: the shadow of Shakespeare

## James P. Bednarz

The sustained theoretical focus on collaboration in recent scholarship of early modern English drama has demonstrated the apparently limitless number of influences that can be factored into the process of theatrical production. Yet one of its most revealing forms remains the most literal: the writing of a play by a pair or group of authors working on a single text at the same time. About half of the Middleton canon is collaborative in this restrictive sense. But considering how important collaboration was to Middleton, there were few occasions on which he composed with others outside of his paired work with Thomas Dekker and William Rowley.[1] Indeed, Middleton's co-writing with Dekker and even greater involvement with Rowley was such a large part of his career that it even informs his few group compositions. His métier was to write with a single partner at a time – a process that yielded some of his best work – and he rarely joined larger syndicates.

Current scholarship has identified three group collaborations in which Middleton participated. The earliest record that we have of Middleton as a dramatist, *Henslowe's Diary*, notes that in 1602 he worked with Dekker, Anthony Munday, Michael Drayton, John Webster, and "others" on the lost "Caesar's Fall." Then, around 1618 or the following year, he co-wrote *An/The Old Law* with Rowley and perhaps Thomas Heywood. Finally, in 1623, he probably plotted and wrote about 303 lines (in different sections) of *The Spanish Gypsy*, along with John Ford, its principal author, aided by Dekker and Rowley.

Aside from these three group compositions, Middleton partnered only twice on plays with a single collaborator other than Dekker or Rowley. Although *Timon of Athens* could conceivably have been written any time between 1605 and 1607, the strongest evidence, I believe, suggests that Middleton worked on it between 1605 and 1606, and that he composed *Anything for a Quiet Life* with Webster in 1621. It was on these two occasions that he engaged in the kind of concentrated dual authorship that he practiced in his sustained relationships with Dekker and Rowley. And in each instance, Middleton's stints, first with Shakespeare and then with Webster, early and late in his career, were brief departures from his ongoing partnerships that duplicated their mode of production.

Yet Middleton's joint enterprises with Shakespeare and Webster arose under surprisingly varied circumstances. With Webster there was so much less at stake. Co-writing *Quiet Life* for the King's Men with Webster near the end of their contemporaneous careers, Middleton reunited with a playwright of about the same age with whom he had labored as a fledgling dramatist on "Caesar's Fall." Webster's work as a playwright was channeled into three bursts of activity: 1602–5, 1612–17, and 1621–5. And it was in the last of these three periods, when his great tragedies were behind him, that he returned with Middleton to a genre – city comedy – through which they had established their theatrical reputations. By 1621 each was so adept at composing this kind of play, and so willing to edit each other's passages – as equals – that the attempt to ascribe specific parts of *Quiet Life* to either is especially controversial. (The situation is further complicated by the fact that it was not published until 1662 in an edition that set its verse almost entirely as prose.) What Middleton and Webster jointly produced was a nostalgic variation on the familiar New Comedy plot formula they had each separately perfected with Dekker in *The Roaring Girl* and *Westward Ho*. How different this belated project with Webster consequently appears in light of Middleton's earlier, edgy collaboration with Shakespeare on *Timon*, their provocative experiment in satirical tragedy.

On the one occasion in which Middleton collaborated with the greatest writer of his age, the situation was far more challenging. Shakespeare, who was then reaching the end of his great tragic sequence, was still searching for ways to extend its range into new areas of experience, and he found in Middleton someone who might impart a contemporary urgency to classical drama. *Timon* nevertheless initially appeared in the Shakespeare First Folio of 1623 as a single-authored tragedy, and there has been a long-standing reluctance to cede any part of it to others. But Brian Vickers is right to insist that the combined studies from the early nineteenth century to the present by Charles Knight, N. Delius, F. G. Fleay, E. H. Wright, William Wells, H. D. Sykes, David Lake, MacDonald P. Jackson, Jonathan Hope, Gary Taylor, John Jowett, and R. V. Holdsworth "prove beyond any doubt" that Middleton collaborated on it with Shakespeare (*Shakespeare*, p. 281). Rarely has the cumulative case for collaboration been so thorough and convincing. The main reason for this success is that the Folio seems to have been printed – with little alteration by its main compositor – from a holograph manuscript drafted by both authors. It consequently preserves observable traces of Shakespearean and Middletonian idiosyncrasies of thought and style.

A wide range of readily observable features – such as Middleton's rapid vacillations between prose, blank verse, and rhyme in single speeches – correlate positively with his characteristic semantic, grammatical, and orthographic choices. Jowett writes that "Middleton's presence in the play" suggests a "joint venture," but he also maintains that "it appears from the text as a whole that Middleton wrote his contributions after Shakespeare had stopped working on his" (*Companion*, p. 357). Yet despite much that can be known about each writer's contribution to *Timon*, there are also passages in the play in which Shakespeare's and Middleton's writing seems so closely intertwined that it is difficult, if not impossible, to understand how they were produced. Questions persist about the extent to which, perhaps through imitation, they successfully accommodated their personal styles to each other, blurring in places the ordinary linguistic markers used to distinguish them. It is impossible to know, for instance, if there was an interval between their writing or if Shakespeare supervised or revised what Middleton submitted.

For mainstream Shakespeareans, *Timon*'s authorship has long been a problem, and by 1904 A. C. Bradley had already been convinced on stylistic grounds that "Shakespeare did not write the whole play" (*Shakespearean Tragedy*, p. 351). But despite the growing strength of the argument for collaboration, the authority of E. K. Chambers, who famously excoriated the "disintegration" of Shakespeare's plays by scholars set on arbitrarily assigning his work to others, based on loose parallels of expression and thought, dominated twentieth-century criticism. Searching for any other solution than collaboration, in an uncharacteristic lapse of judgment, Chambers, who was himself troubled by the play's stylistic dissonances, resorted to the biographical fiction that *Timon* was written "under conditions of mental, and perhaps physical stress, which led to a breakdown" (*William Shakespeare*, vol. 1, p. 181). Recent analysis, however, has restored a sense of Shakespeare's sanity by discovering, with considerable consistency, Middleton's involvement in about 33 to 38.7 percent of the play.[2]

When Shakespeare and Middleton composed *Timon*, the latter was the young genius of city comedy at Paul's, the author of plays, between 1602 and 1606, such as *A Trick to Catch the Old One*, *A Mad World, My Masters*, and *Michaelmas Term*. What brought him into Shakespeare's orbit was that he had just begun to write tragedies for the King's Men at the Globe. By the end of 1605, Middleton had completed *A Yorkshire Tragedy* for Shakespeare's company, and it was at about the same time that he might have worked on *The Revenger's Tragedy* for them as well.[3] Attuned to Middleton's peculiar facility with satiric city comedy and his renewed interest in tragedy, Shakespeare probably asked him to coauthor *Timon*, met with him to outline its plot, and divided the work between them in ways that scholars are just starting to understand. Middleton, who admired and imitated Shakespeare (even going so far as to publish *The Ghost of Lucrece* in 1600), must have been thrilled at the invitation. But even though their collaboration must have been particularly close, scholars have not been able to ascertain, because of its many inconsistencies, loose ends, and army of unnamed characters, whether the text first printed in the Folio was either: (a) based on an early draft – "foul papers" – later revised for an undocumented production, or, instead, (b) evidence of a failed venture that never reached the stage. Selected for publication in the First Folio only at the last minute to fill the gap left when *Troilus and Cressida* was temporarily not available for printing, *Timon* remains a problematic text in the Shakespeare-Middleton canon.

Shakespeare might have written *Timon* in response to the manner in which Ben Jonson, by March of 1606, had energized *Volpone*, his latest comedy for the King's Men, with scenes of perverted gift-giving, deception, and greed. The idea might have occurred to Shakespeare to apply the same kind of economic satire to tragedy when he turned to one of his favorite sources, North's translation of Plutarch's *Lives*, for his subject. *Volpone* was Jonson's first play to be centered on legacy hunting, a theme that Middleton had popularized in such comedies as *Trick*, and Jonson modeled its closing episode, depicting the trickster's faked death, on Quomodo's disastrous ploy in *Michaelmas*. In responding to *Volpone*, Shakespeare might consequently have turned for assistance to the writer who had inspired Jonson (although the latter subsequently dismissed Middleton as a "base fellow" [*Jonson*, vol. 1, p. 137]). But as the senior dramatist on the project, Shakespeare, who was about sixteen years older than Middleton, not only composed most of the tragedy but reserved its passionate conclusion for himself.

Although he allowed Middleton sufficient room for improvisation, Shakespeare gave the play its definitive structure. In plotting it, Shakespeare utilizes some of the same basic elements he deploys in *King Lear* at about the same time: in each the tragic hero indulges in excessive giving that is met with ingratitude, triggering his withdrawal into a wilderness where he rages and curses mankind. But was Shakespeare in *Timon* recreating effects he had already more successfully achieved in *Lear*, or was he staking out new territory in *Timon* for further exploration in the greater play? Our answer goes a long way in determining how we view *Timon*'s place in Shakespeare's and Middleton's careers. Yet there is currently no consensus about whether *Timon* anticipates or echoes *Lear*. In the Oxford single edition of the play published in 2004, for instance, John Jowett laments that "it is impossible to be sure which was written first" (Shakespeare, *Timon*, p. 8), but three years later, without explanation, he ventures that it "probably precedes" *Lear* (*Companion*, p. 356). My own suspicion, however, is that the opposite is true. Even though Jowett credibly assumes that *Timon* was probably written early in 1606, he might be wrong in concluding that it was written before *Lear*, since Holdsworth has recently identified echoes of *King Lear* in *Yorkshire*, which, by all accounts, was written in 1605 ("Middleton's Authorship," pp. 4–6).

Shakespeare's work with Middleton was the first in a series of collaborations that he engaged in with younger playwrights from 1606 to 1613, including his involvement with George Wilkins on *Pericles* and John Fletcher on *Henry VIII*, *Two Noble Kinsmen*, and the lost "Cardenio." His goal was probably to rejuvenate his writing by drawing on the varied talents of a new generation. In each case, the older, established dramatist collaborated with a younger, promising playwright who had just become successful. Of these three collaborators, however, Shakespeare's project with Middleton, perhaps due to its experimental, biting, satiric nature, was the least likely to be popular. With Wilkins, whose writing he also completed, Shakespeare had an immediate hit that reignited his interest in the possibilities of romance, which he continued to develop on his own in *Cymbeline*, *The Winter's Tale*, and *The Tempest*. And with Fletcher he felt comfortable enough to explore history, tragicomedy, and romance in his only sustained collaboration. But the precise circumstances concerning the success or failure of Shakespeare's work with Middleton are harder to determine. The many unnamed characters and loose plot ends of the version we possess have led to the assumption that it was never originally performed, abandoned as unwatchable. But since the First Folio text of *Timon* might have been printed from a rough draft, it tells us nothing definite about whether or not the play was initially produced.

What the First Folio text of *Timon* reveals, however, is an intricately constructed collaboration in which Middleton responds to Shakespeare's dramatic cues and elaborates on his patterns.[4] In the first scenes of *Timon*, for instance, Middleton builds on Shakespeare's opening. But his signal contribution to the play is an artfully constructed insert (scenes 5–10 or act 3.1–6) in which he depicts the failed efforts of Timon's servants Flaminius and Servilius to secure financial aid from his false friends, and his subsequent dunning by these once congenial creditors on whom he has lavished gifts. Here Middleton was in his element, since he had adeptly handled similar material in creating the voracious lenders of *Trick*. When he started working at the Globe he had already become what Jowett calls "a poet of debt" (Shakespeare, *Timon*, p. 47), attuned to the language of finance, and it is in this capacity that he framed the peculiar dilemma of *Michaelmas*, in which the generous and unsuspecting Sir Richard Easy almost suffers Timon's fate when he temporarily loses his estate through fraud. Easy, like Timon, is "a fair free-breasted gentleman, somewhat too open" (1.2.57). And his erstwhile downfall, like Timon's, is the result of a vice of prodigality so closely aligned with the virtue of liberality that the con-man Shortyard attributes it benignly to his "good confidence" (4.3.16) in humanity.

It was to these six scenes in *Timon* that Middleton brought a kind of comic gusto that exposes basic social relations to be duplicitous expressions of economic knavery. Middleton specialized in the representation of those inhumane qualities that make Timon, rendered mostly passionately by Shakespeare, a misanthrope. Middleton consequently provides the background for Timon's powerful tirades, written by Shakespeare, that echo the peculiar alternation of screed and curse that punctuates *King Lear*. In both *Lear* and *Timon*, the overly generous, but foolish, giver is maddened by ingratitude and retreats into a barren wilderness where he denounces existence as bestial and diseased and calls for the dissolution of the world.

Continuing this pattern of division in scene 11 (3.7), Middleton then builds on Shakespeare's work by ringing his collaborator's portrait of an increasingly irate Timon in the mock banquet scene with the arrival of his false friends and their enforced departure in a hail of stones. In assigning Middleton this embellishment, however, Shakespeare also allowed him the opportunity to branch out in a new creative direction by developing a sympathetic characterization of Flavius, Timon's steward, who, in scenes 4, 13, and 14 (2.2, 4.2–3), like the counselor Kent in *King Lear*, remains faithful to his master in adversity. In doing so, Shakespeare elicited from Middleton a sentimental and moralizing tone that contrasts with his usual satiric edge. The result is an oddly Shakespearean sequence. Middleton was prepared to attempt something new: a more earnest form of dialogue based on sympathy and commiseration, rather than knavery and deceit.

The question of the extent and the nature of Middleton and Shakespeare's collaboration is particularly troublesome in those parts of the play for which attribution is more uncertain, especially scenes 3, 4, 11, 13, and 14, in which both hands have been variously identified. In scene 4, for example, in what is perhaps the most interesting of these conjoined passages, characteristic Shakespearean forms are so melded to Middleton's style that parts of the scene defy explanation or, rather, make numerous competing interpretations possible. Middleton might have done most of the writing, but the witty banter among Apemantus, the Fool, and the usurers' servants closely parallels the subject of Lear's dialogue with his similarly unnamed Fool.

In each play, the Fool's function is to universalize folly as a fundamental human characteristic and to serve as a "shadow" self whose specter dissolves any normative conception of identity. (Shakespeare first articulated the philosophical conceit of "shadow" and "substance" as existential doubles in the Temple Garden scene (2.4) of *Henry VI Part I*, and it became a favored trope in his poetic repertoire.) In *Timon*, Varro's first servant hails the jester, "How dost, Fool?" and is subjected to Apemantus's curt response, "Dost dialogue with thy shadow?" (scene 4, 49–50), and in *Lear*, the king's self-questioning, "Who is it that can tell me who I am?" is greeted (in the Folio text) by the Fool's reply, "Lear's shadow" (1.4.189–90). Impressed by the Fool's wit, Varro's servant then admits, "Thou art not altogether a fool," only to be told, "Nor thou altogether a wise man. As much foolery as I have, so much wit thou lack'st" (scene 4, 111–13). Similar phrasing, but deployed with greater subtlety, appears again in *Lear*. "This is not altogether fool, my lord," Kent tells Lear, to which the Fool adds, "No, faith, lords and great men will not let me" (1.4.125–6 in Q only). He is not "altogether" (i.e. "the only") fool, the jester implies, since the powerful insist on sharing his title. In *Timon*, the Fool with his relatively diminished wit appears only in this one scene, and it is possible that in writing it Middleton looked to the recently composed *Lear* for guidance but was unable to duplicate its brilliant wordplay. If this is true, however, Shakespeare must have looked to *Lear* as well, since the bitter king's curse on "ingrateful man" (3.2.9), reiterated twice by Timon, appears in a section of the play he wrote (scene 14 [4.3], 189 and 195).

Any study of Middleton's occasional collaboration might seem at first to take us solely to the accidental periphery of the canon. But insofar as it involves his work on *Timon* with Shakespeare, it places us at its conceptual core, revealing his curious status as a writer who, for different readers in different periods, produced work that was deemed *either* equal or inferior to Shakespeare's. From the beginning of the nineteenth century, some readers began to complain that despite the misconception fostered by the First Folio, *Timon* was not entirely Shakespeare's, since parts of it appeared to be the work of an inferior dramatist whose involvement was signaled by his defective style. The overwhelming proof that Middleton collaborated on *Timon*, however, has finally freed critics to reevaluate his contribution on its own terms, and this has encouraged a new paradoxical appreciation of the dramatist as *both* Shakespeare's "double" and "other."

NOTES

1. Even when working on city pageants, Middleton only wrote an insert of fifty-nine lines for *The Whole Royal and Magnificent Entertainment* for James I in 1604, under Dekker's direction, and never shared the give-and-take of composing with others.
2. These estimates by Gary Taylor and David Lake are cited by Vickers, *Shakespeare*, p. 281.
3. Dawson and Minton's introduction to Shakespeare and Middleton, *Timon*, p. 18, speculates that the tragedy was probably written in 1607. The strongest evidence it presents for this dating, however, is the theory that Shakespeare was inspired to write about Timon after having read a brief account of him embedded in Plutarch's "Life of Antony," the main source for *Antony and Cleopatra*, composed that year. But Shakespeare had long been familiar with Plutarch's *Lives*, and the links between *Timon, King Lear, A Yorkshire Tragedy*, and *Volpone* connect it more firmly to the theatrical context of 1605–6 than to later plays such as *Antony* or *Coriolanus*. The earlier dating also coincides with a period during which Middleton is known to have worked for Shakespeare's company.
4. The best extended commentary on this issue is offered by Jowett, "Pattern of Collaboration," pp. 181–205.

CHAPTER 24

# Collaboration: sustained partnerships

*Heather Hirschfeld*

At the end of the romp that is Middleton's *A Mad World, My Masters* – a play centered on a grandson's efforts to dupe his wealthy grandfather, Sir Bounteous Progress, into giving him money – the young protagonist, Follywit, disguises himself and his comrades as a company of players in order to perform at his grandfather's estate. The theatrical enterprise is a hoax to begin with, designed to allow the men to steal from the grandfather during their prologue and then sneak away, but Follywit himself is taken by surprise when his "plot's betrayed" and his company caught by the local Justice of the Peace (5.2.47). Improvising with abandon, Follywit tricks the JP into freeing his men; they all escape, leaving Sir Bounteous to recognize that he has been."gulled, i'faith, I am gulled" (5.2.176). When Follywit returns, "in his own shape" (5.2.205 SD), Sir Bounteous tells his grandson that "We had a play here":

FOLLYWIT: A play, sir? No.
SIR BOUNTEOUS: Yes, faith, a pox o'th' author!

(5.2.229–31)

Sir Bounteous is, of course, addressing the very "author" he curses, a delicious piece of dramatic irony. But also to be savored is the rich notion of the "author" implicit in the grandfather's complaint. "Author" encompasses here a wide range of dramatic activities fully consonant with a cultural climate which "did not carefully insulate the writing of scripts from the acting of plays" (Masten, *Textual Intercourse*, p. 15): Follywit organizes the men into a company, conducts them to the Bounteous estate, devises a plot for them to act (appropriately entitled "The Slip"), introduces it to the audience in a prologue, and rescripts it in the face of impending disaster. The fact that Sir Bounteous cannot recognize the author when he stands in front of him only highlights the latter's command – however vulnerable to outside forces such as the JP – over a fiction that has intervened materially in the men's lives.

219

As a dramatist, Thomas Middleton was interested in sharing these kinds of activities and this kind of command. Having gotten his theatrical start in 1602 by contributing, along with Thomas Dekker, Michael Drayton, John Webster, and Anthony Munday, to the lost "Caesar's Fall" (Henslowe, *Diary*, p. 202), Middleton continued to compose with other dramatists even as he was successfully writing plays, pageants, and pamphlets on his own, eventually earning the position of City Chronologer of London in 1620. In addition to occasional joint enterprises with William Shakespeare and John Webster (see James P. Bednarz's essay in this volume, p. 211), Middleton worked with Dekker between 1603 and 1611 on two pamphlets and three plays (*News from Gravesend* and *The Meeting of Gallants at an Ordinary*, and *The Patient Man and the Honest Whore*, *The Bloody Banquet*, and *The Roaring Girl*), and then again in 1623 on *The Spanish Gypsy*; and with William Rowley between 1613 and 1623 on five plays (*Wit at Several Weapons*, *A Fair Quarrel*, *An/The Old Law*, *The Changeling*, and *Gypsy*), as well as on a masque (*The World Tossed at Tennis*). Fully acquainted with the ways in which dramatic authorship for the early modern stage was "a relational form, a contest, a negotiation," Middleton remained committed to writing scripts with other playwrights at the same time as he juggled a solo career (N. Johnson, *Actor as Playwright*, p. 4).

Middleton's interest in joint work was not an anomaly in the world of the early modern professional theatre; G. E. Bentley calculates that over half of the plays for the London stage between 1576 and 1642 were scripted by more than one dramatist (*Profession of Dramatist*, p. 199). This kind of collaborative writing has long been a focus for modern scholars, at first for those interested in attribution studies (the determination of who wrote what parts of which plays), a form of stylistic analysis which, although sometimes criticized for its anachronistic assumptions about early modern writing practices and for its "decomposition" of texts, is fueled by a commitment to verbal or stylistic personality appropriate for the Renaissance and which has allowed for the determination of the canon of Middleton collaborations upon which the discussion below relies (M. P. Jackson, *Studies in Attribution*; Lake, *Canon*; Taylor, *Companion*, pp. 335–446; see also Eric Rasmussen's essay in this volume, p. 229). But collaboration has also become a focus for theatre historians concerned with the stage's sociocultural and political conditions and their effect on the construction and meaning of dramatic authorship. The frequency of joint writing for the early modern stage, as Jeffrey Masten explains in his important book *Textual Intercourse*, "poses challenges to the ideology of the author," those entrenched notions about the playwright as a single, inspired literary genius in full, intentional control over his work and its production. "Collaboration is . . . a dispersal of author/ity, rather than a simple doubling of it; to revise the aphorism, two heads are different than one" (p. 19). And this difference, other scholars remind us, reflects the fundamentally collaborative nature of the dramatic enterprise itself, which involved company sharers, bookkeepers, scribes, and censors, as well as actors and audiences, and finally printers "in shaping the text." Thus it was "motivated and sustained" by "networks of dependency, both discursive and institutional" (Cox and Kastan, "Introduction," p. 2).

These networks were not homogeneous. The history of the early modern stage shows us that collaboration – whether between writers or between writers and other invested parties – was not a one-size-fits-all category; it took different forms at different times and places and among different people. (Perhaps the most poignant form is the one set by the little-known dramatist Robert Daborne, who, desperately past a deadline, tried to placate his creditors by promising that "I have not only labord my own play which shall be ready before [the company] come over but given Cyrill Tourneur an act of y^e Arreignment of london to write y^t we may have y^t likewise ready for them" [*Henslowe Papers*, p. 72]). Distinct models of joint writing emerge from the payment records of *Henslowe's Diary*, the account book of the entrepreneur Philip Henslowe which records money lent to and received from theatre personnel from 1592 to 1603. In 1598 Henslowe lent money to be paid to George Chapman for "ii ectes of A traged*i*e of bengemens [Jonson's] plott*e*," suggesting a very particular division of labor (*Diary*, p. 100). Such a division is less transparent in payments to the pair of Dekker and Drayton for three plays about the French civil wars, but the fact that they continued to write as a team to produce a trilogy (although Dekker alone was paid for the fourth play, called "the firste Intreducyon") suggests a model of consistency in collaborative work across a topic or theme (*Diary*, pp. 98–103). The *Diary* also records payments not only to pairs of writers but also to larger syndicates, including quartets like that of Dekker, Drayton, Chettle, and Wilson, or quintets such as Dekker, Webster, Chettle, Heywood, and Wentworth Smith (pp. 89–91, 88–92, 218–19).

Middleton joined just such a quintet in 1602 to compose "Caesar's Fall" for the Admiral's Men. But, as James P. Bednarz notes in this volume (p. 211), he quickly came to concentrate on writing with a single partner, returning to the syndicate model only late in his career when, with Dekker, Rowley, and Ford, he participated in *The Spanish Gypsy*. Indeed, the collaborative duo seems to have become the dominant mode in the early decades of the seventeenth century, as the theatre, under the patronage of the royal family starting with the accession of James in 1603, became more and more a respected pastime for audiences and a respectable profession for writers. Francis Beaumont and John Fletcher were the period's most visible couple; they began writing together for the children's companies as early as 1606, but by 1610 they were scripting plays as a team primarily for the King's Men, Shakespeare's company and London's leading troupe, creating emotionally labile tragicomedies that were popular both in the city and at court. Later seventeenth-century commentators were to look back nostalgically on the two as the "Castor and Pollux" of the stage, who each found resources in the other's wit or judgment and thus "succeeded in Conjunction more happily than any Poets of their own, or this Age, to the reserve of the Venerable *Shakespeare*, and the Learned and Judicious *Johnson*" (Langbaine, *An Account*, p. 203). When Beaumont retired from the stage in 1613, Fletcher found other partners to work with repeatedly: Shakespeare, Nathan Field, and Philip Massinger.

Middleton's sustained ties with Dekker, beginning in 1604, and then with Rowley, beginning in 1613, could be said to foreshadow and then to mirror those of Fletcher with his collaborators. But there is an important difference in the ways these men operated. Fletcher was what G. E. Bentley calls an "attached" professional playwright, tightly connected to a single acting company (*Profession of Dramatist*, pp. 28–35). Slowly but surely, and despite forays for the Lady Elizabeth's Men as late as 1614, Fletcher established himself exclusively as a King's Man, inheriting the role of the company's principal playwright from Shakespeare and passing it on to Massinger in the 1620s. This was not Middleton's way: he worked, as Brian Jay Corrigan has suggested, "freelance" ("Crisis Literature," p. 287). "Freelance" is a nineteenth-century coinage, but it expresses accurately the kind of "protean relationship" with the theatre companies that Middleton enjoyed in the decades after James's accession, as he wrote for the Children of Paul's, the Children of the Chapel, the King's Men, Prince Henry's Men, Lady Elizabeth's Men, and Prince Charles's Men. And joint writing was central to his flexibility. Given that the bulk of Middleton's solo plays – from *The Revenger's Tragedy* of 1606 to the fantastically popular *A Game at Chess* of 1624 – were written for the King's Men, and given that the bulk of his plays with Dekker and Rowley were written for Prince Henry's Men and Prince Charles's Men, respectively, it seems that he relied on collaboration as a way to write plays for different companies. Or, to put it another way, he was willing, and able, to write for companies other than the King's Men in order to join up with Dekker and Rowley.

It is possible to imagine what appealed *personally* and *dramatically* to Middleton about these specific partners: Dekker's earnest Protestantism, his extensive experience writing for the theatre, his sensitivity to social hierarchy, and his intimacy with the London landscape; Rowley's boisterous sense of humor, his special fondness for writing about travel and travelers, and his acting credentials (Rowley was a leading member of Prince Charles's company and himself specialized in clown roles). But it is also possible to imagine what appealed to Middleton *institutionally* about them. If, as Grace Ioppolo has written, "dramatists seem to have chosen their own collaborators rather than accepting those forced on them by Henslowe or other entrepreneurs," then Middleton's choice of Dekker and Rowley allowed him to maintain the prerogatives of a freelance playwright unconstrained by rigid allegiances to a single company, exercising an authorial agency and intentionality within the intensely collective, communal environment of the early modern theatre (*Dramatists*, p. 32).[1] The fact that Middleton made the choice of Dekker and Rowley consistently over stretches of time suggests that, even if he was skeptical of permanent professional commitments, he was respectful of personal loyalties developed over long periods. How did these loyalties manifest themselves in their texts, which span such a wide range of genres, topics, and issues?

Middleton shared with Dekker an intensely theatrical perspective, a way of seeing and describing the world as a stage even when writing prose. Thus their pamphlet *Gravesend* (1603–4) summarizes in a poem, with a shockingly visceral vocabulary, the effects of the plague on London.

> These are the tragedies, whose sight
> With tears blot all the lines *we write*.
> The stage, whereon the scenes are played
> Is a whole kingdom. What was made
> By some (most provident and wise)
> To hide from sad spectators' eyes
> Acts full of ruth, a private room
> To drown the horror of death's doom,
> That building now no higher rear:
> The pest-house standeth everywhere,
> For those that on their biers are borne
> Are numbered more than those that mourn.
>
> (934–45 [emphasis added])

The deliberate use of "we" – replacing the undifferentiated "Somebody" of the dedicatory epistle – calls attention not only to the writers' joint work but also to their joint horror at the London before them: "how can we choose / But have a sad and drooping muse / When corpses do so choke the way / That now thou look'st like Golgotha" (768–71). A similar horror informs their tragedy *The Bloody Banquet*, not published until 1639 but dated to 1608–9, which juxtaposes a Senecan plot of infidelity, revenge, and canni- balism (an adulterous young queen is made to eat the lover she herself murders) with the large-scale betrayals common to warfare, here between the ancient empires of Lydia, Lycia, and Cilicia. Dekker seems to have set up the first three scenes of the play and two scenes of the second act, with Middleton taking over until the final act, to which both contributed. But they are clearly united in portraying and then critiquing the kind of political and sexual lusts that drive the characters. And what seems to disturb them most is not simply the fact of the bloodthirsty or passionate pursuits but the motivations and machinations behind them. As the Tyrant admonishes his adulterous wife immediately after he discovers her dead lover and immedi- ately before he schemes to make her eat him, "The deed is not so monstrous in itself / As is the art which ponders home the deed" (4.3.160–1).

Although the Tyrant himself is guilty of unspeakable crimes, his horror at the abuse of art – particularly the art of plotting – is a resonant one for the two playwrights. They take up the issue from a more comic perspective in their two other joint plays, *Patient Man* (1604) and *Roaring Girl* (1611), the first extremely popular in its own time (it was published five times between 1604 and 1635) and the second widely read today. *Patient Man* involves interconnected stories that highlight the self-defeating foolishness of trying to manipulate people or events. In one plot, a citizen wife, Viola, schemes to offend her preternaturally patient husband, Candido, because she "wants that virtue which all women's tongues have – to anger their husbands" (2.87–8). This plot is explicitly intertextual: when Viola hints at her attrac- tion to an apprentice dressed in her husband's clothes, he suggests that their sleeping together "'Twere a good comedy of errors" (12.25). Middleton and Dekker follow the arc of Shakespeare's 1590s play by having Candido (like Antipholus of Ephesus) imprisoned for being mad; they twist their source by showing the wife's torment when she wants her husband back. The other plot involves an obsessively protective Duke who tries to keep his daughter Infelice from her lover Hippolito by feigning her death and burial; his plans are betrayed by the very doctor he hires to poison Hippolito, and in the final scene the Duke presides over their marriage as well as that of Bellafront, the converted prostitute of the title, to Matteo, the only man whom she has actually slept with.

The most celebrated of the Middleton-Dekker collaborations is *Roaring Girl*, whose cross-dressing protagonist Moll Cutpurse, a romanticized ver- sion of a real woman (Mary Frith) from the London street scene, fore- grounds the period's concerns with changing notions of gender, power, and sexuality. Scholars believe that the real-life Frith may have appeared onstage during a performance, thus serving as a collaborator herself in the production of the play;[2] the fictional Moll serves a similar purpose, facilitating the marriage of Sebastian Wengrave, against the will of his father, to his beloved Mary Fitzallard. Along the way to the happy ending, Moll (a woman who parades about in men's clothes) unsettles expectations and disturbs sensibilities. To Sir Alexander Wengrave, Sebastian's father, she is "'a creature ... nature hath brought forth / To mock the sex of woman'" (2.129–30). To the gallant Laxton, who assumes that she must be a prostitute, she is both highly desirable ("I would give but too much money to be nibbling with that wench") and, after she scolds and beats him, intimidating: "I think I fight with a familiar, or the ghost of a fencer! She's wounded me gallantly" (5.125–6). To a set of gentlemen unfamiliar with the ways of the London underworld she is both a rescuer – she saves them from being taken by local thieves – and a figure of suspicion: "I wonder how thou camest to the knowledge of these nasty villains," a lord asks her (10.322–3). At every turn, the dramatists have Moll defend her honor and her autonomy in monologues that are also deft social critiques. In her most famous outburst, against Laxton, she accuses men of trafficking in rumors about women's sexual availability:

> How many of our sex by such as thou
> Have their good thoughts paid with a blasted name
> That never deserved loosely or did trip
> In path of whoredom beyond cup and lip?
> But for the stain of conscience and of soul,
> Better had women fall into the hands
> Of an act silent than a bragging nothing:
> There's no mercy in't.
>
> (5.81–8)

She then goes on to accuse men not only of making false claims about women but of seducing the most vulnerable.

Because she enables a heterosexual marriage at the play's close, some critics have seen the dramatists' presentation of Moll as socially conservative,[3] but their collaborative work in the creation of the character seems more deliberately designed to "boldly challenge established social and sexual values" (Rose, "Women in Men's Clothing," p. 368; Hirschfeld, "What Do Women Know?," pp. 123–46). Indeed, no value is more challenged by Moll than marriage, which she roundly rejects for herself: "I have no humor to marry. I love to lie o' both sides o'th'bed myself; and again o'th'other side" (4.37–9).

Challenging received social and sexual values – and in particular paternal control over children's marital options – also lies at the core of the Middleton-Rowley partnership, widely considered "one of the most successful collaborations of the Jacobean era" (Shaw, "Introduction," p. xx). Their joint enterprises (which began after Middleton's work with Dekker had ceased) were inaugurated in 1613 with *Weapons*, a comic exercise in strategic one-upmanship; the protagonist, Wittypate, designs various projects to outsmart his father, while a host of other characters develop various schemes to achieve their preferred couplings. The juggling of plots and disguises, culminating in what one character aptly calls "the harvest of our designs," is a collaborative tour de force which ironically underscores the threat to individual choice posed by rigid social structures (5.1.1). The dramatists treat a similar threat, this time to male friendship, in *Quarrel* (composed between 1615 and 1616), a rich satire on cults of honor and female chastity. And in *Old Law* (composed between 1618 and 1619), a comedy based on a seventeenth-century version of a modest proposal – the newly devised "old law" of the state of Epire mandates that men and women be executed when they reach 80 and 60 years old, respectively – they target the amoral greed of children for their parents' estates and the impatient lust of spouses for fresh, younger partners, while calling into question the rights of citizens to oppose the government. In the final scene the dramatists reveal the law to be an elaborate trick of the Duke of Epire to test his citizens, but the bulk of the play is a concentrated meditation on one of the playwrights' chief concerns: the perversion of language by characters who use the conventions of legal discourse to invalidate essential human bonds and virtues.

This concern is central to the playwrights' greatest collaborative achievement, *Changeling*, a dark, psychologically explosive tragedy composed and performed around 1622 for Lady Elizabeth's Men (their earlier collaborations had all been for Prince Charles's Men). The play accommodates two intersecting plots: in the tragic plot, assigned by scholars to Middleton, Beatrice-Joanna, daughter of the nobleman Vermandero, wants to extricate herself from a marriage to one man, Alonzo de Piracquo, in order to marry the dashing Alsemero; in order to do this, she arranges for her father's servant, De Flores, whom she loathes as much as he obsessively desires her, to murder Alonzo. The second plot, assigned to Rowley and set in a madhouse on the outskirts of the first plot's Alicante, features a jealous old doctor, Alibius, who locks his beautiful young wife away from the world, only to have some of his patients – gallants who infiltrate the hospital by pretending to be fools and madmen – woo her. The gallants, Antonio and Francesco, are the play's most explicit "changelings," but the most provocative one is Beatrice, who starts the play as a virginal and sympathetic, if spoiled, young woman, but quickly stains body and soul by arranging the murder of her suitor and then her waiting-woman and by becoming De Flores's sexual toy. Beatrice's descent reverberates with tragedy's – and Protestantism's – deepest concerns about issues of human will and destiny, posing the tortuous question of whether the murderous Beatrice of the play's close is different from, or simply the inevitable realization of, the court coquette of the beginning. Likewise the gallants, whose disguises as fools and madmen can be seen not as masks but as the purest expression of their passionate selves. So even if the two plots literally intersect when the madmen come to perform for the court, they converge more profoundly in their sustained meditation on characterological and linguistic metamorphosis, on "ring[ing] changes on the meaning and structure of language" in ways that reveal their characters' control – or lack of control – over the words and worlds around them (Bueler, "Rhetoric," p. 96).

Although visible throughout the play, differentials in verbal power are most stunningly on display during Beatrice's exchange with De Flores after he has murdered Alonzo. He expects payment in sex; she cannot follow his meaning:

> DE FLORES: Do you place me in the rank of verminous fellows
>    To destroy things for wages? Offer gold
>    For the life-blood of man? Is any thing
>    Valued too precious for my recompense?
> BEATRICE: I understand thee not.
> DE FLORES: I could ha' hired
>    A journeyman in murder at this rate,
>    And mine own conscience might have lain at ease,
>    And have had the work brought home.
> BEATRICE [*aside*]: I'm in a labyrinth!
>    What will content him?
>
> (3.4.66–74)

When Beatrice, finally comprehending that the only thing that will content him is her virginity, protests that they are of different social classes ("Think but upon the distance that creation / Set 'twixt thy blood and mine"), De Flores seizes and revises her understanding of her "creation": "You're the deed's creature," he tells her, "by that name you lost / Your first condition, and I challenge you, / As peace and innocency has turned you out, / And made you one with me" (3.4.140–3). She should thus "Look but into your conscience, read me there. / 'Tis a true book; you'll find me there your equal" (3.4.135–6). De Flores, in an act foreshadowing his eventual rape of Beatrice,[4] declares that he has written himself into her mind even as she had been trying to write herself out of an unwanted marriage and into a desired love affair.

Such verbal violence and violation is the precise opposite of the kind of writing relationship that scholars suggest Middleton and Rowley enjoyed in all their plays, but especially in *Changeling*, where "the effect of the collaboration was especially potent" (Bueler, "Rhetoric," p. 97). I would suggest that the power of their relationship is based on a collaborative ideal best observed in its allegorized perversion: De Flores's verbal and sexual threat. The ideal, then, is the mutually desired sharing of words and plots, and it informs the canon of Middleton's plays. Whether or not it was ever completely achieved, it remained important to him. Even after *Changeling*, he continued to work collaboratively with his two sustained partners, joining forces with both Dekker and Rowley (and John Ford) on *Gypsy*, a drama which makes playwriting and performing central to the plot. Perhaps most meaningfully, he likely carved out a clown part (the Fat Bishop) for Rowley in what would be the Renaissance stage's blockbuster hit, *Game*; his collaborator, if not collaborative writing, was a part of Middleton's most successful solo composition.

## NOTES

1. For an important challenge to collaboration as the governing paradigm of playwrighting and a discussion of the single author as the pervasive model for the playhouse, see Knapp, "What Is a Co-Author?"
2. Hutchings and Bromham suggest that the performance of the real Mary Frith represents dramatic collaboration as "a trope that produces a creative, unmanageable friction" (*Middleton*, p. 53).
3. See for instance Baston, who suggests "that the vision of the play is far more reactionary than radical" ("Rehabilitating Moll's Subversion," p. 320).
4. For an important discussion of this sexual relation as a matter of rape, see Burks, "'I'll want my will else'."

## CHAPTER 25

# Collaboration: the determination of authorship

## Eric Rasmussen

The entry on "collaboration" in the *Shakespeare Encyclopedia* (P. Parker [ed.]) asserts that "Shakespeare was a frequent collaborator in the writing of scripts, especially at the beginning and end of his career." Indeed, it is pleasant to think of Shakespeare getting a toehold in the profession by contributing a few scenes to plays such as *Edward III*, going on to produce single-authored works for the next twenty years, and then passing the baton of principal dramatist for the King's Men to John Fletcher by collaborating with the younger playwright on *Henry VIII*, *The Two Noble Kinsmen*, and the lost "Cardenio." By encouraging such a narrative, however, the author of that encyclopedia entry (yours truly) occludes the thriving collaborative relationship that Shakespeare appears to have maintained for several years with Thomas Middleton.

Thomas Kyd observed that when he and Christopher Marlowe would write "in one chamber," papers which were "affirmed by Marlowe to be his" would on occasion become "shufled" with some of Kyd's own (cited in Brooke, *Life of Marlowe*, p. 104). Whether or not Shakespeare and Middleton ever shared a writing chamber, their work was clearly "shuffled" to a certain extent in the early seventeenth century. Middleton appears to have had a hand in *Measure for Measure* (1604) and *Macbeth* (1606), perhaps revising them after Shakespeare's retirement. In 1607, the two playwrights seem to have collaborated on *Timon of Athens*.[1] In that same year, Middleton's *The Puritan Widow* was published with a title-page attribution to "W. S.," later expanded to "Will. Shakespeare" in Archer's 1656 play list, and subsequently included in the Third (1664) and Fourth (1685) Shakespeare Folios. The following year, Middleton's *A Yorkshire Tragedy* was registered as "written by WYLLIAM SHAKESPERE" and published, with a slightly more muted attribution on the title page, as "*Written by* VV. Shakespeare"; it later formed part of Thomas Pavier's aborted 1619 collection of Shakespeare's plays, and then appeared in both the Third and the Fourth Folios.

Given this "shuffling" of Middleton and Shakespeare, it may be worth remembering that in 1607 – the year in which *Timon* was written by the two – no plays of Shakespeare's appeared in print, neither first editions nor reprints. On the other hand, 1607 was a banner year for Middleton's presence in the bookshops, with the publication, along with *Puritan*, of first editions of *The Phoenix*, *The Revenger's Tragedy*, and *Michaelmas Term*, all published anonymously. In 1608, three Shakespeare plays appeared (Q1 *Lear*, Q4 *Richard II*, and Q5 *1 Henry IV*), as did three first editions of Middleton plays, all now published with his name or initials featured on the title pages (*Your Five Gallants*, *A Mad World, My Masters*, and *A Trick to Catch the Old One*), along with *Yorkshire*. What emerges from the publication record of 1607–8 is a picture of Middleton as an up-and-coming playwright who had twice as many plays appearing in print during this period as did Shakespeare – although *Puritan* and *Yorkshire* were credited to Shakespeare. Perhaps these were mistakes in attribution – understandable given the close working relationship of the two playwrights. But it may be that the plays were, in fact, collaborations in which the senior partner was accorded all of the available credit. Similarly, although "Thomas deckers & midelton" received a payment from Henslowe for *The Patient Man and the Honest Whore* in 1604 (Henslowe, *Diary*, p. 209), the title page of the quarto attributes the play only to Dekker. The difficulties that Middleton, as a junior collaborator, may have had getting acknowledged are nicely documented by Henslowe's 1602 payment for "Caesar's Fall" to "antoney Monday & mihell drayton webester & the Rest," where "mydelton" is later interlined in the manuscript above "the Rest" (Henslowe, *Diary*, p. 201).

In trying to imagine the process by which Middleton and Shakespeare may have collaborated, Shakespeare's editors – perhaps not surprisingly – have tended to view him as the figure firmly in control. Speculating about the genesis of *Timon*, the editors of the 2008 Arden Shakespeare edition, Anthony Dawson and Gretchen Minton, maintain that since Shakespeare "was the foremost playwright of the time, while Middleton was just coming into prominence," Shakespeare "probably took the lead ... and took the meatiest scenes for himself ... he reserved most of the final two acts for himself" (pp. 4–5). On the other hand, John Jowett, the editor of the play in the Oxford *Middleton*, gives Middleton the active verb as the one who "took the banquet scene, the central scenes with Timon's creditors, Alcibiades's confrontation with the Senate, and most of the episodes figuring the Steward," such that "Shakespeare was left to concentrate on the opening" (*Companion*, pp. 357–8). It should be noted that both of these scenarios represent collaboration, at least on the verbal level, as selfish appropriation rather than mutual interaction.

In fact, early modern playwrights who worked together on plays tended to work apart (see Rasmussen, *Textual Companion to* Doctor Faustus, p. 30). Famously, Thomas Nashe, who wrote the induction and first act of *The Isle of Dogs*, complained that Ben Jonson, who wrote the other four acts, did not have "the least guess of my drift or scope" (Nashe, *Works*, vol. III, p. 154). Shakespeare used a different source book for his contribution to *The Two Noble Kinsmen* than Fletcher used for his: in Shakespeare's section, the name Pirithous is trisyllabic and spelled *Pirithous* (the spelling in North's Plutarch); in Fletcher's share, it has four syllables and is spelled *Perithous* (the spelling in Chaucer's *Knight's Tale*). So, too, in *Timon*, Middleton preferred "Apermantus" and "Ventidgius" to Shakespeare's "Apemantus" and "Ventidius." Indeed, it is such patterns of difference that often encourage scholars to speculate about a text's collaborative origins.

Apparently there was often a spatial separation in a collaboration: Shakespeare was writing in his chamber where he had a Folio of North's Plutarch; Fletcher was writing in another location where he had a Chaucer Folio. But the temporal dimension is more complex. A text produced by two or more dramatists during a single period of composition is generally termed a "collaboration" (*Timon*); if the work of the two is separated by a period of time, however, then the resultant text is an "adaptation" (*Macbeth*, *Measure for Measure*). These categories are formalized in the headnotes to these three plays in the Oxford *Middleton*. Although James P. Bednarz's essay in this volume (p. 211) offers a lively and detailed reconstruction of what he characterizes as a "particularly close" collaboration between Middleton and Shakespeare on *Timon*, Jowett concludes that "Middleton wrote his contributions after Shakespeare had stopped working on his" (*Companion*, p. 357). How, then, should we view Middleton's work on *Timon* – as collaborating, revising, or adapting?

Scholars who undertook the study of Middleton's asynchronic collaborations with Shakespeare were seeking solutions to obvious problems: Why do the cue-lines for two songs from Middleton's *The Witch* (1616) appear in Shakespeare's *Macbeth*? Why does a song from Fletcher's *Rollo, Duke of Normandy* (c. 1617) appear in *Measure for Measure*? A solution to the first problem was proposed in 1869 by W. G. Clark and W. A. Wright, who wrote, "we incline to think that the play [*sic*] was interpolated after Shakespeare's death, or at least after he had withdrawn from all connection with the theatre. The interpolator was, not improbably,

Thomas Middleton" (cited in Shakespeare, *Macbeth*, Furness [ed.], p. 266). This solution was further fleshed out by Gary Taylor, first in the *Textual Companion* to the *Oxford Shakespeare* (Wells and Taylor [gen. eds.], 1987) and then in the Oxford *Middleton* (2007), in which Inga-Stina Ewbank's introduction argues that Middleton, after Shakespeare's retirement, added to *Macbeth* two songs and a dance from his "ignorantly-ill-fated" play *Witch*, which had "fallen foul of the censor," and that, "in order to motivate the appearance of Hecate in these [scenes], he added the rest of what is now 3.5 and some lines in 4.1" (*Middleton*, p. 1166). The adaptation would have brought a proto-operatic dimension to the play, with music, dancing, and spectacular stage effects. Although the idea that Middleton may have adapted *Macbeth* is cautiously accepted by many scholars, Brian Vickers's *Shakespeare, Co-Author* (2002), an extensive study of the collaborations that Shakespeare engaged in with Peele, Middleton, Wilkins, and Fletcher, dismisses as "ungrounded" the argument that "several scenes in *Macbeth* had been supplied by Middleton" (pp. 123–5). More recently, Vickers reports that a computer-assisted authorship study of the Hecate scenes reveals "absolutely no trace of Middleton's hand, but extensive proof of Shakespeare's" (Vickers, "Disintegrated," p. 15). Tellingly, in Robert Miola's Norton Critical Edition of the play (2004), Middleton is nowhere mentioned.

The possibility that Middleton adapted *Measure for Measure* was first proposed in the *Oxford Shakespeare* (Wells and Taylor [gen. eds.]), with Taylor and Jowett detailing their arguments in a subsequent duograph, *Shakespeare Reshaped* (1993), and providing additional support in the Oxford *Middleton*. Editors since Theobald had known that the song that begins the fourth act, "Take, O take those lips away," also appears in a John Fletcher play, *The Bloody Brother*, written c. 1617, but, perhaps naturally, they assumed that Fletcher borrowed the song from Shakespeare. Jowett and Taylor, however, presented reasons for believing that the song was original with Fletcher and represents, instead, a late interpolation into Shakespeare's text. If the song is removed from the opening of act 4 of *Measure for Measure*, and two of the Duke's soliloquies are transposed, a few minor textual tangles can be straightened out as well.

Jowett and Taylor also drew attention to the famous duplication in the play's second scene, where Mistress Overdone enters and informs Lucio that Claudio is being taken to prison, and will soon be executed, for getting a woman pregnant; Pompey then enters and tells her what she has just told Lucio. It is clear that one of the passages was intended to replace the other, but most previous textual editors had assumed that the duplication was the result of a Shakespearean false start. However, Jowett and Taylor detected the presence of another hand. They pointed out that the act divisions in *Measure for Measure* and the evident censorship strongly suggest that the Folio text derives from a theatrical manuscript. They also observed that the Folio page on which these passages appear is particularly cramped, as if the compositor had included a number of lines that had not been taken into account when casting off copy for the stint. Interestingly, the compositor took spacing measures that would allow for seven extra lines, precisely the length of the Pompey passage. In other words, the Pompey passage was seemingly marked for omission, and so perhaps not counted when the compositor's stint was cast off, but the compositor misread the deletion marks and mistakenly set both the Pompey passage and the Lucio-Overdone passage that was intended to replace it. Jowett and Taylor made the point that Shakespeare's primary source provides a precedent only for the Pompey passage. Stylometric, linguistic, and vocabulary evidence in the Lucio-Overdone passage points away from Shakespeare (and most other dramatists) and towards Middleton. Overdone's allusions to "the war," which Jowett and Taylor argued would hardly have been topical in 1604 (the putative date of *Measure for Measure*), would have been more so in 1619–24, the years that saw England's first military engagement since the peace declared upon James's accession in the spring of 1603; similarly, the ironic allusion to the King of Hungary's peace would have had more force in the 1620s in the wake of Hungary's abandonment of its allies at the beginning of the Thirty Years War. Jowett has since bolstered this argument by observing that a newssheet published on October 6, 1621, recording the incursions of the Budianer Hungarians, makes particularly detailed reference to a number of dukes meeting with the King of Hungary (*Companion*, p. 419). Finally, a set of verbal parallels and specific features of dramatic technique link the Lucio-Overdone passage to Middleton's writing in the early 1620s. This accumulation of evidence points rather decisively to Middleton as the author of the interpolation and strongly suggests a date of composition *c.* 1621.

Reviewing Jowett and Taylor's arguments in 1996, I found them to be "compelling" (Rasmussen, "Review," p. 36), but few other textual scholars are as enthusiastic. In her 1996 edition of *Measure for Measure*, Grace Ioppolo wrote that the arguments are "extremely interesting," but found them to "depend upon too much unsupported speculation to be conclusive" (p. 21). Vickers's *Shakespeare, Co-Author* does not even mention the possibility that Middleton adapted *Measure for Measure*. And Angela Stock, in her update of the Cambridge edition (2006), pulls no punches: "If posthumous adaptation could explain the plays' defiant ambiguity, this writer for her part would like to know who co-authored *Richard II* and *The Merchant of Venice*, not to mention *Henry V* and *Coriolanus*" (p. 71).

It has to be said that Jowett and Taylor's increasingly assured insistence about the validity of their hypothesis has done little to persuade skeptics. Their appropriately tentative suggestion in 1986 that the play "may have undergone adaptation after Shakespeare's death" by "Someone – perhaps Thomas Middleton, to judge by the style" (Wells and Taylor [gen. eds.], *Oxford Shakespeare*, p. 789) had become a virtual certainty by 2004: "the evidence for posthumous adaptation of *Measure* is now even stronger than the evidence for posthumous adaptation of *Macbeth*" (G. Taylor, *Mediterranean*, p. 249). Moreover, the narrative in the *Companion* to the Oxford *Middleton*, in which John Jowett refutes, in the third person, the earlier tentative conclusions of Jowett and Taylor, is a bit strange:

They gave three reasons for doubting Middleton's authorship of the interpolated lines after the song; none of them, however, is compelling . . . Jowett and Taylor's third reason for dismissing Middleton was the 'general blandness' of these lines. This is poor evidence for an attribution (*Companion*, p. 419)

Anthony Davies's entry on *Measure for Measure* in *The Oxford Companion to Shakespeare* (Dobson and Wells [eds.], 2001) has the virtue of greater judiciousness: "the first part of 1.2 was probably added to the promptbook by a later adapter, probably Thomas Middleton. This later exchange was probably meant to replace the original." Probably.

NOTE

1. The year 1607 is the date adduced by Anthony Dawson and Gretchen Minton in the introduction to Shakespeare and Middleton, *Timon*, p. 18. Cf. James P. Bednarz's arguments for an earlier date of composition in footnote 3 of his essay in this volume, p. 218.

## CHAPTER 26

# Middleton and dramatic genre

## Suzanne Gossett

"Is it a tragedy plot, or a comedy plot?" This characteristically inappropriate response of young Sam to his conniving mother's announcement, "I have a plot in my head, son" (*A Trick to Catch the Old One*, 2.1.374–6), would nevertheless resonate with early modern audiences. Readers and viewers alike apparently wished to be prepared for the aesthetic experience of a play by advance notice of its generic classification. Thus the Shakespeare First Folio catalogued plays as "comedy" "tragedy," and "history," and the 1647 Beaumont and Fletcher First Folio was entitled *Comedies and Tragedies*. In his 1616 Folio Ben Jonson placed generic markers on the individual title pages. However, from the beginning of Middleton's career these categories were bleeding into each other. Polonius notoriously assures Hamlet that the traveling actors are the best in the world "for tragedy, comedy, history, pastoral, pastoral-comical, historical-pastoral, tragical-historical, tragical-comical-historical-pastoral, scene individable or poem unlimited" (2.2.379–82, Folio text), and this definition was recalled almost two decades later when the fake players in Middleton's *Hengist, King of Kent* (1616–20) announce they are "comedians, tragedians, tragicomedians, comi-tragedians, pastoralists, humorists, clownists and satirists" (5.1.70–3).

These two lists reflect contemporary attention to the "new" genre of tragicomedy, whose uncertain parameters were much discussed in Italy and England at the turn of the seventeenth century. Marston's *The Malcontent* was entered into the Stationers' Register as a tragicomedy in 1604, just as Middleton started writing for the stage (the term had first appeared in the Register in 1598); in 1609 Fletcher felt it necessary to define tragicomedy for readers of *The Faithful Shepherdess*. At the same time Shakespeare, whose comedies and tragedies of the 1590s had been models of the traditional forms, began experimenting with plays that are still troublesome to categorize, sometimes called problem plays, sometimes tragicomedies, sometimes romances. Even his tragedies could stray from expected norms, yielding a play as disconcerting as *Timon of Athens*, on which the young Middleton collaborated.

Middleton was well chosen for this task; plays throughout his canon resist traditional generic limitations. From his earliest independent work he tended to satirize the formal divisions. Once more established, he wrote a number of plays – examples are *The Witch, Hengist, An/The Old Law*, and *A Game at Chess* – which only with difficulty can be forced into familiar categories. A general overview of his canon suggests that it falls into groupings where similarity of content forms connections stronger than ostensible differences between genres.

The difficulties of defining the genres are well known to literary theorists. Working deconstructively, Derrida found within genre itself a "law of impurity" and concluded that it is impossible *not* to mix genres ("Genre," p. 57). Thomas Pavel similarly noted "the mixture of stability and flexibility of the notions that designate literary and ... cultural genres," and recommended seeing genre as "a set of good recipes, or good habits of the trade" ("Literary Genres," pp. 202, 210). In *Kinds of Literature* (1982) Alastair Fowler accepted genre "as the basis of the conventions that make literary communication possible" (p. 36), but adopted Wittgenstein's concept of "family resemblance" to account for persistent variation. In this way Fowler could acknowledge that "every literary work changes the genre it relates to" (p. 23) and yet conclude that the individual genres are best viewed as "coded structures" for interpretation. By 2003 Fowler had loosened his definition, proposing that genres instead be considered "fields of association" or "virtual contexts" ("Formation," p. 190), but his original distinctions between genre (or kind), subgenre, and mode remain helpful in gauging the parameters of Middleton's experimentation. For example, tragedy is a *genre*, revenge tragedy is a recognizable *subgenre*. But in *The Revenger's Tragedy* it is the *modal* treatment of the form, with its unexpected grotesquerie and darkly comic moments, which is characteristic of Middleton. It is thus necessary to distinguish Middleton's repeated, ironic tweaking of recognized genres from the more general slipperiness of the terms.

Even Middleton's early city comedies, a flourishing, recognizable subgenre, push against formal limits. At first glance his string of plays for Paul's Boys from 1603 to 1606 – *The Phoenix, Michaelmas Term, Trick, A Mad World, My Masters*, and *The Puritan Widow* – with their urban settings, economic satire, complex plotting, and dependence on such elements of Roman comedy as intergenerational competition, seem clever but conventional. Unlike Middleton's later comic plays, which characteristically have female central figures like Moll in *The Roaring Girl*, Mistress Low-Water in *No Wit/Help Like a Woman's*, and the Duchess in *More Dissemblers Besides Women*, the boys' plays center on intriguing young men like Follywit and

Witgood. Yet as early as *Trick* (1605) there are anomalous elements. For example, the usurer Dampit, a "trampler of the law," is apparently a typical figure of satiric city comedy, but from the early comment that "if you put in the devil once, riches come with a vengeance" (1.4.29–30) there are unexpected religious overtones. His maidservant sings that "There's pits enough to damn him, before he comes to hell"; he lies sick and drunk "like the devil in chains"; and Audrey's ambiguous final comment, "His hour's come upon him," may even suggest that Dampit dies behind the bed curtains, leaving comedy far behind (4.5.2–195.)

Middleton's violations of conventional genre appear to come from two different impulses. The first is literary, a flaunting of originality that repeatedly defies audience and reader expectations. Whether doubling the final masque in *Revenger* or assisting in turning heroic tragedy towards satire in *Timon*, Middleton persistently stretches the "coded structures." But equally important is the dominance of other "fields of association." Calvinism, topical comment, and attitudes toward gender link plays across the tragic/comic divide, connecting sections of the canon by content rather than by structure or form.

Middleton's religious attitudes emerge even in comedy, where they tend to darken the form. Occasionally he does not seem to be playing with the genre so much as losing control of it. For example, in *Mad World* (1605), Penitent Brothel has a familiar role: the clever seducer of a jealous man's wife. But unlike Jonson's Volpone the following year, Brothel is appalled by his sin even while plotting to achieve his goal. At his first entrance he wonders, "Why in others do I check wild passions / And retain deadly follies in myself?" (1.1.100–1). After the successful seduction he berates himself as "divorced from heaven, / Thou wretched unthrift that has played away / Thy eternal portion" (4.1.3–5). As Peter Saccio says, Brothel's repentance creates "tonal dissonance" between his sense of sin and the play's "amoral intrigue" (*Middleton*, p. 415). The lines in which he preaches continence to the woman he has seduced – "None for religion, all for pleasure burn" (4.5.58) – could come from a sermon.

Equally serious are the conversion and repentance of Sir Walter Whorehound in *A Chaste Maid in Cheapside* and the Colonel in *A Fair Quarrel*. *Chaste Maid* is structurally comic, ending with multiple marriages and a double resurrection from the dead for the romantic leads. However, the wounded Whorehound's speeches, in which he concludes that he might have "everlastingly slept out all hope / Of grace and mercy" (5.1.30–1) had he not been awakened by his injury, are precisely similar to those of the Colonel in the tragicomic *Quarrel*. True, the Colonel feels more assurance that "seeing me armed with penitence and forgiveness" his "invisible enemy flies" (4.2.45–6), but in Calvinist terms it is impossible to know who is saved. If comedy requires the restoration of order and the confirmation of community, all of these repentances – even Beatrice-Joanna's in *The Changeling* – are comic. Although he languishes in the Knight's Ward, Sir Walter is "resurrected" as much as are Touchwood Jr. and Moll.

The inadequacy of traditional generic divisions for the Middleton canon becomes more obvious in his later plays. The Oxford *Middleton* classifies *Game* and *Hengist* as English histories, *Witch* and *Old Law* as tragicomedies, *Changeling* and *Women Beware Women* as tragedies. But the integration of topical material modifies the conventional forms, and the focus on female central figures tends to ironize even tragic emotion.

Middleton was apparently fascinated by the greatest scandal of the period, the murder of Sir Thomas Overbury by the twice-married Frances Howard, probably with the assistance of her second husband, King James's former favorite Robert Carr. Perhaps regretting the part he had played in writing the lost "Masque of Cupids" to celebrate that marriage, Middleton built almost all of *Witch* (1616) on elements of Howard's lurid life that had recently emerged in her trial. These included the rendering of a rejected husband selectively impotent; an aristocratic woman's resort to witchcraft and magic for murderous ends; and the pregnancy of Francesca (= Frances Carr, pregnant during the trial) (see Alastair Bellany's essay in this volume, p. 117). Although *Witch* can pass as a tragicomedy, its conclusion seems to mock the form. Not only has the undesired husband of Isabella, one of the three female characters who share the Howard references, conveniently died by falling into a dungeon, but when the Duchess is confronted with the body of the husband whose murder she has arranged, like Howard she accepts responsibility for murder but is outraged to be called an adulteress. Only once the Governor condemns her to "Die, then, a murdress only" (5.3.124), does the Duke – whose body has been propped up like that of the Duke in *Revenger* – revive. The self-parody seems intentional, particularly because the plots of both plays make prominent use of a skull. *Witch* really only makes sense if one realizes its topical import. Unsurprisingly it was not published in the seventeenth century, but being a practical man of the theatre Middleton reused some of the supernatural materials in revising *Macbeth*.

He returned to Frances Howard in the equally puzzling *Hengist*. This play, as Grace Ioppolo writes, "mocks any attempt to give it a generic tag" (*Middleton*, p. 1448), combining as it does a Jack Cade-like uprising based on a contemporary crisis in the cloth trade, the farcical tale of the Mayor of

Queenborough, and a full-blown political tragedy derived from Holinshed's *Chronicles*. Roxena, daughter of the Saxon Hengist and lover of Hersus, like Howard proves her purity with the help of a fake chastity test, arranges a murder, gains political power but ultimately betrays her husband and her lover. Ioppolo defends Roxena for demonstrating "the cruel, destructive, and ultimately fraudulent control that men assume they exert over the women" (*Middleton*, p. 1450), but once again the topical references – besides the Overbury murder and the failed Cokayne Project, the play apparently recalls a quarrel between James's deputies on the Isle of Jersey and the crisis in Bohemia (Taylor, *Companion*, p. 412) – overshadow character study.

Arguably, Middleton only gained full control of the tragic implications of the Howard story in *Changeling*. Here again are the fake virginity test and the murderous willingness to destroy a man inconveniently blocking a desired marriage. Yet the development of Beatrice-Joanna, from ethical unawareness to a recognition that "'Tis time to die when 'tis a shame to live" (5.3.179), raises the echoes of Frances Howard from titillatingly topical to grandly and convincingly psychological. Nevertheless, the play continues to violate generic expectations: Taylor notes that *Changeling*, like *Hengist*, juxtaposes a tragic and a comic plot, rather than integrating them as in Middleton's tragicomedies (*Companion*, p. 413), and McMullan ("*Changeling*") argues that the focus on the ugly and the interwoven "hospital" plot keeps *Changeling* "hybrid, multiple, grotesque," simultaneously exemplary of revenge tragedy and self-parodying.

Middleton's most striking subordination of generic form to topical reference came with his scandalous success, *Game*. Although unquestionably based on current "history," formally *Game* is *sui generis*. Reading Shakespeare's *Henry IV* or Marlowe's *Edward II* would hardly equip one with the "coded structures" for interpreting this *Game*, which instead draws on allegorical traditions that look back to Spenser and forward to anti-Catholic polemic. Taylor argues that for its early viewers the play was full of recognizable contemporary figures (*Middleton*, p. 1826), and it may be that he is right for some – some of the figures, and some of the audience. The players staged the Spanish Ambassador Gondomar with his characteristic accoutrements, and many references note the Gondomar satire. Nevertheless, much of the plot concerns the unidentified White Queen's Pawn. Even Taylor admits that "the play forces us to imagine characters who are both persons and [chess] pieces" (*Middleton*, p. 1773). Significantly, an early reader asserted he was unable to understand it, not because he was unaware of the confrontation with Spain but "because I have no skill in the game" (*Middleton*, p. 1826). It was Middleton's last play, presumably because he only achieved release from prison by a promise to this effect. And it stands as a symbol of his willingness to stretch the genres almost beyond recognition.

Attitudes towards gender also help reshape genre in Middleton's plays. Even his more conventional comedies tend to distort the usual sexual tropes. For example, the clever Courtesan in *Trick* is far from a simple whore; Moll in *Roaring Girl* fights rather than faints at the sight of a sword; the cross-dressed page in *Dissemblers* falls into naturalistic labor and rather than achieving a happy marriage is attacked by her impregnator as a quean. The later tragedies with female figures at their centers are most clearly differentiated from the codified model. Where even powerful women are usually secondary in tragedy, in *The Lady's Tragedy* the Lady's heroic suicide contrasts with her ineffectual lover's hesitation; in *Changeling* both plots center on women, and Beatrice-Joanna initiates murder.

*Women Beware* best epitomizes Middleton's modifications of tragic form. The title immediately signals that the action will not concern kingdoms and battles; instead the play is a study of the moral, spiritual, and sexual disintegration of women at various life stages. As in *Othello*, the opening of this domestic tragedy occurs *after* a runaway marriage, but private events are not combined with a larger political framework or a heroic protagonist. Instead, as in a city comedy, the early scenes give a material exposition of the environment. For example, one consequence of the rape is Bianca's dissatisfaction at the absence of "a cushion-cloth of drawn-work, / Or some fair cut-work pinned up in my bedchamber, / A silver and gilt casting bottle hung by't" (3.1.19–21). Similarly, in her sudden infatuation with Leantio, Livia undertakes to "buy me my desires" (3.2.64), assuring Leantio that she has enough "To make my friend a rich man in my life, / A great man at my death" (3.2.362–3). Her obsession with her toy boy borders on black comedy: she reassures herself, "I am not yet so old but he may think of me" and decides to "paint" again (3.2.140–2).

The final masque, in which Livia is killed by fumes, Isabella by flaming gold, Hippolito by poisoned arrows, and Guardiano by falling into the trap, suggests Middleton challenging himself to outdo the double masque in *Revenger*, with its blazing star and thunder on demand. Despite the deaths, the conclusion of *Women Beware* risks evoking laughter. However, the religious viewpoint ultimately prevails. The Cardinal's declaration that the Duke's action "sets a light up to show men to hell" (4.1.228), and his sententious conclusion, "where lust reigns, that prince cannot reign long" (5.1.266), are among the few things in the play that cannot be reduced to parody.

Not long after *Women Beware* the Shakespeare First Folio reified critical concepts of the dramatic genres and the divisions between them. That same year, 1623, *The Spanish Gypsy* was licensed and performed. The play is paradigmatic of Middleton's relation to his theatrical environment. First, it is the collaborative product of four authors: Middleton and William Rowley, named on the title page, and John Ford and Thomas Dekker, not named but dominant. Middleton probably wrote only small sections of the play but was responsible for its "polyphonic" structure, both cause and manifestation of the generic mixture (Taylor, *Companion*, p. 437). The play combines the comic antics of the clowns Sancho and Soto with three nearly tragic plots: Luis de Castro's revenge for his father's death, the false accusation of theft that leads Juan de Carcamo to wound his accuser's lover, and, centrally, Clara's rape.

Once again we see the influence of the three factors that dominated Middleton's relation to conventional genre. First, the shape of the play is partly distorted by its topicality. As I have argued elsewhere, each runaway son recalls some element of Prince Charles's secret trip to Spain earlier in the year (*Middleton*, pp. 1724–6). Specific historical events occasionally intrude, like the accident caused by "the jester that so late arrived at court" (3.2.246). In addition, the fortune-telling gypsies who are really metamorphosed aristocrats are modeled on the roles James's courtiers took in Jonson's *Gypsies Metamorphosed* (1621). Next, women are central to several of the plots, and Clara's attitudes, in particular, are critical to the tragicomic outcome. Raped, she nevertheless has enough presence of mind to steal a crucifix from the room she finds herself in, and unlike Lucrece she believes herself unstained by an act she did not invite. Thus she can suffer yet survive. Finally, critical to the mixed tone are the powerful scenes of religious repentance. Roderigo feels immediate remorse for his "deed of wickedness" (1.3.83); later he meditates on "what vile prisons / Make we our bodies to our immortal souls" (3.1.1–2). As all ends happily, with the finding of a lost child, marriage to the rapist, and recovery of the wounded, the play is technically tragicomedy. But in fact it is more like the complex mixture described in *Hengist*, including not only comedians and tragedians, but clownage and satire, dancing and rape. As the gypsies promise, a "merry tragedy" (4.2.37).

*Gypsy* bears the imprint of Middleton and was the last play he was involved in writing before *Game*. If Jowett's date of summer 1621 for *Women Beware* is correct (*Companion*, pp. 414–16), then between 1621 and August 1624, the date of *Game*, Middleton reached a new peak of inventiveness and literary strength. Though he clearly counted on his audience to recall the very forms he was stretching, he was restricted not by the gradual solidifying of the genres but by greater powers. Silenced as a dramatist, by 1627 he was dead. His willingness to reach beyond conventional generic limits is one of his strengths; it also no doubt contributed to the difficulty that reduced critical appreciation for so long.

CHAPTER 27

# Writing outside the theatre

*Alison A. Chapman*

Thomas Middleton's best non-dramatic writings have a scrappy and kaleidoscopic realism, one that comes from their immediate engagement with the foibles and vices of late sixteenth- and early seventeenth-century London. Judging simply from the tenor of these works, it is easy to see why Middleton later in life fared well as London's City Chronologer: here was an author possessed of a Nashean sensibility, a sharp appreciation for the grubby, comic, venal urban world he lived in and the ability both to celebrate and to censure it. This sensitivity to his immediate social milieu is echoed by Middleton's awareness of other contemporary texts. His non-dramatic works are highly intertextual, but not in the lofty manner of Ben Jonson alluding to Horace or John Milton revising *The Aeneid* and Genesis. Rather Middleton directs his authorial gaze laterally towards the ground-level textual debates of his own day. He was a bit too young to have participated in the Marprelate Controversies, but the fact that he so often modeled his work on the writings of Nashe and Robert Greene (key voices for the anti-Martinist side) suggests his relish for contemporary satire and contentiousness, his readiness to identify a textual mêlée and to jump in. Readers of Middleton's *Macbeth* and *Measure for Measure* know of his ability to adapt prior plays, but fewer readers may know – because Middleton's non-dramatic works are not widely read – that his poetry, pamphlets, and almanacs show this same propensity to take a preexisting text and to revise or adapt it in new ways. This adaptive impulse was allied to a pervasive concern with social morality and a sympathy for the oppressed. That is, the intertextuality so characteristic of his works shows not only Middleton's flair for intellectual one-upmanship, but also his sense that literature has an overriding ethical imperative. In Middleton's view, since the highest function of writing is to correct human error, every work is morally bound to respond to, extend, or overturn the works preceding it, all in the interests of reforming vice and praising virtue.

Middleton published a cluster of three early works, and all of them – *The Wisdom of Solomon Paraphrased* (1597), *The Ghost of Lucrece* (probably written around 1598 but not published until 1600), and *Microcynicon: Six Snarling Satyres* (1599) – show this commingling of the intertextual and the ethical. *Solomon* is noteworthy as Middleton's first work, a rendering of the Apocryphal Wisdom of Solomon into 705 pretentious and labored stanzas (to be fair, Middleton was only 17 when he wrote it). Yet while it has generally and rightly been panned for its lack of artistic merit, as David M. Holmes points out, Middleton's decision to reprise the Wisdom of Solomon's social and moral critique is also characteristic of his view that literature is "an instrument of human edification" (*Thomas Middleton*, p. 8). Where *Solomon* shows Middleton engaged with one text from the Apocrypha, his next work, *Ghost*, ups the ante. Here we see him reprising and responding to several contemporary sources, a pattern characteristic of so many of his subsequent works. First, by presenting Lucrece as a ghost come back to earth to tell her story, Middleton echoed the stories in the popular and frequently reprinted *Mirror for Magistrates*. Second, by featuring a lamenting female speaker, he capitalized on the contemporary vogue for female complaints, as evidenced by works like Michael Drayton's *Matilda* (1594) and Samuel Daniel's *Complaint of Rosamond* (1592). Third, as Norman Brittin notes, throughout *Ghost* Middleton borrows freely from Robert Greene's *Ciceronis Amor* (1589), noteworthy as the first of many times that he would look to Greene's works (*Thomas Middleton*, p. 21).

Finally, and most obviously, Middleton also responds to Shakespeare's *Rape of Lucrece* (1594). Middleton effectively writes the sequel to Shakespeare's work, showing Lucrece, after an extended stay in Hell, returning to earth to pour invective on Tarquin. Middleton seems concerned to outdo Shakespeare. For instance, Shakespeare suggests that one tragic result of the rape is a kind of union or mirroring of victim and victimizer, as when Lucrece enacts on herself a version of the same sexual violence that Tarquin has enacted on her. Middleton takes this sense of psychic union born of forced physical intimacy and pushes it a step further. Lucrece likens the two of them to breastfeeding mother and nursing child: "Thou art my nurse-child, Tarquin, thou art he. / Instead of milk, suck blood and tears and all," and she says, "Here's blood for milk, suck till thy veins run over, / And such a teat which scarce thy mouth can cover" (136–7, 141–2). Significantly, Middleton seems much more concerned than Shakespeare with pinning down the nature of Lucrece's guilt. Shakespeare leaves this issue ambiguous: on the one hand, in his poem Lucrece refers to her "fault" and her "sable ground of sin," but on the other, Collatine and his companions say that since her mind is "untainted," she bears no sin or stain (1072, 1073, 1710). Middleton, in contrast, stakes out a clearer ethical position by specifying that Lucrece lives in Hell. He even has her forcibly indict her own moral failings: "'Twas thou, O chastity, m'eternal eye, / The want of thee made my ghost reel to hell" (507–8). As G. B. Shand notes, in this rendering Lucrece sinned by not struggling against Tarquin, despite his threats to kill her and lodge her body in bed beside a dead groom's (*Middleton*, p. 1988). Furthermore, Middleton makes it clear that, as a pagan, she has no hope of redemption. As she exclaims, "Lucrece, I say, how canst thou Lucrece be, / Wanting a god to give a life to thee?" (561–2). So while the text is a searing commentary on male lust and leaves no doubt about the degree of Lucrece's victimization, it also presents an uncompromising (and, for most modern readers, an uncomfortable) vision of the victim's responsibility for her own tragic fate.

Like *Ghost*, Middleton's third early work, *Microcynicon: Six Snarling Satyres*, also contains a textual allusion in its title and engages with the conventions and presuppositions of other contemporary works. Joseph Hall's *Virgidemiarum* was arguably the first truly satiric work in English. Hall subtitled the first three books as *Tooth-less satyrs* (1597) and the second three as *byting satyres* (1598). By calling his stories *Snarling Satyres*, Middleton positions them as the heirs to Hall, and they fall into the same category of swingeing social critique. Indeed, Hall's work had triggered an outpouring of satires in the 1590s, and as Wendy Wall points out, by writing in this vein Middleton joined a fashionable vogue, putting himself alongside authors like John Marston, Everard Guilpin, and John Donne (who wrote a manuscript *Satires* around 1593) (*Middleton*, p. 1970). Like most satirists, Middleton presents stock vice characters such as the insolent Superbia, the prodigal Zodon, and the sodomitical Pyander, all of whom lay bare their own sins for the reader's edification.[1] Satire IV, however, is an interesting departure from satiric conventions, and here we see Middleton reaching out to a different kind of text. As Brittin observes, this part of the text is modeled on Greene's 1592 cony-catching pamphlets, since Middleton lays out the five easy steps by which cheating Droone, an underworld rogue, cons a rich gentleman out of his cash (*Thomas Middleton*, p. 24). In *Microcynicon* Middleton has one foot in the world of contemporary satire and another in the vogue for stories from London's criminal underclass.

It is worth giving the full title of one of Greene's cony-catching pamphlets – *The Blacke Bookes Messenger. Laying open the Life and Death of Ned Browne one of the most notable Cutpurses, Crosbiters, and Conny-catchers that ever lived in England* (1592) – since five years after *Microcynicon*

Middleton was again to borrow from Greene and to signal this borrowing in his title. In *The Black Book* (1604) Middleton continues in Greene's vein by anatomizing a series of criminals in a mock-encomiastic fashion. But although Middleton has a significant debt to Greene, his debt to another contemporary writer is even more pronounced. Middleton's *Black Book* is a direct continuation of Nashe's *Pierce Penniless, His Supplication to the Devil* (1592).[2] In Nashe's work Pierce is forced to send a plea for patronage to Lucifer, and the work ends with Pierce dying in neglected penury (a fate that Nashe suffered soon after the publication of *Pierce*). Nashe had even imagined the possibility of a continuation of his work. In *A private Epistle of the Author to the Printer* in *Pierce* he imagines that, had he the leisure, he might "write the retourne of the *Knight of the Post* from Hell, with the *Devils* answer to the *Supplication*" (sig. €2v). Seemingly taking Nashe's cue, Middleton begins where *Pierce* ends, in much the same way that *Ghost* picks up the narrative threads of *Rape of Lucrece*, evidence of what Shand calls Middleton's "powers of supplementary invention" (*Middleton*, p. 204). The main part of *Black Book* begins, "No sooner was 'Pierce Penniless' breathed forth but I, the light-burning Sargent Lucifer, quenched my fiery shape and whipped into a constable's nightgown, the cunning'st habit that could be, to search tipsy taverns, roosting inns and frothy alehouses" (p. 208). Lucifer has been so moved by Pierce's supplication that he has come to earth to explore London's underworld and to arrange a pension for Pierce. Settling the details of his own last will and testament, Lucifer bequeaths Pierce about one-tenth of a penny on every act of prostitution, which "will be such a fluent pension that thou shalt never need to write *Supplication* again" (p. 218).

*Black Book*'s exuberant engagement with Nashe's *Pierce* and with other works purporting to expose the vices of London's criminal class is echoed in its sidelong glances at two other kinds of works: the mock testament tradition so popular in the period and sixteenth-century editions of the Bible. *The Wyll of the Deuyll, and last Testament* (1548), *Wyl Bucke his testament* (1560), and Isabella Whitney's *Wyll and Testament* (1573) are just three examples of the popular mock testament tradition, a tradition intended "to expose the madness and hypocrisy of 'things as they are' in the real world" (Hutson, *Usurer's Daughter*, p. 127).[3] *The Wyll of the Deuyll* was an early Reformation attack on Roman Catholic clerical abuses, and this text shows how closely the mock testament could align with religious writing. Like so many early modern sermons, Middleton's *Black Book* excoriates human vice, although it does so through means of comedy and mock encomium rather than through sober invective. Gary Taylor argues that Middleton, in *Black Book*, is looking towards the ultimate religious work of the period and that the text's woodcut-like appearance mimics "the typography of sixteenth-century English Bibles, the 'good book' of which Lucifer's 'black book' is a parody" ("End of Editing," p. 137).

As the above discussions suggest, Middleton had a particular relish for inserting himself into the center of a textual conversation and volleying its terms, conventions, and presuppositions about. Indeed, so pronounced is this proclivity that it is hard to find a non-dramatic work where Middleton is *not* pointedly engaged with some prior text in what is ultimately a debate about morality. For example, Middleton's *The Penniless Parliament of Threadbare Poets* (1604) was designed to be a continuation of a 1601 jestbook entitled *Jack of Dover, His Quest of Inquiry for the Veriest Fool in England*, and in Middleton's hands the jests have an increased awareness of social injustice: as Middleton's mock Parliament decrees sardonically, "it is ordered and agreed upon that bakers, woodmongers, butchers, and brewers shall fall to a mighty conspiracy so that no man shall either have bread, fire, meat, or drink without credit or ready money" (*Middleton*, p. 2005). Middleton's ability to adapt a prior text and his sympathy with the oppressed are also evident in his *Father Hubburd's Tales: or, the Ant and the Nightingale* (1604), which – as both a beast fable and a social critique – continues in the vein of Edmund Spenser's *Mother Hubbard's Tale* (1590). We see a similar engagement both with public morality and a prior body of texts in *The Peacemaker, or Great Britain's Blessing* (1618). By attacking both drunkenness and the practice of dueling, Middleton participates (albeit in a less overtly theological way) in the contemporary puritan "reformation of manners" campaign being waged from pulpits and printing presses.

Middleton's forays into the genre of the mock almanac and the mock prognostication show his intertextual impulse arguably at its most pronounced. For instance, *Penniless Parliament* is both a continuation of a prior jestbook and also, as F. P. Wilson first noted, a revision and condensation of Simon Smellknave's *Fearful and Lamentable Effects of Two Dangerous Comets* (1591), itself a mock prognostication that burlesqued popular texts foretelling the ill effects of various astrological phenomena ("Prognostications," p. 25). Similarly, both *Plato's Cap* (1604) and *The Owl's Almanac* (1618) are parodies of astrological almanacs, by 1600 the most popular kind of text in early modern English culture. For example, in *Plato*, Middleton's prediction that when the sun enters into Virgo "maidenheads will be cheaper than mackerels" is a tongue-in-cheek version of the language of traditional almanacs, with their dire predictions about how the various phases of the zodiac will affect human affairs (*Middleton*, p. 200). Again, we see here a love of intertextual play layered with a pervasive concern for social morality. *Owl* continues in the same vein, although in this work Middleton is not only satirizing serious almanacs, he is also self-consciously trying to outdo Thomas Dekker's parodic *Raven's Almanac* (1609), in much the same way that *Penniless Parliament* built atop Smellknave's *Fearful and Lamentable Effects*, which was itself a response to a whole genre of more serious astrological *works*.

Middleton engages yet another category of contemporary texts in his *News from Gravesend* (1604, coauthored with Thomas Dekker) and *The Meeting of Gallants at an Ordinary* (1604). Both are part of a long tradition of plague works, a tradition reaching back at least as far as Boccaccio's *Decameron* and given contemporary voice in works like Nashe's plague-conscious satires, written in the 1590s, and also in Dekker's eclectic *Wonderful Year* (1603), which chronicles the various tragedies of plague victims. *Meeting* is a particularly inventive modulation of the plague literature tradition. It opens with a literal "meeting of gallants" in the central aisle of St. Paul's, a fashionable meeting-place for London's aristocratic young bloods. In a bleak twist Middleton shows that since plague has driven off all the human aristocrats (London's upper classes fled to Winchester during the waves of plague), the only "gallants" left are Famine, War, and Pestilence. These three strut their stuff in the cathedral, and each claims precedence and insults the others' powers. Pestilence ultimately gains the upper hand by narrating a set of blackly funny plague tales. The "meeting of gallants" in St. Paul's thus becomes the framing device for a "meeting of gallants at an ordinary." That is, Pestilence tells of a number of human gallants who meet at a tavern (an "ordinary") to escape the plague and listen to their Host – a "mad, round knave, and a merry one" – tell a number of tales, usually involving insensate drunkards being mistaken for plague victims (*Middleton*, p. 190). This conjoining of upper-crust tale-telling and the plague is an obvious nod to Boccaccio, and Middleton's garrulous, rotund Host is also deeply Chaucerian. As Robert Maslen observes, works like *Gravesend* and *Meeting* also resemble other plague works in their defiance of conventional generic boundaries: there is no traditional textual category into which these works can be fitted (*Middleton*, p. 128). For example, in addition to its layering of tales within tales and its patchwork of different voices and settings, *Meeting* also merges the tragic and the comic in dizzying ways. For instance, the Host tells of those who died on the roads and were "Rolled into ditches, pits and hedges so lamentably, so rudely and unchristianlike, that it would have made a pitiful and remorseful eye bloodshot to see such a ruthful and disordered object, and a true heart bleed outright" (*Middleton*, p. 194). And yet having said that any "true heart" would bleed at the tragic spectacle, he adds "– but not such a one as mine, gallants, for my heart bleeds nothing but alicant [wine]." Where so many contemporary writers had responded to the plague with moralizing jeremiads on the state of contemporary vice, Middleton in *Gallants* has a "drier, tougher, and funnier view" (Yachnin, *Middleton*, p. 185). Middleton suggests that the only realistic response to such whole-scale tragedy is a continuing affirmation of life. As the Host tells his listeners, "But let not this make you sad, gallants. Sit you merry still" (*Middleton*, p. 194).

Middleton's degree of intertextual engagement in his prose and poetic works is evidence of his essentially theatrical imagination. At many points in his works, one gets the sense that he was imagining them being spoken aloud as dialogue. For instance, the preening argument of Plague, War, and Pestilence in *Meeting* could be readily transposed to the stage, and Shand points out that *Ghost* was performed in 1996 and proved surprisingly powerful in a dramatic venue (*Middleton*, p. 1986). Similarly, the conversations and tableaux that Middleton creates in *Black Book* – as Lucifer pokes his nose into one den of iniquity after another – could come right out of stage plays. Middleton's tendency to show characters in dramatic dialogue with one another, even in non-dramatic texts, is echoed on a larger scale by his habit of entering into conversation with other texts. Middleton, it seems, had a fundamentally collaborative habit of mind, such that even when he was not actually coauthoring with another writer, he tended to write works that needed the voices of others in order to make sense. Furthermore, he was not interested in using other texts in order to display his erudition or to create a vision of English literature's relationship to the classics. To the contrary, reading the polyphonic and contentious energy of Middleton's non-dramatic works suggests how much he simply enjoyed the literary equivalent of the donnybrook.

NOTES

1. The outpouring of satires during this period triggered a backlash from the authorities, and, depending on one's view, Middleton – along with Marston and Hall – was either lucky or unfortunate enough to have his book burned by order of the Archbishop of Canterbury and the Bishop of London on June 4, 1599.
2. For Middleton's debt to Nashe in *Black Book*, see Rhodes, *Elizabethan Grotesque*, pp. 57–60.
3. See Hutson's more extended treatment of mock testament tradition in *Thomas Nashe*, pp. 127–51.

## CHAPTER 28

# Medieval remains in Middleton's writings

## Anke Bernau

By the time Thomas Middleton was born, in 1580, the initial printing boom of the works of "medieval" authors, with the exception of those associated with Geoffrey Chaucer, had already started to recede, not to be revived until the eighteenth century (Gillespie, *Print Culture*; Kelen, *Langland's*; Lerer, "William Caxton"). Yet the potent – and ideologically charged – interpretations of what first came to be known as "the Middle Age"[1] had begun to be articulated in the decades before Middleton's birth and continued beyond his lifetime. Foremost among the uses to which the term was put by both Humanists and Protestant reformers (though for different ends) was the articulation of a new age. Thus, one of the most powerful and persistent tropes of Western historiography emerged at this time; what Lee Patterson has called "the gigantic master narrative by which modernity identifies itself with the Renaissance and rejects the Middle Ages as by definition pre-modern" ("On the Margin," p. 92).

One of the main challenges faced by Protestant reformers in the sixteenth century was the creation of a national narrative that allowed for change without positing it as a rupture. At a time when precedent and the authority of antiquity were concepts under review, the various complex and even contradictory developments which are rather misleadingly referred to under the unifying heading of "the Reformation" required the present to be understood and presented as a *renewal* of something ancient and thus "original," rather than as a break with the past altogether. The reformation was to be a purification – a rectification of the errors and perversions introduced by the Catholic (medieval) Church – a return to the foundations of Christianity (McCulloch, *Reformation*). Thus, while it would be misleading to think of the intellectual and religious upheavals and developments in this time as in any way teleological or univocal, it would be fair to say that this doubled desire – for change as well as for continuity – shaped many representations and understandings of the past, both distant and recent.

Whether rejected or embraced, the "medieval" was integral to what came to be fashioned as the Renaissance or Reformation. What was urged for erasure, most officially in injunctions issued under Elizabeth I and Edward VI against a range of Catholic forms of worship, as well as what was earmarked for remembrance (the works of Chaucer or Langland; the ancient, "pure" English Church), became part of the battleground on which political, religious, and intellectual debates were played out. As a result, a vocabulary or set of tropes emerged that were closely associated with medieval history and historiography, its cultural productions and its religious forms. Prominent among these tropes were those that depicted the "middle age" as an unenlightened, superstitious, even barbarous age that could not distinguish truth from falsehood. The period in which Middleton lived and produced his work offers "a complicated picture of continuity and change, of the triumph of new doctrine and the persistence of traditional practice" (Ferrell, "Religious Persuasions," p. 48).

### USES OF THE PAST: GENERIC CONTINUITY AND TRANSFORMATION

Middleton's drama tends to be commended for its insistent focus on the "here and now" of his time. There is not much overt "medievalizing" in his plays, either in the sense of a sustained, self-conscious representation of the medieval past, or of an explicit interest in its cultural legacies. However, there are formal and generic aspects, as well as numerous references to familiar and widespread tropes, that suggest a medievalizing tendency in this most modern of Jacobean playwrights.

The many diverse forms of medieval drama continued to coexist along-side newer forms throughout the sixteenth century; even the mystery plays were performed until the very late sixteenth century. Some medieval dramatic forms were used deliberately by Protestant writers (such as John Bale) as vehicles for a new world view. Such use of familiar forms could serve to underline the difference of the "message," or it could present new ideas in a manner that made them seem already familiar. The continuities between medieval and later dramatic forms have frequently been noted.[2] While he posits a break in dramatic traditions around 1580, Raphael Falco also observes that "older medieval forms do not simply drop away," but "undergo a complicated process of integration" ("Medieval," p. 255).

This is also evident in Middleton's work, which in addition draws on tropes that were commonly associated with the Middle Ages by the time he wrote. These tropes could refer either to a specific historical moment or to qualities and behaviors that were thought to be indicative of the mindset of that past. Thus, a belief in magic and supernatural beings, one of the period's most common stereotypes of the "middle age," was combined with a negative representation of Catholicism in *A Game at Chess* in a way that owed much to contemporary discourses about the medieval past. *Game* is a history play, albeit one that reveals its "radical originality" by "conspicuously reject[ing]" two earlier features of the genre: "the focus on individual prowess, and the representation of a distant past" (G. Taylor, *Middleton*, p. 1774). Nonetheless, because the medieval had become so thoroughly aligned with magic and Catholicism, use of these tropes brings with it "medieval" associations – signaling, usually, that which is treacherous, regressive, cruel.[3] The refusal to focus on a single individual is a common feature of morality drama and medieval allegorical writing. Furthermore, the conceit of the chess game was not only drawn on in the writings of such late medieval poets as Chaucer and Lydgate, but its "allegorical treatment" featured in "[o]ne of the most popular of late medieval ethical manuals" (Carruthers, *Book*, p. 144). These texts continued to circulate: William Caxton, for instance, printed an English translation of such a manual in 1474 (reprinted in 1483), as *The Game and Playe of Chesse*. The fact that this genre had long been associated with diverse didactic functions arguably makes Middleton's use of the conceit in *Game* all the more striking and suggestive.

Even in the plays Middleton wrote for the "new" commercial theatre, we see persistent reference to medieval forms and tropes.[4] Middleton's partiality for allegory, his referencing of aspects of the morality play, and even the liveliness (and scatology) of his language continue a tradition present in numerous earlier plays – for instance, *Mankind* (*c.*1470) or pageants from the York cycle. Many of Middleton's plays feature characters whose names are reminiscent of the personified "virtues" and "vices" of the morality tradition: "Infelice," "Lucre" or "MoneyLove," "Sir Bounteous," "Master Penitent," "Lussurioso," "Ambitioso," "Supervacuo," "Castiza." Other characters are identified by professional or familial status, as in Chaucer's *Canterbury Tales*: "Country Wench," "A Poet," "A Painter," "A Jeweller," "A Merchant," "A Mercer." Middleton explicitly refers to Chaucer twice in his plays: once in *No Wit/Help Like a Woman's* and once in *More Dissemblers Besides Women*. This is perhaps not surprising, since "thirteen plays based on Chaucer's work were composed" between 1558 and 1625 (Machan, *Textual*, pp. 20–2). Middleton also seems to be acknowledging, albeit ironically, the ongoing popularity of medieval romance in his inclusion of a "Sir Lancelot" ("the only gentleman of England") and a servant called

"Arthur" in *A Trick to Catch the Old One* (4.5.91–2).[5] His use of genres that were already popular with late medieval audiences extends to beast fables, debate poetry, collections of stories ordered within a frame narrative, and praise of, or complaints by, women. His introduction of a "ploughman" in *Father Hubburd's Tales* participates within a tradition of "Ploughman-Tales" that stretches back to Langland's *Piers Plowman* (Cummings, "Reformed Literature"). Finally, continuity with earlier discourses and tropes, such as those of humoral physiology or of female chastity, are evident in Middleton's work.[6]

### USES OF THE PAST: NATIONAL HISTORY

Ongoing debates over the nature and value of the national past were waged not just in antiquarian or theological circles, but also in sixteenth- and seventeenth-century drama. Gordon McMullan has counted forty-two plays dealing with the national past in the period 1560–1625. Of these, seventeen deal with Arthur, Brutus, or other legendary material, six with the Saxon invasions, eight with pre-Conquest history, and four with the Norman Conquest (McMullan, "Colonisation," pp. 138–40; see also Griffin, *Playing*). Middleton would have been aware of these, as well as collaborating with a number of their authors.[7]

The importance of national origins and historical precedent was a familiar truth for medieval writers. Antiquity conferred authority; a glorious ancestry could be emulated, and helped to shape a people's self-understanding. When Geoffrey of Monmouth wrote his *History of the Kings of Britain* in the twelfth century, he offered his audiences two venerable ancestors: the Trojan, Brutus, and the Briton, Arthur. Geoffrey's work, though contested in his own time, became instantly and hugely successful. Overcoming the aboriginal giants they encountered when first arriving in Britain, Brutus and his men cultivated the land and built a city, "New Troy" (or "Troynovant"), which was now known as "London." Arthur, in turn, is in Geoffrey's version not only a heroic king, but an imperial conqueror, even defying Rome's claim to overlordship. In 1534 Polydore Vergil's *Anglica Historia* was first published. A history of the English begun at the request of Henry VII, it stated in no uncertain terms that Geoffrey's account of Brutus and Arthur was nothing but falsification and error. This unleashed a passionate debate over whether or not these two foundational figures should – or could – be relinquished. During the sixteenth century, as Helen Parish notes, "the medieval past was first rejected, then explored, exploited and employed in the defense of the Reformation" (*Monks*, p. 37).

Middleton wrote three plays that have been called historical, two of which are set in the medieval past: only *Hengist, King of Kent* (1620) survives. This popular play combines a dual medievalist temporality: the story of the Saxon Hengist is told through the figure of the fourteenth-century monk and chronicler, Ranulf Higden, whose universal history, the *Polychronicon*, was first translated into English by John Trevisa in the late fourteenth century and then printed by William Caxton in 1482. It remained popular throughout the Tudor period and was drawn on by, among others, Raphael Holinshed, whose *Chronicles of England, Scotland, and Ireland* supplied numerous playwrights with source material for their historical dramas.

At the very opening of *Hengist*, "Raynulph" praises the value of old stories:

> Ancient stories have been best:
> Fashions that are now called new
> Have been worn by more than you
>
> (1.0.10–12)

These lines set up a relationship between the present and the past that is both based on analogy and thus likeness (the present is like the past), and on precedence and difference (ancient stories are best; the new is a version of the old). The exemplary value of the past was commonly exhorted by medieval writers and by early modern authors such as George Puttenham. In his *The Arte of Englishe Poesie* (1589), Puttenham explains that of all rhetorical techniques, none is more persuasive than the "example, which is but the representation of old memories." The past functions as a mirror ("glasse") in which one can see "the lively image of our deare forefathers, their noble and virtuous maner of life" (cited in G. A. Sullivan, *Memory*, p. 3).

*Hengist* relates the "establishment of Anglo-Saxon Britain," using it to provide a commentary on current affairs at the same time as drawing on a figure who featured prominently in the writings of medieval and early modern historiographers (Ioppolo, *Middleton*, p. 1448). While some critics have read the play as straightforwardly anti-Saxon, it is not straightforwardly antimedieval. The qualities that the play condemns – insatiable ambition and ungovernable lust – are, as Raynulph's opening speech suggests, not historically specific. While the Saxons are certainly not idealized, the ultimate treachery comes from within, from Vortiger, a Briton. The two most virtuous characters, Constantius and Castiza, both long for a reli-gious – that is, a monastic – life. Although Constantius's otherworldliness makes him a weak king, it is also true that the religious figures in this play – all of whom belong to a Catholicized past – are presented sympathetically.

The emphasis on native sinfulness, which mars an otherwise "chosen" people and allows foreign invaders such as the Saxons to conquer Britain, can be found in chronicles from the sixth century onwards (Bernau, "Saint" and "Britain"). In *Hengist* one can read the past both as providing a historical allegory about flawed native politics and as a timeless moral exemplum about individual human sinfulness. Both suggest a transhistorical (or ahistorical) temporality; both partake of a mode of thought that has been seen as representative of a medieval inability to think historically, but which is really a particular understanding of the ethical function of the past for the present. Thus, while Middleton is not necessarily interested in a medieval past for itself, he is, in good "medieval" fashion, using the past in the interests of the present.

## USES OF THE PAST: CIVIC PAGEANTRY AND THE CITY

While Middleton's interest in history is suggested by his appointment as London's first official City Chronologer in 1620, it is in his civic pageants that we find the most frequent references to the medieval past. The city in which he lived, and for which he wrote, enabled his most sustained encounter with the "medieval": its "most prominent landmarks ... were principally of medieval origin," and it still maintained its "traditional culture of urban secular entertainment" (Seaver, *Middleton*, pp. 60, 73). And while reforms did suppress some of the city's traditional religious observances and practices, Lawrence Manley reminds us of the "*longue durée* of customary civic events" ("Civic Drama," p. 294).

The medieval past and its present uses surrounded Middleton from the day he was born. The man who baptised him in his parish church of St. Lawrence Jewry was Robert Crowley, a "famous preacher and non-conformist" (G. Taylor, "Lives and Afterlives," p. 28), but also the man who brought out an edition of Langland's *Piers Plowman* in 1550 (Kelen, *Langland's*, p. 77). Growing up in Cheapside, close to Guildhall, Middleton lived among medieval structures and traditions: the parish itself (Seaver, *Middleton*, p. 68); the parish church of which he was a member; the Livery Companies for whom he wrote and to which his father belonged; the university he attended (though it too had become a force for reform). Presumably Middleton would also have been utterly familiar with the Guildhall giants, "two immense statues erected before the mid-sixteenth century," which "regularly featured in mayoral processions" as well as coronation processions (Cohen, *Of Giants*, p. 29). Although they were referred to by various different names over time, they represented the very giants that Brutus and his men were said to have vanquished when they first founded Britain in Geoffrey of Monmouth's contested account. In the sixteenth century and beyond they literally stood at the heart of London civic life.

Two forms of civic drama that Middleton was involved in were the royal entry, a medieval tradition that continued in Middleton's time, and the Mayor's Inaugural Show, of more recent date, but also invested in claiming historical continuity.[8] Here again is that mutable and flexible combination of the old and the new, what Manley calls the "reinvention" of tradition ("Civic Drama," p. 295). Thus, *The Whole Royal and Magnificent Entertainment, with the Arches of Triumph* (1604), celebrating the royal entry of James I into London, to which Middleton contributed one speech (2122–81), both looks "back to inherited medieval forms of public display and allegory" and "anticipates the development of a cosmopolitan, classicizing and relatively exclusive court culture under the early Stuarts" (Smuts, *Middleton*, p. 221). A significant national moment is being celebrated through references to the hotly contested medieval version of national origin.

In the first pageant of *Magnificent*, the *Genius loci* of London recalls the origins of the city by referring to it as "Troy" or "Troynovant," clear references to Geoffrey's Trojan foundation myth (*Magnificent*, Pageant 1, 314, 357).[9] Later on in the second pageant *Genius* gives a brief overview of the history of Britain, which has progressed from when "Brutus' plough first gave [it] infant bounds" (Pageant 2, 782) to the present day, the point at which its destiny has been fulfilled (768–72). National history is presented here as an accumulation of stages; the present is the apotheosis of what was prophesied at the origin: "for thou now art blessed to see / That sight for which thou didst begin to be" (780–1). The gloss on "Brutus" given by the authors states that: "Rather than the city should want a founder, we choose to follow the received story of Brute, whether fabulous or true, and not altogether unwarranted in poetry . . ." (note *c*).[10] Like their medieval antecedents, these writers recognize the affective and symbolic power of origins – and of its most (in)famous articulation.

It is in the mayoral pageants that we can see Middleton's own uses of the medieval past. In his third, *The Triumphs of Love and Antiquity* (1619), history is once again a repository of worthy "examples" for the present: these examples function as a "crystal glass / By which wise magistracy sets his face" (113–16). This appears to reference the widespread medieval "Mirror for Princes" tradition, which was carried on in the sixteenth century by such writers as Thomas More, Sir David Lindsay, or in *A Mirror for Magistrates* (1559, 1563, 1578, 1587), itself conceived as a sequel to Lydgate's *Fall of Princes* (*c.*1431–8; printed in 1554). Not only are earlier mayors commemorated as exemplars in *Antiquity*, but the personification of "Antiquity" recalls "Plantagenets twenty-one," from King Edward III onwards.

In his fourth mayoral pageant, *The Sun in Aries* (1621), Middleton uses a range of symbolic devices to link "the political and the natural, the social and the supernatural, the historical and the mythical" (Berlin, *Middleton*, p. 1586). Following the opening speech by "Jason," which highlights the blessings that wise governance brings on "those past, thyself, and those to come" (88), the mayor proceeds to the Tower of Virtue, on whose battlements stand, "as virtue's standard-bearers or champions" (99), numerous illustrious personages from the city's past, including Henry fitz Ailwin, "London's first elected mayor (1189–1212)" (*Middleton*, p. 1590, n. 105). Yet here, too, the uses of the past are carefully delineated: the "true heirs" (180) of these venerable antecedents turn out to be "[j]ust six in number" (181), rulers from Henry VII to James I.

In his 1622 pageant for the Company of Grocers, *The Triumphs of Honour and Virtue*, Middleton once more draws on the "heritage of the morality play ... with the newly appointed mayor cast as a sort of Everyman" (Loomba, *Middleton*, p. 1714). Here the historical tradition of glory and honor is continued in new arenas of activity: trade and colonization. In *The Triumphs of Integrity* (1623) we see an accumulation of the tropes that recur so frequently in Middleton's civic pageantry: a genealogical list of mayors, and the ethical precedent they set, spelled out in a speech by "Memory":

> We by great buildings strive to raise our names,
> But they more truly wise built up their fames,
> Erected fair examples, large and high,
> Patterns for us to build our honours by
>
> (152–8)

Patterns, mirrors, examples: these are the functions to which Middleton puts the medieval past time and time again. It is here that the dual function of communal memory and forgetting is most evidently at work.[11] These processes are enabled by a city that provides the framework within which tradition can be praised, though often in the name of change.

This seemingly paradoxical combination finds one of its most explicit expressions in *The Triumphs of Health and Prosperity* (1626), which opens with a direct comparison between written histories and the city as historical stage. The city is shown to be more effective, since it provides a concrete focus and context for its citizens' memories and emotions. The pageant includes the almost ritualistic invocation of mayoral antecedents and also draws on the enduring medieval trope of the "body politic," in which the realm is likened to a human body, with respective professions or social orders playing divinely assigned and thus naturalized parts. Yet Middleton also deviates from that model, in assigning to a *place* – London – the life-giving function of the heart: "It has, as in the body, the heart's place, / Fit for her works of piety and grace" (146–7). London's "meridian" position makes it "the fountain of the body's heat, / The first thing that receives life, the last that dies" (162, 163–4). Here, the figure of the king is displaced by the city as lifeblood of the realm – a city whose own lifeblood depends on all those who have worked and lived within it. London functions both as personification[12] and as living monument; her buildings and the crowds that throng her streets are participants in the national drama that unfolds in relation to, and within, London – a London, whose medieval remains can be (selectively) incorporated in the present.

Throughout the sixteenth and seventeenth centuries the "medieval" was a malleable category, one that could be used either to assert historical continuity or to argue for a "modern" present that needed the past in order to define itself. Middleton did not turn frequently to medieval myth or history; nonetheless, he used medieval literary techniques and referred to medieval historical precedent, particularly in his civic pageants. For these, London itself provided the framework and the stage – and London, like the "medieval," was capacious enough to encompass multiple temporalities and meanings, as well as to provoke a range of powerful emotions.

## NOTES

1. The first use of the term "middle age" is said by the *Oxford English Dictionary* to occur in John Foxe's *Actes and Monumentes* (1563, with numerous reprints until 1684).
2. For an overview, see Emmerson, "Dramatic History."
3. There are other instances of the "medievalized" supernatural in Middleton's *oeuvre* – for instance, the succubus in *A Mad World, My Masters*.
4. On Middleton's indebtedness to late medieval literary, devotional, and visual genres and practices, especially the *danse macabre* and *ars moriendi*, see Neill, "Death," and Holdsworth, "Introduction," "*The Revenger's Tragedy* as a Middleton Play," "*The Revenger's Tragedy* on Stage," and "*Women Beware Women*." I am very grateful to Roger Holdsworth for his generous help and suggestions.

5. On the immense popularity of "medieval" themes and figures in the seventeenth century, taken from saints' lives, chivalric literature, and folk stories, see Spufford, *Small Books*.

6. For an overview of continuities in medical, legal, and literary discourses in relation to female chastity, see Bernau, "'Saint'" and *Virgins*.

7. Thus, for instance, Middleton was involved in the revival (1602) of Robert Greene's *Friar Bacon and Friar Bungay*, which "offers a near-comprehensive collection of popular images of the Middle Ages" (Williams, "*Friar Bacon*," p. 31).

8. Manley argues that the importance of the Inaugural Show increased from 1541 and describes this development as a "new kind of civic myth-making" ("Civic Drama," pp. 302, 307).

9. In Pageant 5 there is a whole song dedicated to "Troynovant" (1535–66).

10. Brutus is again referred to in Pageant 5, in which the speaker refers to Brutus as James's "grand grandsire Brute" (1501), and in Pageant 6 (2160), among the lines written by Middleton.

11. See also his poem "The Temple of St James" (25–8), which includes a commemoration of the medieval foundress of that church, Queen Matilda (1080–1118).

12. In *The Triumphs of Truth* (1613) London is presented as "a reverend mother" who welcomes the new Lord Mayor "with motherly love" (119, 136).

PART V

*Social and psychological contexts*

## CHAPTER 29

# Gender and sexuality

## Caroline Bicks

Female sexuality operated across multiple, sometimes contradictory discourses in early modern culture, and Middleton used them all to evoke the complexities of male–female relationships in his works and time. On the one hand, popular beliefs, informed by patristic tradition, constructed all women as the daughters of Eve: they had strong sexual appetites, but no self-control. Hersus, in *Hengist, King of Kent*, epitomizes this view when he describes how a woman's "cunning"/cunnus makes her wild: "'tis her cunning, / The love of her own lust, which makes a woman / Gallop downhill as fearless as a drunkard" (2.4.171–3). On the other hand, early moderns believed in a humoral body whose fungible fluids needed regular purgings to restore a healthy balance of humors and spirits. One of these fluids was sperm, which women's bodies, as well as men's, allegedly produced. According to the popular Galenic model of reproduction, this female seed, once released through the heat of orgasm, contributed to conception. The exercise of sexual desire, then, was considered natural and healthy: "Moderate venerie is very expedient for preservation of health" as well as the human race (Vaughan, *Naturall*, p. 38).

Greensickness, a disease imagined to trouble unmarried women, was caused by the unhealthy retention and corruption of their seed. The condition was best treated by marriage, the remedy Maudline Yellowhammer prescribes for her daughter Moll, who must "quicken [her] green sickness" with "A husband" (*A Chaste Maid in Cheapside*, 1.1.5–6). A mutually agreeable wedding was the ideal way to manage a maid's desires: as long as her sexuality remained within the bounds of marriage, to be directed toward procreation, her urges were not only licit, but desirable. Leantio pleasurably anticipates his wife's welcome: "After a five days fast / She'll be so greedy now, and cling about me" (*Women Beware Women*, 3.1.106–7); and the fertility of the Touchwoods, according to Touchwood Senior, springs from their mutual desire, the passion of "our wills" and "our bloods," not just his (*Chaste Maid*, 2.1.13–14).

But what happened if a woman remained unwed, or if she married for lust rather than children? Widows who chose to remarry were especially suspect because they had experienced sex and perhaps just wanted more of it. As the Lord Cardinal states: "Second marriage shows desires in flesh; / Thence lust and heat and common custom grows." A woman who weds once, on the other hand, is the model of purity, for "she's part virgin who but one man knows" (*More Dissemblers Besides Women*, 2.1.79–81).

Medical writers believed that 14 was the age at which females begin to turn, in body and mind, towards that one man: "womens paps begin to swell and they think upon husbands" (Crooke, *Microcosmographia*, p. 192). Most women in early modern England, however, did not wed until their late twenties, if they wed at all (Mendelson and Crawford, *Women*, p. 108). This model of female maturation and desire, then, maps out a culturally recognized stretch of time during which female sexuality was operating outside a husband's control. The writers of *The Practice of Physick* were not alone in advising that "if the patient can not so conveniently be married ... some advise that the Genital Parts should be by a cunning midwife so handled and rubbed, as to cause an Evacuation of the over-abounding Sperm" (Culpeper *et al.*, p. 419).

This graphic image of a midwife servicing a virgin body dramatizes how men generally were one step removed from the female body's sexual operations. A culture of modesty discouraged women from consulting with physicians about female matters; England was the last European country to have men attend regular labors; and in the courts women were brought in to search other women's bodies to determine virginity and pregnancy. Diaphanta fears, for example, that Beatrice-Joanna will search her, like "the forewoman of a female jury," to determine her virginity (*The Changeling*, 4.1.103). The trial of Frances Howard, a woman famously rumored to have faked her court-ordered virginity test in 1613 (with the help of two corrupt midwives and a jury of matrons) in order to annul one marriage and pursue another, informs many of Middleton's plotlines.[1]

As a result of these cultural and legal codes, men were often at a loss when it came to interpreting the female body's secrets. In his Epistle Dedicatory to *The Sicke-Womans Private Looking-Glasse*, John Sadler complains that a woman "afflicted with any disease of the wombe" will refuse, for modesty's sake, to "divulge and publish the same unto the Physitian." The Physician whom the secretly pregnant Jane Russell must consult in *A Fair Quarrel* is equally frustrated by his patient's reticence. He cannot read her body's condition, but must rely on her to "ope to the physician / All her dearest sorrows" (2.2.2–3). Claiming that she has "blushes that will stop my tongue" from exposing herself to him, Jane asks for someone "of mine own sex" (2.2.45, 4).

Middleton's plays often hinge on the problems that this secretive, female body presented for fathers and husbands. Peter Stallybrass has argued that the threshold of a man's house, and the vagina and mouth of his daughter or wife, were analogous and anxiously guarded spaces in early modern culture ("Patriarchal Territories," p. 129 ). Middleton repeatedly calls on this trope to dramatize the problem of keeping female sexuality (and, by extension, the patriarchal home) enclosed and under a man's watchful eye.

Try as they might to pen up their desiring females, the men in the plays are unable to keep them hidden and unpenetrated. As *Women Beware*'s Bianca argues, it is no good "To keep a maid so strict in her young days," for "Restraint breeds wand'ring thoughts" – the kind that may involve future husbands, but rarely ones their fathers have chosen for them (4.1.31–2). Moll – a piece of "vent'rous baggage," according to her irate father – escapes twice from his home to pursue marrying Touchwood Junior (*Chaste Maid*, 4.1.275); Aurelia literally runs away to join the gypsies rather than marry her father's choice of husband (*Dissemblers*); and Bianca's desires drive her from her "father's window / Into these [Leantio's] arms at midnight" (3.2.254).

While such transgressions are ultimately forgiven in the service of comic convention, they lead to punitive penetrations in the tragedies: "For as at a small breach in town or castle / When one has entrance, a whole army follows; / In woman, so abusively once known, / Thousands of sins has passage made with one" (*Hengist* 4.2.227–30). Bianca's original crossing of her father's threshold foreshadows her willful movement to the window of Leantio's home, against his orders that she stay "mew[ed] up / Not to be seen" (3.1.218–19); this in turn triggers the sequence of events that leads to her rape by the Duke. In the same vein, Beatrice-Joanna's betrayals origi- nate with her initial crossing of her father's will and walls: what was once his "spacious and impregnable fort" becomes open to murder and adultery because she has let her desires run unchecked, bringing Alsemero in to have "the liberty of the house" (*Changeling*, 3.2.4, 3.4.12). Her "giddy turning" away from her father's choice of husband marks her as a whore (1.1.159). De Flores uses this argument when he blackmails her into sleeping with him (or, arguably, being raped): "Thou whore in thy affection, / 'Twas changed from thy first love, and that's a kind / Of whoredom in thy heart" (3.4.145–7).

Given this prevalent (and, for women, punitive) attitude towards inde- pendent female desire, it is not surprising that many of Middleton's female characters go to extremes to preserve the illusion of their virginity and,

once married, their chastity. Beatrice-Joanna fakes her virginity twice –
manipulating her husband's liquid test (gleaned from the scholar Mizaldus)
and substituting Diaphanta for herself on her wedding night. The Young
Queen of *The Bloody Banquet* shoots her lover dead when he fails to keep his
promise to stay hooded and blind to her identity, for "There are more loves;
honours, no more than one" (4.3.118).

While many of the plays depict such overly desiring and deceptive
women, they feature many more women who are perfectly capable of
keeping their bodies chaste, even when the patriarchal home is penetrated.
Isabella proves her husband Alibius a jealous fool for keeping her enclosed in
his madhouse while she staves off the advances of the intruder Antonio
(*Changeling*); and although the merchant wives of *The Roaring Girl* toy with
the gallants who enter their husbands' shops, they all prove to be loyal
spouses. Even the Duchess in *Dissemblers*, who feels the desires of the flesh
after going to her window and spotting Andrugio, repents before acting on
them, enclosing herself in a religious sanctuary so she can "knit . . . up my
vow" to her dead husband's memory (5.2.204). Truly good, chaste women
keep their bodies enclosed, or at least ensure that no future breach will occur
if it has been forced upon them: Gloriana accepts death over rape (*The
Revenger's Tragedy*); Castiza reveals her rape to her husband (for which she
swiftly faces punishment) rather than prove herself an untrustworthy spouse
(*Hengist*); and Antonio's wife saves him from the dishonor of her rape by
killing herself (*Revenger*).

Even the most chaste of wives, however, was subject to anxious scrutiny
once she was pregnant. In a pre-DNA era, men had to rely on a woman's
word when it came to identifying a pregnancy and naming paternity. As the
Captain in *Quarrel* laments: "who lives / That can assure the truth of his
conception" (2.1.14–15). Middleton foregrounds this problem by making
most of the advanced pregnancies in his plays undetectable. This is a notable
departure from the works of his contemporaries: Shakespeare's Hermione,
by comparison, has "spread . . . / Into a goodly bulk" (*The Winter's Tale*,
2.1.19–20); and Webster's Duchess of Malfi "waxes fat i'th'flank" (*The
Duchess of Malfi*, 2.1.69). The Page in *Dissemblers*, however, is nine months
pregnant, yet no one detects it; Francisca's "great belly" goes equally unno-
ticed (*The Witch*, 1.1.134); Sordido claims he cannot "see through a great
farthingale" to discover Isabella's pregnancy; and even her husband, who felt
that "something stirred in her belly the first night I lay with her," could not
identify her pregnancy at the time (*Women Beware*, 4.2.112, 102–3).

The pregnant body was imagined to be full of mysteries, such as its
strange and bestial cravings: the Page longs to eat a human nose

(*Dissemblers*, 5.1.8–9) and Mistress Allwit longs for "pickled cucumbers / And his [Sir Walter's] coming" (*Chaste Maid*, 1.2.6–7). Moralists and medical writers anxiously debated why it was that women like Mistress Allwit still desired sex once they were pregnant. One popular handbook quotes Aristotle's argument that "The woman with child ... ought not to have the company of her husband" (although sex was allowed just before labor, in order "to shake the child, and make him come the more readily forth" [Guillemeau, *Childe-birth*, p. 24]). The belief that a woman could conceive again after a first conception – "the womb opening it self by reason of great delight in the action" – added a further troubling dimension to the pregnant body's sexual illegibility (Sharp, *Midwives*, p. 77). Even if a husband could be secure in his paternity, his pregnant wife's body could open up and make room for a second, adulterous conception.

The fear of a woman's "wand'ring thoughts" informed other early modern concerns about the pregnant woman's ability to misshape and potentially deceive. Male writers enjoined her to have a quiet mind; if not, she might "imprint that stamp upon her child, which she conceives unto herself" (Burton, *Anatomy*, p. 221). Craving strawberries could lead to a strawberry-shaped birthmark; a longing for hare could lead to a child with a harelip. Most threatening of all, if a woman desired another man at the time of conception, the child might end up resembling him and not the husband. Tomazo, suspicious of Beatrice-Joanna, tries to warn his brother not to marry her:

> If ever pleasure she receive from thee,
> It comes not in thy name, or of thy gift;
> She lies but with another in thine arms,
> He the half-father unto all thy children
> In the conception – if he get 'em not,
> She helps to get 'em for him in his absence.
> (*Changeling*, 2.1.134–9).

For men, fathering children was a definitive mark of manhood, which makes Tomazo's image especially emasculating. Describing men's stones, or testicles, Nicholas Culpeper wrote that they are called "*Testes*, that is, Witnesses, because they witness one to be a Man" (Culpeper, *Directory*, p. 11). Upon discovering that his wife is pregnant, Sir Oliver cries, "Ho, my wife's quickened; I am a man for ever!" (*Chaste Maid*, 5.3.1). Although Allwit claims he is happy to have Sir Walter father his wife's children for him, his servant mocks him behind his back, claiming that Allwit is "out of work," and "falls to making dildoes" (1.2.58).

When a couple were not able to conceive, their barrenness was attributed to either the man or the woman. Typically, however, the woman carried the bulk of the blame. After pages describing the various failures of the womb to provide fertile ground, for example, *The Birth of Mankind* devotes one sentence to the "defect and lack in the man," before declaring that the other causes of his infertility "shall not need here to be rehearsed" (Raynalde, p. 189). Ever protective of the patriarch, dominant early modern discourses were loath to identify men's reproductive shortcomings as organic. This may help explain why male infertility was sometimes attributed to witchcraft. Sebastian goes to Hecate to get "charmed and retentive knots" to render Antonio incapable of impregnating his wife (*Witch*, 1.2.166).

In *Chaste Maid* the fault lies clearly with Sir Oliver's "brevity," a reference either to his impotence or premature ejaculation (*Chaste Maid*, 2.1.150); yet he blames his wife for having had too many sexual partners (2.1.149). Prostitutes were considered prone to barrenness since they allowed different men's seeds to enter them. Hippolito lectures Bellafront on her whoredom, describing the "fruitless riot" of her customers: "for what one begets / Another poisons; lust and murder hit. / A tree being often shook, what fruit can knit?" (*The Patient Man and the Honest Whore*, 6.401–3). One or both parents' sin could cause a fatal birth as well as infertility: as Livia describes the incestuous fruit of Hippolito and Isabella's union, "The deed cries shortly in the midwife's arms, / Unless the parents' sin strike it stillborn" (*Women Beware*, 4.2.69–70).

Although fatherhood made a man in certain respects, the inordinate and uncontrolled spreading of his seed could undo him by expending too much of his heat and humoral spirit. Lussorio is so full of "heat" that he "would not be contained, he must fly out" (*Revenger*, 1.1.82, 84); and Tarquin's "ardent hot desire" leads to the foul breach of Lucrece and the law (*The Ghost of Lucrece*, 149). In Touchwood Senior's case, he has threatened his manhood by fathering too many children – a comic situation that compels him to stop sleeping with his wife and declare that "the feast of marriage is not lust but love / And care of the estate" (2.1.50–1).

Once a woman gave birth, she continued to be a figure of physical excess, threatening the man's finances and home. Allwit claims that he "heard a citizen complain once / That his wife's belly only broke his back" (*Chaste Maid*, 3.2.66–7). The gossips' gathering that invades his home is lavish and expensive, a female take-over of his home: "nurse upon nurse, / Three charwomen, besides maids and neighbours' children!" (2.2.6–7). Such gatherings took place throughout the lying-in month, during which time the mother stayed in her bed, attended by her friends, while the husband, barred from sleeping with his wife, paid to entertain them. These feasts were frequently satirized as sites of verbal and physical excess: gossiping, eating, and (in the case of Mistress Allwit's gathering) pissing (3.2.196).

This potential for post-partum excess informed the continued scrutiny of the new mother's sexuality. According to humoral theory, the blood from the uterus transformed into milk once the baby was born. ("Thou art my nurse-child, Tarquin," wails Lucrece's ghost. "Here's blood for milk; suck till thy veins run over" [*Ghost*, 136, 142]). The nursing mother needed to keep her blood pure of disruptive feelings or risk passing them on to the infant; hence she was "to avoid all passions and venerous actions" (Sharp, *Midwives*, p. 271). Although women commonly hired wet-nurses if they could afford it, there was a puritan movement in the beginning of the seventeenth century that encouraged maternal breastfeeding. While it is impossible to know how far the Calvinist Middleton's sympathies may have extended in this case, he certainly places great value on the Old Queen in *Banquet* who nurses her own child back from the brink of death and is thus able to provide, with her "constant breast," a "hopeful heir" for the troubled kingdom (5.1.232, 235).

Most of the births in Middleton's plays, however, dramatize the plight of the undomesticated female body. Roughly 4 percent of babies born in 1600 were bastards, the result primarily of broken nuptial contracts and the exploitation of single women working and living away from home. Furthermore, up to 25 percent of brides were pregnant at their weddings, a statistic that highlights the sexual activity of partners who were betrothed, but not yet married. For the woman, bastard-bearing could result in imprisonment, or worse if she chose not to identify the father; if a man was discovered to have fathered a bastard, he would be obligated to take full financial responsibility for the child (Cressy, *Birth*, pp. 73–5).

Middleton's plays are full of the fruits of these potentially hazardous unions, a feature that allows him to explore the day-to-day realities and consequences of sex outside of marriage. As a point of comparison, Shakespeare's plays often feature bastard adults, but none – with the notable exception of *Measure* – give sustained focus to men and women confronting the births of bastard children. (Middleton likely adapted the latter play in 1621 to accentuate the presence of the pregnant Juliet [Jowett, *Middleton*, p. 1543].) For the men of Middleton's plays, these scenarios highlight the financial burden of claiming a child and the desire to dispose of it quickly and at minimal cost. Touchwood Senior must pay off one of the many wenches he impregnates (*Chaste Maid*, 2.1), an act that supports Aberzanes's claim that "you can swell a maid up / And rid her for ten pound" (*Witch*,

2.3.13–14). He disposes of his and Francisca's bastard by paying off an Old Woman to leave the child on a tailor's doorstep.

For the women of Middleton's plays these births present an equally real, but quite different problem: the loss of one's reputation and future as a respectably married woman. Jane Russell quickly agrees to have her new-born raised by a Dutch Nurse, "For else what husband would choose me his wife, / Knowing the honour of a bride were lost?" (*Quarrel*, 3.2.56–8); Isabella hastens to marry the witless Ward before her pregnancy is revealed (*Women Beware*); and Lactantio's pregnant, cast-off mistress begs him to "stir your care up to prevention" and marry her before it is too late (*Dissemblers*, 3.1.11).

In this sense, the secretively pregnant women in Middleton's plays (unlike those imagined in medical, philosophical, and other popular discourses) are not at all empowered: they lack strong female confidantes and instead depend on and fall prey to particular men. There are no women to protect the pregnant and newly delivered mother, as happens in *A Midsummer Night's Dream* and *The Winter's Tale*, or Jonson's *The Magnetick Lady*. The Black Queen's Pawn was "poisoned with child, twice" by the Black Bishop's Pawn when she was a probationer at Brussels. He hid the pregnancies, advertising them as spirit possessions, and leaving her ruined (*A Game at Chess*, 5.2.104); Francisca must rely on Aberzanes to arrange for her secret delivery (*Witch*); the Page is forced to sing and dance until she falls on the floor in labor pains; and although Jane's reputation is saved at the eleventh hour by the Physician's sister, she is largely left alone to fend off his sexual blackmail. Although Middleton at times uses early modern discourses of female sexuality to give his female characters the upper hand, they rarely maintain their grip; more often than not, they barely escape permanent damage to their bodies and reputations, or they fall to their deaths and disgrace.

### NOTE

1. For more on the Frances Howard case, see Lindley, *Trials*.

## CHAPTER 30

# Women's life stages: maid, wife, widow (whore)

## Jennifer Panek

By titling a play "The Puritan Maid, the Modest Wife, and the Wanton Widow," Middleton invoked his culture's traditional categorization of women's life stages, as determined by their relationship – past, present, future – to men. While no one knows whether his maid, wife, and widow lived up to their billings, as the play survives only as an entry in the Stationer's Register of 1653 (Feldmann and von Rosador, *Middleton*, p. 330), the same triad is a staple in literature of the period, from Samuel Rowlands's verse narrative *Tis Merrie When Gossips Meete* (1602), in which a wife and widow advise a maid while getting tipsy at a tavern, to Nathan Field's *Amends for Ladies* (1611), where comic convention provides fifth-act husbands for the maid and widow, giving the wife the last word: "mine is now approved the happiest life, / Since each of you hath changed to be a wife" (5.2.300–1). As Shakespeare's Lucio in *Measure for Measure* irreverently reminds us, however, not all women fit into these categories – "she may be a punk, for many of them are neither maid, widow, nor wife" (5.1.178–9) – and the women of Middleton's plays tend to complicate such neat divisions even further: Beatrice-Joanna outwitting a virginity test after a murder costs her her maidenhead (*The Changeling*); Mrs Allwit placidly committing adultery with her husband's full approval (*A Chaste Maid in Cheapside*); the courtesan Jane expertly impersonating a wealthy widow (*A Trick to Catch the Old One*). In a patriarchal society where maids, wives, and widows lived with the threat of being one sexual misstep away from recategorization as a whore, theatre audiences were evidently fascinated by women who challenged the boundaries of their prescribed roles.

The word "maid" itself – a synonym for virgin – encapsulated what a young unmarried girl in early modern England was taught to consider her primary duty. While moralists enjoined abstinence to unmarried people of both sexes, overwhelming emphasis was put on the need for women to maintain their virginity until marriage. Robert Cleaver's much-reprinted domestic handbook, *A Godlie Forme of Householde Government* (1598), is particularly clear on this point:

Maides and young women are to be put in mind, and alwaies to remember, that the best portion, the greatest inheritance, and the most precious jewell that they can bring with them on the marriage day, is Shamefastness: the want whereof is most hurtfull in all women ... A man needeth many things: as wisedome, eloquence, knowledge of things, remembrance, skill in some trade, or craft to live by, justice, courage, and other things and qualitites moe, which were too long to rehearse: and though some of these be lacking yet he is not to be disliked, so that he have many of them. But in a maide, no man will looke for eloquence, great wit, ordering of the Common-wealth, prudence, etc. Finally, no man wil looke for any other thing of a woman, but her Honestie: the which onely if it be lacking, she is like a man that wanteth all that hee should have. For in a maide, the honestie and chastitie is in stead of all. (p. 351)

Underlying such exhortations was the common belief that sexual purity did not come naturally to young virgins, since a woman's comparatively weaker powers of reason made her more susceptible to her passions, including sexual desire, than a man. Sir Thomas Overbury's character of "A Very, Very Woman" (1614) is "Mariageable and Fourteene at once; and after shee doth not live but tarry" (4); lusty little Moll Plus in *The Puritan Widow* (1606) reduces that to "presently after twelve" for London girls (5.2.15), although actual first-time London brides wed at about twenty (Elliott, "Single Women," p. 86). When Diaphanta eagerly agrees to the bed-trick that will deflower her in Beatrice-Joanna's place, and then prolongs her pleasure so far that she risks discovery, she merely confirms conventional assumptions about even the most inexperienced woman's inherent sexual voracity.

The culture's fixation on female chastity, that invaluable yet uncertain commodity, is repeatedly interrogated by Middleton in plays where "maids" desperately (or in some cases, mercenarily) conceal the loss of their virginity. Beatrice-Joanna, who feigns the appropriate symptoms after her suspicious husband presses on her a pre-consummation swig from glass M, is one of a sizeable company that includes Francisca, secretly pregnant at only 16 (*The Witch*); Roxena, who stages "proof" of her chastity by curing an epileptic with "a virgin's right hand stroked upon his heart" (*Hengist, King of Kent*, 2.4.224); and Frank Gullman, who has sold her maidenhead on fifteen separate occasions (*A Mad World, My Masters*). The commodification of chastity pervades Middleton's comedies. Both *Michaelmas Term* and *Your Five Gallants* feature virginal country girls recruited by London pimps, an all too common hazard for young female migrants seeking work in the city;

in the latter play, Primero passes off an entire brothel of prostitutes as innocent music-students, who "blush . . . to hear of a stop, a prick, or a semiquaver" (2.1.93). The market value assigned to what authors like Cleaver insisted was a maid's supreme moral value is made brutally literal by Sir Walter Whorehound, who salivates over Moll's dowry of "two thousand pound in gold" and her "sweet maidenhead worth forty" (*Chaste Maid*, 4.4.54–5). On the streets of London Whorehound could have paid a good deal less: in 1603, the Bridewell court heard from a servant girl named Katherine Williams, whose mistress sold her virginity for only 40 shillings (Griffiths, "Structure of Prostitution," p. 47).

Like Moll Yellowhammer, a young woman needed more than her chastity to compete on the London marriage market: a dowry or "portion" and an education befitting her class were also requisite. The latter varied widely, depending on a family's social standing, income, and attitudes towards female education. Among the middling sort, girls learned reading and (somewhat less commonly) writing, "housewifery," and enough arithmetic to keep basic household accounts; other subjects might include music or French (Charlton, *Women, Religion, and Education*, pp. 126–53). The social-climbing Yellowhammers lavish a classical education at Cambridge on their dim-witted son Tim while his sister gets music and dancing lessons, accomplishments her mother believes necessary to make her a desirable bride (*Chaste Maid*). Mrs Openwork, on the other hand, "a gentlewoman born," claims to have learned not only French but Latin while in service to a lady; her love-match with a mere London sempster takes her several steps down the social ladder (*The Roaring Girl*, 3.344–52).

All but the very poorest girls expected to bring a portion to their marriages, whether amassed from inheritances, gifts from relatives, or savings from their own labor (Erickson, *Women and Property*, pp. 79–97). Moll Yellowhammer's £2,000 portion is exceptionally large for a goldsmith's daughter, four times that of the wealthiest girls of her class. Mary Fitzallard, a knight's daughter, is above average for her station with a portion of just over £3,000; Sir Alexander's insistence that his son do better is just plain greedy (*Roaring Girl*). Further down the social scale, Frank Gullman's merchandisable maidenhead has allowed her and her mother to save up a portion of £300, about average for the daughter of a well-off tradesman (*Mad World*). A girl with no portion whatsoever risked being considered, like Castiza in *The Revenger's Tragedy*, only "good enough to be bad withal" (1.3.104): the daughter of a late, bankrupt courtier, she has "no other child's-part but her honour" (2.1.3) and is accordingly beset with propositions, not proposals.

Accepting a proposal of marriage was a serious matter. Whether performed before witnesses or alone, betrothal or "contracting" to marry was
understood to bind a couple irrevocably to each other, even though solem-
nization in church was required for moral and social legitimacy. A betrothed
individual who broke promise or married someone else could face a lawsuit
in the ecclesiastical courts, such as the one Mrs Gallipot conjures up in her
ruse to obtain money for Laxton: the pre-contract she claims to have had
with him would annul her current marriage, its three-year duration and two
children notwithstanding; her husband accordingly pays Laxton not to sue
(*Roaring Girl*). The legal and moral weight of a contract contributes to the
anguish of Mary Fitzallard, vowed "in sight of heaven" to Sebastian before
his father forbids the marriage (*Roaring Girl*, 1.60); of Fidelio's betrothed,
whose incestuously inclined uncle would rather keep her dowry for himself
(*The Phoenix*); and of Govianus's Lady as she fends off the Tyrant (*The
Lady's Tragedy*).

As binding as betrothal was, one did not have to resort to murder, with
Beatrice-Joanna, to escape it: an unconsummated contract could be dissolved by mutual consent, as Witgood and Jane pretend to do in *Trick*.
Marriage, on the other hand, was for life. A "divorce" in Middleton's time
referred primarily to a church-court-approved separation that allowed the
couple to live apart but prohibited remarriage; only if the original marriage
was proven invalid for reasons such as pre-contract or consanguinity did a
divorce – more accurately, an annulment – release the couple to marry
again. Wife-sale, as attempted by the Captain in *Phoenix*, was certainly not a
legal option, nor is there evidence it was widely practiced even as a folk
custom in this period.[1] With "till death do us part" standing in full literal
force, even moralists dedicated to upholding parental authority deplored
coerced marriage: matches such as the one the Yellowhammers try to force
on Moll or the one Fabritio tragically imposes on Isabella (*Women Beware
Women*) fall foul of injunctions like William Gouge's in *Of Domesticall
Duties* (1622), which advises that parents "may use all manner of faire
meanes to move their children to yeeld to that which they see good for
them: but if they cannot move them to yeeld, to referre the matter to God,
and not against their childrens minds to force them" (p. 564).

As *Women Beware*'s Isabella points out, however, even women who choose
their own husbands "do but buy their thraldoms, and bring great portions /
To men to keep 'em in subjection" (1.2.172–3). If maids were required to be
chaste, moralists insisted that the chastity of wives was inextricably tied up
with subjection and obedience to their husbands. "Set downe this with thy
selfe," William Whately instructs wives in *A Bride-Bush, or a Wedding Sermon*

(1617): "mine husband is my superiour, my better; he hath authority and rule over mee: Nature hath given it him . . . God hath given it him . . . I will not strive against God and nature" (p. 36). "A wife," specifies Gouge, "must yeeld a chaste, faithfull, matrimoniall subjection to her husband" (p. 28). When a wife failed to obey, insubordination was assumed to go hand in hand with infidelity; in the popular imagination, the man who could not govern his wife was inevitably a cuckold, with all the emasculating humiliation that entailed. But while wives did fiercely defend themselves against imputations of sexual misconduct – as revealed by Laura Gowing's study of defamation suits – their insistent focus on sexual behaviour may have actually functioned to uncouple chastity from obedience: the more women elevated the importance of sexual fidelity as the defining characteristic of a good wife, the more freedom they had to determine the rather more nebulous limits of subjection.[2]

While the theme of marital infidelity is ubiquitous in Middleton, as in much early modern drama, he rarely deals in the typical Shakespearean pairing of irrationally jealous husband and innocent wife. On the contrary, jealous Middletonian husbands are usually punished with the cuckolding they deserve, especially if they confine or unreasonably test their wives: Harebrain in *Mad World* offers a hilarious example, Anselmus in *Lady* a horrifying one. Even more idiosyncratically, Middleton repeatedly explores the question of what might happen if a wife's adultery were in fact synonymous with her obedience: *Lady*, *Anything for a Quiet Life*, and *Chaste Maid* all feature wives whose husbands *want* them to sleep with other men. In the first, the courtier Sophonirus eagerly proffers his wife to the powerful Tyrant; in the second, Knavesbe seeks advancement through persuading Sib to sleep with Lord Beaufort (she pretends to comply, only to treat Knavesbe to the full-on stereotype of a cuckold's domineering wife). The prosperous and fertile ménage of Allwit, Mrs Allwit, and Whorehound in *Chaste Maid* provides the richest and least morally straightforward portrayal of a wittol (a complaisant cuckold) and his wife, with Allwit enjoying a most unorthodox assuagement of both the sexual and the economic anxieties that wives were conventionally held to provoke: "I am as clear / From jealousy of a wife as from the charge," he exults, "O, two miraculous blessings!" (1.2.49–51).

City wives in particular were commonly satirized as voracious consumers of their husband's resources; however, the actual economic situation of most married women in early modern England combined the disabilities of coverture – the system which deprived married women of a legal identity and granted husbands sole ownership of their wives' property and earnings – with significant participation in productive labor. In addition to the usual tasks of running a household, the wife of a London craftsman or tradesman typically worked alongside her husband.[3] The citizen wives of *Roaring Girl*, where Mrs Gallipot shreds tobacco and serves customers in the family's apothecary shop while Mrs Openwork updates her husband on which custom orders of undergarments she has completed, offer a more realistic picture of women's place in the economic order than the indolent Mrs Allwit, for whom childbirth is an excuse to demand so many luxury goods that she looks "as if she lay with all the gaudy-shops / In Gresham's Burse about her" (1.2.34–5). Middleton, in fact, is fairly even-handed when it comes to wives and money: in the satirical *Five Gallants*, Mrs Newcut's extravagance ruins two husbands (like the Jeweller's Wife in *Phoenix*, her consumption extends to men paid for sex), but Kate Low-Water (*No Wit/Help Like a Woman's*) and Lady Cressingham (*Quiet Life*) prove to have more financial acumen than their husbands and use it to their households' good. Coverture did not necessarily prevent wives from considering the household wealth to be as much theirs as their husbands', and from handling it accordingly.

Freed from coverture, the widow – provided she was wealthy – was a figure of much interest for practical-minded bachelors and early modern dramatists alike. A widow had full rights to her property, and, in most cases, far more freedom than a first-time bride to bestow herself and it on a husband of her own choosing. And although she might be criticized if she made a poor choice – like Lady Plus in *Puritan* or Castiza in *Phoenix* – remarriage in and of itself was considered morally neutral; far more threatening is a widow like Livia, who eschews remarriage while using her wealth to entice a lover and her experience to toy cynically with the chastity of younger women (*Women Beware*). The widows of London crafts- and tradesmen, who were entitled by city custom to a third of their late husbands' estates, and in practice often inherited much more, had a particular tendency to remarry quickly, often with slightly younger men of the same company (Brodsky, "Widows," pp. 122–54). While many such matches in real life no doubt involved financial prudence on both sides, comic plots about rich widows eager to marry attractive but penniless young men (or about men who hoped as much) were popular fare on the early modern stage. In plays such as George Chapman's *The Widow's Tears* and Lording Barry's *Ram Alley*, the stereotype of the lusty widow ensured that the most virile suitor carried the day. Middleton, while exceptionally fond of plots involving widows – seven appear in his comedies alone – is more likely to satirize the mercenary suitor than the desirous widow: the frenzied chase after the fictitious Widow Medlar in *Trick*; Lady Goldenfleece's houseful of ludicrous and/or despicable suitors in *No Wit*; Ricardo's underhanded tactics to win Valeria's fortune in *The Widow* (1615–16).

Middleton's own upbringing may have influenced his attitude towards such matches: his mother Anne, widowed and remarried in 1586 (the year her son turned 6), spent the remaining seventeen years of her life in litigation as her second husband, Thomas Harvey, tried to seize control of her property. If Harvey and Anne are immortalized as the vile Captain and the foolishly generous Castiza of *Phoenix*, Middleton's earliest play featuring a remarried widow, the tribute is flattering to neither.[4]

Later in Middleton's career, a more attractive figure can be found in the titular figure of *Widow*, who also has something in common with the playwright's mother: the foresight to make a premarital settlement, a legal means of evading the full weight of coverture. A woman who wanted to retain control of her property on marriage could sign it over to a close friend or relative, who would hold the property in trust for the married woman's own unrestricted use. Anne conveyed over £300 and several leases to three family friends who also happened to be lawyers; had she not, Harvey could have spared his lawsuits and simply disposed of it as he pleased. In *Widow*, Valeria conveys her entire fortune to her brother-in-law, leaving the suitors who have been wrangling for her hand in court to discover that the winner is entitled to marry her, but not to touch a penny of her wealth. Both on and off the stage, widows were the women most likely to make such settlements – "she'll ha' convey'd her state safe enough from thee, an' she be a right widow" (1.3.101–2) grumbles Quarlous in Ben Jonson's *Bartholomew Fair* (1614) – contributing to a popular belief that the balance of marital power was stacked against the man who married a widow rather than a maid, especially if she brought more money to the match than he did.[5] The London widow Martha Moulsworth, author of a 1632 autobiographical poem and veteran of three marriages, describes how she had her "will in house, in purse, in store" with her beloved third husband, concluding, "The virgin's life is gold, as clerks us tell, / The widow's silver: I love silver well" (207–8). No widow could go back to "the virgin's life," but she may have had reason to hope that a second round of wifehood might be better than the first.

1. On betrothal, see Ingram, *Church Courts*, pp. 189–218, and O'Hara, *Courtship and Constraint, passim*; on divorce, see Ingram, *Church Courts*, pp. 145–50, 171–88, and Stretton, "Marriage," pp. 18–39.
2. The hypothesis that emphasizing chastity de-emphasized obedience is in Amussen, *Ordered Society*, pp. 121–2. Concerning popular perceptions of adultery, see Gowing, *Domestic Dangers*, pp. 180–206; Foyster, *Manhood*, pp. 103–39.

3. Women's work is discussed in Mendelson and Crawford, *Women*, pp. 256–344, and in Fletcher, *Gender, Sex, and Subordination*, pp. 223–55. On coverture, see Erickson, *Women and Property*, pp. 24–6; Mendelson and Crawford, *Women*, pp. 37–9.
4. The "lusty widow" stereotype is discussed in Panek, *Widows and Suitors*, pp. 77–123; for Anne Middleton and *Phoenix*, see pp. 65–6 and 132–8.
5. On settlements, see Erickson, *Women and Property*, pp. 102–13, 122–4, 147–9; on wives' perceived power in second marriages, see Panek, *Widows and Suitors*, pp. 46–76.

CHAPTER 31

# Disguise and identity in the plays of Middleton

## Farah Karim-Cooper

The second unlawfull Circumstance of Actors apparell, is its over-
costly gawdinesse, amorousnesse, fantastiquenesse, and disguizednesse
(Prynne, *Histrio-Mastix*, p. 890)

Despite antitheatrical invectives, playgoing in the early modern period was a
popular activity, largely because of the theatre's reliance on what Andrew
Gurr has termed "implausible illusion," a term referring to the tricks,
devices, and performance strategies available to playwrights and acting
companies (*Shakespearean Stage*, p. 7). Dramatists playfully gestured
towards the illusion of stage-playing while acknowledging its practical
realities. This dialogic combination of illusion and reality is at the heart of
the theatrical encounter in this period and defines its conventions. One of
the most commonly deployed stage tricks was disguise. In England disguise,
long a principal feature of festival pageants, medieval mysteries, and morality plays, became a crucial component of early modern drama, practically
because it was sometimes an essential plot driver, and metaphorically
because it alluded to the fluidity of identity, providing a visual metonym
for the *dissembling* art of theatre itself. Cotgrave's French-to-English dictionary translates *desguisé* as "to disguise; to counterfeit, or set a false coat or
glosse on; to alter, adulterate, falsifie, sophisticate" (*Dictionarie*, Sig. Bbᵛ),
implying that at its root, disguise signified hypocrisy and deception, common antitheatrical charges against stage-playing.

In most instances theatrical disguise depends on collusion between
character and audience; only on rare occasions is the audience unaware of
who really lies beneath the layers of disguise (the plot twists in Jonson's
*Epicoene* and Middleton's *The Widow* are two exceptions). This cooperation
is a by-product of the architectural and lighting conditions of the playhouses; whether outdoors or indoors, theatrical spaces enabled a collaborative encounter between actors, playwrights, and audiences. Like
Shakespeare, Middleton richly exploited such conditions of performance,

279

and audiences, whose cognitive engagement helped to construct dramatic identities, willingly accepted the implausibility of the theatrical illusion. Although many disguise plots are highly conventionalized, playwrights like Shakespeare, Jonson, and Middleton deployed the device in a complex variety of ways: disguise may enable mobility, or lead to romantic love, redemption, liberation, renewal, or reunion; disguisers may be motivated by the need for concealment, greed, or social revenge. Middleton's plays are heavily populated with disguisers who deceive others, usually for financial or sexual gain. But more so than in the work of any other playwright, the convention of disguise in Middleton is punctuated with irony and parody.

Middleton often explores identity and how the perception of the self is influenced by the social and economic environment. Most of the deception plots in Middleton's plays circulate around economic greed, social revenge, or material acquisition, during this period all provocative of anxieties about a changing market economy and an upwardly mobile middle class. Early modern playwrights added a new dimension to the trickster figure, "an unrelenting disgust of the economic imperatives by which society was organized" (Dynes, "Trickster," p. 366). Equally, Middleton's use of disguise reveals a preoccupation with the enactment of gender and the materials that enable it. Although this chapter will take its examples from *The Revenger's Tragedy*, *A Mad World, My Masters*, and *Widow*, it is important to stress that disguise is a prominent feature throughout Middleton's canon. For Middleton, the theatre, with its performative audience and illusionistic principles, provided the right conditions for exploring the nature of identity.

### IDENTITY IN EARLY MODERN ENGLAND

Stephen Greenblatt's seminal study, *Renaissance Self-Fashioning* (1984), opened up critical discussion of the ways in which early modern selves were constructed. Courtesy manuals, conduct books, sermons and homilies, and puritan attacks on cosmetics, theatre, gambling, dancing, and masking all register a cumulative cultural anxiety about the ways in which selves are not only constructed by but also conducted in their social worlds. The factors that contributed to the shifting perspectives on self-fashioning are too many to recount here, but economic and religious changes were key contributory factors to ways of discovering the self that were threatening to particular religious and political factions. Antitheatrical writers viewed altering one's body as a dangerous activity that would produce monstrosity and deformity. William Rankins's significantly titled antivanity tract, *A*

*Mirrour of Monsters* (1587), calls players "monsters" who "in outward shew seeme painted sepulchers, but digge up their deeds, and finde nothing but a masse of rotten bones" (p. 2). Rankins argues that "under the colour of humanitie, they present nothing but prodigious vanitie" (p. 2). References to the doubleness of players in such vituperative attacks are common.

As early as 1952, M. C. Bradbook defined Elizabethan theatrical disguise "as the substitution, overlaying or metamorphosis of dramatic identity, whereby one character sustains two roles" ("Disguise," p. 160). Thus disguise enables the retention of two theatrical selves, which explains why early modern dramatists frequently and self-reflexively gesture towards the doubleness of identity. More recently Nancy Selleck's work on selfhood provides a helpful strategy for understanding early modern conceptions of identity. She argues that "selves," during this period, "share a tendency to locate selfhood beyond subjective experience, in the experience of an *other*" (*Interpersonal Idiom*, p. 2). To move beyond the one-person model of selfhood means "addressing the ways that other bodies and other perspectives fashion the self" (p. 3). Disguised bodies are doubled bodies, as Bradbrook points out, so sometimes disguise *reveals* a character's identity even while it attempts to conceal it. Although disguisers in Middleton hide their primary identities beneath layers of clothing, prosthetic beards, or makeup, continuity between disguiser and disguise simultaneously reveals and blurs essential qualities. For example, when Follywit in *Mad World* pretends to be an actor or prologue in the final play within a play, his wife, the courtesan, does not recognize him, but she admits, in an aside, to being sexually intrigued by him, illustrating Follywit's appeal to her as a performer: "O' my troth, an I were not married, I could find in my heart to fall in love with that player now, and send for him to supper" (5.2.33–5). In this example, the disguise plot is underlined with irony. The audience would laugh here as they recognized that the character playing the "actor" is actually an actor playing a character, who, in fact, is the courtesan's husband. From Follywit's activities throughout the play, we learn that he is a brilliant performer, and his final disguise as an actor reveals this trait.

Disguise, then, is also a metatheatrical device gesturing towards the beguilement of acting. Playwrights used it to exploit the theatrical practices of cross-dressing, doubling, and masking, conventions that remind audiences of the protean quality of social identity. However, it was this proteanism that worried the antitheatrical writers who spoke out against acting, because it destabilized not only the status quo but the legibility of human selves. William Prynne, for example, objects to "this counterfeiting of persons, affections, manners, vices, sexes, and the like, which is inseparably incident to the acting of Playes; as it transformes the Actors into what they are not" (*Histrio-Mastix*, p. 159). The shape-shifting effects of performance and its conventions resembled too closely the activities of the devil himself.

Middleton prods this anxiety in one of the most critically discussed moments of his work. In *Mad World* (4.1) Sir Penitent Brothel is visited by a succubus disguised as Mistress Harebrain, with whom he has consummated his adulterous relationship. In this extraordinary scene, Sir Penitent Brothel decides to give up his affair and immediately repent. The very sight of the succubus alters his course, and he finally manifests the double-sided quality that his name reveals about his identity when he chooses contrition. In 4.5 he then sees it as his mission to convince Mistress Harebrain to do the same:

> The very devil assumed thee formally:
> That face, that voice, that gesture, that attire
> E'en as it sits on thee, not a pleat altered,
> That beaver band, the colour of that periwig,
> The farthingale above the navel, all
> As if the fashion were his own invention.
>
> (4.5.26–31)

This speech outlines the mechanics of impersonation; not just the assumption of the wig and the farthingale, but also voice and gesture contribute to the enactment of identity. Bradbrook reminds us of the early associations between disguising and the devil: "the two archetypes were the disguise of the serpent and the disguise of the Incarnation" ("Disguise," p. 161). In Middleton's example, the devil in disguise, functioning as a deliberate parody of the antitheatrical link between the satanic and playing, ironically inspires a sinner's contrition.

Part of Nancy Selleck's aim was to revise our current understanding of what words such as "character," "personality," "individual," "self," and "identity" meant in an early modern context. For example, "individual" acquired its current meaning in the eighteenth century; however, it has a longer history, "stemming from the word's original meaning of *indivisible*, which includes its use in the early seventeenth century to describe two distinct persons or things as *inseparable* from each other" (*Interpersonal Idiom*, p. 38). This reformulation of the early modern vocabulary of the self illuminates the many instances in Middleton's work where it is clear that, for him, identity is dialogic, relying on an "interpersonal" exchange between characters, double selves (the hidden and disguised self), or character and audience. The cultural reception of disguise was dichotomous, characterized first by the argument that any device, activity, or object that would blur identity and create social confusion was of the devil, and, second, by the consumptive demands of performative audiences who loved the illusions of theatre. Playwrights like Middleton took great pleasure from exploiting the theme of social confusion, particularly the blurring of sexual identities at a time when the early modern theatre employed boy actors to play women – who occasionally had to disguise themselves as men – and there were steadily increasing numbers of female audience members.

## MIDDLETON AND THE PROSTHETICS OF GENDER

Principally, disguise is constructed through parts. Gowns, petticoats, doublets, hose, stockings, cloaks, beards, wigs, and cosmetic ingredients constitute the prosthetics of identity and were easily available to theatre companies. The combined meaning of these outward signifiers of the self depended on a specific cultural understanding of each individual part. Clothing was socially encoded as the primary sign of one's gender, social status, age, marital status, or profession. The desire to make sexual and social identity obvious at a glance is evident from the very existence of Tudor sumptuary laws, which dictated the colors and fabrics that were permissible within each social bracket. Related to the social regulation of apparel is the fact that clothes were essential to the construction and memorialization of identity:

We need to understand the animatedness of clothes, their ability to 'pick up' subjects, to mold and shape them both physically and socially, to constitute subjects through their power as material memories. Memories of subordination (e.g. of the livery servant to the household to which he or she 'belongs'); memories of collegiality (e.g. of the member of a livery company with his or her guild); memories of love (e.g. of the lover for the beloved from whom he or she receives a garment or a ring); memories of identity itself. (Jones and Stallybrass, *Clothing*, p. 2)

In *Widow* Middleton parodies the notion that clothes capture and retain identities. In act 5, scene 1 Philippa and Violetta decide to dress "Ansaldo" in Philippa's clothes. When Brandino enters and sees "Ansaldo" disguised like a woman in his wife's clothes, he feels compelled to kiss her, as the image recalls the memory of his young wife. Middleton colorfully illustrates the transferable properties of clothing in the making and unmaking of gender, for the final coup of the play is that "Ansaldo" is actually a woman. This shocking revelation, apart from being a brilliant piece of theatre, highlights the problem with the ways in which identity was established during this period. John Harrington provides the moralistic articulation of this problem in 1597 when he writes:

Wee goe brave in apparell that wee may be taken for better men then wee bee; we use much bumbastings and quiltings to seeme better formed, better showlderd, smaller wasted, and fuller thyght, then wee are; wee barbe and shave oft, to seeme yownger then wee are; we use perfumes both inward and outward to seeme sweeter then wee be; corkt shooes to seeme taller then wee bee. (*A Treatise on a Play*, cited in Gurr, *Shakespearean Stage*, p. 9)

Theatrical disguise depended on the "memories of identity," which is why it provoked anxieties about status and the sartorial transgressions that led to social confusion. Sermons and pamphlets railing against the sumptuous display of the body register the palpable tension between prescription and practice. Nervousness about difficulty in distinguishing reality from appearance is evident in the language of diatribes against bodily adornment, cosmetic alteration, and excesses of apparel. In *The Excellency of Good Women* (1613), Barnabe Rich asks "how many vices are hidden under these painted faces, what deformitie covered with vailes & masks, what crooked minds under streightned bodyes" (p. 21)? Here beautifying the self is seen as an act of concealment, suggesting that deformity lies beneath cosmetic masks and ornate clothing. This argument is fantastically materialized by the dressed and painted skull of Gloriana in *The Revenger's Tragedy*. This prop, the normative symbol of death, invites audiences not only to contemplate mortality, but also to question what constitutes womanhood, fueling fears about the increasing ease with which identity could be manipulated, an anxiety also provoked by the cross-dressing that was a necessary condition of early modern theatrical performance.

Such deliberate manipulation of identity was seen primarily as a female proclivity. Aligning the deceptive qualities of their ruse with a woman's inclination to disguise her body through sexually entrapping cosmetic materials, Vindice asks his brother Hippolito before the masque of death,

> Art thou beguiled now? Tut, a lady can,
> At such all-hid beguile a wiser man.
> Have I not fitted the old surfeiter
> With a quaint piece of beauty?
>
> (3.5.51–4)

Ironically, the attack is discharged even while he congratulates himself about his own skills as a cosmetician. In this context disguise parodies cultural assertions about the toxicity of female sexuality since, once kissed, the skull will prove a deathtrap to the lascivious Duke.[1] In this scene the memory of Gloriana as she once was – a virtuous and natural beauty – is buried beneath the cosmetic disguise and its cultural associations. We learned in Vindice's opening apostrophe to the skull that "then 'twas a face / So far beyond the artificial shine / Of any woman's bought complexion" (1.1.20–2). Although theatrical disguise depends on the socially encoded "memories of identity," Vindice attempts to strip away his earlier memory of Gloriana through the materials of disguise because of the function the skull is about to perform; however, the two meanings ascribed to it in the play continue to coexist. Episodes involving cosmetic disguise such as this one deliberately provoke the cultural anxieties aroused by the beautifying practices of women and the toxicity of their cosmetic ingredients. Cosmetic masks call to mind the simultaneous presence and absence of the hidden self.

During the early modern period, the antivanity movement shared the same vocabulary with the antitheatrical tracts. Writers who spoke out against women "now beclad in a varnish Excrement; & so bedawbed in a glittering Rubbish" (Gaule, *Distractions*, p. 86), aligned female cosmetic practice with the deceptive counterfeiting of theatrical disguise designed to obfuscate identity. Middleton parodies this discourse when in *Mad World* the appearance of the succubus disguised as a woman provokes a satirical attack that rehearses a tired old metaphor comparing a sumptuously dressed woman to a German clock:

> What is she, took asunder from her clothes?
> Being ready, she consists of hundred pieces,
> Much like your German clock, and near allied:
> Both are so nice they cannot go for pride.
>
> (4.1.19–22)[2]

Middleton is not necessarily railing against overly dressed women; rather, through his theatrical appropriation of antivanity discourses, the playwright challenges the assumption that women should not be in control of their own representation. This interrogation seems self-consciously ironic when we consider the play was written for a commercial theatre that excluded women entirely from performance.

### CONCLUSION

As I have been arguing, Middleton deploys disguise to explore questions about identity. Although the material elements of performance are all prosthetic reminders that identity is visually constructed, one further method of disguise is the gestural act of impersonation. The word "personate" in early modern English had two meanings, to sound out a loud noise and, as John Florio defines it in *A Worlde of Wordes, Or Most copious, and exact Dictionarie in Italian and English* (1598), the act of imitating another. This was the most common sense of the word, used often in relation to stage playing. In *Widow* Ricardo is a debt-ridden spendthrift and something of a lady's man. He brags that he has loved a thousand women, half of them married. Francisco, however, is less confident in his abilities and worries that he is too shy to talk to Philippa. When Ricardo offers to help Francisco, he decides to impersonate her: "I'll show you her condition presently" (80). Here "condition" means "essential nature." As Taylor and Warren gloss the word, "in English it develops a complex of senses related to modes or states of being; here Ricardo protests that he will show (act out for) Francisco her true character as he understands it" (*Middleton*, p. 1086), which, in essence, is what defines the act of disguise. In this final twist of *Widow* the playwright establishes that the self cannot be determined or identity unlocked based simply on appearances. Thus disguise was the most effective way of illustrating the tantalizing elusiveness of identity, and this device as well as other "implausible illusions" was fundamental to the artistry of Middleton and his contemporaries.

NOTES

1. Middleton's *The Lady's Tragedy* (1611) also stages a dead female body painted with toxic cosmetics, which acts as a prop to administer revenge against a lascivious Tyrant, clearly a recurrent theme for Middleton and the King's Men (both plays performed in their repertory just four years apart).
2. This misogynistic analogy can also be found in Shakespeare's *Love's Labour's Lost* (3.1.190–200) and Jonson's *Epicoene* (4.2.88–90).

## CHAPTER 32

# Drugs, remedies, poisons, and the theatre

## Tanya Pollard

From tobacco to strange poisons, paints, and potions, drugs play central roles in Thomas Middleton's plays. Their prominence is not surprising in itself: drugs and poisons were proven crowd-pleasers in early modern England, attracting fascination both on- and offstage. Increased travel and trafficking over the course of the sixteenth century brought exotic new substances such as tobacco and opium to England, while changes in medical theory and practice stirred controversies about pharmaceutical preparations and consequences, heightening the intrinsic ambiguity of medicines (J. G. Harris, *Foreign Bodies*; Pollard, *Drugs and Theater*). Accordingly, drugs offered attractive material for playwrights looking to captivate, alarm, and delight their paying audiences.

Yet although Middleton's interest in drugs is not unusual, his dramatic use of them is distinctive and illustrates his playful responses to both social and generic conventions. As playwrights experimented with the effects of drugs onstage, individual genres developed affinities with specific substances. City comedies explored the pleasures of new urban fashions such as smoking tobacco; revenge tragedies identified horror with the sly villainy of poison; and tragicomedies exploited the possibilities of ambiguous drugs that could delay, thwart, and reverse expectations. Middleton wrote about all of these drugs, in all of these genres, and self-consciously forged connections between them. The drugs in his plays showcase his self-conscious awareness of contemporary trends, allowing him to simultaneously mock them and capitalize on their marketability.

### PLEASURES OF THE CITY

A lifelong Londoner, Middleton began his commercial playwriting career with city comedy, a new genre that he was instrumental in creating. It is fitting, then, that the drug featured most prominently in his plays is tobacco, a fashionable new substance that introduced recreational drug use

to England (Mathee, "Exotic Substances"; Pollard, "Pleasures and Perils").
After making its way to Europe from the New World in the sixteenth
century, tobacco entered England in the 1560s and had become wildly
popular by the 1590s. When Middleton began writing, then, tobacco was
not only a well-established part of urban life, but a convenient symbol for
the pursuit of pleasure and all its complications. Like the pranks and
protagonists of city comedy, it evoked novelty, wit, sociability, and reckless
spending; also like them, it was of questionable moral and financial value,
and quickly reduced to hot air.

Tobacco's original claims were therapeutic. According to the dominant
medical theory inherited from the Greek physician Galen, it was believed to
heat and dry the body, strengthening manly vigor by driving out sluggish
cold and wet humors. The drug's dramatic popularity, however, quickly
undermined its strictly medicinal status. Barnabe Rich scoffed that "if all be
diseased that doth vse to take Tobacco, God helpe *England*, it is wonder-
fully infected, and his Maiestie hath but a few subiects that be healthfull in
his whole dominions" (*Irish Hubbub*, p. 46). The drug became associated
with "wantonnesse and delight" (Venner, *Briefe and Accurate Treatise*, B2v),
as well as with masculinity and its social bonds; William Barclay claimed
that tobacco "worketh neuer so well, as when it is giuen from man to man,
as a pledge of friendshippe and amitie" (*Nepenthes*, A4r). Tobacco offered
especially apt material for the theatre: not only was it linked with urban
pleasure and sophistication, but it was routinely sold and consumed in
playhouses, even on the stage itself.

Throughout his city comedies Middleton uses tobacco to evoke the idle
and self-indulgent habits of urban gallants, the fashionable men-about-
town whom the genre both mocked and celebrated. In one of his earliest
plays, *The Phoenix* (1603–4), one such gallant is the Captain, a mercenary
cad trying to rid himself of an unprofitable marriage. Lamenting the
contrast between the constraints of marriage and the freedoms of the city,
he encapsulates the latter with the image of smoking:

O, that a captain should live to be married! . . . What a fortunate elder brother is he,
whose father being a rammish plowman, himself a perfumed gentleman, spending
the labouring reek from his father's nostrils in tobacco, the sweat of his father's
body in monthly physic for his pretty queasy harlot (2.55–61)

Tobacco, to the Captain, epitomizes consumption. Implicitly evoking the
humoral system's interchangeability of fluids and vapors, he identifies its
fumes with the evaporation of labor. This smoke and its accompanying
sensual pleasures offer a microcosm not only for the leisurely life he has

haplessly signed away, but for the greed and carnality that the title character must confront in order to rule the city justly. Strictly speaking, the Captain is an antihero, and the drug is a sordid accessory in his self-interested fantasies. Yet despite the moralizing ending, this image of the gallant with his tobacco is a crucial part not only of the play's jaunty comic tone, but of the urban pleasures that Middleton is selling to his audiences.

Tobacco has similarly mixed connotations throughout Middleton's comic canon. In *The Patient Man and the Honest Whore* (1604), written with Thomas Dekker, the gallant Castrucchio revels in "most Herculean tobacco," though the identification with classical heroism is quickly deflated by the whore Bellafront, who complains that it "[m]akes your breath stink like the piss of a fox" (6.100, 102–3). In *A Mad World, My Masters* (1605) Sir Bounteous Progress is bemused after kissing his mischievous nephew, disguised as his mistress:

i'faith I cannot forget to think how soon sickness has altered her to my taste. I gave her a kiss at bottom o'th' stairs, and by th' mass, methought her breath had much ado to be sweet, like a thing compounded methought of wine, beer and tobacco. (4.4.2–7)

The tobacco that very nearly gives away Follywit's scheme suggests the younger man's witty masculine bravado. Since Follywit's smoke-fuelled pranks ultimately result in his marrying his uncle's whore, their value proves mixed at best, but the equanimity with which he accepts his fate suggests that the pleasure he accrues is worth its cost.

While Middleton's city comedies frequently mention tobacco in passing, the drug plays an especially central role in *The Roaring Girl* (1611), written with Dekker. Not only does it pervade Laxton's flirtation with Mistress Gallipot, but the titillating scandal of Moll Cutpurse's androgyny hinges significantly on her shocking consumption of tobacco (Rustici, "Smoking Girl"). Early in the play, as the gallants approach the apothecary shop, Mistress Gallipot is identified as one "that minces tobacco."

LAXTON: Ay: she's a gentlewoman born, I can tell you, though it be her hard fortune now to shred Indian pot-herbs.

GOSHAWK: O sir, 'tis many a good woman's fortune, when her husband turns bankrupt, to begin with pipes and set up again.

LAXTON: And indeed the raising of the woman is the lifting up of the man's head at all times: if one flourish, t'other will bud as fast, I warrant ye.

(3.8–17)

Set against the commercial backdrop of the apothecary's drugs, the gallants' bawdy banter evokes tobacco's associations with virility. Its phallic pipes offer a masculine counterpoint to the open vessel evoked by Mistress Gallipot's name, and their raising, lifting, flourishing, and budding link profit with sexual activity. Fittingly, the apothecary's shop is also the site of Moll's first appearance, in which the gallants are smitten by her swagger and ply her with tobacco. Her erotic charge is as firmly linked to the heat and delight of the surrounding tobacco smoke as to her masculine attire and manner. And ultimately this heat proves potent: although Moll shakes off her suitors, and Laxton's exploitation of Mistress Gallipot goes up in smoke, Sebastian succeeds at shocking his father into letting him marry his true love. Throughout Middleton's city comedies, tobacco may be tainted, damaging, and elusive, but – at least some of the time – it provides the pleasures it promises.

## PAINTS, POISONS, AND REVENGE

Although Middleton was a pioneer with city comedy, he arrived late at the scene of revenge tragedy. By the time he wrote *The Revenger's Tragedy* (1606) the genre that had exploded in popularity nearly two decades earlier was ripe for parody. The self-conscious wit and artifice of city comedy and, increasingly, tragicomedy threatened to make the raw grief of conventional revenge tragedy look outmoded and unsophisticated. Middleton, accordingly, brought the satirical force of these genres to the traditional conventions of revenge tragedy, especially in his use of drugs.

By the seventeenth century poison had become almost synonymous with revenge. While early revenge tragedies such as *The Spanish Tragedy* (*c.*1587) and *Titus Andronicus* (*c.*1592) hinged on wit and physical violence, the genre's escalating identification with Italian settings, themes, and sources led to stealthier schemes and strategies. Throughout England as well, poison acquired a striking notoriety: in 1602 Lord Chief Justice Sir Edward Coke asserted that of all crimes, poison is "the most horrible, and fearfull to the nature of man" (Coke, *Third Part*, p. 48). In *Hamlet* (*c.*1600) Shakespeare exploited this fascination by changing the public stabbing found in his source into a secret poisoning. With its melancholic malcontent revenger, its use of a skull as a memento mori, and the play within the play furthering its murder plot, *Revenger* marks its debts to *Hamlet* self-consciously, but the play's use of poison illuminates Middleton's sardonic divergence from his model. Vindice's poisoning plot conjoins Hamlet's morbidity with the farcical homicidal glee of Barabas from Marlowe's *The*

*Jew of Malta* (*c*.1590), the violent erotic passions of Kyd's *Tragedy of Soliman and Perseda* (*c*.1592), and the playful opportunism of a city comedy prankster.

*Revenger* showcases its irreverent wit in its farcical allegorical names (Vindice, Lussurioso, Supervacuo), exaggerated caricatures, and colorful plot twists, but it finds its apotheosis in Vindice's poisoning plot. The play's pervasive vocabulary of figurative poisons becomes spectacularly literal when Vindice costumes, paints, and poisons the skull of his former love Gloriana to set a fatal trap for the lecherous Duke. "This very skull," he vaunts,

> Whose mistress the Duke poisoned with this drug,
> The mortal curse of the earth, shall be revenged
> In the like strain, and kiss his lips to death.
>
> (3.5.102–5)

With the dark symmetry characteristic of revenge tragedy, Gloriana's remains are transformed into a weapon against her murderer. Her kiss serves the Duke the figurative poisons of his own lust, turned into the literal poisons he fed her. Vindice's trick is playful, theatrical, erotic, and ridiculous: what sort of a man fails to notice that the woman he's seducing is only a skull? Above all, it is grotesquely comic, stripping the genre of its classical seriousness and reveling in an exaggerated version of its morbidity.

If *Revenger* mocks revenge tragedy while simultaneously paying homage to its pleasures, *The Lady's Tragedy* (1611) echoes and extends its parody. Rather than being deceived into kissing a painted skull, a tyrant willfully deceives himself into kissing a painted corpse. Even more than *Revenger*, the play features allegorically named stereotypes, as if in a morality play; the Tyrant, who usurps the throne, is in love with the Lady, who loves the true king, Govianus. After the Lady kills herself rather than surrender to the Tyrant, he dotes on her corpse, and hires a painter – Govianus, in disguise – to restore her color and, as it turns out, to poison him. Ironically, the drugs that turn toxic in both plays are intended as remedies. Cosmetics, or "face-physics," as they were sometimes called in the period, were understood as forms of medicine, potions used to preserve and heighten natural beauty. Just as tobacco suggests the decadent and ephemeral pleasures of city comedy, face-paints here point to the capacity of illusions to offer both delight and danger.

The play's climactic final scene is simultaneously horrifying, melodramatic, and comic. Elated by the Lady's apparent revival, the Tyrant explodes with joy – "O, she lives again!" – until after kissing her:

TYRANT: Ha!
  I talk so long to death, I'm sick myself.
  Methinks an evil scent still follows me.
GOVIANUS: Maybe 'tis nothing but the colour, sir,
  That I laid on.
TYRANT:          Is that so strong?
GOVIANUS:               Yes, faith, sir.
  'Twas the best poison I could get for money.
        [*He reveals himself*]

                     (5.2.114, 121–6)

Govianus's smug pride in his trick evokes that of Vindice, who cannot resist taking credit for his revenge: "We may be bold / To speak it now. 'Twas somewhat witty-carried, / Though we say it. 'Twas we two murdered him" (*Revenger*, 5.3.96–8). Like city comedy wits whose smoke-borne confidence helps them wrest money and women from naive gulls, these men employ drugs not only to achieve their goals, but to display their cleverness. In doing so, they make audience members not only confront their complicity with their desires and crimes, but recognize the parallels between the cruel schemes of city comedy and the sly wit of revenge.

### STRANGE POTIONS

Although Middleton is best known for his city comedies and revenge tragedies, he also wrote tragicomedy, a genre typically linked with threats, delays, and reversals. Tragicomedies often exploit ambiguous drugs such as sleeping potions to bring about their plot twists, but Middleton's supernatural pharmacy in *The Witch* (1616) characteristically exaggerates this trend. At the play's opening Ferdinand responds to Sebastian's lament over his betrothed's wedding by wondering, "But where's the remedy now?" (1.1.5). As if in response, the witch Hecate offers up a plethora of potions, multiplying plot twists in a spectacular parody of the genre's reliance on pharmaceutically induced transformations.

    The play's central remedy is an anti-aphrodisiac, perhaps the only one in the period's drama. In order to undo Isabella's marriage, which she contracted under the misimpression that her betrothed had died in battle, Sebastian stalls its consummation by obtaining a drug that Hecate promises will "strike a barrenness in man or woman," such that neither "performs the least desires of wedlock" (1.2.151, 158). While Antonio and Isabella fume and fret over their unconsummated marriage, the courtier Almachildes turns to the witches for "charms and tricks to make / A wench fall backwards"

(1.1.91–2), and successfully wins Amoretta's lust – until the charm is dislodged and turns its effects on the Duchess. Meanwhile the Duchess's revenge plot is triggered by another potion of sorts: her husband's morbid "strange health" drunk from a cup made of her father's skull infuriates her with the reminder of his murder of her father (1.1.104).

The play's twists hinge not only on aphrodisiacs, counter-aphrodisiacs, and drinking games, but on poisons and placebos. As the various plots come together towards the end, Antonio gives his sister and her husband "subtle poison" (5.1.54) to punish them for premarital fornication, and drinks it himself in remorse at having apparently killed his innocent wife. Upon lamenting his act, however, he is delighted to learn that all is well: not only is his wife still alive, but his faithful servant had only pretended to give him poison. This discovery leads to all the play's cures: in quick succession, his sister is forgiven, he annuls his marriage and surrenders Isabella to her true love Sebastian, and the Duke recovers from his wife's attempted murder. Throughout the play, Middleton invents and multiplies colorful drugs to catalyze the delays, disasters, reversals, and eventual triumphs at the heart of tragicomedy.

While *Witch*'s plot twists rely on strange but ultimately benign drugs to toy with audience expectations on the way to a happy conclusion, the switchbacks of *The Changeling* (1622), written with Rowley, pursue a similar strategy towards a darker end. Beatrice-Joanna's goal of marrying Alsemero is first obstructed by her betrothal to Alonzo, then facilitated by De Flores's murder of Alonzo, and then again jeopardized when she loses her virginity to De Flores as payment for his work. Intriguingly, the play departs from its source and creates yet another switchback, with the invention of a drug to test Beatrice-Joanna's virginity: like the anti-aphrodisiac, the only one of its kind in the period's drama.

The virginity potion showcases Beatrice-Joanna's skill at playing a city comedy schemer, and at first she does very well at outwitting Alsemero (Garber, "Insincerity"). Before her wedding night she discovers a book in his closet and reads its instructions on "How to know whether a woman be a maid or not" (4.1.41). It advises giving the suspected party a potion, "which – upon her that is a maid – makes three several effects: 'twill make her incontinently gape, then fall into a sudden sneezing, last into a violent laughing, else dull, heavy, and lumpish" (4.1.48–51). After trying the potion on her maid Diaphanta to ensure that she will serve as a reliable substitute during the wedding night consummation, Beatrice-Joanna memorizes Diaphanta's response, and persuasively performs it for Alsemero after he gives her the potion. "Chaste as the breath of heaven," he exults (4.2.150).

While the happy reversals of tragicomedy often depend on a benign drug masquerading as poison, however, the virginity potion ultimately leads to a second, unhappy, counter-reversal. The potion's initial impact on Beatrice-Joanna is threatening, and when Alsemero offers her the glass, she feigns concern that it is poison: "I fear 'twill make me ill" (4.2.137). Apparently thinking herself a heroine of city comedy or tragicomedy, however, she in fact trusts that the drug will prove benign: she has neutralized its danger with her wit. The ingenious trickery of city comedy wits, however, is almost exclusively reserved for men – even the roaring girl is ultimately only a prop in the schemes of the play bearing her name – and Beatrice-Joanna is not allowed to enjoy this role long. Ultimately she is exposed, and dies disgraced and miserable. In a double reversal, the virginity potion proves poisonous after all, turning a potential tragicomedy back to tragedy.

## CONCLUSION

Throughout Middleton's plays, drugs, potions, and poisons mark the playwright's witty self-consciousness towards dramatic genres and their conventions. The pleasurable haze of tobacco, the seductive allure of cosmetics, the invisible threat of poison, and the ambiguous possibilities of sleeping potions, aphrodisiacs, anti-aphrodisiacs, and virginity potions, all serve as catalysts for crucial turning points in the plays, bringing about transformations, toying with audiences' expectations, and creating the unexpected reversals that shape genres' endings and emotional effects. Drugs, for Middleton, offer the double triumph of the popular success that comes of giving audiences what they want, and the witty one-upmanship of exposing, exaggerating, and parodying popular conventions.

## CHAPTER 33

# Middleton and the supernatural

## Michael Neill

Supernatural phenomena belonged to the sensational stock-in-trade of Elizabethan and Jacobean theatre: they were at once part of its classical inheritance and a development of native conventions. Here the vengeful ghosts of Senecan tragedy rub shoulders with witches and evil spirits whose energetic antics recall the devils and vice-figures of medieval morality drama. Thomas Middleton, however, showed an interest in the paranormal even before he began to exploit the theatrical potential of such devices: prominent amongst his juvenilia is *The Ghost of Lucrece* (1600), in which Shakespeare's virginal suicide is summoned from the underworld to broadcast her story to the world; while among the works that helped to establish him on the London literary scene was *The Black Book* (1604), a prose satire in which Lucifer rises from hell to denounce the "adulterous circles" of Jacobean London in bilious monologue (57).

The supernatural trappings of these early works are largely conventional, of course: *Ghost* belongs to the long-established genre of "female complaint," typically imagined as uttered by the ghost of an abandoned or violated woman; while *Black Book* answers a plea for hellish patronage in Nashe's *Pierce Penniless*, to whose starving poet Lucifer now promises "a standing pension" (109). Middleton gives a slightly new cast to the complaint poem by framing it with a prologue and epilogue that place unusual emphasis on the horrors of mortification, endowing the normally disembodied voice of lament with a grisly physicality: "the ghost of gored Lucretia" (34) is no airy spirit, but an animated corpse whose "teats . . . [give] suck" (641–6) to Death, and whose flesh is rendered horribly vivid in a kind of anti-blazon: "That hair which danced in beams before her breath / Serves now to stuff the gaping ribs of death" (618–19). *Black Book* has its own Grand Guignol moments, as when Lucifer comes across Pierce lying "upon a pillow stuffed with horse-meat, the sheets smudged so dirtily as if they had been stolen by night out of St Pulcher's churchyard when the sexton had left a grave open and so laid the dead bodies woolward" (422–5). But in both cases there is a self-conscious theatricality

295

about Middleton's handling of supernatural detail that prevents readers from taking it too seriously. Not only does the choric framework present Lucrece's complaint as if it were a stage performance, but she is made to imagine her heart as a "tragic scene" on which "black appetites" perform their parts (241–8), as if in a drama of Tarquin's composition: "The actor he, and I the tragedy. / The stage am I, and he the history" (398–9). In *Black Book* Lucifer similarly appears "*as Prologue to his own play*," announcing his intention to "turn actor, and join companies" in "this dusty theatre of the world ... this earthen Globe" (38–41, 61–2); while his encounter with Pierce is orchestrated by the flagrantly histrionic ghost of Mistress Silver-pin, "who suddenly risse out of two white sheets and acted out of her tiring-house window" (400–2).

As if commenting on his own fictionality, Lucifer declares that "There are more devils on earth than are in hell" (43); and, in spite of Middleton's fondness for the language of the demonic, there is a recurrent suggestion in his writing that human wickedness needs no diabolic encouragement. So in *Michaelmas Term* (1604–6), for example, the cozening draper Quomodo is assisted by two so-called "spirits," Shortyard and Falselight, who, despite the latter's Luciferian name and their habitual shape-changing, are merely mortal swindlers. Similarly, in *A Trick to Catch the Old One* (1605) – a play whose title seems to promise a gulling of Satan himself – the vice-like nomenclature of Dampit, Lucre, and Hoard announces nothing more supernatural than a trio of London usurers.

By contrast, in *A Mad World, My Masters* (1605), the powers of hell seem to make an actual appearance when Penitent Brothel is visited by a succubus in the guise of Mistress Harebrain; but even this creature proves surprisingly substantial ("Feel, feel, man: has a devil flesh and bone?" [4.1.36]); and since it comes in the "shape" of his mistress (4.1.29 SD), the audience (like Penitent) will initially assume that it is indeed the adulteress herself. When Pentitent shouts "Devil!" at the creature's seductive dancing, and "conjure[s her] ... By that soul-quaking thunder to depart" (4.1.69–70), he speaks metaphorically. It is only when his injunction puts the succubus to flight that Penitent begins to fear that he is indeed dealing with an evil spirit. The testimonies of his servant and Mistress Harebrain finally convince him that his visitor was "the devil in [her] likeness" (4.5.24); but Middleton's audience, confronted by two seemingly identical "shapes" embodied in the same boy actor, may be less certain: their assumptions schooled by the proliferating disguises of a plot that emphasizes the theatrical deceptiveness of appearance, they face the teasing possibility that the "damned art" attributed to the succubus may be nothing more than a fetch of Mistress Harebrain's craft.

Middleton's next comedy, *The Puritan Widow* (1606), places conjuring at the very center of its action; but in this case it is quite transparently fraudulent – a device contrived by the penurious scholar George Pieboard to secure the release of his highwayman friend, Captain Idle, from prison and probable execution. Constrained to live by the "shifts, wiles, and forgeries" of his wit, Pieboard has "put on the deceit of a fortune-teller" (1.2.79, 84–5) – a role he boasts of playing "as well as if I had a witch to my grandam" (2.1.287–8). Planning to deceive a wealthy knight, he comes to the Marshalsea, bringing with him a magic circle "ready charactered" for the purpose (3.5.33–4). Idle is at first reluctant to join in his practice, fearing that "in this false conjuration a true devil may pop up indeed" (106–7). Pieboard, however, quells his anxieties with a dismissive quibble – "A true devil, captain, why there was ne'er such a one" (108–9) – and Idle undertakes to demonstrate "the power of [his] art" to Sir Godfrey, while carefully feigning trepidation that he may fall foul of "the Act passed in Parliament against conjurors and witches" (170, 134–5). There ensues some elaborately theatrical hocus pocus, in which the conjuror's fustian is conveniently accompanied by the menacing peals of thunder. Successfully convincing his victim that he is a powerful arch-magician, the highwayman is temporarily accepted as a "man of parts" fit for the Widow Plus to marry (4.2.259–61), while Pieboard wins the promise of her daughter with a climactic display of supernatural fakery, in which he appears to raise his co-conspirator, Corporal Oath, from his coffin.

Oath's mock funeral and spectacular rising exemplify one of Middleton's favorite games with the supernatural – one that impudently harks back to medieval resurrection plays. Beginning with the fake deaths of Infelice in the collaborative *The Patient Man and the Honest Whore* (1604) and Quomodo in *Michaelmas*, the trick achieves its most outrageously theatrical form in *A Chaste Maid in Cheapside* (1613), where Touchwood Junior and Moll use it to soften the hearts of her mercenary parents. With the lavish funeral rites accorded the young lovers in the final scene, the comedy appears to have taken an unexpectedly tragic turn – an impression confirmed by the protracted lament with which Touchwood's elder brother berates the penitent mourners. Having milked the spectacle for pathos, however, he astounds his audience by summoning the lovers to rise from their coffins, urging them (in a witty reversal of seventeenth-century funeral custom) to convert their shrouds to wedding sheets (5.4.45–7).[1]

The mock resurrection that concludes *The Witch* (1616) is managed without the histrionic pomp of a mock funeral; but in keeping with the play's tendency to burlesque tragicomic convention, its absurdity is underlined by comic duplication: first, Sebastian throws off his disguise, announcing: "I was dead, sir, / Both to my joys and all men's understanding, / Till this my hour of life" (5.3.51–3); and then the corpse of the supposedly murdered Duke revives to reclaim his errant wife from execution. This play's concern with supernatural matters extends well beyond such straightforward trickery, however; for its most spectacular scenes involve Hecate, the witch of the title, with her acolytes, spirits, and feline familiar.

An odd gallimaufry of a play, *Witch* makes sense once it is recognized as a satiric response to the Overbury scandal (see Alastair Bellany's essay in this volume, p. 117). In keeping with this anticourt bias, the play's treatment of the supernatural draws extensively on a text detested by King James – Reginald Scot's skeptical *Discoverie of Witchcraft* (1584). Convinced that he himself had been the object of malign spells, the king was a firm believer in necromancy; and Hecate's boast of her ability to "confound some enemy on the seas . . . [with] sudden ruinous storms / That shipwreck barques" (1.2.131–4) seems designed (like a similar spell in *Macbeth*) to recall the alleged attempt by a North Berwick coven to drown the youthful James and his bride on their voyage home from Denmark in 1589. In *Witch*, however, Hecate's spells prove ridiculously ineffectual; and, though she bears the name of *Macbeth*'s pagan tutelary, this old hag is confessedly mortal (1.2.64–5).

Early in the first scene, the lecherous courtier, Almachildes, frustrated in his wooing of Amoretta, resolves to visit the coven whom he credits with "charms and tricks to make / A wench fall backward" (1.1.91–2); but on his first sighting of Hecate's crew, they strike him as ridiculous – mere fairground cheats: "Call you these witches? / They be tumblers, methinks, very flat tumblers" (1.2.193–4); and though Almachildes almost immediately reverts to his former credulity, the action generally confirms this contemptuous dismissal. For all the lurid sensationalism of diabolic recipes that include serpents, bat's blood, and an unbaptized baby, the witches' spells have no grander aims than satisfying Hecate's sexual voracity and her appetite for petty revenge. They are no more able to force a girl's affections or to undo an enforced marriage than they can injure Almachildes himself when the Duchess seeks his destruction. Though Hecate promises the lovelorn Sebastian that she will "raise jars, / Jealousies, strifes and heart-burning disagreements" between Antonio and Isabella, she is constrained to admit her inability to "disjoin wedlock," since "'Tis of heaven's fastening" (170–2). The charm with which "her hagship" supplies Almachildes (2.2.9) proves to be another blind alley, serving only to lure the gullible courtier into a plan to make away with the Duke, and fobbing him off with a bed-trick in which the favors of a strumpet are substituted for those of the Duchess.

The two remaining scenes of conjuring (3.3 and 5.2) do even less to advance the plot: the first merely provides a spectacular opportunity for Hecate to fly about the stage with her familiar, *"A spirit like a cat"* (3.3.48 SD). In the second, the coven responds to the Duchess's request for a spell to destroy Almachildes with more crude doggerel, dancing around a cauldron into which they toss such macabre ingredients as "bear-breach and lizard's brain … three ounces of the red-haired girl / I killed last midnight … blood of a bat … juice of toad, [and] oil of adder" (5.2.56–73). Apart from its further echoes of Scot, this scene is clearly indebted to the very play whose conjuring scenes it would subsequently be used to embroider – *Macbeth*. But Middleton's version is conspicuously shorn of prophetic ghosts, while its "villainous burden" of revenge (85–6) comes to nothing.

*Witch* remained unpublished in Middleton's lifetime, and in the dedicatory epistle that adorns its one surviving manuscript, he describes it as "ignorantly ill-fated," suggesting that it fell foul of authority because "Witches are … by the law condemned." If their patron's annoyance had placed the King's Men and their dramatist in an awkward position, this might account for the company's decision to revive *Macbeth* – a play rather more flattering to James's superstitions – and to employ Middleton as its reviser.[2] It certainly seems significant that, in expanding Shakespeare's scenes of conjuring, Middleton should have installed Hecate as the menacing goddess of witchcraft, even while equipping her with some of the same chants and spells deployed by her mortal namesake in *Witch*. Whatever the motives behind his refurbishment, however, it is difficult to believe that the reviser's heart was entirely in the project.

The metatheatrical self-consciousness with which Middleton so often handles scenes of witchcraft, conjuring, and ghostly resurrection can give the impression of a thoroughgoing skepticism. Yet it would be a mistake to assume that this represents any consistent philosophical position. In *The Lady's Tragedy* (1611), for example, Sophonirus's boast that he can procure the heroine for the Tyrant's bed by means of "special charms" taught him by a witch (2.3.67–8) is rendered absurd by the crude materiality of the "dear stone" with which he attempts to bribe her (3.1.25).[3] However, the sinful "witchcraft" that "beguiles" Votarius when he kisses the wife of his friend Anselmus has a more ominous suggestiveness – not least because the adulterous Wife imagines herself as surrendering to "the arms of death, and kiss[ing] destruction" (1.2.247–54). In this iteration of the Death and the Maiden trope, there is an uncanny anticipation of events later in the play: when the Tyrant learns of the Lady's suicide he describes her as "married to death and silence" (4.2.27); and when he visits her tomb the very monument seems to "woo" him, so that he must "run and kiss it" (4.3.9) – an action that looks forward to the macabre eroticism of the final scene and his fatal embrace of the Lady's painted corpse. By identifying her dead body with *Mors* itself ("Why, 'tis not possible death should look so fair," [64]) the Tyrant unwittingly prophesies his own doom.

Even in this play Middleton teases the conventional expectations of his audience, for the Tyrant's impious outrage on the tomb is framed by the ridiculous timidity of the soldiers who accompany him. No ghost appears, despite the compounding of their master's blasphemy with a parodic recollection of Christ's resurrection, when he orders them to "Remove the stone" from the door of the tomb (4.4.53).[4] Yet the following scene offers spectacular confirmation of the soldiers's fears when Govianus comes to kneel at his wife's empty monument:

> *On a sudden in a kind of noise like a wind, the doors clattering, the tombstone flies open, and a great light appears in the midst of the tomb; his Lady, as went out, standing just before him* (4.4.42 SD)

Govianus responds by promising to "make myself / Over to death too" (81–2); but that privilege is reserved for their oppressor: in the final scene the Lady's ghost returns, its appearance once again uncannily mirroring that of the corpse which is the object of the Tyrant's necrophiliac "idolatry" (5.2.153 SD; 5.5.20). When Govianus, disguised as a painter, is commanded to use his "art [to] hide death" upon his wife's face (81), it appears to the bedazzled Tyrant as though he has effected a magical resurrection; but – fittingly enough, since cosmetic disguise is imagined as the epitome of courtly corruption – the paint is a poison which transforms the Lady's body into the figure of that "death" to which the Tyrant unwittingly abandons himself (122). When he calls for assistance, her ghost appears "*in the same form as the Lady is dressed in the chair*" (153 SD), as if to claim him as her victim. Then, in the closing moments of the play, as the Lady's cadaver is formally enthroned and crowned alongside her living husband, her spirit makes one last appearance before leaving "*with the body, as it were attending it*" (206 SD), body and soul finally reunited in a ritual that is at once coronation, funeral, and reenacted wedding.

The spectacular stage business involving the Lady's sudden rising from her illuminated monument was powerful enough to prompt John Webster to rework it two years later, using the same stage property, in the Echo scene of his *Duchess of Malfi* (5.3) (Bergeron, "Wax Figures," pp. 331–2). But for modern audiences the momentary frissons produced by the play's uncanny repetitions and the weird double images of spirit and corpse are likely to prove more disturbing. These indeed recall the technique of Middleton's two most powerful works, *The Revenger's Tragedy* (1606) and *The Changeling* (1622).

*Revenger* is a ghost play without a ghost. As its opening spectacle of a young man interrogating a skull seems designed to remind us, Middleton's tragical satire is in many ways parasitic upon *Hamlet*; yet at first glance it appears almost devoid of the supernatural machinery that characterizes Shakespeare's play of haunting. It is true that its later action is punctuated by fearful portents – bursts of thunder and a "wondrous dreadful" comet (5.3.17) – that usher in the apocalyptic massacre of the final scene. But the effect of the latter is undermined by the comic desperation with which Lussurioso's flattering courtiers compete to give it a happy construction (5.3.29–34); while the thunderclaps which Vindice salutes as portents of divine vengeance are rendered absurd by the comic patness with which they respond to his indignant appeal: "Is there no thunder left . . .? There it goes" (4.2.197–8). The heavens rumble again at the bloody conclusion of his masque in 5.3; and this time Vindice's ecstatic response renders the histrionic character of the moment even more explicit: "Mark, thunder! / Dost know thy cue, thou big-voiced crier? . . . When thunder claps heaven likes the tragedy" (42–8).

Equally stagey, but much more disconcerting in their effect, are the scenes involving Vindice's grisly puppeteering with the skull of his mistress, Gloriana. In the course of the play's opening sequence, his imagination begins to change this relic from a conventional *memento mori* into an instrument of revenge that seems charged with its own sinister agency. This fantasy is made grotesquely real in the scene where his "bony lady" (3.5.121) is transformed, with the aid of tires and cosmetics, into the luscious but deadly beauty with whom he offers to satisfy the Duke's senile lechery:

> I have not fashioned this only for show
> And useless property. No, it shall bear a part
> E'en in it own revenge.
>
> (100–2)

While Vindice's language again emphasizes the theatricality of the occasion, the perfect symmetry with which Gloriana's poisonous embrace mimics her own murder gives it an uncanny resonance, identifying the skeletal puppet as a fearful doppelgänger, like the grim *gefehrten* who sweep away their mortal partners in Dance of Death paintings (Neill, *Issues of Death*, pp. 74–5).

From one perspective, of course, the reanimation of Gloriana as a sexually available "country lady" (133) amounts to another of Middleton's mock resurrections; and in this it resembles the equally weird sequence involving Vindice's own alter ego, "Piato" – the creature hired by Lussurioso to secure the favors of Vindice's sister, Castiza. When this supposed malcontent falls under suspicion for the old Duke's murder, Vindice is forced to switch disguises, now assuming the role of "Vindice" (whose fictive character is marked by his rustic accent). To the revenger's incredulous dismay, this new persona is promptly hired by Lussurioso to murder "Piato"; but, in a grimly farcical twist, Vindice solves the problem by dressing up the Duke's corpse as the former hireling, whom he can now pretend to stab. This last encounter with the twice-murdered Duke, who has become his own self-constructed double, leaves Vindice convulsed with a strange mixture of horrified amusement and near panic:

> I must kill myself.
> Brother, that's I; that sits for me. Do you mark it?
> And I must stand ready here to make away myself
> yonder – I must sit to be killed and stand to kill myself.
>
> (5.1.4–7)

For all its transparent theatricality, this episode develops a queasy suggestiveness from the way in which it renders concrete the protagonist's gathering loss of holdfast on his own selfhood. Vindice's is the condition described in Freud's classic essay on "The 'Uncanny'" – one in which "the subject identifies himself with someone else, so that he is in doubt as to which his self is, or substitutes the extraneous self for his own [so that] there is a doubling, dividing and interchanging of the self."[5] "What, brother," Vindice crows on first assuming a disguise, "am I far enough from myself?" (1.3.1). The effect of his masquerades is precisely to make him "forget [his own] nature" (1.3.182) – to the point where his identity seems to have become a perplexingly plural thing ("All this is I" [4.2.130]), leaving him "in doubt / Whether I'm myself or no!" (4.4.24–5). There is an eerie appropriateness, then, in the self-betrayal that ensures Vindice's destruction at the end of the play, for he has no one to blame but his selves – "'Tis time to die when we are ourselves our foes": just as well, he jests, that Piato died: "he was a witch" (5.3.109–18).

This gathering sense of uncanny fatality is equally apparent in the last – and arguably the greatest – of Middleton's tragedies. Although co-written with William Rowley, *Changeling* bears the distinctive marks of Middleton's imagination, especially in the main plot for which he was largely responsible. By contrast with *Revenger*, this play makes some use of supernatural machinery in the form of an accusatory ghost; but this haunting says more about the psychology of Middleton's central characters than about the reality of the paranormal. Having murdered Alonzo at the behest of Beatrice-Joanna, De Flores is twice confronted by the spectre of his victim (4.1.0 SD; 5.1.57 SD): unlike its eloquent predecessor in *Lady*, however, this revenant never speaks; it is visible, moreover, only to De Flores and his equally guilty mistress. Thus, while her glimpse of the apparition persuades the nervous Beatrice that "Some ill thing haunts the house" (5.1.62), audiences are likely to concur with De Flores's rationalizing dismissal of it as "but a mist of conscience" (60).

The play's title, of course, arouses its own supernatural expectations – only to confound them; for it proves to refer not to any sinister fairy exchange, but (as the original list of dramatis personae informs us) to an altogether different kind of "changeling" – the lecherous courtier, Antonio, who changes himself into an idiot (or "changeling") in order to gain access to Isabella, the beautiful wife of the madhouse keeper in Rowley's subplot. Yet as the play traces the process by which "beauty [is] changed / To ugly whoredom" (5.3.197–8), transforming Beatrice-Joanna into her own dark double, the idea of evil substitution gradually reasserts itself. Just as the impressive "outward view" of Vermandero's castle serves only to conceal its vicious "secrets" (1.1.67–9), so his daughter's loveliness is merely the "visor" masking a "deformed" changeling (5.3.46, 77). So too, De Flores, the pliant model of "servant-obedience," will stand exposed as the agent of a "master-sin: imperious murder" (5.3.198–9). "O cunning devils," cries the baffled Alsemero, "How should blind men know you from fair-faced saints?" (5.3.108–9): the answer, of course, is that in the uncanny world of *Changeling*, with its contradictory, doubled selves, there is no way of knowing.

This preoccupation with secret doubles[6] and with emotions and desires hidden from the conscious self can make *Changeling* appear like a dramatic gloss on the mysterious "Book of Experiment, called *Secrets in Nature*" that Alsemero keeps locked in his closet (4.1.24–5); at the same time it anticipates Freud's notion of the uncanny as involving "something which ought to have remained hidden but has come to light" (*Standard Edition*, vol. XVII, p. 241)."[7] The principal characters in the main plot are haunted by a sense of fatality that they cannot properly account for, even to themselves. In the play's opening speech, Alsemero seeks to persuade himself that his sighting of Beatrice "in the temple" amounts to a blessed "omen" (1.1.1–12); yet he admits the uneasy possibility that his passion is simply the product of "some hidden malady / Within me, that I understand not" (24–5). This hint of mysterious sickness is mirrored in the strange obsession that "ails" De Flores when he contemplates the woman they both desire (2.1.27): "I must see her still! / I shall have a mad qualm within this hour again, / I know't . . . What this may bode I know not" (2.1.79–83). Beatrice-Joanna is troubled with an equally perplexed sense of foreboding that leaves her "trembling of an hour after" at the very sight of "This ominous ill-faced fellow," De Flores (2.1.92, 52). By the end of the play she will understand the meaning of that visceral reaction only too well: "Beneath the stars, upon yon meteor / Ever hung my fate, 'mongst things corruptible; / . . . my loathing / Was prophet to the rest, but ne'er believed" (5.3.154–7). "The rest" of which she speaks includes not merely the horror of her own newly discovered damnability, but the perverse sexual attraction, masking as revulsion, to which she has learned to give the name of "love" (5.1.70).

"The uncanny," according to Freud, "is something which is secretly familiar, which has undergone repression and then returned from it," and it is characteristically revealed in patterns of weird repetition – "the constant recurrence of the same thing" (*Standard Edition*, vol. XVII, pp. 245, 234). In *Changeling* it takes the visible form of the phallic token that forces Beatrice to confront the repressed truth of her obsession with De Flores. Sighted first in the gesture that concludes the opening scene, where De Flores (seeking to "haunt her still") attempts to force his fingers into the "sockets" of Beatrice's glove (1.1.237–40), its critical reappearance is in 3.4, the scene on which the whole plot pivots. Here De Flores returns from killing Alonzo with a proof of success that is simultaneously the sign of Beatrice's tie to her murdered fiancé and of her deeper bond to the murderer himself – the finger and betrothal ring that leave them "engaged so jointly" (l.91): "I could not get the ring without the finger . . . for it stuck / As if the flesh and it were both one substance" (29, 39–40). For Freud, "dismembered limbs" are in themselves "peculiarly uncanny" (*Standard Edition*, vol. XVII, p. 244); and the last recurrence of the severed finger occurs in a literal haunting, as De Flores is startled by the ghost of Alonzo "*showing him the hand whose finger he had cut off*" (4.1.0 SD).

Of all the ghosts, spirits, demons, and witches who pass across Middleton's stage it is perhaps only this one, charged with the unaccountable menace of the uncanny, that for a moment makes the functioning presence of the supernatural appear fully convincing. Yet it can hardly be a coincidence that this eerie dumb show is immediately followed by the "precious craft" (4.1.16) of Beatrice's raid on Alsemero's closet and her discovery of a book which, for all its magical auspices, proves to be an encyclopedia of practical experiment by means of which, like some ambitious Baconian inquisitor, this recalcitrant wife plans to "beguile / The master of the mystery" (4.1.38–9). In Middleton's world it is human guile that holds the audience's fascinated gaze, while the supernatural, though seldom quite absent, keeps sliding unnervingly out of sight.

NOTES

1. Gittings, *Burial and the Individual*, pp. 111–12; Neill, *Issues of Death*, pp. 165, 329, 339–40. The Lenten setting of the play, combined with the Easter parody in 2.2, helps prepare for the lovers' resurrection.
2. For the dating and scope of Middleton's revisions, see *Companion*, pp. 383–98.
3. All citations from A (original) text.
4. See, for example, Matthew 28:2–13 for a number of striking parallels with Middleton's scene.
5. Freud, "The 'Uncanny'," in *The Standard Edition*, vol. xvii, pp. 217–52 (p. 234).
6. A material correlative of the double motif is produced by the conventional bed-trick device, in which Beatrice's maid, Diaphanta, becomes a substitute (or "changeling"), taking the place of her mistress as Alsemero's "false-bride" (5.3.161).
7. On secrets in *Changeling*, see Neill, "Introduction" to Middleton and Rowley, *The Changeling*, pp. xix–xxvi.

## CHAPTER 34

# "Distracted measures": madness and theatricality in Middleton

## Carol Thomas Neely

In the early modern period only a handful of plays and playwrights represent madness and then only sporadically; just three models beget variations. The first and most studied model, eschewed almost entirely by Middleton, is the representation of tragic madness: prestigious, elevated, characterized by thematically rich and disjointed speech and behavioral excess. This model is instigated by Kyd's Hieronymo, in *The Spanish Tragedy*, whose performance of madness circulates throughout the period and is developed by Shakespeare in the figures of Ophelia, King Lear, and the Jailor's Daughter. The second model, a comic one, is that of a nominally mad figure such as Diccon the Bedlam in *Gammer Gurton's Needle* or Trouble-All in *Bartholomew Fair*, that maddens others to catalyze plot chaos. Middleton pioneers the third model: the play-within-play performance by Bedlamites for the sane, which he and Thomas Dekker introduce in *The Patient Man and the Honest Whore* (1604), one of Middleton's earliest plays. *The Changeling*, with Rowley (1622), one of Middleton's last plays, provides the final example (of just five) of this brief theatrical fad.

Middleton's two Bedlamite plays within plays and those he catalyzed by others have long remained a touchstone for mimetic views of theatre and hence for understanding Bethlehem Hospital and its practices. But as I have shown in my book, *Distracted Subjects*, these plays tell us next to nothing about early modern Bedlam; instead the madhouse performances hold the mirror up to art (pp. 84–204). They are a means for Middleton (and others) to parody and exploit the themes and play types, the material strategies, and the actor–audience alliance that guarantee success to early modern playwrights, and to foreground theatre's core elements: bodies and illusion, costumes and props, disguise and role-shifting. Madness is also represented through metatheatrical performativity in at least three other Middleton plays – metaphorically in *A Mad World, My Masters*, glancingly in *The Lady's Tragedy*, and centrally in *The*

*Nice Valour; or, The Passionate Madman.* Middleton's representations of madness through performative excess in comedy, tragedy, and tragicomedy blazon his exuberantly self-conscious art and concur with early modern understandings of mental disorder.

Medical treatises, doctor's case notes, Alderman's repertories, and Bedlam censuses all reveal that the term "madness" is not widely used in the period except in literature and drama. Like "distraction," its more ordinary early modern synonym, madness is an umbrella term that covers a wide variety of excessive emotions and non-normative behaviors, from mildly amusing to deadly serious. Madness, like distraction, exists on a continuum: it may refer to commonplace anger or uncontrollable wrath and one state can shift into the other. But whatever the diagnostic term used – melancholy, lovesickness, fury, fits – all mental disorder is understood as caused by unbalanced bodily humors. Its diagnosis is made by onlookers, based on aberrant behaviors (or speech), and madness is believed transient and curable (Neely, *Distracted Subjects*, pp. 2–4). Cured patients are released from Bethlehem Hospital (pp. 175–81), and distracted subjects are routinely said to be "restored to memory" and to go about their business (p. 3). But whereas Middleton's foolish, lovesick, or humor-driven main characters are reabsorbed into the community, his Bedlamites, less characters than performative fragments, vanish without cure.

This contrast is especially vivid at the denouement of *Patient Man*, when all the characters converge on Bethlem monastery, "six or seven miles" from Milan (14.106–7), and three madmen perform. The characters are cured of their excessive and selfish passions, whereas the three caricatured madmen stage satiric riffs and disappear. The "monastery" is a stage locale that provides the ingredients needed for the denouement: a chapel for a clandestine wedding with a friar to officiate, friars' robes for disguises, and a diversion so the marriage can be completed before the on-hand heavy father, the Duke, can stop it.[1] The metatheatrical show by the mad insistently foregrounds Middleton's theatre practices. The Master of Ceremonies enters, stage directions indicate, as Thomas "Towne, like a Sweeper," and speech prefixes (previously normalized) reiterate this well-known comedian's name. The Friar who introduces the mad performance promises comedy and sadness: "they do act / Such antic and such pretty lunacies, / That spite of sorrow they'll make you smile" (15.163–5), and in fact we see the onstage audience respond in unison as cued, with laughter ("Ha ha ha" [15.207]) and with sympathy ("A very piteous sight" [256]) – what playwrights hope for from their audiences.

The three madmen's monologues illustrate stage types: Madman 1 has lost his speculator's livelihood, and his children, like the Duke's daughter,

have disappointed their father; Madman 2 has lost his beloved, like
Hippolito in this play; and Madman 3 is a wildly jealous husband, the
opposite of the patient Candido here, but a frequent Middleton type.
Although the sweeper declares all mad and the Duke declares his reform
has occurred "in place fit / to bridle me" (15.416–17), it is in fact Bellafront
the honest whore, disguised as a madwoman, who triggers the denouement
by exposing the eloping couple's disguises and securing a husband for
herself. The characters, perhaps because they have viewed the obsessions
of the mad performers, abandon their own. The Duke embraces his
daughter's marriage, Matteo resigns himself to marrying a whore, and
Viola ceases to goad her husband, Candido, out of patience. The central
characters may be cured of their foibles, but the mad performers vanish –
marking the transience of stage performance itself – although this play left
its mark.[2]

In *Mad World* (1606), madness and performance, virtually synonymous,
permeate the play. The protagonist, Follywit, an actor who scripts his own
performances, represents excessive folly controlled by wit. Others too
perform illusory roles for gain, and the labor required to stage them is
made explicit. Frank Gullman the prostitute can simulate maiden coyness
with tears and bashful withdrawal (4.6.78–80) to sell her virginity for the
sixteenth time – and marry. But her finest scene – of feigned illness in act 3
scene 2 – requires props (gallipots, plate, an hourglass, a chamber pot), a
fake doctor, and a virtuoso performance. She feigns vomiting or farting to
drive away her unwanted suitors and then hides the sounds of Mistress
Harebrain and Penitent Brothel's offstage adulterous lovemaking from the
eavesdropping Master Harebrain by improvising her side of a dialogue with
the wife, punctuated with simulated erotic tears, groans, and sighs – "huff,
huff, huff," "Hey, hy, hy," "Suh, Suh" (3.2.170 SD, 216–18) (Daileader,
*Eroticism*, pp. 32–5). In a second spectacle in act 4 scene 1, the actor playing
Mistress Harebrain appears to her lover as a "succubus" (in speech prefixes),
or a "devil," as Brothel, torn between lust and penitence, imagines; the
audience likely sees the character, silly and seductive as ever. Brothel
hilariously exorcizes the figure in, perhaps, a parodic glance at the feigned
demonic possession of Edgar as Poor Tom in *King Lear*, staged a year earlier
in 1605.

The three devices that Follywit stages to steal money from his tightfisted
grandfather, Sir Bounteous Progress, wittily expose the mechanisms of early
modern performance practices. In what Peter Saccio calls a "kind of green-
room scene" (*Middleton*, p. 414), he and his men devise plot lines and
costumes for his first role as Lord Owemuch, who visits Bounteous, robs his

grandfather and himself – and is richly reimbursed. While he is preparing for his second robbery, we watch him dress as a prostitute, donning a skirt, hairpiece, mask, and chin-clout (3.3.83–135) – just as boy actors would have done to play women. His final performance, "The Slip," reenacts the main play's action, but also, like Shakespeare's devices in great houses, goes hilariously awry. This play within play highlights the hazards of performance for traveling troupes – the "uncertain" lives of actors, threatened by puritan attacks and restraints on performance (5.1.33–7, 64–8). Designed to distract Sir Bounteous from a third robbery, the play is mounted with props "borrowed" from the host: a chain which turns Follywit into a Justice and a watch that, ringing, reveals his subterfuge. But the brilliance of his improvised prologue, soliloquy, and substitute plot redeems him. "The Slip" is received as "the maddest piece of justice" (5.2.129–30). Like the Bedlamite performances in *Patient Man*, it produces laughter and self-knowledge: "Ha ha . . . Troth, I commend their wits. Before our faces, make us asses while we sit still and only laugh at ourselves" (5.2.187–90).

In three tragedies larded with comedy – *Lady* (1611), *Changeling*, and *Valour* (1622) – madness is deepened but remains a catalyst for juxtapositions of the distracted and the healthy, and for metatheatrical spectacle. In *Lady*, the darkest of the three, both plots are driven by men who are mad with what the period diagnosed as lovesickness. In the main plot the Tyrant will let nothing stop his possession of the Lady – not her refusal, love for another, or suicide. His insatiable lust parallels the oft-cited and most extreme case history in Renaissance lovesickness treatises: the fetishistic love of a man of Athens for a statue. The stricken young man, like the Tyrant with his corpse, "cannot be out of the sight of [the statue]," but remained "embracing and kissing it, as if it hath been a living soul," and then decked the statue out, as Tyrant does the corpse, with "a rich crowne," "sumptuous ornaments," and "precious vestments" (Boaistuau, *Theatrum*, pp. 199–200). Tale and play exemplify love-madness at its most appalling, because statues, like corpses, cannot return love.

The Tyrant's story culminates in shocking metatheatrical spectacles that flaunt theatrical convention and mislead spectators by revising scenes in Shakespeare's *The Winter's Tale*, also performed by the King's Men at Blackfriars theatre earlier in the same year. In act 4 scene 3, the crazed Tyrant, to possess the dead Lady, breaches the discovery space/tomb, opens the coffin and orders the corpse carried off, accompanied by a sardonic chorus of servants. Just forty lines later the corpse rises from that coffin in a spectacular *coup de théâtre* with multiple stage effects: "*On a sudden in a kind of noise like the wind, the doors clattering, the tombstone flies open, and a great*

*light appears in the midst of the tomb; his Lady, as went out, standing just
before him all in white, stuck with jewels and a great crucifix on her breast*
(4.4.42 SD). The marked-for-performance version of the text (B) continues:
"*Enter Lady: Rich. Robinson*," naming the boy actor who played the role.
Theatre audience and reader alike are amazed by the rare appearance of a
female ghost, especially one so recently a corpse. They are encouraged to
attend to the skill of the boy actor who plays a Lady in black, then her corpse
in white, then her identical Spirit in quick succession. Some might recall
Antigonus's dream of what he believes is the ghost of dead Hermione, all in
white, giving orders regarding Perdita in *Winter's Tale* (3.3). The Tyrant's
macabre madness produces another performance in the last scene as, to music,
he adorns, caresses, and kisses the corpse to restore its "warmth," "heat," and
even speech (5.2.96–114). The beloved, Govianus, disguised as a painter,
contributes to her makeover, using stage makeup, representing poisoned
cosmetics, to paint the body (and kill the Tyrant). This scene is especially
uncanny for audience members who might have gasped just months earlier as
the faith and longing of the onstage audience restored life to Hermione's cold
statue at the end of *Winter's Tale*. There is no resurrection here; but the Lady's
Spirit reenters, dressed in black like her corpse, and accompanies it offstage,
breaking commonsense boundaries of body and spirit, life and death.
Audiences surely wondered at the mechanics of the spectacle. Who portrays
corpse and spirit: a dummy? a secondary actor? Richard Robinson?

Middleton and Rowley's *Changeling* is Middleton's second representation of a madhouse, this one extended into a full second plot that unfolds in
Spain in a house called Bedlam with likely specific allusion to the London
hospital's currently embattled keeper, Helkiah Crook. It is the last of the
five early modern plays in which Bedlamites appear; here they exist only as
disembodied voices or dumb performers. Action instead focuses on others
who inhabit the madhouse and engage with the mad: Alibius, the owner;
Isabella his wife; Lollio, the keeper; Antonio, disguised as a fool; and
Franciscus, disguised as a madman. The scenes set in the madhouse
(1.2, 3.3, 4.3) provide numerous dramatic and thematic parallels with the
main plot in the castle (Malcolmson, "As Tame"; Middleton and Rowley,
*Changeling*, Thompson [ed.], pp. xxii–xxiv; Neely, *Distracted Subjects*,
pp. 195–8, and "Hot Blood," pp. 62–5). Like the aristocratic Beatrice-
Joanna in the castle plot, the middling-sort Isabella in the madhouse plot
is pursued by three suitors, who hope to seduce and sleep with her
notwithstanding that she is locked up by her jealous husband. Whereas
Beatrice-Joanna blindly slides into lust and murder, and dies for it, Isabella
self-consciously and wittily dons a mad disguise to enjoy "the pleasure of

your bedlam" (3.3.24) and to test her suitors, restrain herself, and mock the untrammeled desires that cause a conflagration, literal and figurative, in the castle. Here, too, contact with mad performance proves salutary.

The identification of the madhouse with theatre is cemented in act 4 scene 3, as we watch Isabella "practise" or perform for her would-be lover, Antonio. To put on "this habit of a frantic," she gets from Lollio "the key of the wardrobe" (4.3.50–1, 133). But her foolish suitor Antonio, also feigning madness, refuses to see himself in the mirror her performance provides: "Thou wild unshapen antic; I am no fool, / You bedlam" (4.3.131–2), so dismisses and disillusions her. At the end of the scene, Lollio, Isabella, and Alibius watch the mad themselves rehearse the dance they have prepared for Beatrice-Joanna's wedding festivities to gain "coin and credit" (4.3.219–26). The wedding and the performance, like Isabella's own, are aborted. But whereas the main plot protagonists die, those in the second plot are sobered and reformed, if not transformed, as the play ends (5.3.185–215). More explicitly than *Patient Man*, but less fully than *Valour*, this play suggests that performing theatre or watching it performed might curb excess.

Middleton's next play, *Valour*, was likely first performed half a year after *Changeling*, in September 1622 (G. Taylor, *Companion*, pp. 424–26; G. Taylor, "*Nice Valour*"). Madness is concentrated in one title character who performs the standard subdivisions of distraction – "all the passions of mankind" (1.1.51) – in discrete vignettes: lovesickness (1.1, 2.1), melancholy (3.3), fury (3.4), and laughing madness (5.1).[3] The courtiers humor his "fits" to glut them (1.1.67–72). Each successive condition is represented by theatrical devices: by a song for each malady, by a costume embodying the marks of melancholy (3.3 SD), by a masque of Cupid and an antimasque of Kicks. The song representing melancholy so successfully encodes the standard signs of the prestigious aristocratic condition (e.g. "folded arms" and "fixed eyes" [3.3.36–54]) that it became the most widely circulated dramatic song in the period (G. Taylor, *Companion*, p. 1071). The Madman's stylized and silly performances, however, have brutal material consequences. When furious, he viciously beats up others. His serial seduction attempts are poignantly shadowed by the plight of the woman he has seduced and impregnated, ironically disguised as the "Cupid" to whose reign she is victim, as she desperately seeks marriage before she gives birth. Through representing madness, the play self-consciously explores the ingredients of theatre – devices and material bodies, songs, dances, and blows – to reveal its "frightful pleasure" (*Changeling*, 3.3.281).

The Passionate Madman's antic shows are both foil and trigger to the folly of Chamont. Although the lability of the "man in fragments" (1.1.241) seems the opposite of the rigidity of Chamont's "so precise a manhood"

(1.1.194), these two self-absorbed characters similarly live by illusions that ignore the reality of the body and do harm. The Lord flattens his servant Galoshio to a "cullis," to "very pap and jelly" (3.1.36–8), leaves Lepert nearly dead, impregnates the Page, and orders the Soldier, an imaginary love rival, beaten up. Chamont, similarly jealous and distracted by this "court-ship," wildly overreacts to the duke touching him with a switch as an irrevocable loss of honor. His idealism blinds him to his Lady's desires as the Lord is blind to the Page's pregnancy, and both indulge in solitary melancholy, an aristocratic self-indulgence. The health of Lepert, author, masque-presenter, and coward contrasts to the others' blindness. He provides antidotes to illusions of honor and madness by acknowledging the body and by theorizing, absorbing, or displacing violence. He practices and advocates receiving instead of giving blows to short-circuit the dueling code and produce "the dissolution of all bloodshed" (3.2.21). His treatise within the play, *The Uprising of the Kick And the Downfall of the Duello*, and his staged masque (5.1.79–86), whose dancers costumed as fools perform the postures of receiving blows, demonstrate how performing bodies (and printed texts) usefully displace violence.[4] In the play, material blows absorbed do penetrate self-willed illusions and facilitate social and sexual relations. When, during the masque of blows, the Passionate Madman is stabbed and badly wounded by the Soldier, his fits end and he marries the Page. Together, the need to save his brother from the consequences of this blow and the earlier tap with the switch jolt Chamont into valuing "human-ity" over honor, enabling reconciliation and marriage to his Lady.

The play's epilogue, spoken most aptly by Lepert, underscores, as do all the plays discussed, that theatre performance, like madness, is strenuous, extravagant, physical work. It exists through the "labor" of the playwright, the bodies of players "over-acting passions," and an audience that absorbs the blows which plays "shoot round" at them. Lepert understands his masque "practitioners" as "Endurers of the time," who bring health by "overcloy[ing]" the passions of the lord (4.1.363–4). Alibius in *Changeling* likewise understands performance as measured, disordered, educational, and health-bringing: "to teach it in a wild distracted measure, / Though out of form and figure, breaking Time's head – / (It were no matter, 'twould be healed again / In one age or other, if not in this)" (3.3.283–6). Theatrical performance, like distraction, violently "breaks" the passage of everyday time and space, but mysteriously "heals," allowing performers and audi-ence, like the mad and those who encounter them, to return to their everyday business, sobered. We watch this process play itself out in each of the five Middleton plays discussed in this chapter.

NOTES

1. Bethlehem Hospital, from its founding in 1247, was a religious foundation, never a monastery. But *The History of Bethlem* uses the play as evidence that "By the early sixteenth century, it was believed that Bethlem had begun life as a monastery" (Andrews *et al.*, *History*, pp. 40, 53 n. 4), and Paul Mullholland also accepts its fiction as fact, referring to "the monastery from which it (Bethlem Hospital) historically sprang" (*Middleton*, p. 284).

2. *Patient Man* was among the most popular of early modern plays, as editions, revivals, and citations show (Mulholland, *Middleton*, p. 280). It quickly generated a sequel, Dekker's *Honest Whore Part II*, and a series of London comedies variously authored and performed by rival companies in 1604 and 1605: Dekker and Webster's *Westward Ho*, Chapman, Jonson, and Marston's *Eastward Ho!*, and then Dekker and Webster's *Northward Ho* (with its visit to Bethlem in London). The Bedlamite motif is further imitated and developed in Webster's *The Duchess of Malfi* and Fletcher's *The Pilgrim*.

3. In "*Nice Valour*," pp. 13–18, Gary Taylor analyzes how the play's representation of these conditions parallels their description in Robert Burton's *Anatomy of Melancholy*, a compendium of traditional views of madness, first published in 1621. All four types are pictured on Burton's frontispiece, added in the 1628 edition.

4. Authorship too is represented as material labor – as selling books, correcting printer's proofs, and savoring typefaces – and texts as made of "blows upon pot paper" (4.1.245), a metaphor capturing the mechanics of early modern printing.

PART VI

*Afterlives*

## CHAPTER 35

# *Invisible Middleton and the bibliographical context*

## Sonia Massai

The publication of *Thomas Middleton: The Collected Works* in 2007 marked a dramatic development in the fashioning of Middleton as a major writer and playwright in print. The large body of works now collected under Middleton's patronym (fifty-three in total, besides occasional poems and juvenilia) has transformed his reputation from a writer of popular city comedies to a more versatile and accomplished author of many genres, including city pageants, masques, entertainments, prose and verse satires, and compelling tragedies. The Oxford *Middleton* also fulfilled what Joseph Quincy Adams described in 1938 as "a crying need" for a scholarly edition of this important playwright ("Foreword," p. vii). Middleton's works had only been collected once before, by Alexander Dyce in 1840. Arthur Henry Bullen reprinted Dyce's edition in 1885–6, introducing new errors into texts that were already falling short of the standards associated with the editing of Shakespeare and other non-dramatic early English authors in the period. Dyce's approach to the establishment of Middleton's texts was inconsistent. While he collated three quarto editions and two manuscripts to establish his text of *A Game at Chess*, he relied on the received text of other plays. In his preface to *An/The Old Law*, for example, he provides the following rationale for choosing his control text: "The [earliest edition] abounds in the grossest typographical errors. I have followed, except in some trifling particulars, the text of Gifford, who published *Old Law* in the IV$^{th}$ volume of his Massinger" (*Middleton*, vol. 1, p. 3). Dyce's text, reprinted by Bullen and subsequently used for smaller collections of selected plays in 1887, 1894, 1904, and 1915, provided the only available version of the vast majority of Middleton's works during the nineteenth and twentieth centuries.

Adams was also struck by the relative invisibility of Middleton's works when compared to other major early modern playwrights: "It is strange that of the major English dramatists contemporary with Shakespeare Thomas Middleton, who at several points touched the master, has been the most neglected by modern scholarship" ("Foreword," p. vii). By 1938 Shakespeare's works had been printed and reprinted in over twelve hundred editions.[1] The editorial attention paid to the transmission of Shakespeare's works into print is unmatched by that for any other early modern playwright, but the number of important collected editions is at least comparable for some of his contemporaries. The dramatic works first printed and ascribed to Beaumont and Fletcher by Humphrey Moseley in 1647 and by Henry Herringman in 1679 were followed by ten other major collections, ranging from Jacob Tonson's 1711 edition to the multivolume edition launched under the general editorship of Fredson Bowers for Cambridge University Press in 1966. Roughly the same number of editions of Jonson's complete works was published from the mid-eighteenth century to the mid-twentieth century, when the Clarendon Press issued the last volume of C. H. Herford and Percy and Evelyn Simpson's Oxford edition. By contrast, Middleton was only available to readers of early modern English drama either in single-text editions of his most popular plays or in Dyce's imperfect edition. It was only in 2007, with the publication of the Oxford *Middleton*, that his works were finally re-membered into an imposing scholarly edition that makes it possible for students, scholars, and theatre practitioners to experience the full range of Middleton's achievements as a major writer and playwright.

The reasons for Middleton's marginalization in the context of the transmission of early English drama in print are complex and worth exploring, because they shed light on Middleton's afterlife in print and his attitude to dramatic publication. A peculiar feature in the history of Middleton's reception in print is that even those who edited his works believed that they would not appeal to large numbers of readers. Dyce, for example, presented his edition to "the lovers of our early literature" (*Middleton*, vol. 1, p. vii) rather than to the general reader. Its publication was delayed because the publisher, as Dyce reports in a letter to William Wordsworth dated 7 December 1837, "was frightened at the state of the trade" (de Sélincourt (ed.), *Wordsworth*, vol. 11, p. 907n) and presumably feared that the edition would not sell well.[2] Similarly, a publisher's note in Bullen's edition states that "Four hundred copies of this Edition have been printed and the type distributed. *No more will be published*" (*Middleton*, vol. 1, p. b2). This figure contrasts strikingly with the expectation of how many copies a new edition of Shakespeare's works would sell at the time. When Alexander Macmillan joined forces with Cambridge University Press and the team of editors who were preparing the Cambridge Shakespeare, he wondered how popular a single-volume version of the Cambridge Shakespeare would be. Writing to a fellow publisher in 1864, he asked: "I want you to tell me whether you think I have a reasonable chance of selling 50,000 of such a book in three years. For if so I can do a nice stroke of business" (Murphy, *Shakespeare in Print*, pp. 175–6). As Andrew Murphy explains, "What Macmillan was proposing . . . was the 'Globe Shakespeare'," which exceeded expectations, "reach[ing] its fifth edition [by 1867], with each printrun amounting to 20,000 copies" (*Shakespeare in Print*, p. 176).

While Shakespeare's first collected edition, the First Folio of 1623, was addressed "To the Great Variety of Readers . . . From the most able to him that can but spell," Dyce and Bullen prepared their editions for those readers who had an antiquarian interest in early English drama. More generally, Middleton's appeal was deemed to be limited to a few dramatic masterpieces. As Bullen puts it, "Had [*The Changeling, Women Beware Women,* and *The Spanish Gypsy*] been destroyed, the loss to our dramatic literature would have been serious, for only here is Middleton's genius seen in its full maturity" (*Middleton*, vol. 1, p. lix). Even the editors of miscellaneous collections of early English drama, like Robert Dodsley, included some of Middleton's most popular plays without remarking on his stature as a playwright. Walter Scott's preface to *The Ancient British Drama in Three Volumes,* a miscellaneous collection published in 1810, is representative in stating that "besides the immortal Shakespeare, there flourished, during this period, Beaumont and Fletcher, Jonson, Ford, Massinger, and Webster; and the lesser, yet respectable names of Shirley, Daniel, Brome, Marston and Dekker, and others, adorn the same age" (vol. 1, pp. b–bᵛ).[3] Middleton remains tellingly unnamed. Middleton did not fare much better among his twentieth-century editors. F. L. Lucas, who edited *Anything for a Quiet Life* as part of his edition of *The Complete Works of John Webster,* sardonically remarked: "It would have given me great pleasure to suppress this play: it has certainly given me none to edit it." Also indicative is Lucas's assessment of Webster's and Middleton's respective stature: "it seems to some almost incredible . . . that the author of *The White Devil* should have stooped, even in the company of another, to write such trash as this" (*Webster,* vol. IV, p. 69).[4]

Middleton's lack of critical clout would therefore seem to account for his bibliographical invisibility. In this respect Middleton is comparable to other "minor" early modern playwrights, including Thomas Heywood. The latter's best-known play, *A Woman Killed with Kindness,* was included in Robert Dodsley's miscellaneous *Collection of Old Plays* (1744), and his *Four Prentices of London* was then added to the expanded reprint of Dodsley's *Collection* in 1780. The same plays were included in *The Ancient British*

*Drama* and, except for a handful of single-text reprints, readers of early English drama had to wait until 1874 for the first collected edition of Heywood's *Dramatic Works*. However, Middleton's invisibility cannot be justified entirely by the perceived modesty of his literary achievements, because some of the plays now wholly or partly attributed to Middleton *were* regularly edited and published, but under a different patronym or anonymously. For example, *Timon of Athens* was included in Shakespeare's First Folio (1623) and *Wit at Several Weapons* and *The Nice Valour* were included in Beaumont and Fletcher's *Comedies and Tragedies* (1647); all were regularly re-edited and reprinted as part of different canons. *The Revenger's Tragedy* was traditionally attributed to Cyril Tourneur, and *A Yorkshire Tragedy* was mostly presented to its reader as written by an anonymous author or authors.

The main difference between Middleton and other major playwrights clearly has more to do with the fact that his works were not collected in a substantial folio edition during his lifetime or shortly after his death than with the intrinsic quality of his achievements. Some of Middleton's most popular plays were not published until after his death in 1627. *A Chaste Maid in Cheapside* was first printed in 1630, *Changeling* and *Women Beware* in 1653, and some plays, including *The Witch* and *The Lady's Tragedy* (traditionally known as *The Second Maiden's Tragedy*) survive only in manuscript. As MacDonald P. Jackson explains,

> The [First] Folio is crucial to our sense of Shakespeare's achievement. Modern editors accept its definition of his dramatic canon with only minor additions ... Also, it is widely acknowledged that at least one or two of the plays in the Folio (and in subsequent editions of *The Complete Works*) are collaborative, containing material by dramatists other than Shakespeare. But these adjustments to the Folio's canon have little effect on our sense of 'Shakespeare' ... [By contrast,] Middleton's corpus of plays, poems, entertainments, and pamphlets was dispersed over sundry quartos, octavos, and manuscripts of widely varying dates. Uncollected, Middleton disappeared from view, 'untalked of and unseen'. (*Companion*, p. 81)

Unlike Shakespeare, Jonson, and Beaumont and Fletcher, Middleton never became a patronymic category within which a body of works could be gathered, edited, and published during the early modern period for future generations of readers.

Another circumstantial reason for the dispersal of Middleton's works is that, unlike Shakespeare, he did not write his dramatic works for a single company, who then acted as guardians and custodians of the deceased author's scattered textual remains. Even more crucially, Middleton never displayed a proactive interest in the transmission of his commercial plays into print.[5] Middleton did woo prospective patrons through the medium of print, but not through dramatic publication. For example, he dedicated *The Ghost of Lucrece* (1600) and *Sir Robert Sherley his Entertainment in Cracovia* (1609), and the language of his dedications is predictably conventional and rhetorically inflated. In *Ghost*, William, Second Baron Compton, of Compton Wynyates, Warwickshire is addressed as "patron to the child-house of my vein," "godfather to th'issue of my brain," and "baptiser of mine infant lines" (5–8). Similarly conventional is the dedication to Sir Thomas Sherley attached to one surviving copy of *Sherley*, where Middleton devotes his efforts to the "eternizing memory of [the Sherley brothers'] virtues and fortunes" (Additional Passages, 14–15). Middleton probably failed to secure Lord Compton's patronage in 1600, as suggested by his fierce attack against patronage in *Father Hubburd's Tales*, published in 1604.[6] However, Middleton continued to dedicate his pageants, his masque, and his entertainments. What is remarkable is the absence of dedications in any of the single-authored commercial plays published during his lifetime. By contrast, Middleton personally wrote the dedications in two presentation manuscript copies of *Game* and *Witch* prepared by the professional scribe Ralph Crane. It would therefore seem reasonable to assume that Middleton distrusted print as a viable medium through which he could secure textual patronage as a commercial playwright.

Middleton's selective use of dedications may be due to the fact that commercial plays were not dedicated as often as masques, entertainments, and city pageants, the latter being occasional pieces specifically commissioned at court or by the city authorities and more likely to be sponsored by a powerful patron. Middleton was therefore relying on well-established practice when, with his coauthor William Rowley, he dedicated their masque *The World Tossed at Tennis* (1620) to "Charles, Lord Howard, Baron of Effingham, and to his virtuous and worthy lady, the Right Honourable Mary, Lady Effingham" or his *Honourable Entertainments* (1621) to the city fathers. Even so, Middleton does not seem as committed to textual patronage as some of his contemporaries. Thomas Heywood, for example, who wrote a comparable number of city pageants, included full dedications not only to the new mayor but also to the two sheriffs of London. By contrast, Middleton wrote two full dedications, interestingly eulogizing the civic function of this type of entertainment as well as his dedicatees, in *The Triumphs of Truth* (1613) and *The Triumphs of Honour and Industry* (1617), but then appended merely perfunctory dedications to later pageants. As David M. Bergeron puts it, "after these rousing arguments for the moral purpose of the pageants, Middleton contents himself in his five remaining pageants to offer dedications of brief, undistinguished verses. Perhaps in the epistles dedicatory of 1613 and 1617, he had said all that he wanted or needed to say about his art and textual patronage" (*Textual Patronage*, p. 66).[7]

The paratext included in *The Roaring Girl*, written with Thomas Dekker and published in 1611, confirms Middleton's reluctance to entrust his livelihood or reputation to the custom or patronage offered by readers of plays originally written for the commercial stage. In the dedicatory epistle addressed "To the Comic Play-readers, Venery and Laughter," signed by Middleton, the playbook is described as "fit for many of your companies, as well as the person itself, and may be allowed both gallery-room at the playhouse and chamber-room at your lodging" (18–20). The playbook is never invested with literary status or any higher purpose than keeping the reader "in an afternoon from dice, at home in your chambers" (12–13). On the other hand, in Middleton's dedicatory poem included in John Webster's *The Duchess of Malfi* (1623), Webster is praised for overseeing the publication of his play and compared to those benefactors who commit to good works while they can, instead of relying on the good will of the executors of their wills. Yet even in this poem, other lines – "every worthy man / Is his own marble, and his merit can / Cut him to any figure and express / More art than death's cathedral palaces, / Where royal ashes keep their court" – suggest Middleton's distrust of the monumental editions published posthumously as ostentatious repositories for their authors' textual remains.[8]

Invisibility among common readers or future generations of readers is what Middleton may have regarded as "a consummation devoutly to be wished," at least for the plays he wrote for the commercial stage. Although unsigned and attached to a collaborative play, the epistle dedicated "To the well-wishing, well-reading understander, well-understanding reader" in *Tennis* offers a fitting image of an early modern writer shunning the reading market created by the efforts of early modern stationers and booksellers: "How [this masque] will be now tossed in the world I know not – a toy brought to the press rather by the printer than the poet" (6–8). The visibility granted to Middleton as a major writer and playwright may therefore be the product of our desire to re-member and monumentalize him rather than his wish to build his literary reputation as a successful playwright through the medium of print. The readers Middleton wanted to reach were potential patrons, as shown by the signed paratext attached to his occasional dramatic works and his personal involvement in the production of manuscript copies of *Game* when the play was banned from the stage in August 1624.

Middleton did seem poised to become a popular dramatist in print in 1607–8. *The Phoenix* and *Michaelmas Term* were published anonymously, but *A Mad World, My Masters* appeared bearing the initials "T. M." on its title page, *A Trick to Catch the Old One* was reissued with a variant title page in order to include the initials "T. M.," and *Your Five Gallants* was published and attributed to "T. Middleton." However, after 1607–8, plays now attributed to Middleton were published anonymously and some of his most successful plays were not published at all until several years after his death. Far from being a reflection of his stature as a writer and a playwright, his invisibility in the bibliographical context would therefore seem to stem from his hope that he should "pass still by the fair way of good report" (*Tennis*, pp. 23–4) among those he lived to entertain.

NOTES

1. For a full list of Shakespearean editions, see Murphy, *Shakespeare in Print*, pp. 279–410.

2. I am grateful to John Lavagnino for drawing my attention to this letter.

3. Walter Scott did not sign this preface, but his "continual involvement" in the preparation of this collection is documented by correspondence with its publisher, as reported in Todd and Bowden, *Sir Walter Scott*, pp. 170–2 (John Lavagnino, in conversation).

4. I am again indebted to John Lavagnino, who helped me identify Lucas as a striking example of the poor reception of Middleton among his editors.

5. Middleton scholars disagree when it comes to establishing his overall attitude to print culture and the opportunities offered by the book trade. Gary Taylor, for example, argues that "Middleton actively exploited the potencies of print" ("Lives and Afterlives," p. 42), and Cyndia Clegg detects "significant author involvement" in Middleton's "associations ... with particular publishers and printers" (*Companion*, p. 251), while John Jowett refers to "Middleton's characteristically weak or entirely absent control of [his] texts' circulation" (*Companion*, p. 286). This divergence of views may be at least partly due to the fact that some types of literary and dramatic publications were more popular than others and Middleton's attitude to publication would seem to have varied accordingly.

6. For further details, see Middleton, *Ghost*, J. Q. Adams (ed.), pp. xxiii–xxxi.

7. In noting the absence of dedications or addresses to readers in the printed editions of Middleton's single-authored commercial plays and his modest contribution of paratextual materials to his city pageants, I qualify Gary Taylor's remark that "after 1611 editions of Middleton's dramatic texts published during his lifetime regularly contained ancillary authorial material addressed to readers" and depart from his conclusion that "Middleton's attention to the potentials of print also extends to the published texts of plays." Taylor's further

argument – "No authorized Shakespeare text, printed in his lifetime, is illus-
trated; between 1611 and 1625, five separate title page illustrations are printed in
editions of dramatic texts by Middleton" ("End of Editing," p. 138) – is also
problematic: three of these illustrations are attached to collaborative plays and
their inclusion cannot be ascribed wholly and firmly to Middleton; moreover,
title-page illustrations often feature in editions published anonymously, posthumously, or without the author's permission, so their inclusion seems to stem
from non-authorial agents, most probably their publishers. All title-page illustrations from the period are reproduced in Foakes, *Illustrations*, pp. 87–147.

8. This commendatory poem has also been read as an allusion to the publication of
Shakespeare's First Folio and as a warning against the potential for textual
corruption suffered by the text of plays published posthumously. For further
details, see Akrigg, "Allusion," p. 26.

CHAPTER 36

# Afterlives: stages and beyond

## Diana E. Henderson

FIRST AND SECOND COACHES
Chapter I
*O, think upon the pleasures of the palace!*
*Securéd ease and state! The stirring meats*
*Ready to move out of the dishes, that e'en now*
*Quicken when they are eaten...*
*Banquets abroad by torchlight! music! sports!*
*Nine coaches waiting – hurry – hurry – hurry –*
*Ay, to the devil....*
                    TOURNEUR: *The Revenger's Tragedy*

So begins Mary Stewart's 1958 romantic thriller, *Nine Coaches Waiting* (p. 9). Citing as an epigraph lines now attributed to Middleton and dividing her novel into nine "coaches" – or stages, to invoke the resonant word linking transport and theatricality – her popular fiction reminds us that Middleton has often been performed without our conscious knowledge, his aphoristic wit and "stirring" speeches echoing unexpectedly across media. Like Shakespeare, Middleton is more often recalled in pieces than as whole cloth, allowing a freedom of use through recontextualization. Arguably this is what any canonical theatre text provides living artists: simultaneously a poaching ground, a foundation, and a springboard for "music! sports!" and more. The playtext itself becomes a vehicle, allowing us to "hurry – hurry – hurry" forwards as the material world stirs into imaginative action, "ready to move" and "quicken" in order to provide the theatrical consumer with "pleasures."

This dynamic (and sensual) view of Middleton stands in contrast to the standard accounts of his plays' performance history, often distinguished from that of Shakespeare and other first-tier dramatists. It is usually claimed that he "disappeared" from the stage after the English Restoration and did not "reappear" until British theatrical censorship was finally challenged in the wake of John Osborne's *Look Back in Anger* (1956). Middleton's frank rendition of court corruption and mercenary city life then resonated with the contemporary emphasis on angry young men unmasking class pretension, often through their domineering sexual relations as well as explosive speech. Formative productions cited to illustrate this narrative include *The Changeling* at the Royal Court in 1961 directed by Tony Richardson, the Royal Shakespeare Company's 1962 *Women Beware Women* directed by Anthony Page, and the RSC's *The Revenger's Tragedy* directed by Trevor Nunn in 1966.

Such an account is broadly accurate but nonetheless incomplete. Focusing narrowly on the English professional stage, it ignores earlier salvos such as Joseph Papp's Shakespeare Workshop *Changeling* in 1956 directed by Earl Sennett, as well as subsequent American performances: notable US productions of *Changeling*, for example, include Elia Kazan's at Lincoln Center in 1964, Robert Brustein's at Boston's American Repertory Theater in 1985, and Robert Woodruff's at the Theatre for a New Audience in 1997. This latter New York production interpolated scenes from Webster's *The White Devil* and cited J. G. Ballard's *Crash* in its program, reinforcing the extremity and contemporaneity of its provocative combination of sexual passion and violence; its mixing of authorial voices, moreover, reminds us of the always collaborative nature of theatrical voicing (especially apt when considering the afterlives of a writer who was himself such a frequent coauthor and adaptor). One should note, too, a number of thoroughly modern adaptations, such as Brad Fraser's *The Ugly Man* (1993) set in Prairie Canada or Melanie Marnich's *Tallgrass Gothic* (2007), which renames Beatrice-Joanna "Laura" and similarly moves her to the US Great Plains.

This process of adaptation has a long history, complicating the assumption that Middleton "disappeared" from the stage after the 1660s. To cite an instance from Middleton's comic repertory, *A Mad World, My Masters* was not only among the first plays revived at the Restoration, but became one of two Middleton plays Aphra Behn drew on in composing *The City Heiress* (1682), and was subsequently a source for Charles Johnson's *The Country Lasses* (1715). Not only was the latter playtext frequently performed during the eighteenth century in Britain, but it became the first "Middleton" performance in the American colonies during the 1760s and continued to be "revived into the nineteenth century" (Steen, *Ambrosia*, p. 11). Thus Barrie Keeffe's 1977 adaptation (collaboratively developed with William Gaskill and the Joint Stock Theatre Company) – which restores Middleton's title but reworks the play in a late capitalist context of thwarted class struggle – is as much a dynamic continuation of long-established theatrical practices as an act of radical revival.

Drama in performance is always a complex dance, pairing continuity and change. Although *Changeling's* comic subplot had been praised for its popularity later in the seventeenth century, it was the main plot that was adapted by William Hayley as *Marcella* (1784) and performed with substantial success at Covent Garden in 1789 – though the playwright considered the "house rather thin" and averred "it is not calculated to be a popular play" (Steen, *Ambrosia*, p. 77). It was nevertheless better received than the Elizabethan Stage Society's *The Spanish Gypsy* a century later (1898), despite that amateur production being directed by the famous champion of "original staging practices," William Poel, and including an enthusiastic prologue penned by the poet Algernon Charles Swinburne – and being overtly advertised as a play by Middleton. Although the influential critic William Archer thought the first four acts showed promise in realizing the group's revivalist goals, he excoriated the fifth act's departures from a play he nevertheless found inferior to *Changeling* (whose main plot he too would later adapt as *Beatriz Juana* [1927]). Perhaps it was the very attempt at authenticity rather than adaptation that hoist Poel on his own petard: the tension between his "relentless fidelity" to *Gypsy's* inferior comic plot and his rearrangements and "excisions mainly in the blank-verse passages" of the main plot drew Archer's most acid response (reprinted in Steen, *Ambrosia*, pp. 215–17). By Poel's time historicist habits of reading carefully edited and complete playtexts and an attitude of seriousness about dramatic tradition collided with the freedom of stage play.

Thus it would take more radical re-vision, rather than a return to fidelity, to make Middleton's plays theatrically vital in the later twentieth century. In this process, the theories of Antonin Artaud, Brecht's Marxist adaptations of early modern plays, the remaking of Shakespeare as "our contemporary," the 1960s "sexual revolution," and the politics of anticensorship British theatre would each play a part. All these contexts made overt the legitimacy – indeed, necessity – of employing old texts to current ends, reintroducing their immediacy to the present-tense artistic experience that is theatrical performance.

The corruption of privilege, social deviance, and sexual power represented in Middleton's playtexts – and the anger and passion they conveyed – did indeed resonate in early 1960s Britain, motivating the theatrical revival of his tragedies in particular. Far from coincidentally, the 1961 *Changeling* was directed by the man who five years earlier had directed the theatre-changing production of *Look Back in Anger* in the same space; as Beatrice-Joanna it starred Mary Ure, who had created Alison Porter in both the Osborne stage production and the film version Richardson subsequently directed

Figure 36.1 The Royal Court Production of *The Changeling*, starring Robert Shaw as
De Flores and Mary Ure as Beatrice-Joanna, 1961.

(see Figure 36.1). One wonders whether journalistic criticism of Ure's performance as too passive, not sufficiently sexually willful, was influenced by
memory of that earlier production, or conversely indicated an urgent desire
for a more explosive second challenge to British propriety in its wake.
Certainly the following year's RSC *Women Beware* prompted Kenneth
Tynan – later the creator of *Oh! Calcutta!* – to claim that "where sexual
vagaries are concerned there is more authentic reportage in *The Changeling*
and *Women Beware Women* than in the whole of the First Folio" of
Shakespeare (cited in McLuskie, *Renaissance Dramatists*, p. 19). The now-
familiar pattern of deploying Middleton to expose the limitations of conventional storytelling (identified with Shakespeare) had already been established.

So too the perception of his plays' direct applicability to modern life through the theatrical illusion of "authentic reportage."

How one viewed such "reportage" varied, of course, depending on one's position within the modern audience and the performance choices made. Over the ensuing decades, numerous productions brought to the fore Middleton's complex roles for women, presenting welcome opportunities for actresses in classical repertory companies where male parts geometrically outnumber female. That said, most productions tended to reinforce dominant (male) perceptions of the sexual politics involved even when they were deemed socially subversive or radical. Having actresses play roles originally designed for boys or men reduced the audience's ability to discern these as male projections of women, and increased the realism (and disturbing quality) of scenes involving forced sex. But in 1962 it was enough simply to stage *Women Beware* without attending to the titular message, be it sententious or ironic: for *The Times* reviewer, the "revival of vitality in English drama has ... put things right" – that is, "'modernity' in 1962 was seen as synonymous with the new frankness about sex" (McLuskie, *Renaissance Dramatists*, p. 19). In Terry Hands's 1969 production, the Judi Dench who played Bianca was not yet today's M or a Dame to be reckoned with, but the beautiful trapped ingénue who had been Zeffirelli's similarly doomed Juliet. Not until the 1970s would the women's movement bring to more general consciousness the paradoxes of lauding "free sex" in a culture that had not changed its structures of labor and (re)production – and even then few theatrical producers, directors, or reviewers were women.

The disjunction between sexual representation and female liberation came to a head most famously in two English productions during the 1980s. Both the possibility and limits of gendered social critique were evident when Helen Mirren took the lead role in the RSC's 1983 production of *The Roaring Girl* (see Figure 36.2). Towards the end of that decade Kathleen McLuskie aptly highlighted the misplaced antifeminism of reviewers who criticized Mirren's combination of a "thigh-thrusting strut" and physical attractiveness ("her provocative body") in the role of cross-dressing Moll Cutpurse, remarking that "[t]he confusion of sexual discourses and the blatant voyeurism of such remarks revealed the problems around the representation of women and the debates on heterosexuality which were currently preoccupying the women's movement at large" (McLuskie, *Renaissance Dramatists*, pp. 4, 5). Nevertheless, in retrospect the production seems to herald something of the more capacious third-wave feminism that has since evolved, embracing a broader definition of sexual, performative femaleness and self-assertion without demanding that each

Figure 36.2 Helen Mirren as the Roaring Girl. Royal Shakespeare Company, 1983.

woman be a consistent advocate for sisterhood or a direct agent of broad social change. Opening the main theatre's season with a story of female triumph was one sign of the times. Like so many who assert, "I'm not a feminist, but. . .," director Barry Kyle told *Ms London* that he "didn't sit down to do a *grande oeuvre* of quasi feminist Jacobean dramas, but . . . [these plays] have working class heroines and women who really lived in the London of their day . . . the leading figure is a woman, victimized for a number of reasons, often just because she is a woman" (cited in McLuskie,

*Renaissance Dramatists*, p. 2). Interest in the working class was no longer confined to angry young men, as the rise of socialist female playwrights and feminist collective theatre in the 1970s had made clear; moreover, this consciousness took on new urgency (as well as posing new challenges for gender analysis) with the advent of Thatcherism.

Indeed, Kyle reversed the opening scene sequence to establish the London commercial street as the action's frame, its timely rebuke to the prime minister's denial of "society" including a crippled beggar dragging himself about behind privileged shoppers. The set "dominated by cog-wheels" emphasized that world's nascent industrial capitalism, and Sir Alexander Wengrave's provincial accent signaling his "new money" status reinforced the context of fluid societal change (O'Callaghan, *Thomas Middleton*, pp. 59–60). The performance emphasized the speech of Gull, Jack Dapper's servant, stressing the outrageous "disparity between the rich lifestyle and diet of the wealthy and the poverty of those who serve them" (O'Callaghan, *Thomas Middleton*, p. 64). As with Keeffe's modernization of *Mad World*, performance allowed Jacobean city comedy to become a vehicle for immediate economic satire and protest, while in this instance also celebrating an unconventional woman.

More starkly, Howard Barker's "collaborative" text of *Women Beware* for the Royal Court in 1986 aimed to jolt its audience out of their bourgeois capitalist complacency, but ultimately generated more criticism for its transformation of rape into a device for psychological liberation and social justice. Rewriting the latter part of the tragedy to eliminate "mass murder," but at the cost of a more focused emphasis on the violation of Bianca's body, Barker's changes in one sense extend the Court's 1960s tradition of working-class vengeance and sexual challenge; in describing his enlarge-ment of one non-aristocratic role into Bianca's putatively revolutionary rapist, Barker writes, "Sordido is a model of modern youth, culturally embittered, a redundant genius who lives the life of the gutter" (*Arguments*, p. 28). At the same time Barker regards his work as breaking through both gendered and sexual traditions by refusing Middleton's con-clusion that "says lust leads to the grave. I say desire alters perception . . . Middleton knew the body was the source of politics. He did not know it was also the source of hope" (cited in O'Callaghan, *Thomas Middleton*, p. xxiv). Imaginatively addressing the dead playwright, Barker compared their treat-ments of the scheming Livia: "In yours, a woman engineers the fall of a woman, for a man. That is the role of women in your time. In mine, a woman engineers the fall of a woman, but for her own enlightenment. But the pain is terrible" (*Arguments*, p. 28).

The pain, and other emotions, experienced by audience members did not always accord with Barker's theory. McLuskie observes that even Livia's "liberation" resulted from "Leontio's phallic energy" and wryly concludes, "Women, it seems, have to be raped into knowledge, men gain revolutionary knowledge and power by abstaining" (*Renaissance Dramatists*, pp. 21–2). No doubt Barker upends the culture's dominant scripts, thereby revealing how often "ravishment" or "seduction" become metaphorical cover-ups (a pattern common in *Changeling* productions; see Barker and Nicol, "*Changeling*"). Barker's "theatre of catastrophe" shares Brecht's goal of forcing the audience to confront material realities as well as Artaud's sense that cruelty is necessary to expose conventionally licensed violence. Nevertheless, as Anthony Dawson argues, Barker's play "ends up exploiting male fantasies against and about women as a mode of resolution"; indeed, "[h]ere we have a much more dangerous voyeurism-sadism than the Ward's in Middleton, though it may indeed be one that is prevalent in our own society. But the problem is that it is here given the full weight of the play's authority" ("*Women Beware*," pp. 317–18). These criticisms juxtaposed with Barker's theory, like the comments of the critics and director of *Roaring Girl*, serve as salutary reminders that performance scholarship must look beyond stated intentions and single documentary accounts. Clearly Barker attempts to reject straightforward identification with "role models," but the tensions between representation and endorsement remain, as does the potential of intense affect to short-circuit rather than spark a liberatory vision – at least during performance.

Yet what better description might there be of Middleton and Rowley's *Changeling* as well? Featuring two remarkable antiheroes *avant la lettre*, this tragedy deploys asides, architecture, and horror to create claustrophobia and catastrophe, leaving actors and audiences to "solve" its mystery, often by resorting to modern psychological theories, traumatic back-stories, or deep parody of social corruption. Its rich performance history includes television, radio, and film adaptations, with Beatrice-Joanna variously played by such actresses as Mirren, Diana Quick, Emma Piper, Miranda Richardson, Elizabeth McGovern, Marin Hinkle, Cheryl Campbell, and Olivia Williamson (about which, see Solga, *Violence*, as well as Barker and Nicol, "*Changeling*"). Her blackmailing servant/master De Flores has been reinterpreted as a nineteenth-century black slave (George Harris, in Richard Eyre's 1988 production), a contemporary Asian (1991 British Chinese Theatre), and a bisexual Canadian (*The Ugly Man*; see Bennett, *Performing Nostalgia*, pp. 91–3). In the generally pedestrian 1993 BBC televised production, which eliminated the madhouse subplot and featured Hugh Grant as a

Figure 36.3 Bob Hoskins as De Flores thrusts his fingers into Beatrice-Joanna's glove in the BBC televised *Changeling*, 1993.

flowing-tressed (and callow) Alsemero, Bob Hoskins reprised some of the working-class glee and mastery of the whispered aside of his 1981 BBC Iago (see Figure 36.3). The close-up potential of small screen also allowed the vivid materiality of his glove and finger "play" to evoke the kinds of squirming discomfort live theatre should similarly register, especially in the sordid scene wherein De Flores retains the displayed, dismembered digit somewhere on his body as he forces sex.

The sustained juxtaposition of sex and violence in *Revenger* raises similar issues about the "entertainment value" of audience witnessing, while provoking complex emotions through its disturbing mixture of sardonic wit, performative liveliness, and horrific objectifications and violations. Also performed under Tourneur's name, its lively international history includes US productions by the Washington-based Folger Theatre Group (1972, directed by Louis W. Scheeder), New York's Jean Cocteau Repertory (1982, directed by Toby Robertson), and NYC's Red Bull Theater (2005–6, directed and adapted by Jesse Berger), as well as Di Trevis's 1987 RSC production starring Antony Sher and the 2008 Manchester Royal Exchange production directed by Jonathan Moore. In the 2008 National Theatre production directed by Melly Still, the metamorphic swirl of the revolve stage and Rory Kinnear's dynamic Vindice captured a very contemporary sense of decadent privilege (see Figure 36.4). But perhaps it also revealed the extent to which we in the audience have become too inured by media saturation to register adequately the shock contained within

Figure 36.4 *The Revenger's Tragedy*, directed by Melly Still, National Theatre, 2008.
Rory Kinnear as Vindice, Ken Bones as Duke, Jamie Parker as Hippolito. Cf. 3.5.195–6,
"Now with thy dagger / Nail down his tongue."

theatrical pleasure. My own viewing was influenced by sitting behind a
well-heeled young city couple, who had smuggled in a bottle of red wine
rather than purchasing the allowed plastic cup's worth, and seemed more
intent on two forms of oral gratification than the fictional action – even
during Kinnear's direct audience address reminding us that, despite our
lusts and sumptuous veneers, we too would eventually resemble the "bony
lady." (Soon after, the couple snuck out, leaving the dregs for the ushers to
clean up.) A more Middletonian irony seems hard to stage.

Yet as I write, two New Hampshire teenagers await trial for the grisly
torture and murder of a randomly selected mother and child, an action
carried out simply to see how it felt and about which they showed no
remorse; media reports emphasized grotesque details such as their using
iPod lights to find the bedroom and their regret at the unexpected survival
of the stabbed, battered daughter. Against this backdrop of increasingly
familiar brutality, the cavalier evil of the Duke and his sons pales, and some
of the satire in 1980s productions looks almost precious (say, the Beatrice-
Joanna/Princess Diana parallelism in the wake of Royal Wedding fever – a
connection whose cynicism was subsequently confirmed in ways worthy of

Middletonian tragic farce). In such a post-Artaudian context, it seems increasingly difficult – and all the more important – to seek fresh ways to reconceive Middleton's ethical urgency through vivid performance.

The inaugural productions of *A Chaste Maid in Cheapside* and *Mad World* at the Globe remind us that there is a wide range of tonality possible for modern Middleton, including more lighthearted approaches to giddy commercial and sexual exchange (see cover illustration). Likewise tragicomic works such as *An/The Old Law* (as adapted by Max Hafler for the 1990 Lyric Studio, Hammersmith, or as performed by the 2005 RSC) have found contemporary resonance in both their formal rejection of generic clarity and their representations of generational power-shifts and callousness. Enlarging the range of approaches, be it through adaptations of comedies like Edward Bond's 1966 *Chaste Maid* or the deployment of new screen and digital resources, as in the National's *Revenger*, increases the likelihood of more, and more vital, Middletonian afterlives. Given the precedent of Robert Chetwyn and Nick Bicât's 1981 musical version of *Eastward Ho!* and the importance of music and song within many Middleton works, might there even be a musical just around the corner? Of the multiple possibilities we might say, echoing the theatrical transport of Samuel Pepys after attending the 1661 *Changeling*, "it takes exceedingly."

## CHAPTER 37

# Middleton in the cinema

## Pascale Aebischer

Instead of harking back to texts regarded as sacred and definitive, we must first break theatre's subjugation to the text ... If theatre is as bloody and as inhuman as dreams, the reason for this is that it perpetuates the metaphysical notions in some Fables in a present-day, tangible manner, whose atrocity and energy are enough to prove their origins and intentions in fundamental first principles ...

**PROGRAMME:** Disregarding the text, we intend to stage: ... Elizabethan theatre works stripped of the lines, retaining only their period machinery, situations, character and plot.

Antonin Artaud, "The Theatre of Cruelty" (1938)

Artaud's call for a new way of staging early modern drama had a tangible impact not only on Middleton's fortunes on the twentieth-century British stage, as Diana Henderson suggests in this volume (p. 325), but also on his afterlife in the cinema. While all three cinematically released, commercially available Middletonian films are influenced by Artaud, none takes his manifesto as seriously as does Jacques Rivette's *Noroît (une vengeance)* (1976). The French New Wave director's adaptation of *The Revenger's Tragedy* is a Western-turned-pirate-film revolving around the attempts by Morag (Geraldine Chaplin) to avenge her brother's death at the hands of the pirate Giulia (Bernadette Lafont) and her gang. It is also, more importantly, an experiment in literary adaptation, cinematic narration, and the use of music and language as soundscape. For Rivette, *Revenger* holds the key to Artaud's "Theatre of Cruelty" (Wiles, "Theatricality," p. 170). Artaud had dreamed of directing *Revenger* and recovering its mythical, ritualistic essence; he described the play as a "great, noisy machine, grandiose, exalting" (cited in Pollock, "Le Théâtre," p. 172, my translation), the very opposite of a "sacred text." Through his adaptation of *Revenger*, Rivette attempts a cinema of cruelty in which he pushes further the exploration of *auteur*ship characteristic of New Wave cinematic practice and writing, challenging the boundaries between theatre and cinema, past and present, the mythic and the real.

Scénario: Eduardo de Gregorio
Marilù Parolini
Jacques Rivette
d'après
The Revengers Tragaedie
de Cyril Tourneur
(printed by G. Eld, in Fleet-Lane, 1608)

Figure 37.1 Credit sequence of Jacques Rivette's *Noroît*. *Noroît* (1976). Dir. Jacques Rivette. 128 minutes. Color. France. Mono D'Origine.

Rivette's preoccupations are evident from the moment the title sequence attributes the scenario of the film to a team of scriptwriters while proclaiming it to be based on "The Revengers Tragaedie / de Cyril Tourneur / (printed by G. Eld, in Fleet-Lane, 1608)." In the competition for authority over the film, the scriptwriters lose out to the play, whose large font size and authenticating old spelling catch the eye (see Figure 37.1). The attribution "de Cyril Tourneur" is equally striking: the choice of French highlights Rivette's desire to attribute the play to *someone*, however inauthentically. Rivette's own sandwiched position in the middle of the screen is the ostentatiously self-effacing gesture of an "anti-auteurist" director who dreams of "communal films" but cannot imagine an abdication of authority to a troupe of performers as total as the anonymity of the 1608 title page suggests (Monaco, *New Wave*, p. 316).

Rivette's conflicted relationship with *Revenger* is evident throughout the film. True to Artaud's call for plays to be stripped of their text in order to recover the atrocity of the fable, the film almost entirely dispenses with both the text and plot of *Revenger*, retaining merely the essence of the drive to revenge the death of a loved one, the theatricality of the play's violence, and the atmosphere of sexual debauchery coupled with lust for power. Whereas the film's dialogue is spoken entirely in French, the few lines of the play preserved in the film are spoken in English, out of context, rendering them "obscure and allusive, and most of all separate from all other exchanges, doubly theatrical and potentially magical" (Smith and Morrey, *Rivette*, p. 160). As part of the film's experimental soundscape, the theatrical, magical Middletonian text comes to stand for the medium of theatre, which Rivette has described as cinema's "elder brother" (cited in Ménil, "Mesure," p. 78). For Rivette, integrating theatre in a film enables cinema to understand its own distinct identity. As embodied by *Revenger*, theatre is the archaic medium through which *Noroît* reaches for its mythological roots and against which it defines itself as cinema. In the film's opening scene, the camera pans across an empty beach and settles on Morag/Vindice, huddled over the corpse of a man. As Morag raises herself and starts stroking the corpse, she proclaims, in accented French: "Shane, my brother, I have been looking for you. I have found you in the ocean, on the rocks, scattered, shredded. With my breath, with my hands, I have reassembled you. There is your body, as it was before." We are invited to identify this dismembered body of the elder brother with the fragmented theatrical text of *Revenger*, which is about to be reconstituted by Morag. As she raises her head to intone Vindice's "Thou goddess of the palace, mistress of mistresses, / To whom the costly-perfumed people pray . . . let me blush inward" (1.3.6–10), Morag breathes new, cinematic life into the theatrical text. The point of the citation is not intelligibility or even reference, but mystery and alienation, stripping the play of its text through the very act that celebrates its rebirth in the medium of cinema.

*Revenger* thus is and is not part of the film. Act and scene divisions that periodically interrupt the flow of the action do not correspond to their counterparts in the play, reminding the viewer of the film's theatrical origin while negating its significance (Smith and Morrey, *Rivette*, p. 158). Indeed, *Revenger* seems oddly absent from the first half of the film, until the play's significance is brusquely reasserted in a cluster of scenes that reenact the Duke's poisoning with Gloriana's skull in a manner that destabilizes the boundaries between play and audience, fiction and reality. The play first resurfaces when Morag and her accomplice Erika (Kika Markham in a Hippolito-like role) circle around the shrouded body of Shane, chanting "Now to my tragic business . . . I have not fashioned this only for show / And useless property. No, it shall bear a part, / E'en in it own revenge. This very skull, / . . . with this drug, . . . shall be revenged" (3.5.99–104) (see Figure 37.2). Part magical incantation, part significant information about the role Shane's body is about to play, this quotation seems also to be addressed to the viewer. That there may be more here than meets the eye becomes clear when "I have not fashioned this only for show" recurs a few scenes later, as Morag laces the lips of Shane's corpse with poison, ready to be kissed by Giulia's blonde sister Régina (Babette Lamy), who mistakes Shane for her lover Jacob (both men are played by Humbert Balsan). What looked at first like a ritual incantation now appears to have been the rehearsal for an actual murder.

Figure 37.2 Erika and Morag chanting Vindice's lines over Shane's body. *Noroît* (1976). Dir. Jacques Rivette. 128 minutes. Color. France. Mono D'Origine.

Figure 37.3 The play within the film: Morag/the Duke spitting out a snake to signal her poisoning by Erika/Vindice. *Noroît* (1976). Dir. Jacques Rivette. 128 minutes. Color. France. Mono D'Origine.

The lines recur, once more, in the next scene, in which Erika and Morag in a blonde wig give a highly theatrical performance of the scene of the Duke's murder in *Revenger* before the assembled audience of Giulia and her fellow pirates (see Figure 37.3). The play within the film is now both the

performance of the scene that had previously been rehearsed by the two
conspirators and a theatrical repetition of the "real" murder of Régina we
have just watched. French *répétition* means both rehearsal and repetition,
and this is what we are witnessing here: performance as *répétition* with a
difference. The elder brother of *Noroît*, the theatrical text of *Revenger*, is
repeated again and again in the film, always fragmented, reassembled with a
difference, ever more theatrically, until it is brought to a provisional stand-
still at the end of this scene by the intrusion of cinema's "reality" and "fixity"
in Giulia's seemingly unmotivated gory murder of one of the audience
members – the only time Rivette's film shows us blood. What had been a
cruel piece of theatre is transformed here into Rivette's unsettling attempt at
creating a cinema of cruelty, in which the spectator can never be certain of
the status of the images presented and in which the "situations, character
and plot" of *Revenger* take precedence over text and meaning.

Rivette's attempt to distil the mythical essence of the Middletonian text
stands alone in its radical application of Artaudian principles. But while
there is no clear line of descent from Rivette to Marcus Thompson and Alex
Cox, the two independent filmmakers who have, more recently, turned to
Middleton's tragedies for inspiration, what nevertheless unites their films
is the sense, put into words by Peter Greenaway, that Jacobean drama is
part of

an alternative tradition, that starts with Seneca and goes on through Jacobean
drama to be picked up later by people like de Sade, and then . . . continues with
[Artaud's] Theatre of Cruelty . . . and perhaps it is also picked up by filmmakers like
Buñuel . . . I'm fascinated by an alternative examination of cultures, which . . .
examines the center of the human predicament by going to the edges, to the
extremes, to see in fact how far one can stretch the examination of various forms of
aberrant behavior. (cited in Rodgers, "*Prospero's Books*," p. 12)

Key to this view of Jacobean drama, for better or worse, is the notion of
"extremes," of excess and deviance.

The wish to portray extreme aberrance drives Marcus Thompson's 1998
adaptation of *The Changeling*. Like Rivette, Thompson puts the name
of the play's author(s) at the center of his field of tensions: although a
caption proclaims the authors to be "Thomas Middleton AND William
Rowley," with a "SCREENPLAY BY Marcus Thompson," the film's
name is *Middleton's Changeling*. This, then, will be neither the play collaboratively written by Middleton and Rowley, nor the Marcus Thompson
screenplay with its "Yo, sister!" interjection, but something more akin
to Baz Luhrmann's conspicuous authorial incorporation in *William*

*Shakespeare's Romeo + Juliet*, released two years earlier. The film turns out to be all of these options rolled into one: there's enough Rowley left in it to justify his inclusion, so much Thompson that the director/screenwriter's input cannot possibly be overlooked, and plenty of Middleton and oblique references to the Shakespearean performance tradition (and in particular Orson Welles's *Othello*). This is the tragedy of a director who could not make up his mind.

Thompson's tendency towards excessive signification that ultimately frustrates interpretation is evident in the choice of artists involved in the film. Ian Dury as De Flores brings to the part not only his reputation as the singer of "Sex and Drugs and Rock'n'roll," but also his cameo appearance in Peter Greenaway's "Jacobean" *The Cook, The Thief, His Wife and Her Lover*. Art-house engagement with the "alternative tradition" to which Jacobean drama and its Artaudian successors belong is thus signposted, but how this relates to the casting of popular comedian Billy Connolly as Alibius in a truncated subplot and the introduction of punk poet John Cooper Clarke reciting one of his poems remains unclear.

The multiplication of references is compounded by a trail of allusions – partly through visual imagery, partly through the use of wedding-dress designer Elizabeth Emanuel – to the life and death of Princess Diana, drawing on the tabloids' fascination with celebrity, fashion, and sex between a member of the aristocracy and her riding instructor. If there is one consistent interpretation of the play in this film, it is the unequivocal representation it offers of the sexual relationship of Beatrice-Joanna and De Flores as a rape. This stands in stark contrast to the way the relationship has been portrayed on the twentieth-century stage, where its representation as the fulfilment of Beatrice-Joanna's repressed desire for De Flores has become "virtually canonical" (Barker and Nicol, "*Changeling*," p. 3). But the portrayal of the relationship as a rape does not, in *Middleton's Changeling*, amount to Barker and Nicol's wished-for "provocative feminist reading" in which "Beatrice Joanna's career can be (re-)read as critiquing every aspect of patriarchal ideology" (p. 43). Rather, the film proposes a reading in which Beatrice-Joanna is punished for her attempts to choose her own sexual partners, a punishment that is carried out against a backdrop of stables, horses, and carriages that insistently returns us to the fantasized location of Diana's adultery.

In a scene reminiscent of Lavinia's rape in *Titus Andronicus*, Thompson has De Flores brutally raping Beatrice-Joanna on top of a wooden trunk containing the dismembered corpse of her fiancé, while blood seeps through the slats and pours down the walls of the castle. After the rape, in another evocation of bulimic Diana, Beatrice-Joanna tries to be sick. A black-and-white montage shows her re-experiencing the rape as a love scene featuring herself and Alsemero in a stylish modern apartment, with De Flores as a violent intruder. The scene taps into class-driven fantasies of defilement: while it is clear that the rape is traumatic for Beatrice-Joanna, this sequence also fulfils a pornographic desire to subdue the inaccessible upper-class woman in front of her defenseless husband. The film's conclusion, in which Diana's wedding is conflated with the scene of her death with yet another upstart lover, sees De Flores jumping on the black wedding carriage containing Beatrice-Joanna and slaughtering her in an erotic frenzy that leaves her panting and covered in blood from head to toe. Her objectification is complete as the camera tracks over her bloody body over which De Flores gloats, his – and the implied audience's – deepest desires satisfied.

The objectification of the female upper-class body that is thus central to Thompson's vision is also at the heart of Alex Cox's *Revengers Tragedy* (the absence of the apostrophe in the title signals both authenticity and alienation, performing work very similar to Rivette's spelling of *The Revengers Tragaedie*). This film, too, cashes in on the ways in which non-Shakespearean Jacobean drama is associated with the Artaudian Theatre of Cruelty and the opportunity for an alternative exploration of culture. What distinguishes *Revengers* from *Middleton's Changeling*, however, is the wit and coherence with which Cox references his artistic precursors and draws the battle lines with the Shakespearean heritage industry. Drawing on the punk aesthetic of Derek Jarman's *The Last of England* (1988) and *Edward II* (1991), and invoking Buñuel in the credit "an exterminating angel film," *Revengers* contributes to the marked rise in the number of low-budget independent filmmakers in Europe reacting against the mass-market Shakespeare films associated with Hollywood.

But while Cox aligns himself with a counter-cinematic and politically engaged tradition of filmmaking, the film does not break with the Shakespeare film as a cinematic genre altogether: not only does another credit reveal that *Revengers* is produced by "Bard Entertainments," but the film features *Hamlet* and Branagh veteran Derek Jacobi, cast as the dissolute old Duke clinging to power, youth, and sexual potency alongside the Duchess of Diana Quick (an actress associated with the Royal Shakespeare Company). The alternative to the Duke's corrupt regime is embodied by the husband-and-wife team of Antonio and his Lady, whose name – Imogen – links them to the Shakespearean canon, too. Sophie Dahl's Imogen, like Beatrice-Joanna in Thompson's film modelled on Diana, is destroyed by the media which pursues her, rendering her an object

Figure 37.4 Lussurioso (Eddie Izzard), driver (Alex Cox), Ambitioso (Justin Salinger), and Duchess (Diana Quick). *Revengers Tragedy* (2003). Dir. Alex Cox.

of popular desire, as instrumentalized in death as in life, a two-dimensional screen icon in both. The political and cultural contest, it appears, is between two alternative versions of Shakespeare that turn out to be equally corrupt: one the camp and superannuated Shakespeare of the theatrical establishment, the other the kitsch Shakespeare of the twenty-first-century popular media, cross-contaminated by celebrity culture. Christopher Eccleston's working-class Liverpudlian Vindici (the spelling adopted by Cox) emerges as the third term in this equation: a Middletonian revenger attacking the Shakespearean establishment through ventriloquism, parody, and corrosive wit.

That the film represents a corrosive attack on Shakespeare and political inertia is made explicit on Alex Cox's website, where the director opposes Shakespeare's reactionary politics and his status as "a dessicated work of 'quality literature'" with Middleton's "more modern" language and political nonconformism. For Cox, *Revenger* enables a critique of the oppressive class barriers that have remained unchanged since the seventeenth century, and the anachronisms that pervade his film are there to highlight this continuity. His own appearance in the film in the guise of the Duke's driver gives physical expression to the shift in class attitudes and cultural authority he wants to see: the driver who starts off being obtrusively deferential to his boss ends up sitting at the bottom end of the ducal breakfast table, drinking beer and wrapped in the Duke's massive coat to signal his gleeful usurpation of Jacobi's place in the film (see Figure 37.4).

Like Rivette, Cox uses the corpse of the lover as a cipher for the Middletonian text, which is brought back to uncanny life when Vindici picks up Gloriana's skull and ventriloquizes her cry for "Revenge! Revenge! Revenge!" As the film progresses, this ventriloquism increasingly leads to the conflation of Vindici and the three women with whom his revenge is connected: his poisoned and posthumously raped bride Gloriana, his sassy sister Castiza, who is the object of persistent sexual harassment, and Imogen, whom Castiza assists after her rape. In the climactic scene of the Duke's murder, Vindici's ventriloquism of the skeletal Middletonian text leads to the graphic corrosion of the mouth(piece) of Shakespearean author-ity when Jacobi's Duke starts spitting blood, his lower face disintegrating under the effect of the poisoned kiss.

Imogen's double association, with kitsch, two-dimensional media Shakespeare on the one hand, and with the group of Middletonian victims-turned-revengers on the other hand, might seem contradictory, but it follows its own distinct logic. Cox gives all three of the play's sexually victimized women a far more prominent role than they have in the play, involving them actively in Vindici's revenge. While in Middleton's text Antonio's Lady only appears in her death and speaks only through the signs with which she has surrounded her body, Cox portrays the build-up to her rape in the soccer stadium, lets us hear her off-screen screams, and, crucially, shows her being rescued and comforted by Castiza and her brothers, who take up her cause and set their revenge in the stadium that was the scene of her rape. Meanwhile the flashbacks to Vindici and Gloriana's wedding that punctuate the film link the rape of Imogen, which employs the iconography of rape by androgynous tattooed youths viewers will recognize from Julie Taymor's *Titus* (1999), to the murder of Gloriana who, Lavinia-like, vomits blood over her white gown. After her death, a parodic version of the gravediggers' squabbling over the legal status of Ophelia's death by two punters in a pub links Imogen to yet another Shakespearean victim of male aggression.

A distinction thus emerges between Imogen the rape victim, whose cause is defended by the Middletonian revengers, and the two-dimensional version of Imogen as a screen icon, whose political abuse by Antonio is critiqued by the film. There is a Shakespeare Cox finds worth saving, it seems, but it is the Shakespeare of the disempowered, not that of the mainstream Shakespeare industry and the media, who watch Vindici being gunned down by the assembled powers of the army, a moribund judge, a beefeater and, in a witty invocation of historical censorship, "a bailiff dressed as a Master of the Revels" (Lehmann, "Performing,"

p. 214). As Cox's ending makes clear, these forces of conservatism might be able to defeat the revolution embodied by Middleton's revenger in the short term, but their annihilation is not far off: the camera pans up towards a portrait of Queen Elizabeth II, which is converted into grainy black-and-white pixels and transformed into a mushroom cloud while the disembodied voice of Vindici/Gloriana screeches "Revenge! Revenge! Revenge!" If Cox's film, as Courtney Lehmann suggests, makes a case for "the removal of Shakespeare from his position of priority and privilege in the history of film adaptation" ("Performing," p. 217), then it is only fitting that in his alternative examination of twenty-first-century English culture at its most extreme and aberrant, it is Middleton who has the last word.

## CHAPTER 38

# Middleton's presence

## Simon Palfrey

"All narrative forms make of the present something past; all dramatic form makes of the past a present" (Schiller, "On the Tragic Art," p. 356; see Meisel, *How Plays Work*, Chapter 6). So claims Schiller of the necessary present tense of all drama, in that the event of the play can only happen *now*, in the moment shared by actors and audience. But plays, like all artworks, are also in some basic way out of time, such that the very notion of a present and indicative "context" is dubious. Art is imperative, optative, subjunctive: it urges things, wishes things, imagines things. So plays are never simply continuous with the world offstage. They have their own rules and physics, and do all kinds of violence to time and space as habitually experienced. For one thing they force us to *see* relational structures that we usually take for granted; they denature space, through radical semiotic attenuation. They speed things up and break things down; they contract things at will, make invisibilities visible; they magnify particularities by the simple fact of choosing specific actions, which thereby become exemplary, and ne-glecting others, which thereby disappear, as they never quite can in life. Mimesis demands change; it enacts and argues for transformation. A play, then, is less taken with re-presenting what can be witnessed outside the magic box than with pushing, often with the most thrilling peremptory briskness, backwards or forwards from this presentness: into causes; into consequences.

And of course a play is written for future presents – or at least any play that is still worth bothering with centuries after its first composition. It necessarily generates what Kierkegaard called a "forward repetition": its passionate appropriation by others, so that iteration is subjective possession and spiritual transformation (see especially *Repetition*). Such afterlives are hard to track and impossible to program. But the fact of them is never separate from a potential inhering in the source; they are not impositions of willful posterity. In other words, future possibilities depend on realizing (in various senses) what is already present. Anachronism is absolutely necessary if a work is to live beyond its moment; but some anachronisms are better than others, and the best of all, I think, find the anachronies already lurking in the source.

Presence to us depends on presence to Middleton. If he does not feel it pressing upon him or swelling into apparency, nor will we. But by presence I mean *real presence*, rather than a shadow or simulacra: one that bears ethical responsibility, which in turn means facing history foursquare and recognizing the inheritance. History is an active presence for Middleton, but it is only accidentally characterized by James's court or the city of London. More essentially, history means a specifically Calvinist understanding of *consecution*, in which the cause of events is at once transcendent (in God), original (in sin), and immanent (because both are forever active in things). Presence is defined by compulsion and necessity. It is a qualitative thing, not a securely measurable one. For we are speaking of art: the point to hold to is that necessity precisely means *possibility*.

Leibniz, early modern philosophy's great theorist of possibility, understands "possibles" as the ideas that actually subsist in the mind of God. All have a disposition to exist, but only those possibles with the most essence *do* exist. Actuality, therefore, must be the "best of all possible worlds," in line with the principle of sufficient (God's) reason (*Shorter Texts*, pp. 32, 195). Now, Middleton can seem to be the gloomy negative to Leibniz's technicolor optimism. Possibility is in God's keeping, all right, but things in the world are cast off from all deserving, sordid repetitions of original susceptibility and perversion, indentured to fleshly love, indentured to death. To reach to such an apprehension of presence, we have to put aside more familiar models of possibility, like Shakespeare's, with its abundant feeling for imminence and alternatives. In Middleton, possibility is a kind of *redaction* of necessity: personal divagations must return home; all shades of color bleed back to the white and black of the original chessboard; the plot has been written. To the extent that other motives are breeding, it is in *despite* of this known scenario, which remains immovable.

The plot is unusually determining for Middleton. His *Ur*-scene of the Fall is one such, with its fatal bite and the kiss that trades it all in. But it is also true at a more basic compositional level. Writing the plot scenario, and then writing the play *to* this plot, was Middleton's foundational technique (Stern, *Documents*). We know this because he wrote for many different companies, men and boys by turns, in numerous different theatres; and because he often wrote collaboratively. It was not possible for Middleton to develop the intimate relations with actors that Shakespeare did over many years, nor the intense part-sensitive scripting that Shakespeare did, in which an overarching plot seems regularly to have deferred to part-engineered diversions, densities, intervals, and opportunities (Palfrey and Stern, *Parts*). Only the plot scenario could have given the mobility and concision that Middleton required. Furthermore, this plot scenario determined whether or not there would *be* a play: if the company did not buy it, there would not be.

But the plot scenario is much more than merely a technical aid or an invitation to treat for potential producers. The scenario claims knowledge, and a kind of originating possession, of the fundamental reasons for the play's being. Whether it dilates on a specific "seeding" scene, or chops up a long and unwieldy story into fractal bites, the scenario seeks to abstract the logic, the basic rules of motion and motive, which give to the playworld its purposive drive. Consequently, to *believe* in plot scenarios – to accept that they are indeed prehensions of the larger play – might usefully subserve Middleton's presumed theology: events cannot outrun their source; improvisation must play inside defined permissions; the world is written, rather than unfinished or unpredictable; irruptiveness does not produce the new, either subjectively or historically, and still less in terms of metaphysical teleology, but rather proves the truth of what has been foreordained. Above all, it turns the full play into a repetition – a backward-casting *execution* of the predicative model (plot scenario/Eden).

This is not to say that plotting in scenes is all about sequential uniformity. When Dr Johnson writes of "the disposition and consecution of the scenes of a play," the word "consecution" comes from the Latin *consecutio*, meaning to follow closely or to overtake (*Dictionary*, 23F2a). Sequence is imbued with purpose, volition, a kind of appetite. It is not an inert succession of points on a line. Almost more important is the space in between each point, suddenly volatized by necessity, as one scene strives to overtake another, or as the later scene is dragged or magnetized back to the previous one. *Consecution* can propose scenic relationships of a Hegelian or Freudian intensity, in which only a scene's relative *conatus*, its soul-appetite, can determine its presence to us. Drama's present, then, really is tense.

Since consecution speaks of causes and fates, some scenes will necessarily possess more than others. Often Middleton's plays seem to be catalyzed from a single, specifically imagined scene, which is also the point to which all the action is heading: it is both origin and completion, trigger and climax. *The Changeling* is an obvious example: everything waits for and turns upon the moment when Beatrice catches up, as it were, to De Flores, when their contract is sealed, dependency acknowledged, and they are charged fully into their destined form. The "scene" is staggered, so that De Flores sees it, then we do, then Beatrice, then Alsemero, then everyone. The duo are revealed less as flesh-and-blood humans than as holograms of original degradation – as though all the time just waiting to be turned at the right angle, towards the jaundiced light, and recognized in all foulness as the crouched beasts that they are. The scene garners *iconic* animation; it delivers a picture, as though from well-known tales, mythic and immovable, horribly returnable. Such moments are the acme of Middletonian possibility.

Middleton's decisive scenes always show the central characters truly *entering* in this fashion – as though demonic inversions of St. Paul's "putting on the new man."[1] This true entrance can occur at any moment in the play, delineating in a frieze-like, almost sculpting fashion – or what Kierkegaard might denote as *mimical* – the attitude-to-the-world of the character (*Anxiety*, pp. 131–2). An original vision is at once revealed, in all its ghastly purity. For example, *A Yorkshire Tragedy* is generated by, and duly fulfils, a single image. Middleton finds it in the pamphlet source, but memorably recreates it:[2]

> He sits and sullenly locks up his arms,
> Forgetting heaven, looks downward, which makes him
> Appear so dreadful that he frights my heart,
> Walks heavily, as if his soul were earth
>
> (2.15–18)

To realize Middleton's aims we simply need to realize the moving sculpture. We have already heard (from Sam the servant) of Husband's brutality – he "beats his wife ... has consumed all, pawned his lands ... calls his wife whore and his children bastards" (2.42–58) – but now his hideous carelessness gathers a kind of plastic iconicity. When not sitting moodily, he is walking without purpose, shaking the floorboards and scowling. The violence of the walking repeats the violence of the locked arms, rendered strangely simultaneous by the present-tense facticity of the actions: he sits, he locks his arms, he looks downwards, he walks heavily. The tragedy is that, even in imagination, he can effect nothing but pleonasm – his walk reverberates with the heaviness of earth, just as his gaze is magnetized downwards and his arms are locked, as though horizontal in burial. And indeed there are hints of horrible, ghoul-like automatism, as though movement is no longer simple and natural, but spectral or zombie-like. So, he *is* sitting, and violently pressing his body inwards; this intensified constriction gives morbid energy to the "downward" look, which is not simply "downcast," as in depressed or defeated, but appetitive, yearning, even plunging. He is in despair, doubtless, but he is not catatonic, nor is he curled in a ball like a hedgehog. He wants more – he wants to punish. All this makes his walking continuous with his downward look, as an affect of it, in the way of a casting after some correspondent action, perhaps to repair or, more likely, to embed him still further in his despair. In this way, Husband is given something like Macbeth's violent wistfulness, marooned in his situation, pegged to the boards like fate's clown, and pushing imaginatively into releasing action that can only compound his sin and loss.

The sum effect is more than a conventional allegory of a man gone to the devil. Stillness moves, or movement is stilled; his body is *ahead of itself,* enacting things rehearsively, feeling nothing, overcoming the mental obstacles to their achievement in the future. The geography is metaphysical, just as his journey is. He is already there, in hell. With one glance, his unbodied body walks ahead of him, like a spirit released into dreadful commission. With another, he remains where he was, where he is, all the more emptied for having done, imaginatively, that which will end everything. As he sits in his knot he is killing his family, ridding himself of all burdens, shutting the eyes of those whose look produces shame. This portrait, then, is the mime that will come true – that will walk into sound and commission any moment: "O, yonder he comes." The mimical, then, is precisely the *possible*, in all its enormity.

Such predictive scenic capsules may bring to mind what the phenomenologist Marion says of Kant: "before any phenomenal breakthrough toward visibility, the horizon waited in advance." Or as Hippolito's pithy summary has it: "Lust and forgetfulness has been amongst us, / And we are brought to nothing" (*Women Beware Women*, 5.1.184–5). We are never free to forget: the anterior concept will not only catch up with us, it will determine our horizons. But is this the limit of Middleton's present? Are his phenomena always apprehended – preemptively seen and inevitably arrested – by his concepts? Marion apposes this understanding of experience with what he calls "saturated phenomena." By this he denotes a sublime occurrence, "phenomena with $n + 1$ horizons," in which the phenomenal experience *exceeds* any governing concept. These "saturated phenomena" are "neither foreseeable (on the basis of the past), nor exhaustively comprehensible (on the basis of the present), nor reproducible (on the basis of the future)." They are instead "absolute, unique, occurring," and assume the "character and the dignity of an event" ("Saturated," pp. 32–42). Is this not also true of Middleton's most present, most *necessary* scenes?

Marion's key terms are astonishment, bedazzlement, revelation, when an access of affect embarrasses conceptual understanding or intellectual preparation and we are left to absorb something truly new. The object is no longer constituted by the subject's intention. In a sense, we can return to the strictly *naïve* affects that theatre so often depends on, and the simple fact that the phenomenology of attendance – what we feel or apprehend as we witness the play – always has a capacity for disobedience, for fugitive stirrings or unexpected sympathies.

By definition, such phenomena cannot be programed in the way of Middleton's habitual scenic teleology. Accordingly, Middleton's more overtly revelatory gestures do not elicit the requisite astonishment: Lady's resurrection as a white-robed angelic ghost in *The Lady's Tragedy*, for instance, is always likely to be weighed down precisely by allegorical "intentionality." But consider the violent penance of Husband in *Yorkshire*. The devil, he cries, "[d]eparts at every joint, heaves up my nails" (8.19). Simultaneously we hear spiritual renewal; exorcism (the devil now separate from him); a returning human feeling that is also murderous guilt, and thus self-dissolving or even self-murdering; present torture (secret and foul) and anticipated judicial punishment (public and right). There are many such moments in this play's visionary final scene. No one could be guiltier than Husband, more a proof of inveterate sinfulness, yet he is found turning in a gyre between punishment and redemption, with the wounds he dealt turning to tears for him, the tears turning to jewels to cherish, as the innocent eyes of those he slaughtered "shoot" upon his cheeks (8.39). Dead and living bodies are savagely, miraculously shared, in the most audacious return of family and love. His necessary exile from heaven is suddenly the locus of the deepest pathos.

At his most present, Middleton is tense with such impossible possibilities – this despite the fact that the mathematics of sin allows no exceptions, that the equation always comes to nought. For these big scenes produce a paradoxical effect, akin to Marion's "saturation." The fact that story catches up with itself, and is no longer impatient to reach the necessary consequence, grants space to dress – and, more than that, to address – the stakes of the moment. The words achieve a self-sculpting, almost baroque spatiality – a frame inside the frames, invested with strangely resistant possibility. The pre-articulated idea comes true, but precisely via a phenomenal excess whose intensity stuns rather than teaches the imagination. We witness a literal recklessness – seeing the stakes of sin and persisting, almost joyfully. An irradiating *permission* floods the scene.

Consider Tyrant in *Lady*. He is the only character dignified with a personal metaphysical geography ("I stand as in a shade … I keep the valleys / The place that is last served" [1.1.212–16]), and it is *into* this that he is always headed. The culminating episode sees him smash his beloved's tomb, take the corpse back to his palace, dress it in honey and restoratives, and cherish it as his sex-doll. It invites dismissal, as insane, psychopathic, sacrilegious, degenerate. But if it were only this, the scene would be either comic or lamentable, and it is neither. There is a residue of something else: a passage beyond bourgeois ethics, or a merely grotesque aesthetics, into something more faithful to the playworld's terrible logic.

The scene gets its charge from the contrast between the Tyrant, reverently beholding his Lady, and his soldiers, trembling with holy fear at their transgression. Their fear is normative, and in some ways choric, but it is also time-serving and afraid of ultimacy: "Very fear will go nigh to turn me of some religion or other, and so make me forfeit my lieutenantship" (4.3.47–9). The soldiers are essentially clowns, "slaves" working *for* the hero. Their job is to frame Tyrant, and to point his terrifying absoluteness. So as much as we look with their eyes at his strangeness, they melt away from him as the Tyrant crystallizes into his fate. His beloved appears and the Tyrant is oblivious to all other voices. He is a monomaniac, certainly, but the effect is a gaze that shines hard and exclusively on the only source of value: "O, blest object! / I never shall be weary to behold thee. / I could eternally stand thus and see thee" (62–3). He ascends to a rare lyricism, exalting his Lady as the rising moon, moving into an intimate love-coddle ("Art thou cold? / … 'Tis I, sweet lady, prithee speak / 'Tis thy love calls on thee, the king thy servant. / No, not a word?" [86–90]), calling on her with as fierce and desperate a tenderness as Lear did the dead Cordelia. He is the marooned love-swain, recalling only a kind of fractured carpe diem with which to mockingly rebuke his love: "By th'mass, thou'rt cold indeed; beshrew thee for't! / Unkind to thine own blood? Hard-hearted lady, / What injury hast thou offered to the youth / And pleasure of thy days!" (94–7). He is acting out all the roles that living life has forbidden him, like husband, father, priest: "O I could chide thee with mine eye brim-full, / And weep out my forgiveness when I ha' done" (99–100).

The thing to notice is how Middleton dwells in the moment, in the relationship between the man and the corpse. There is real *duration* given to it – it is the duration of the unlived, the unlivable. Middleton's imperative art rarely dramatizes the subjunctive, but he does so here. But it is not just that he is wistfully imagining "what if?" In the most basic sense he is *doing* it. It requires the annihilation of normative morality to do so. The Tyrant has crossed the threshold. This is why the space for intimacy widens as the soldiers retreat and the Tyrant and his virgin possess the stage. All of Middleton's tragic heroes desire to enter this kind of territory, wanting to enter, or reenter, the unspeakable space where we are most ourselves. They are extrapolations of irrational appetite, or of the violent bias that is love (preferring one above all others and imagining that the remainder of the world diminishes, next to the chosen one's unsurpassable perfection). Tyrant's necrophilia is less perversion than extension, a coming true of love's predicative coupling in death. To be flesh is to be dying; you must live a dying life; to love flesh is to hang on to death, to burrow in it like a maggot.

But the Tyrant's intimacy to the human comedy is still more. He cannot rest in cold morbidity. Having secured his corpse-bride, he wants her color back. The Tyrant is fighting against the life sentence. The only savior is art: "so shall we / By art force beauty on yon lady's face, / Though death sit frowning on't a storm of hail / To beat it off. Our pleasure shall prevail" (5.2.109–12). He attempts what Middleton attempts with Lady's Ghost – some vestige of a return from the wreckage, a "pleasure" in spite of the "everlasting frost": "Our arms and lips / Shall labour life into her. Wake, sweet mistress, / 'Tis I that call thee at the door of life!" (5.2.118–20). In some ways this turns to horrid farce, the Tyrant a clownish and diseased Pygmalion. The comedy is emphasized if the corpse is played by a puppet, flopping from his grip or sagging limply to the stage floor. But Middleton is also deadly serious. For this fatal kiss is the Tyrant's attempt at a birth scene. He is the imaginary mother, "labor"-ing to bring his baby through the "door of life." He would repeat one primal scene by having sex with a corpse; he would repeat another by giving birth to life from death. It is of course all monstrous and grotesque, a belated simulation of loss. But what isn't?

Middleton is not writing theodicies. His subject is human love. Moments like these urge the loneliness of the love-space, and irradiate far beyond any punitive intent. Compared with Shakespeare, Middleton's intersubjective spaces can often seem inert. Everything returns, like a whipped-in coil, to the abandoned monadic subject. But this has its own, very often perverse, integrity. We see it with Bianca, Hippolito, De Flores, Beatrice, Vindice, Tyrant, even Husband: for all of their perversity and violence, they have entered the wounds of possibility.

NOTES

1. Ephesians 4 (Geneva version).
2. The pamphlet has this: "in short time so weakened his estate, that having not wherewithal to carry that port which before he did, he grew into a discontent, which so swaid in him, hee would sit sullenly, walke melancholy, bethinking continually, and with steddy lookes naild to the groud, seeme astonisht, that when his wife would come to desire the cause of his sadnesse, and intreate to be a willing partner in his sorrow ... Hee would eyther sitte still without giving her an aunswer, or rising uppe, depart from her with these wordes; A plague on thee, thou art the cause of my sadnesse" (Middleton, *Yorkshire*, B. Gaines (ed.), pp. 98–9).

# Works cited

Adams, J. Q., "Foreword," in T. Middleton, *Hengist, King of Kent; or, The Mayor of Queenborough*, R. C. Bald (ed.) (New York and London: Charles Scribner's Sons, 1938), pp. vii–viii.

Adamson, S., "The Grand Style," in S. Adamson, L. Hunter, L. Magnusson, A. Thompson, and K. Wales (eds.), *Reading Shakespeare's Dramatic Language: A Guide* (London: Arden Shakespeare, 2001), pp. 31–50.

  "The Literary Language," in R. Lass (ed.), *The Cambridge History of the English Language,* vol. III, *1476–1776* (Cambridge University Press, 1999), pp. 539–653.

  "Varieties, Stereotypes, Satire – and Shakespeare," in Y. Ikegami and M. Toyota (eds.), *Aspects of English as a World Language* (Tokyo: Maruzen, 1993), pp. 225–45.

Agnew, J. C., *Worlds Apart: The Market and the Theater in Anglo-American Thought, 1550–1750* (Cambridge University Press, 1986).

Akrigg, G. P. V, "Middleton: An Allusion to the First Folio?," *Shakespeare Association Bulletin*, 21 (1946), 25–6.

Altieri, J., "Against Moralizing Jacobean Comedy: Middleton's *Chaste Maid*," *Criticism*, 30 (1988), 171–87.

Amussen, S., *An Ordered Society: Gender and Class in Early Modern England* (Oxford: Blackwell, 1988).

*The Ancient British Drama in Three Volumes* (London: James Ballantyne & Co., 1810).

Andrews, J., A. Briggs, R. Porter, P. Tucker, and K. Waddington, *The History of Bethlem* (London and New York: Routledge, 1997).

Appleby, A. B., *Famine in Tudor and Stuart England* (Palo Alto, CA: Stanford University Press, 1978).

Archer, I. W., *The Pursuit of Stability: Social Relations in Elizabethan London* (Cambridge University Press, 1991).

  "The City of London and the Theatre," in R. Dutton (ed.), *The Oxford Handbook of Early Modern Theatre* (Oxford University Press, 2009), pp. 396–412.

Artaud, A., *The Theatre and its Double*, J. V. Corti (trans.) (London: Calder and Boyers, 1970).

Astington, J., "Playing the Man: Acting at the Red Bull and the Fortune," *Early Theatre*, 9 (2006), 130–43.

"Visual Texts: Thomas Middleton and Prints," in G. Taylor and J. Lavagnino (gen. eds.), *Thomas Middleton and Early Modern Textual Culture: A Companion to the Collected Works* (Oxford: Clarendon Press, 2007) pp. 226–46.

Austern, L. P., *Music in English Children's Drama of the Later Renaissance* (Philadelphia: Gordon and Breach, 1992).

"Thomas Ravenscroft: Musical Chronicler of an Elizabethan Theater Company," *Journal of the American Musicological Society*, 38 (1985), 238–63.

Baker, J. H., *An Introduction to English Legal History*, 3rd edn. (London: Butterworths, 1990).

Baker, J. H. (ed.), *The Reports of Sir John Spelman*, 2 vols. (London, 1978).

Bald, R. C., "Middleton's Civic Employments," *Modern Philology*, 31 (1933), 65–78.

Barber, C., *Early Modern English* (London: Andre Deutsch, 1976).

"'You' and 'Thou' in Shakespeare's *Richard III*," *Leeds Studies in English*, 12 (1981), 273–89.

Barbour, R., *Before Orientalism: London's Theatre of the East, 1576–1626* (Cambridge University Press, 2003).

Barclay, W., *Nepenthes, or The Vertves of Tabacco* (Edinburgh, 1614).

Barker, H., *Arguments for a Theater*, 2nd edn. (New York: Manchester University Press, 1993).

Barker, R. and D. Nicol, "Does Beatrice Joanna Have a Subtext? *The Changeling* on the London Stage," *Early Modern Literary Studies*, 10 (May 2004), 3.1–43.

Barroll, L., *Politics, Plague, and Shakespeare's Theatre* (Ithaca, NY: Cornell University Press, 1991).

Barry, L., *Ram Alley*, P. Corbin and D. Sedge (eds.) (Nottingham Drama Texts, 1981).

Barthes, R., *The Rustle of Language*, Richard Howard (trans.) (Berkeley and Los Angeles: University of California Press, 1989).

Barton, A., *The Names of Comedy* (Oxford University Press, 1990).

Baston, J., "Rehabilitating Moll's Subversion in *The Roaring Girl*," *Studies in English Literature, 1500–1900*, 37 (1997), 317–35.

Bawcutt, N. W., "Was Thomas Middleton a Puritan Dramatist?," *Modern Language Review*, 94 (1999), 925–1000.

Bednarz, J., *Shakespeare and the Poets' War* (New York: Columbia University Press, 2001).

Bellany, A., *The Politics of Court Scandal in Early Modern England: News Culture and the Overbury Affair, 1603–1660* (Cambridge University Press, 2002).

"The Murder of John Lambe: Crowd Violence, Court Scandal and Popular Politics in Early Seventeenth-Century England," *Past and Present*, 200 (2008), 37–76.

"Railing Rhymes Revisited: Libels, Scandals, and Early Stuart Politics," *History Compass*, 5.4 (2007), 1136–79.

Bellany, A. and A. McRae (with P. Hammer and M. O'Callaghan) (eds.), "Early Stuart Libels: An Edition of Poetry from Manuscript Sources," *Early Modern Literary Studies*, Text Series 1 (2005) (www.earlystuartlibels.net).

Belling, C., "Infectious Rape, Therapeutic Revenge," in S. Moss and K. L. Peterson (eds.), *Disease, Diagnosis and Cure on the Early Modern Stage* (Aldershot: Ashgate, 2004), pp. 113–32.

Bennett, S., *Performing Nostalgia: Shifting Shakespeare and the Contemporary Past* (New York: Routledge, 1996).

Bentley, G. E., *The Jacobean and Caroline Stage*, 7 vols. (Oxford: Clarendon Press, 1941–68).

*The Profession of Dramatist in Shakespeare's Time, 1590–1642* (Princeton, NJ: Princeton University Press, 1971).

Bergeron, D. M., *Textual Patronage* in *English Drama, 1570–1640* (Aldershot: Ashgate, 2006).

"Stuart Civic Pageants and Textual Performance," *Renaissance Quarterly*, 51 (1998), 163–83.

"The Wax Figures in *The Duchess of Malfi*," *Studies in English Literature, 1500–1900*, 18 (1978), 331–9.

Bernau, A., *Virgins: A Cultural History* (London: Granta, 2007).

"'Britain': Original Myths and the Stories of," in E. Treharne and G. Walker (eds.), with the assistance of W. Green, *The Oxford Handbook of Medieval Literature in English* (Oxford University Press, 2010), pp. 629–48.

"Myths of Origin and the Struggle over Nationhood in Medieval and Early Modern England," in G. McMullan and D. Matthews (eds.), *Reading the Medieval in Early Modern England* (Cambridge University Press, 2007), pp. 106–18.

"'Saint, witch, man, maid or whore'? Joan of Arc and Writing History," in A. Bernau, R. Evans, and S. Salih (eds.), *Medieval Virginities* (Cardiff: University of Wales Press, 2003), pp. 213–33.

Berry, H. (ed.), "Playhouses, 1560–1660," Part III in G. Wickham, H. Berry, and W. Ingram (eds.), *English Professional Theatre, 1530–1660* (Cambridge University Press, 2000), pp. 287–674.

"Where Was the Playhouse in Which the Boy Choristers of St. Paul's Cathedral Performed Plays?," *Medieval and Renaissance Drama in England*, 13 (2001), 101–15.

Blayney, P. W. M., *The Bookshops in Paul's Cross Churchyard*, Occasional Papers of the Bibliographical Society (London: The Bibliographical Society, 1990).

Bloom, G., *Voice in Motion: Staging Gender, Shaping Sound in Early Modern England* (Philadelphia: University of Pennsylvania Press, 2007).

Boaistuau, P., *Theatrum Mundi, the Theatre or Rule of the World*, J. Alday (trans.) (London: J. Wyght, 1581).

Boulton, J., *Neighbourhood and Society: A London Suburb in the Seventeenth Century* (Cambridge University Press, 1987).

Bowers, R., "The Playhouse of the Choristers of Paul's, c. 1575–1608," *Theatre Notebook*, 54 (2000), 70–85.

Bradbrook, M. C., "Shakespeare and the Use of Disguise in Elizabethan Drama," *Essays in Criticism*, 2 (1952), 159–68.

Bradley, A. C., *Shakespearean Tragedy*, repr. (Houndmills: Palgrave Macmillan, 2007).

Brittin, N. A., *Thomas Middleton* (New York: Twayne, 1972).

Brodsky, V., "Widows in Late Elizabethan London: Remarriage, Economic Opportunities, and Family Orientations," in L. Bonfield *et al.* (eds.), *The World We Have Gained: Histories of Population and Social Structure* (Oxford: Blackwell, 1986), pp. 122–54.

Bromham, A. A., "Thomas Middleton's *The Triumphs of Truth*: City Politics in 1613," *The Seventeenth Century*, 10 (1995), 1–25.

Bromham, A. and Z. Bruzzi, The Changeling *and the Years of Crisis, 1619–24: A Hieroglyph of Britain* (London: Pinter, 1990).

Brooke, C. F. T., *The Life of Marlowe* (London: Methuen, 1930).

Brotton, J., *The Sale of the Late King's Goods. Charles I and His Art Collection* (London: Macmillan, 2006).

Bruster, D., *Drama and the Market in the Age of Shakespeare* (Cambridge University Press, 1992).

Bueler, L. E., "The Rhetoric of Change in *The Changeling*," *English Literary Renaissance*, 14 (1984), 95–113.

Bullen, A. H. (ed.), *The Works of Thomas Middleton*, 8 vols., The English Dramatists (London: J. C. Nimmo, 1885–6).

Burks, D. G., "'I'll want my will else': *The Changeling* and Women's Complicity with their Rapists," *ELH*, 62 (1995), 759–90.

Burton, R., *The Anatomy of Melancholy*, F. Dell and P. Jordan-Smith (eds.), repr. (New York: Tudor, 1938).

Butler, M., *The Stuart Court Masque and Political Culture* (Cambridge University Press, 2008).

Cano, D. S., "Entertainments in Madrid for the Prince of Wales: Political Functions of Festivals," in A. Samson (ed.), *The Spanish Match: Prince Charles's Journey to Madrid, 1623* (London: Ashgate, 2006), pp. 51–73.

Capp, B., *The World of John Taylor the Water-Poet, 1578–1653* (Oxford: Clarendon Press, 1994).

Carruthers, M. J., *The Book of Memory: A Study of Memory in Medieval Culture*, repr. (Cambridge University Press, 1998).

Carter, C., "Gondomar: Ambassador to James I," *The Historical Journal*, 7 (1964), 189–208.

Cathcart, C., *Marston, Rivalry, Rapprochement, and Jonson* (Aldershot: Ashgate, 2008).

Caxton, W., *The Game and Playe of the Chesse*, J. Adams (ed.), (Kalamazoo, MI: Medieval Institute Publications, 2009).

Chakravorty, S., *Society and Politics in the Plays of Thomas Middleton* (Oxford: Clarendon Press, 1996).

Chambers, E. K., *The Medieval Stage*, 2 vols. (Oxford: Clarendon Press, 1903).
*William Shakespeare: A Study of Facts and Problems*, 2 vols. (Oxford: Clarendon Press, 1930).

Chan, M., *Music in the Theatre of Ben Jonson* (Oxford: Clarendon Press, 1980).

Charlton, K., *Women, Religion, and Education in Early Modern England* (London: Routledge, 1999).

Christian, M. G., "A Sidelight on the Family History of Thomas Middleton," *Studies in Philology*, 44 (1947), 490–6.

Clare, J., *"Art made tongue-tied by authority": Elizabethan and Jacobean Dramatic Censorship*, 2nd edn. (Manchester University Press, 1999).

Clarke, S., *A Collection of the Eminent Divines* (London, 1662).

Cleaver, R., *A Godlie Forme of Householde Government* (London, 1598).

Clegg, C. S., ""Twill Much Enrich the Company of Stationers': Thomas Middleton and the London Book Trade, 1580–1627," in G. Taylor and J. Lavagnino (gen. eds.), *Thomas Middleton and Early Modern Textual Culture: A Companion to the Collected Works* (Oxford: Clarendon Press, 2007), pp. 247–59.

Cogswell, T., *The Blessed Revolution: English Politics and the Coming of War, 1621–1624* (Cambridge University Press, 1989).

"John Felton, Popular Political Culture and the Assassination of the Duke of Buckingham," *The Historical Journal*, 49 (2006), 357–85.

"Phaeton's Chariot: The Parliament-men and the Continental Crisis in 1621," in J. F. Merritt (ed.), *The Political World of Thomas Wentworth, Earl of Strafford, 1621–1641* (Cambridge University Press, 1996), pp. 24–46.

"Thomas Middleton and the Court, 1624: *A Game at Chess* in Context," *Huntington Library Quarterly*, 47 (1984), 273–88.

Cohen, J. J., *Of Giants: Sex, Monsters, and the Middle Ages* (Minneapolis: University of Minnesota Press, 1999).

Coke, E., *The Third Part of the Institutes of the Laws of England* (London, 1602).

Collinson, P., "The Theatre Constructs Puritanism," in D. L. Smith, R. Strier, and D. Bevington (eds.), *The Theatrical City: Culture, Society, and Politics, 1576–1649* (Cambridge University Press, 1995), pp. 157–69.

Coope, R., "The 'Long Gallery': Its Origins, Development, Use and Decoration," *Architectural History*, 29 (1986), 44–84.

Corrigan, B. J., "Middleton, *The Revenger's Tragedy*, and Crisis Literature," *Studies in English Literature, 1500–1900*, 38 (1998), 281–96.

Cotgrave, R., *A Dictionarie of the French and English Tongues* (London: 1611); repr. (New York and Hildesheim: George Olms Verlag, 1970).

Cowell, J., *The Interpreter* (Menston: Scolar Press, 1972; originally published 1607).

Cox, A., "Directing: *Revengers Tragedy*" (www.alexcox.com/dir_revengerstragedy.htm).

Cox, J. D. and D. S. Kastan, "Introduction," in J. D. Cox and D. S. Kastan (eds.), *A New History of Early English Drama* (New York: Columbia University Press, 1997).

Craig, H., "Grammatical Modality in English Plays from the 1580s to the 1640s," *English Literary Renaissance*, 30 (2000), 32–54.

Crashaw, W., *The Sermon Preached at the Crosse* (London: H. L. for Edmund Weauer, 1607).

Cressy, D., *Birth, Marriage and Death: Ritual, Religion, and the Life-Cycle in Tudor and Stuart England* (Oxford University Press, 1997).

*Bonfires and Bells: National Memory and the Protestant Calendar in Elizabethan and Stuart England* (London: Weidenfeld & Nicolson, 1989).

Croft, P., "The Reputation of Robert Cecil: Libels, Political Opinion and Popular Awareness in the Early Seventeenth Century," *Transactions of the Royal Historical Society*, 6th series (1991), 43–69.

Crooke, H., *Microcosmographia* (London, 1615).

Crystal, D., *A Dictionary of Linguistics and Phonetics* (Oxford: Blackwell, 1985).

Culpeper, N., *Directory for Midwives* (London, 1651).

Culpeper, N., *et al.*, *The Practice of Physick* (London, 1655).

Cummings, B., "Reformed Literature and Literature Reformed," in D. Wallace (ed.), *The Cambridge History of Medieval English Literature* (Cambridge University Press, 1999), pp. 821–51.

Cust, R., "News and Politics in Early Seventeenth Century England," *Past and Present*, 112 (1986), 60–90.

Cutts, J. P., "Jacobean Masque and Stage Music," *Music & Letters*, 35 (1954), 185–200.

*La musique de scène de la troupe de Shakespeare: the King's Men sous le règne de Jacques 1er* (Paris: Centre National de la Recherche Scientifique, 1959).

"The Original Music to Middleton's *The Witch*," *Shakespeare Quarterly*, 7 (1956), 203–9.

"Who Wrote the Hecate-Scene," *Vorträge und Aufsätze/ Shakespeare-Jahrbuch*, 94 (1958), 200–2.

Daileader, C., *Eroticism on the Renaissance Stage: Transcendence, Desire, and the Limits of the Visible* (Cambridge University Press, 1998).

Darby, T. L., "Cervantes in England: The Influence of Golden-Age Prose Fiction on Jacobean Drama, *c.* 1615–1625," *Bulletin of Hispanic Studies*, 74 (1997), 15–31.

Darby, T. L. and A. Samson, "Cervantes on the Jacobean Stage," in J. A. G. Ardila (ed.), *The Cervantean Heritage: Reception and Influence of Cervantes in Britain* (Oxford: Legenda, 2009), pp. 206–22.

Davis, K., "The Urbanization of the Human Population," in R. T. LeGates and F. Stout (eds.), *The City Reader* (London: Routledge, 1996), pp. 2–11.

Dawson, A. B., "*Women Beware Women* and the Economy of Rape," *Studies in English Literature, 1500–1900*, 27 (1987), 303–20.

Day, J., *Law Tricks* (Oxford: Malone Society Reprints, 1950).

Dekker, T. and T. Middleton, *News from Gravesend: Sent to Nobody* and *Meeting of Gallants at an Ordinary*, in F. P. Wilson (ed.), *The Plague Pamphlets of Thomas Dekker* (Oxford: Clarendon Press, 1925), pp. 63–134.

Derrida, J., "The Law of Genre," *Critical Inquiry*, 7 (1980), 55–83.

Dickson, P. G. M., *The Financial Revolution in England: A Study in the Development of Public Credit, 1688–1756* (London: Macmillan, 1967).

Dietz, B., "Overseas Trade and Metropolitan Growth," in A. L. Beier and R. Finlay (eds.), *London 1500–1700: The Making of the Metropolis* (London: Longman, 1986), pp. 115–40.

Dietz, F., *English Public Finance, 1485–1641*, 2nd edn., 2 vols. (London: Cass, 1964).

Dobson, M. and S. Wells (eds.), *The Oxford Companion to Shakespeare* (Oxford University Press, 2001).

Dodsley, R. (ed.), *A Select Collection of Old Plays* (London, 1744).

Dodsley, R. and I. Reed (eds.), *A Select Collection of Old Plays: In Twelve Volumes* (London: printed by J. Nicols for J. Dodsley, 1780).

Duckles, V., "The Music for the Lyrics in Early Seventeenth-Century English Drama: A Bibliography of the Primary Sources," in J. H. Long (ed.), *Music in English Renaissance Drama* (Lexington: University of Kentucky Press, 1968), pp. 117–60.

Duffin, R. W., *Shakespeare's Songbook* (London: W. W. Norton, 2004).

Dyce, A. (ed.), *The Works of Thomas Middleton*, 5 vols. (London, 1840).

Dynes, W. R., "The Trickster Figure in Jacobean City Comedy," *Studies in English Literature, 1500–1900*, 33 (1993), 365–85.

Eccles, M., "Middleton's Birth and Education," *Review of English Studies*, 7 (1931), 431–41.

"Thomas Middleton a Poett," *Studies in Philology*, 54 (1957), 516–36.

Eliot, T. S., *Elizabethan Essays* (London: Faber and Faber, 1963).

Elliott, V. B., "Single Women in the London Marriage Market: Age, Status and Mobility, 1598–1619," in R. B. Outhwaite (ed.), *Marriage and Society: Studies in the Social History of Marriage* (London: Europa, 1981), pp. 81–100.

Emmerson, R. K., "Dramatic History: On the Diachronic and Synchronic in the Study of Early English Drama," *Journal of Medieval and Early Modern Studies*, 35 (winter 2005), 39–66.

Erickson, A. L., *Women and Property in Early Modern England* (New York: Routledge, 1993).

Evans, H. C., "Comic Constables – Fictional and Historical," *Shakespeare Quarterly*, 20 (1969), 427–33.

Fairholt, F. W., *Lord Mayor's Pageants: Being Collections Towards a History of these Annual Celebrations*, part 1 (London: Percy Society, 1843).

Falco, R., "Medieval and Reformation Roots," in A. F. Kinney (ed.), *A Companion to Renaissance Drama*, repr. (Oxford: Blackwell, 2004), pp. 240–56.

Ferrell, L. A., "Religious Persuasions, *c.* 1580–*c.* 1620," in A. F. Kinney (ed.), *A Companion to Renaissance Drama*, repr. (Oxford: Blackwell, 2004), pp. 40–9.

Field, N., *Amends for Ladies*, in W. Peery (ed.), *The Plays of Nathan Field* (Austin: University of Texas Press, 1950), pp. 143–294.

Fincham, K., "Prelacy and Politics: Archbishop Abbot's Defence of Protestant Orthodoxy," *Historical Research*, 61 (1988), 36–64.

Fincham, K. and N. Tyacke, *Altars Restored: The Changing Face of English Religious Worship, 1547–c. 1700* (Oxford University Press, 2007).

Finlay, R., *Population and Metropolis: The Demography of London, 1580–1650* (Cambridge University Press, 1981).

Finney, G. L., *Musical Backgrounds for English Literature: 1580–1650* (New Brunswick, NJ: Rutgers University Press, 1962); repr. (Westport, CT: Greenwood Press, 1976).

Fisher, F. J., "Some Experiments in Company Organization in the Early Seventeenth Century," *Economic History Review*, 4 (1933), 177–94.

Fitzgeoffrey, H., *Satyres and Satirical Epigrams: with Certaine Observations at Black-Fryers* (London, 1617).

Fletcher, A., *Gender, Sex, and Subordination in England, 1500–1900* (New Haven, CT: Yale University Press, 1995).

Florio, J., *A Worlde of Wordes, Or Most copious, and exact Dictionarie in Italian and English* (London, 1598).

Foakes, R. A., *Illustrations of the English Stage, 1580–1642* (London: Scolar Press, 1985).

Folkerth, W., *The Sound of Shakespeare* (New York: Routledge, 2002).

Forman, V., "Marked Angels: Counterfeits, Commodities, and *The Roaring Girl*," *Renaissance Quarterly*, 54 (2001), 1531–60.

Fowler, A., *Kinds of Literature* (Cambridge, MA: Harvard University Press, 1982).

"The Formation of Genres in the Renaissance and After," *New Literary History*, 34 (2003), 185–200.

Foyster, E., *Manhood in Early Modern England: Honour, Sex, and Marriage* (London: Longman, 1999).

Freud, S., *The Standard Edition of the Complete Psychological Works*, James Strachey (ed.), 24 vols. (London: Hogarth Press, 1955–74).

Furdell, E. L., *The Royal Doctors, 1485–1714: Medical Personnel at the Tudor and Stuart Courts* (Rochester, NY: University of Rochester Press, 2001).

Gainesford, T., *The Rich Cabinet* (London: J. B. for Roger Jackson, 1616).

Gair, R., *The Children of Paul's: The Story of a Theatre Company, 1553–1608* (Cambridge University Press, 1982).

Garber, M., "The Insincerity of Women," in V. Finucci and R. M. Schwarz (eds.), *Desire in the Renaissance: Psychoanalysis and Literature* (Princeton, NJ: Princeton University Press, 1994), pp. 19–38.

Gaule, J., *Distractions or The Holy Madnesse* (London, 1629).

Gillespie, A., *Print Culture and the Medieval Author: Chaucer, Lydgate, and Their Books, 1473–1557* (Oxford University Press, 2006).

Gittings, C., *Death, Burial, and the Individual in Early Modern England* (London: Croom Helm, 1984).

Gordon, A., "Performing London: the Map and the City in Ceremony," in A. Gordon and B. Klein (eds.), *Literature, Mapping and the Politics of Space in Early Modern Britain* (Cambridge University Press, 2001), pp. 69–88.

Görlach, M., *Introduction to Early Modern English* (Cambridge University Press, 1991).

Gossett, S., "Sibling Power: Middleton and Rowley's *A Fair Quarrel*," *Philological Quarterly*, 71 (1992), 437–57.

Gouge, W., *Of Domesticall Duties* (London, 1622).

Gouk, P., *Music, Science and Natural Magic in Seventeenth-Century England* (New Haven, CT: Yale University Press, 1999).

"Music, Melancholy and Medical Spirits in Early Modern Thought," in P. Horden (ed.), *Music as Medicine: The History of Music Therapy since Antiquity* (Aldershot: Ashgate, 2000), pp. 173–94.

Gowing, L., *Domestic Dangers: Women, Words, and Sex in Early Modern London* (Oxford: Clarendon Press, 1996).

Greenblatt, S., *Renaissance Self-Fashioning: From More to Shakespeare* (University of Chicago Press, 1984).

Greenblatt, S. (gen. ed.), *The Norton Shakespeare* (New York: W. W. Norton, 1997).

Griffin, B., *Playing the Past: Approaches to English Historical Drama, 1385–1600* (Woodbridge: D. S. Brewer, 2001).

Griffiths, P., *Lost Londons: Change, Crime, and Control in the Capital City* (Cambridge University Press, 2009).

"The Structure of Prostitution in Elizabethan London," *Continuity and Change*, 8 (1993), 39–63.

Griffiths, P. and M. S. R. Jenner (eds.), *Londinopolis: Essays in the Cultural and Social History of Early Modern London* (Manchester University Press, 2000).

Guarini, G., "A Compendium of Tragicomic Poetry", in A. Gilbert (ed.), *Literary Criticism: Plato to Dryden* (Detroit: Wayne State University Press, 1962), pp. 504–33.

Guillemeau, J., *Childe-Birth, or The Happy Deliverie of Women* (London, 1612).

Gurr, A., *Playgoing in Shakespeare's London*, 3rd edn. (Cambridge University Press, 2004).

*Shakespeare's Opposites: The Admiral's Company, 1594–1625* (Cambridge University Press, 2009).

*The Shakespearian Playing Companies* (Oxford: Clarendon Press, 1996).

*The Shakespearean Stage: 1576–1642*, 4th edn. (Cambridge University Press, 2008).

"A New Theatre Historicism," in P. Holland and S. Orgel (eds.), *From Script to Stage in Early Modern England* (New York: Palgrave Macmillan, 2004), pp. 71–88.

Hadfield, A., *Literature, Politics and National Identity: Reformation to Renaissance* (Cambridge University Press, 1994).

Hall, J., *Virgidemiarum. Sixe bookes. First three books, of tooth-less satyrs* (London, 1597).

*Virgidemiarum. The three last bookes. Of byting satyres* (London, 1598).

Hammer, P., *Elizabeth's Wars: War, Government and Society in Tudor England, 1544–1604* (London: Palgrave, 2003).

Hardin, W., "'Pipe-pilgrimages' and 'fruitful rivers': Thomas Middleton's Civic Entertainments and the Water Supply of Early Stuart London," *Renaissance Papers* (1993), 63–73.

Harding, V., "The Population of London, 1550–1700: A Review of the Published Evidence," *London Journal*, 15 (1990), 111–28.

Harrington, J., *A Treatise on a Play* (London, 1597).

Harris, G., "'This is not a pipe': Water Supply, Incontinent Sources, and the Leaky Body Politic," in R. Burt and J. M. Archer (eds.), *Enclosure Acts: Sexuality, Property, and Culture in Early Modern England* (Ithaca, NY: Cornell University Press, 1994), pp. 216–23.

Harris, J. G., *Foreign Bodies* (Cambridge University Press, 1997).

Hebb, D., *Piracy and the English Government, 1616–1642* (Aldershot: Ashgate, 1994).

Heinemann, M., *Puritanism and Theatre: Opposition Drama Under the Early Stuarts* (Cambridge University Press, 1980).

Henslowe, P., *Henslowe's Diary*, R. A. Foakes (ed.), 2nd edn. (Cambridge University Press, 2002).

*Henslowe Papers, Being Documents Supplementary to Henslowe's Diary*, W. W. Greg (ed.) (London: A. H. Bullen, 1907).

Henze, C. A., "Invisible Collaborations: The Impact of Johnson's Original Music," *Text and Presentation*, 22 (2001), 75–87.

Hickman, D., "Religious Belief and Pious Practice Among London's Elizabethan Elite," *Historical Journal*, 42 (1999), 941–60.

Hillebrand, H. N., *The Child Actors: A Chapter in Elizabethan Stage History* (Urbana: University of Illinois Press, 1926).

"Thomas Middleton's *The Viper's Brood*," *Modern Language Notes*, 42 (1927), 35–8.

Hirschfeld, H. A., "What Do Women Know? *The Roaring Girl* and the Wisdom of Tiresias," *Renaissance Drama*, 32 (2003), 123–46.

Holdsworth, R. V., "Introduction," in R. V. Holdsworth (ed.), *Three Jacobean Revenge Tragedies:* The Revenger's Tragedy, Women Beware Women, The Changeling: *A Casebook* (London: Macmillan, 1990), pp. 11–25.

"Middleton's Authorship of *A Yorkshire Tragedy*," *Review of English Studies*, 45 (1994), 4–6.

"*The Revenger's Tragedy* as a Middleton Play (1989)," in R. V. Holdsworth (ed.), *Three Jacobean Revenge Tragedies:* The Revenger's Tragedy, Women Beware Women, The Changeling: *A Casebook* (London: Macmillan, 1990) pp. 79–105.

"*The Revenger's Tragedy* on Stage (1989)," in R. V. Holdsworth (ed.), *Three Jacobean Revenge Tragedies:* The Revenger's Tragedy, Women Beware Women, The Changeling: *A Casebook* (London: Macmillan, 1990) pp. 105–20.

"*Women Beware Women* and *The Changeling* on Stage (1989)", in R. V. Holdsworth (ed.), *Three Jacobean Revenge Tragedies:* The Revenger's Tragedy, Women Beware Women, The Changeling: *A Casebook*, (London: Macmillan, 1990) pp. 247–74.

Hollander, J., "Musica Mundana and *Twelfth Night*," in S. Orgel and S. Keilen (eds.), *Shakespeare and the Arts* (New York: Garland Publishing, 1999), pp. 37–82.

Holman, P., *Dowland: Lachrimae (1604)* (Cambridge University Press, 1999).

*Four and Twenty Fiddlers: The Violin at the English Court, 1540–1690* (Oxford: Clarendon Press, 1993).

Holmes, D., *The Art of Thomas Middleton: A Critical Study* (Oxford: Clarendon Press, 1970).

Hooker, R., *Works*, John Keble (ed.), 7th edn., 3 vols. (Oxford, 1888).

Hope, J., "Second Person Singular Pronouns in Records of Early Modern 'Spoken' English," *Neuphilologische Mitteilungen*, 94 (1993), 83–100.

Hoskins, W. G., *The Age of Plunder: The England of Henry VIII, 1500–1547* (London: Longman, 1976).

Howard, J., *Theater of a City: The Places of London Comedy, 1598–1642* (Philadelphia: University of Pennsylvania Press, 2007).

Hughes, P. L. and J. F. Larkin (eds.), *Tudor Royal Proclamations*, 3 vols. (New Haven, CT: Yale University Press, 1969).

Hunt, M., *The Middling Sort: Commerce, Gender and the Family in England, 1680–1780* (Los Angeles: University of California Press, 1996).

Hutchings, M. and A. A. Bromham, *Middleton and His Collaborators* (Plymouth: Northcote House, 2008).

Hutson, L., *The Invention of Suspicion: Law and Mimesis in Shakespeare and Renaissance Drama* (Oxford University Press, 2007).

*Thomas Nashe in Context* (Oxford: Clarendon Press, 1989).

*The Usurer's Daughter: Male Friendship and Fictions of Women in Sixteenth-Century England* (New York: Routledge, 1994).

Ingram, M., *Church Courts, Sex and Marriage in England, 1570–1640* (Cambridge University Press, 1987).

Ioppolo, G., *Dramatists and their Manuscripts in the Age of Shakespeare, Jonson, Middleton, and Heywood: Authorship, Authority and the Playhouse*, Routledge Studies in Renaissance Literature and Culture, 6 (London: Routledge, 2006).

Ives, E. W., "The Purpose and Making of the Later Year Books," *Law Quarterly Review*, 89 (1973), 64–88.

Jackson, M. P., *Studies in Attribution: Middleton and Shakespeare* (Salzburg: Institut für Anglistik und Amerikanistik, Universität Salzburg, 1975).

"Early Modern Authorship: Canons and Chronologies," in G. Taylor and J. Lavagnino (gen. eds.), *Thomas Middleton and Early Modern Textual Culture: A Companion to the Collected Works* (Oxford: Clarendon Press, 2007), pp. 80–97.

Jackson, T., *The Convert's Happiness* (London, 1609).

James VI and I, *Basilikon Doron, or His Maiesties Instructions to His Dearest Sonne, Henry the Prince* in *The Workes of The Most High and Mightie Prince, Iames* (London, 1603).

*His Maiesties Speach in this last session of Parliament* (London, 1605).

*Political Writings*, J. P. Sommerville (ed.), (Cambridge University Press, 1994).

"The Trew Law of Free Monarchies," in N. Rhodes, J. Richards, and J. Marshall (eds.), *King James VI and I: Selected Writings* (Aldershot: Ashgate, 2003), pp. 259–79.

Jameson, F., *Postmodernism, or, the Cultural Logic of Late Capitalism* (Durham, NC: Duke University Press, 1992).

Johnson, A. H., *The History of the Worshipful Company of the Drapers of London*, 5 vols. (Oxford: Clarendon Press, 1914–22).

Johnson, D. J., *Southwark and the City* (Oxford University Press, 1969).

Johnson, N., *The Actor as Playwright in Early Modern Drama* (Cambridge University Press, 1997).

Johnson, S., *A Dictionary of the English Language*, 2nd edn., 2 vols. (London, 1755–6).

Jones, A. R. and P. Stallybrass, *Renaissance Clothing and the Materials of Memory* (Cambridge University Press, 2000).

Jonson, B., *Ben Jonson*, C. H. Herford, P. Simpson, and E. Simpson, 11 vols. (Oxford: Clarendon Press, 1925–52).

*Epicene, or The Silent Woman*, in G. Campbell (ed.), *Ben Jonson: The Alchemist and Other Plays*, Oxford World Classics, (Oxford University Press, 1995).

Jorgens, E. B., "On Matters of Manner and Music in Jacobean and Caroline Song," *English Literary Renaissance*, 10 (1980), 239–63.

Jowett, J., "For Many of Your Companies: Middleton's Early Readers," in G. Taylor and J. Lavagnino (gen. eds.), *Thomas Middleton and Early Modern Textual Culture: A Companion to the Collected Works* (Oxford: Clarendon Press, 2007), pp. 286–327.

"Middleton's *No Wit* at the Fortune," *Renaissance Drama*, NS 22 (1991), 191–208.

"The Pattern of Collaboration in *Timon of Athens*," in B. Boyd (ed.), *Words that Count: Essays on Early Modern Authorship in Honor of MacDonald P. Jackson* (Newark, DE: University of Delaware Press, 2004), pp. 181–208.

"Thomas Middleton," in A. F. Kinney (ed.), *A Companion to Renaissance Drama* (Oxford: Blackwell, 2002), pp. 507–23.

Kathman, D., "Grocers, Goldsmiths, and Drapers: Freemen and Apprentices in the Elizabethan Theater," *Shakespeare Quarterly*, 55 (2004), 1–49.

"How Old Were Shakespeare's Boy Actors?," *Shakespeare Survey*, 58 (2005), 220–46.

Katritzky, M. A., *Women, Medicine, and Theatre, 1500–1750* (Aldershot: Ashgate, 2007).

Kelen, S. A., *Langland's Early Modern Identities* (New York: Palgrave Macmillan, 2007).

Kellett, J. R., "The Breakdown of Gild and Corporation Control over the Handicraft and Retail Trade in London," *Economic History Review*, 2nd series, 10 (1958), 382–4.

Kierkegaard, S., *The Concept of Anxiety*, R. Thomte (ed. and trans.) (Princeton, NJ: Princeton University Press, 1980).

*Repetition (with Fear and Trembling)*, H. V. Hong and E. H. Hong (eds. and trans.) (Princeton, NJ: Princeton University Press, 1983).

Kitch, A., "The Character of Credit and the Problem of Belief in Middleton's City Comedies," *Studies in English Literature, 1500–1900*, 47 (2007), 403–26.

Knapp, J., "What Is a Co-Author?," *Representations*, 89 (2005), 1–29.

Knutson, R. L., *Playing Companies and Commerce in Shakespeare's Time* (Cambridge University Press, 2001).

"Two Playhouses, Both Alike in Dignity," *Shakespeare Studies*, 30 (2002), 111–17.

Kramer, S., *The English Craft Gilds and the Government* (New York: Columbia University Press, 1905).

Lake, D. J., *The Canon of Thomas Middleton's Plays: Internal Evidence for the Major Problems of Authorship* (Cambridge University Press, 1975).

Lake, P., "Anti-Popery: The Structure of a Prejudice," in R. Cust and A. Hughes (eds.), *Conflict in Early Stuart England: Studies in Religion and Politics, 1603–1642* (London: Longman, 1989), pp. 72–106.

"Calvinism and the English Church, 1570–1635," *Past and Present*, 114 (1986), 32–76.

"From *Leicester his Commonwealth* to *Sejanus his Fall*: Ben Jonson and the politics of Roman (Catholic) virtue," in E. Shagan (ed.), *Catholics and the 'Protestant Nation': Religious Politics and Identity in Early Modern England* (Manchester University Press, 2005), pp. 128–61.

Lake, P. and M. Questier, *The Antichrist's Lewd Hat. Protestants, Papists, and Players in Post-Reformation England* (New Haven, CT: Yale University Press, 2002).

Lancashire, A., "*The Witch*: Stage Flop or Political Mistake?," in K. Friedenreich (ed.), *"Accompaninge the players": Essays Celebrating Thomas Middleton, 1580–1980* (New York: AMS Press, 1983), pp. 161–83.

Langbaine, G., *An Account of the English Dramatick Poets* (London, 1691).

Larkin, J. F. and P. L. Hughes (eds.), *Stuart Royal Proclamations*, 2 vols (Oxford: Clarendon Press, 1973).

Lehmann, C., "Performing the 'Live': Cinema, Simulation, and the Death of the Real in Alex Cox's *Revengers Tragedy*," in S. Werner (ed.), *New Directions for Renaissance Drama* (Houndmills: Palgrave Macmillan, 2010), pp. 195–222.

Leibniz, G., *The Shorter Leibniz Texts*, L. Strickland (trans.) (New York: Continuum, 2006).

Leinwand, T., *Theatre, Finance, and Society in Early Modern England* (Cambridge University Press, 1999).

Lerer, S., "William Caxton," in D. Wallace (ed.), *The Cambridge History of Medieval English Literature* (Cambridge University Press, 1999), pp. 720–38.

Levin, R., "The Four Plots of 'A Chaste Maid in Cheapside'," *Review of English Studies* 16 (1965), 14–24.

Limon, J., *Dangerous Matter: English Drama and Politics in 1623/24* (Cambridge University Press, 1986).

Lindley, D., *The Trials of Frances Howard: Fact and Fiction at the Court of King James* (London: Routledge, 1993).

Locke, J., *An Essay Concerning Human Understanding*, P. H. Nidditch (ed.) (Oxford: Clarendon Press, 1975).

Lockyer, R., *Buckingham: The Life and Political Career of George Villiers, First Duke of Buckingham, 1592–1628* (New York: Longman, 1981).

Long, J. H., *Shakespeare's Use of Music: A Study of the Music and its Performance in the Original Production of Seven Comedies* (Gainesville: University of Florida Press, 1961).

Love, H., *The Culture and Commerce of Texts. Scribal Publication in Seventeenth-Century England*, pb. edn. (Amherst: University of Massachusetts Press, 1998). Originally published as *Scribal Production in Seventeenth-Century England* (Oxford: Clarendon Press, 1993).

Low, J. A., *Manhood and the Duel: Masculinity in Early Modern Drama and Culture* (New York: Palgrave Macmillan, 2003).

Lucas, F. L. (ed.), *The Complete Works of John Webster*, 4 vols. (London: Chatto & Windus, 1927).

MacDonald, M., "Introduction," in M. Macdonald (ed.), *Witchcraft and Hysteria in Elizabethan London* (London: Routledge, 1990).

Machan, T. W., *Textual Criticism and Middle English Texts* (Charlottesville: University Press of Virginia, 1994).

Malcolmson, C., "'As Tame as the Ladies': Politics and Gender in *The Changeling*," *English Literary Renaissance*, 20 (1990), 320–39.

Manley, L., *Literature and Culture in Early Modern London* (Cambridge University Press, 1995).

"Civic Drama," in A. F. Kinney (ed.), *A Companion to Renaisssance Drama*, repr. (Oxford: Blackwell, 2004), pp. 294–313.

Marion, J.-L., "The Saturated Phenomenon," *The Visible and the Revealed*, C. M. Gschwandtner *et al.* (trans.) (New York: Fordham University Press, 2008).

Masten, J., *Textual Intercourse: Collaboration, Authorship, and Sexualities in Renaissance Drama*, Cambridge Studies in Renaissance Literature and Culture, 14 (Cambridge University Press, 1997).

Mathee, R., "Exotic Substances: The Introduction and Global Spread of Tobacco, Coffee, Cocoa, Tea, and Distilled Liquor, Sixteenth to Eighteenth Centuries," in R. Porter and M. Teich (eds.), *Drugs and Narcotics in History* (Cambridge University Press, 1995), pp. 24–51.

McCabe, R., "Elizabethan Satire and the Bishops' Ban of 1599," *Yearbook of English Studies*, 11 (1981), 188–94.

McClure, N. E. (ed.), *The Letters of John Chamberlain*, 2 vols. (Philadelphia: American Philosophical Society, 1939).

McCoy, R., *The Rites of Knighthood: The Literature and Politics of Elizabethan Chivalry* (Berkeley: University of California Press, 1989).

McCulloch, D., *Reformation: Europe's House Divided, 1490–1700* (London: Penguin Books, 2004).

McLuskie, K., *Renaissance Dramatists* (Atlantic Highlands, NJ: Humanities Press International, 1989).

McMillin S., "Middleton's Theatres," in G. Taylor and J. Lavagnino (gen. eds.), *Thomas Middleton: The Collected Works* (Oxford: Clarendon Press, 2007), pp. 74–87.

"Professional Playwriting," in D. S. Kastan (ed.), *A Companion to Shakespeare* (Malden, MA: Blackwell, 1999), pp. 225–38.

McMullan, G., "*The Changeling* and the Dynamics of Ugliness," in E. Smith and G. A. Sullivan, Jr. (eds.), *The Cambridge Companion to English Renaissance Tragedy* (Cambridge University Press, 2010).

"The Colonisation of Britain on the Jacobean Stage," in G. McMullan and D. Matthews (eds.), *Reading the Medieval in Early Modern England* (Cambridge University Press, 2007), pp. 119–40.

McRae, A., *God Speed the Plough: The Representation of Agrarian England, 1500–1660* (Cambridge University Press, 1996).

*Literature, Satire and the Early Stuart State* (Cambridge University Press, 2004).

Meisel, M., *How Plays Work* (Oxford University Press, 2007).

Mendelson, S. and P. Crawford, *Women in Early Modern England, 1550–1720* (Oxford: Clarendon Press, 1998).

Ménil, A., "Mesure pour mesure: théâtre et cinéma chez Jacques Rivette," in S. Liandrat-Guigues (ed.), *Jacques Rivette: Critique et cineaste* (Paris: Lettres modernes: Minard, 1998), pp. 67–96.

Merritt, J. F., "Puritans, Laudians, and the Phenomenon of Church-Building in Jacobean London," *The Historical Journal*, 41 (1998), 935–60.

(ed.), *Imagining Early Modern London: Perceptions and Portrayals of the City from Stow to Strype, 1598–1720* (Cambridge University Press, 2001).

Middleton, T., *A Chaste Maid in Cheapside*, C. Barber (ed.) (Edinburgh: Oliver & Boyd, 1969).

*The Ghost of Lucrece*, J. Q. Adams (ed.) (New York and London: Charles Scribner's Sons, 1937).

*Hengist, King of Kent; or, The Mayor of Queenborough*, R. C. Bald (ed.) (New York and London: Charles Scribner's Sons, 1938).

*A Yorkshire Tragedy*, B. Gaines (ed.) (London: Palgrave, 1988).

Middleton, T. and W. Rowley, *The Changeling*, M. Neill (ed.), (London: A&C Black-Methuen, 2006).

*The Changeling*, P. Thomson (ed.) (London: A&C Black, 1990).

Monaco, J., *The New Wave: Truffaut, Godard, Chabrol, Rohmer, Rivette* (New York: Harbor Electronic Publishing, 2004).

Morley, T., *A Plaine and Easie Introduction to Practicall Musicke* (London: Peter Short, 1597).

Moulsworth, M., "Memorandum," in R. C. Evans and A. C. Little (eds.), *"The Muses Females Are": Martha Moulsworth and Other Women Writers of the English Renaissance* (West Cornwall, CT: Locust Hill, 1995).

Mukherji, S., *Law and Representation in Early Modern England* (Cambridge University Press, 1996).

Muldrew, C., *The Economy of Obligation: The Culture of Credit and Social Relations in Early Modern England* (New York: Palgrave, 1998).

Munro, I., *The Figure of the Crowd in Early Modern London: The City and its Double* (New York: Palgrave Macmillan, 2005).

Munro, L., "Governing the Pen to the Capacity of the Stage: Reading the Red Bull and Clerkenwell," *Early Theatre*, 9 (2006), 99–113.

Murphy, A., *Shakespeare in Print: A History and Chronology of Shakespeare Publishing* (Cambridge University Press, 2003).

Nashe, T., *Pierce Penniless, His Supplication to the Divell* (London: Abell Jeffres, 1592).

*The Works of Thomas Nashe*, R. B. McKerrow (ed.), 5 vols. (Oxford University Press, 1904–10).

National Archives, London (formerly Public Record Office), State Papers Domestic, James I, SP 14.

Neal, L., *The Rise of Financial Capitalism: International Capital Markets in the Age of Reason* (Cambridge University Press, 1990).

Neely, C. T., *Distracted Subjects: Madness and Gender in Shakespeare and Early Modern Culture* (Ithaca, NY: Cornell University Press, 2004).

"Hot Blood: Estranging Mediterranean Bodies in Early Modern Medical and Dramatic Texts," in S. Moss and K. L. Peterson (eds.), *Disease, Diagnosis and Cure on the Early Modern Stage* (Aldershot: Ashgate, 2004), pp. 55–68.

Neill, M., *Issues of Death: Mortality and Identity in English Renaissance Tragedy* (Oxford: Clarendon Press, 1997).

"Death and *The Revenger's Tragedy*," in G. A. Sullivan, Jr. *et al.* (eds.), *Early Modern English Drama: A Critical Companion* (Oxford University Press, 2006), pp. 164–76.

Nichols, J., *The Plea of the Innocent* (London, 1602).

Nicolson, A., *Arcadia. The Dream of Perfection in Renaissance England*, pb. edn. (London: Harper Perennial, 2009). Originally published as *The Earls of Paradise* (London: Harper Press, 2008).

O'Callaghan, M., *Thomas Middleton: Renaissance Dramatist* (Edinburgh University Press, 2009).

O'Hara, D., *Courtship and Constraint: Rethinking the Making of Marriage in Tudor England* (Manchester University Press, 2000).

Orgel, S., *Impersonations: The Performance of Gender in Shakespeare's England* (Cambridge University Press, 1996).

"The Book of the Play," in P. Holland and S. Orgel (eds.), *From Performance to Print in Shakespeare's England* (New York: Palgrave Macmillan, 2006), pp. 13–54.

"Foreword" in R. W. Duffin, *Shakespeare's Songbook* (New York: W. W. Norton, 2004).

Orlin, L., *Locating Privacy in Tudor London* (Oxford University Press, 2007).

Overbury, T., *The Overburian Characters: to which is added, A wife*, W. J. Paylor (ed.) (Oxford: Blackwell, 1936).

*Oxford Dictionary of National Biography*, H. C. G. Matthew and B. Harrison (eds.) (Oxford University Press, 2004–10).

Pahl, R. E. (ed.), *Readings in Urban Sociology* (Oxford University Press, 1968).

Palfrey, S. and T. Stern, *Shakespeare in Parts* (Oxford University Press, 2007).

Panek, J., *Widows and Suitors in Early Modern English Comedy* (Cambridge University Press, 2004).

Parish, H. L., *Monks, Miracles and Magic: Reformation Representations of the Medieval Church* (London: Routledge, 2005).

Parker, G., *The Thirty Years War* (London: Routledge, 1987).

Parker, P. (ed.), *The Shakespeare Encyclopedia: Life, Works, World, and Legacy* (New York: Greenwood, 2010).

Paster, G. K., "Leaky Vessels: The Incontinent Women of City Comedy," *Renaissance Drama*, 18 (1987), 43–65.

Paterson, A. and A. Samson, *Spanish–English Translations Database, 1500–1640* (http://ems.kcl.ac.uk/content/proj/anglo/pro-anglo.html).

Patterson, L., "On the Margin: Postmodernism, Ironic History, and Medieval Studies," *Speculum*, 65 (1990), 87–108.

Patterson, W. B., *King James VI and I and the Reunion of Christendom* (Cambridge University Press, 1997).

Pavel, T., "Literary Genres as Norms and Good Habits," *New Literary History*, 34 (2003), 201–10.

Peck, L. L., *Court Patronage and Corruption in Early Stuart England* (London: Routledge, 1993).

"Building, Buying and Collecting in London, 1600–1625," in L. C. Orlin (ed.), *Material London ca.1600* (Philadelphia: University of Pennsylvania Press, 2000), pp. 268–89.

Peck, L. L. (ed.), *The Mental World of the Jacobean Court* (Cambridge University Press, 1991).

Pennell, S., "'Great quantities of gooseberry pye and baked clod of beef': Victualling and Eating Out in Early Modern London," in P. Griffiths and M. S. R. Jenner (eds.), *Londinopolis: Essays in the Cultural and Social History of Early Modern London* (Manchester University Press, 2000), pp. 228–49.

Perry, C., *Literature and Favoritism in Early Modern England* (Cambridge University Press, 2006).

Peterson, K. L., "The Performing Arts," in S. Moss and K. L. Peterson (eds.), *Disease, Diagnosis and Cure on the Early Modern Stage* (Aldershot: Ashgate, 2004), pp. 3–28.

Phialas, P. G., "Middleton's Early Contact with the Law," *Studies in Philology*, 52 (1955), 186–94.

Pollard, T., *Drugs and Theater in Early Modern England* (Oxford University Press, 2005).

"The Pleasures and Perils of Smoking in Early Modern England," in S. Gilman and Z. Xun (eds.), *A Cultural History of Smoking* (London: Reaktion Press, 2004), pp. 38–45.

Pollock, J., "Le Théâtre et la peste: les dramaturges élisabéthains revus par Antonin Artaud," in F. Laroque and F. Lessay (eds.), *Esthétiques de la nouveauté à la Renaissance* (Paris: Presses de la Sorbonne Nouvelle, 2001), pp. 171–8.

Prestwich, M., *Cranfield: Politics and Profit under the Early Stuarts* (Oxford University Press, 1966).

Prynne, W., *Histrio-Mastix: The Player's Scourge* (London, 1633).

Purkiss, D., *The Witch in History: Early Modern and Twentieth-Century Representations* (New York: Routledge, 1996).

Rankins, W., *A Mirrour of Monsters* (London, 1587).

Rappaport, S., *Worlds Within Worlds: Structures of Life in Sixteenth-Century London* (Cambridge University Press, 1989).

Rasmussen, E., *A Textual Companion to* Doctor Faustus, The Revels Plays Companion Library (Manchester University Press, 1993).

Review of G. Taylor and J. Jowett, *Shakespeare Reshaped, 1606–1623, Modern Philology*, 94 (1996), 233–7.

Raynalde, T., *The Birth of Mankind*, E. Hobby (ed.), (Surrey: Ashgate, 2009).

Read, S., "Puns: Serious Wordplay," in S. Adamson, G. Alexander, and K. Ettenhuber (eds.), *Renaissance Figures of Speech* (Cambridge University Press, 2007), pp. 119–40.

Redworth, G., *The Prince and the Infanta: The Cultural Politics of the Spanish Match* (New Haven, CT: Yale University Press, 2003).

Rhodes, N., *Elizabethan Grotesque* (London: Routledge and Kegan Paul, 1980).

Rich, B., *The Excellency of Good Women* (London, 1613).

*The Irish Hubbub, or, The English Hue and Crie* (London: John Marriot, 1617).

Ricks, C. "The Moral and Poetic Structure of *The Changeling*," *Essays in Criticism*, 10 (1960), 290–306.

"Word-Play in Middleton's *Women Beware Women*," *Review of English Studies*, 12 (1961), 238–50.

Rodgers, M., "*Prospero's Books* – Word and Spectacle: An Interview with Peter Greenaway," *Film Quarterly*, 45 (1991–2), 11–19.

Rogers, J., *Obel or Bethshemesh* (London, 1653).

Rooley, A., *Performance: Revealing the Orpheus Within* (Dorset: Element Books, 1990).

Rose, M. B., "Women in Men's Clothing: Apparel and Social Stability in *The Roaring Girl*," *English Literary Renaissance*, 14 (1984), 367–91.

Rowland, J., *A Choice Narrative of Count Gondamor's Transactions During His Embassy to England*, repr. (London: G. Smeeton, 1820).

Russell, C., *Parliaments and English Politics, 1621–1629* (Oxford University Press, 1979).

Rustici, C. "The Smoking Girl: Tobacco and the Representation of Mary Frith," *Studies in Philology*, 96 (1999), 159–79.

Sadler, J., *The Sicke Womans Private Looking-Glasse* (London, 1636).

Samson, A., "'Last thought upon a windmill'? Cervantes and Fletcher," in J. A. G. Ardila (ed.), *The Cervantean Heritage. Reception and Influence of Cervantes in Britain* (Oxford: Legenda, 2009), pp. 223–33.

Samson, A. (ed.), *The Spanish Match: Prince Charles's Journey to Madrid, 1623* (London: Ashgate, 2006).

Saviolo, V., *Vincentio Saviolo His Practise* (London: Wolfe, 1595).

Schiller, F., "On the Tragic Art" (1792), in F. Schiller, *Essays Aesthetical and Philosophical* (London: George Bell, 1875), pp. 339–60.

Schofield, J., *The Building of London: From the Conquest to the Great Fire* (London: British Museum Publications, 1984).

Schofield, J. (ed. and intro.), *The London Surveys of Ralph Treswell* (London Topographical Society, 1987).

Scot, R., *The Discoverie of Witchcraft* (London: William Brome, 1584).

Scott, T., *The Second Part of Vox Populi or Gondomar appearing in the likeness of Machiavelli in a Spanish Parliament, wherein are discovered his treacherous and subtle Practices to the ruin as well of England as the Netherlands. Faithfully translated out of the Spanish Copy by a well-wisher to England and Holland* (Goricum: Ashuerus Janss, 1624).

*Vox Populi or News from Spain, translated according to the Spanish copy. Which may serve to forewarn both England and the United Provinces how to trust to Spanish Practices* (n.p., 1620).

Seaver, P., *Wallington's World: A Puritan Artisan in Seventeenth-Century London* (Palo Alto, CA: Stanford University Press, 1985).

"Middleton's London," in G. Taylor and J. Lavagnino (gen. eds.), *Thomas Middleton: The Collected Works* (Oxford: Clarendon Press, 2007), pp. 59–73.

Seligmann, R., "The Functions of Song in the Plays of Thomas Middleton" (Ph. D. Dissertation, Brandeis University, 1997).

de Sélincourt, S. (ed.), *The Letters of William and Dorothy Wordsworth: The Later Years, 1821–1850*, 3 vols. (Oxford: Clarendon Press, 1939).

Selleck, N., *The Interpersonal Idiom in Shakespeare, Donne, and Early Modern Culture* (Basingstoke: Palgrave Macmillan, 2008).

Seneca, L. A., *Selected Philosophical Letters*, Brad Inwood (trans.), (Oxford University Press, 2007).

Shakespeare, W., *Hamlet*, P. Edward (ed.), 2nd edn. (Cambridge University Press, 2003).

*Macbeth*, H. H. Furness (ed.), A New Variorum Edition (Philadelphia: J. B. Lippincott, 1873).

*Macbeth*, R. S. Miola (ed.) (New York and London: W. W. Norton, 2004).

*Measure for Measure*, G. Ioppolo (ed.) (New York: Prentice Hall, 1996).

*Measure for Measure*, A. Stock (ed.), updated ed. (Cambridge University Press, 2006).

Shakespeare, W. and T. Middleton, *Timon of Athens*, A. B. Dawson and G. E. Minton (eds.) (London: Arden-Cengage, 2008).

*Timon of Athens*, J. Jowett (ed.) (Oxford University Press, 2004).

Shapiro, B., "Classical Rhetoric and the English Law of Evidence," in L. Hutson and V. Kahn (eds.), *Rhetoric and Law in Early Modern Europe* (New Haven, CT: Yale University Press, 2001), pp. 54–62.

Shapiro, M., *Children of the Revels: The Boy Companies of Shakespeare's Time and their Plays* (New York: Columbia University Press, 1977).

Sharp, J. *The Midwives Book*, E. Hobby (ed.) (Oxford University Press, 1999).

Sharpe, J. A., *Crime in Early Modern England, 1550–1750* (Harlowe, Essex: Longman, 1999).

Sharpe, K., *The Personal Rule of Charles I* (New Haven, CT: Yale University Press, 1992).

Shaw, C., "Introduction," in T. Middleton, and W. Rowley, *The Old Law*, C. Shaw (ed.) (New York: Garland, 1982).

Shute, N., *Corona Charitatis* (London: W. Stansby for Samuel Man, 1626).

Slack, P., "Mirrors of Health and Treasures of Poor Men: The Uses of the Vernacular Medical Literature of Tudor England," in C. Webster (ed.), *Health, Medicine and Mortality in the Sixteenth Century* (Cambridge University Press, 1979), pp. 237–73.

Smith, A. and Morrey, D., *Jacques Rivette* (Manchester University Press, 2010).

Smith, B. R., *The Acoustic World of Early Modern England* (University of Chicago Press, 1999).

Smuts, R. M., "Court-Centred Politics and the Uses of Roman Historians, c. 1590–1630," in K. Sharpe and P. Lake (eds.), *Culture and Politics in Early Stuart England* (Basingstoke: Macmillan, 1994), pp. 25–43.

"Public Ceremony and Royal Charisma: The English Royal Entry in London, 1485–1642," in A. L. Beier, D. Carradine, and J. M. Rosenheim (eds.), *The First Modern Society: Essays in English History in Honour of Lawrence Stone* (Cambridge University Press, 1989), pp. 65–94.

Solga, K., *Violence Against Women in Early Modern Performance* (Houndmills: Palgrave Macmillan, 2009).

Sommerville, J. P., *Royalists and Patriots: Politics and Ideology* (London: Longman, 1999).

*Sophronistes. A Dialogue, Perswading the People to Reverence and Attend the Ordinance of God, in the Ministerie of Their Owne Pastors* (London, 1589).

Spufford, M., *Small Books and Pleasant Histories: Popular Fiction and its Readership in Seventeenth-Century England* (London: Methuen, 1981).

Stallybrass, P., "Patriarchal Territories: The Body Enclosed," in M. W. Ferguson, M. Quilligan, and N. J. Vickers (eds.), *Rewriting the Renaissance: The Discourses of Sexual Difference* (University of Chicago Press, 1986), pp. 123–42.

Steen, S. J., *Ambrosia in an Earthen Vessel: Three Centuries of Audience and Reader Response to the Works of Thomas Middleton* (New York: AMS Press, 1993).

Stern, T., *Documents of Performance in Early Modern England* (Cambridge University Press, 2009).

"Re-Patching the Play," in P. Holland and S. Orgel (eds.), *From Script to Stage in Early Modern England* (New York: Palgrave Macmillan, 2004), pp. 151–77.

Stewart, M., *Nine Coaches Waiting* (London: Hodder and Stoughton, 1958).

Stone, L., *The Crisis of the Aristocracy, 1588–1641* (Oxford: Clarendon Press, 1965).

Stow, J., *Survey of London* (London, 1598).

Streitberger, W. R., "Personnel and Professionalization," in J. D. Cox and D. S. Kastan (eds.), *A New History of Early English Drama* (New York: Columbia University Press, 1997), pp. 337–55.

Stretton, T., "Marriage, Separation, and the Common Law in England, 1540–1660," in H. Berry and E. Foyster (eds.), *The Family in Early Modern England* (Cambridge University Press, 2007), pp. 18–39.

Strong, R., *Art and Power: Renaissance Festivals 1450–1650* (Woodbridge: Boydell Press, 1984).

Sullivan, C., "Thomas Middleton's View of Public Utility," *Review of English Studies*, 58 (2007), 162–74.

Sullivan, G. A., Jr., *Memory and Forgetting in English Renaissance Drama: Shakespeare, Marlowe, Webster* (Cambridge University Press, 2005).

Sutherland, S. P., *Masques in Jacobean Tragedy* (New York: AMS Press, 1983).

Tawney, R. H. and E. Power (eds.), *Tudor Economic Documents: Being Selected Documents Illustrating the Economic and Social History of Tudor England*, 3 vols. (London: Longmans, Green, 1924).

Taylor, G., "Thomas Middleton: Lives and Afterlives," in G. Taylor and J. Lavagnino (gen. eds.), *Thomas Middleton: The Collected Works* (Oxford: Clarendon Press, 2007), pp. 25–58.

"Mediterranean *Measure for Measure*," in T. Clayton *et al.* (eds.), *Shakespeare and the Mediterranean* (Newark, DE: University of Delaware Press, 2004), pp. 243–69.

"Middleton, Thomas (*bap.* 1580, *d.* 1627)," in H. C. G. Matthew and B. Harrison (eds.), *Oxford Dictionary of National Biography* (Oxford University Press, 2004; online edn., May 2008).

"The Renaissance and the End of Editing," in G. Bornstein and R. G. Williams (eds.), *Palimpsest: Editorial Theory in the Humanities* (Ann Arbor: University of Michigan Press, 1993), pp. 121–49.

"Thomas Middleton, *The Nice Valour*, and the Court of James I," *The Court Historian*, 6 (2001), 1–26.

Taylor, G. and J. Jowett, *Shakespeare Reshaped, 1606–1623* (Oxford University Press, 1993).

Taylor, G. and J. Lavagnino (gen. eds.), *Thomas Middleton: The Collected Works* (Oxford: Clarendon Press, 2007).

*Thomas Middleton and Early Modern Textual Culture: A Companion to the Collected Works* (Oxford: Clarendon Press, 2007).

Taylor, G., P. Mulholland, and M. P. Jackson, "Thomas Middleton, Lording Barry, and *The Family of Love*," *Papers of the Bibliographical Society of America* 93 (1999), 213–41.

Taylor, G. and A. J. Sabol *et al.*, "Middleton, Music, and Dance," in G. Taylor and J. Lavagnino (gen. eds.), *Thomas Middleton and Early Modern Textual Culture: A Companion to the Collected Works* (Oxford: Clarendon Press, 2007) pp. 119–81.

Taylor, J., *Prince Charles his Welcome from Spain* (London: G. E. for John Wright, 1623).

Thrupp, S., *A Short History of the Worshipful Company of Bakers of London* (Croydon: Galleon Press, 1933).

Tilly, C., *The Vendée* (Cambridge, MA: Harvard University Press, 1964).

Todd, W. B., and A. Bowden, *Sir Walter Scott: A Bibliographical History, 1796–1832* (New Castle, DE: Oak Knoll Press, 1998).

Tomlinson, G., *Music in Renaissance Magic* (University of Chicago Press, 1993).

Tyacke, N., *Aspects of English Protestantism, c. 1530–1700* (Manchester University Press, 2001).

Unwin, G., *The Gilds and Companies of London* (London: Methuen, 1908).

*Industrial Organization in the Sixteenth and Seventeenth Centuries* (Oxford: Clarendon Press, 1904).

Vaughan, W., *Naturall and Artificiall Directions for Health* (London, 1602).

Venner, T., *A Briefe and Accurate Treatise, Concerning the Taking of the fume of Tobacco* (London, 1621).

Vickers, B., *Shakespeare, Co-Author* (Oxford University Press, 2002).

"Disintegrated: Did Middleton Adapt *Macbeth*?," *TLS* (28 May 2010), 14–15.

Wales, K., "'Thou' and 'You' in Early Modern English: Brown and Gilman Reconsidered," *Studia Linguistica*, 37 (1983), 107–25.

Wells, S. and G. Taylor (gen. eds.), *The Oxford Shakespeare* (Oxford: Clarendon Press, 1986).

Wells, S. and G. Taylor, with J. Jowett and W. Montgomery, *William Shakespeare: A Textual Companion* (Oxford: Clarendon Press, 1987).

Whately, W., *A Bride-Bush, or a Wedding Sermon* (London, 1617).

Wickham, G., *Early English Stages 1300–1600, vol. 3, Plays and their Makers to 1576*, 5 vols. (London: Routledge and Kegan Paul, 1981).

Wikeley, C., "*Honour Conceal'd; Strangely Reveale'd*: The Fool and the Water Poet," in A. Samson (ed.), *The Spanish Match: Prince Charles's Journey to Madrid, 1623* (Aldershot: Ashgate, 2006), pp. 189–208.

Wiles, M. M., "Theatricality and French Cinema: The Films of Jacques Rivette" (Ph.D. dissertation, University of Florida, 2002).

Williams, D., "*Friar Bacon and Friar Bungay* and the Rhetoric of Temporality," in G. McMullen and D. Matthews (eds.), *Reading the Medieval in Early Modern England* (Cambridge University Press, 2007), pp. 31–48.

Willson, D., *King James VI and I* (Oxford University Press, 1956).

Wilson, C. H. "Trade, Society, and the State," in E. E. Rich and C. H. Wilson (eds.), *Cambridge Economic History of Europe*, vol. IV, *The Economy of Expanding Europe in the Sixteenth and Seventeenth Centuries*, 8 vols. (Cambridge University Press, 1967) pp. 487–575.

Wilson, C. R. and M. Calore, *Music in Shakespeare: A Dictionary* (London: Thoemmes Continuum, 2005).

Wilson, F. P., "Some English Mock Prognostications," *The Library*, 4th series, 19 (1938), 6–43.

Wilson, P. H., *Europe's Tragedy: A History of the Thirty Years War* (London: Allen Lane, 2009).

Wirth, L., "Urbanism as a Way of Life," *American Journal of Sociology*, 44 (1938), 1–24.

Wood, N., *Foundations of Political Economy: Some Early Tudor Views on State and Society* (Berkeley: University of California Press, 1994).

Woodbridge, L., *The Scythe of Saturn* (Urbana: University of Illinois Press, 1994).

Worden, B., "Ben Jonson Among the Historians," in K. Sharpe and P. Lake (eds.), *Culture and Politics in Early Stuart England* (Basingstoke: Macmillan, 1994), pp. 67–90.

Wrigley, E. A. and R. S. Schofield, *Population History of England 1541–1871: A Reconstruction* (Cambridge, MA: Harvard University Press, 1981).

Yachnin, P., "Reversal of Fortune: Shakespeare, Middleton and the Puritans," *ELH*, 70 (2003), 757–86.

Yates, F. A., "Elizabethan Chivalry: The Romance of the Accession Day Tilts," *Journal of the Warburg and Courtauld Institutes*, 20 (1957), 4–25.

Young, M. B., *James VI and I and the History of Homosexuality* (Basingstoke: Macmillan, 2000).

# Index

Lightning Source UK Ltd.
Milton Keynes UK
UKOW06f0412010616

275376UK00011B/409/P